The Origins of Macho

Diálogos Series

KRIS LANE, SERIES EDITOR

Understanding Latin America demands dialogue, deep exploration, and frank discussion of key topics. Founded by Lyman L. Johnson in 1992 and edited since 2013 by Kris Lane, the Diálogos Series focuses on innovative scholarship in Latin American history and related fields. The series, the most successful of its type, includes specialist works accessible to a wide readership and a variety of thematic titles, all ideally suited for classroom adoption by university and college teachers.

Also available in the Diálogos Series:

Mexico in the Time of Cholera by Donald Fithian Stevens
Mexico City, 1808: Power, Sovereignty, and Silver in an Age of War and Revolution
by John Tutino
*Tides of Revolution: Information, Insurgencies, and the Crisis of Colonial Rule
in Venezuela* by Cristina Soriano
Murder in Mérida, 1792: Violence, Factions, and the Law by Mark W. Lentz
Nuns Navigating the Spanish Empire by Sarah E. Owens
Sons of the Mexican Revolution: Miguel Alemán and His Generation
by Ryan M. Alexander
The Pursuit of Ruins: Archaeology, History, and the Making of Modern Mexico
by Christina Bueno
Creating Charismatic Bonds in Argentina: Letters to Juan and Eva Perón
by Donna J. Guy
Gendered Crossings: Women and Migration in the Spanish Empire by Allyson M. Poska
From Shipmates to Soldiers: Emerging Black Identities in the Río de la Plata
by Alex Borucki

For additional titles in the Diálogos Series, please visit unmpress.com.

The Origins of Macho

Men and Masculinity in Colonial Mexico

SONYA LIPSETT-RIVERA

University of New Mexico Press ❧ Albuquerque

Library of Congress Cataloging-in-Publication Data
Names: Lipsett-Rivera, Sonya, 1961– author.
Title: The origins of macho: men and masculinity in colonial Mexico /
Sonya Lipsett-Rivera.
Description: Albuquerque: University of New Mexico Press, [2019] | Series: Diálogos
series | Includes bibliographical references and index. | Identifiers: LCCN 2018054773
(print) | LCCN 2018060651 (e-book) | ISBN 9780826360410 (e-book) |
ISBN 9780826360397 (printed case: alk. paper) | ISBN 9780826360403
(pbk.: alk. paper)
Subjects: LCSH: Men—Mexico—History. | Machismo—Mexico—History. |
Masculinity—Mexico—History. | Men—Mexico—Identity. | Mexico—Civilization.
Classification: LCC HQ1090.7.M6 (e-book) | LCC HQ1090.7.M6 L57 2019 (print) |
DDC 305.310972 —dc23
LC record available at https://lccn.loc.gov/2018054773

Cover illustration: Theubet de Beauchamp, *Vistas de México y trajes civiles y militares
y de sus pobladores entre 1810 y 1827* (n.p.: n.p., 1830), n.p.
Composed in Minion Pro 10.25/13.5

For

Fred and Jason José

Contents

❧

Illustrations

Figures

Tables

Preface

This book arose from a question. During the research and writing for my last project, I thought I was coming to grips with some aspects of gender relations in colonial and early national Mexico, but when I encountered incidents with only men involved, their behavior seemed mystifying. For example, one evening in 1799, in Tenancingo, Isidro Juan and his wife were drinking inside their home and strumming on a borrowed guitar. Some friends came by; they joined in with the music and good cheer in what seems to have been a pleasant gathering. Casiano Ortiz was wandering the streets with his friend Blas when they heard the sound of Isidro Juan's gathering. They stood in the doorway, and Blas began to sing. They were not quite part of the party because they stayed on its edge. But when Isidro Juan and his friends asked them to enter, they reacted with hostility, saying that they were not libertines. All of a sudden those inside and outside began to fight, even drawing knives, and as a result several people were wounded.[1]

This episode provoked many questions: Why did Casiano Ortiz and his friend take offense at an invitation? Were these activities part of masculine culture? How did men relate to one another in this period? Run-of-the-mill men were relatively absent in the scholarly literature, so any answers regarding this strange conduct were missing. I embarked on this project using judicial documents, expecting many dark and gloomy incidents between the men who populate the pages of court cases, and although I did find many such episodes, I also discovered much lighter fare, such as horse races on city streets and in the countryside, jokes and humorous nicknames, and examples of banter between men. Along the way I incurred many scholarly debts and many other debts simply of friendship and kindness. Writing a book is mostly a solitary pursuit, but it cannot be done without the assistance of many kindhearted individuals. Nevertheless, I am solely responsible for the contents of this book.

As I decided to embark on this project, it was my great fortune to be awarded a generous grant from the Social Sciences and Humanities Research Council of Canada. This grant allowed me to spend wonderful months in Mexico City doing archival research at the Archivo General de la Nación and the Biblioteca Nacional de México, where the staffs were always helpful. I was also able to employ some superb Carleton University (Ottawa, Canada) graduate students as research assistants in both Mexico City and Ottawa: Christina Parsons, Ana Fonseca, and David Barrios Giraldo. My work was made easier because of their assistance. Without the help of the most generous Linda Arnold and access to her amazing finding aids, my research in the newly relocated documents of the Tribunal Superior Judicial del Districto Federal would not have been as straightforward. Linda continues to be a font of information and the go-to person for research in Mexico. In addition, my lovely friend Carmen Nava helped me discover previously unknown resources for my project, found materials for me, and gave me books. In the last stages of this project I was also extremely fortunate to win the Marston Lafrance Research Fellowship, which allowed me welcome time to write.

Many people helped along the way by providing forums where I could present my work and by reading various portions of the book. Felipe Castro Gutiérrez generously read several chapters, gave me important feedback and corrections, and organized a talk at the Seminario Sociedad Indiana at the Universidad Nacional Autónoma de México (UNAM). Alicia Mayer also invited me to present my work at UNAM's Instituto de Investigaciones Históricas. Verónica Undurraga Schüler invited me to Santiago to present several papers at the Pontificia Universidad Católica de Chile, where she, her colleagues, and her students shared insights and sources. Her warmth, kindness, and sharp intellect made the experience very worthwhile. Margarita Gascón invited me to the Seminario Interdisciplinario sobre Sociedades del Pasado, in Mendoza, Argentina, where between great wine and meals I gained many insights. I also presented papers several times at the Instituto de Investigaciones Históricas de la Universidad Michoacana de San Nicolás Hidalgo at the invitation of Lissette Rivera Reynaldos. I received many excellent suggestions from the faculty and students there, and I particularly appreciate Magali Sánchez Pineda, who originally contacted me from Michoacán and who helped make me so welcome in Morelia. I also shared my ideas at a meeting of the Center for Atlantic and

Global Studies at the Leibniz Universitat Hannover, for which I am very grateful to Ulrike Schmieder and Christine Hatsky.

Several other people helped me by reading a chapter or the whole book. Laura Shelton read an early version of chapter 2 and assisted in sharpening my organization and writing. Jon Truitt kindly read the entire manuscript and provided many corrections and really brilliant ideas about the book's organization. Likewise, Linda Curcio-Nagy read the book and gave me valuable feedback. Zeb Tortorici commented extensively on my work and posed some difficult questions, whose resolution undoubtedly made this a better book. Series editor Kris Lane gave me valuable guidance on various versions and was incredibly encouraging. Copyeditor Judith Antonelli improved my prose immeasurably, and her attentive reading of my manuscript caught many errors. Clark Whitehorn supported this project from the proposal stage and throughout with words of wisdom and down-to-earth advice.

Many other colleagues and friends helped with support or information. Tatiana Seijas generously shared documents with me. Richard Conway helped me understand what a sluice gate is. During many lovely gatherings in Mexico City, Susan Deeds heard me out about my research. Martin Nesvig, Laura Rojas Hernández, Tracey Goode, Anne Rubenstein, Jeff Pilcher, Frances Ramos, Kathryn Sloan, Ann Twinam, Susan Kellogg, Cynthia Radding, Michele McKinley, and Don Stevens have all provided support, in different ways. Juan Ortiz Escamilla introduced me to the images of Theubet de Beauchamp. In Mexico I always enjoy the company and support of my friends and colleagues Rosalva Loreto López and Francisco Cervantes Bello. In addition, I thank my very kind and supportive family: Estela Rivera Ayala and Luis Vera, Antonia Rivera Ayala and Fidel Sánchez, Guadalupe Rivera Ayala, and Raul Rivera Ayala. They are always kind, and they support me not just with their affection but also with lots of good meals and conversations.

At Carleton I enjoyed the support of Dean John Shepherd and my department chairwoman, Dominique Marshall. I have many wonderful colleagues, but I want to specially acknowledge David Dean, Susanne Klausen, Audra Diptee, Susan Whitney, Norman Hillmer, Jen Evans, Jan Siltanen, Jill Wigle, Lorena Zarate, Laura MacDonald, and Cristina Rojas. Outside work, many friends help keep me sane: Antonio Cazorla Sánchez and Céline Bak, Diane Marleau and Neil Farish, Christine Rivas, Colin Coates and Megan Davies, Ann Clark McMunagle, Diane Forbes, Jamie and Garry Lombardo, and all my horse-riding and equine friends.

Family is central to my life, and during the final stages of this project my father, Fred Lipsett, entered a sad decline and died. I think often of his intellectual example, his wide-ranging curiosity, and his quiet brand of masculinity. My son, Jason José, has grown into a fine young man—one who is wise beyond his years. It is to these two men in my life that I dedicate this book.

CHAPTER 1

Many Masculinities

✣ MEXICAN HISTORY IS FULL OF MEN. THEY POPULATE CONQUEST accounts and chronicles, battles and acts of bravery, and political struggles. Within colonial gender studies, however, men have been relatively absent. They have often occupied a formulaic role—cardboard figures dominating their wives, daughters, and mistresses. Because of this absence and the small number of works on colonial Mexican masculinity, it has been simple to rely on the easy stereotype of the violent Mexican man—the explosively violent, virile man who dominates women and other men. Quick to anger, his passions are deadly.[1] Although historians have begun to dispel this mythology, the Mexican macho remains a powerful representation that seems to work as a type of shorthand to categorize and define a large swath of people.[2]

In counterpoint to this clichéd portrayal of Mexican men, this book argues that there were, in fact, many types of masculinity in colonial Mexico. Although there were certainly violent men with explosive tempers in New Spain, the ideal to which men aspired and that they tried to embody was one of emotional control. This was a society born of the violence of conquest, but as the colony—New Spain—was established, norms of composure and self-possession were imposed, thus keeping a lid on potential aggression. As in many colonial societies, a hierarchy of both status and ethnicity forced men to exhibit a masculinity deemed appropriate for their place. On a daily basis, men of lower status had to act out their submission and sublimate their frustrations; this precarious balance of power and compliance worked up to a certain point, at which men's anger was periodically released in rebellious acts. As New Spain's society and political regime changed in the eighteenth century, with campaigns to impose orderly conduct on plebeian society as well as the militarization of society, the colonial authorities' capacity to contain plebeian men's resentment and frustration was challenged. It was in this crucible that the beginnings of the masculinity associated with the Mexican macho developed; as colonial subjects overthrew their rulers, the type of violent man that had been unacceptable under colonial rule became useful, thus providing the origins of the stereotypical macho.

Although this book explores the origins of the masculinity associated with the macho, it is also a first attempt to comprehensively examine men's lives and masculinity in colonial Mexico and to write men's gender perspective into the history of New Spain. These men have been present in various histories, but I bring to the subject a more nuanced vision of the ways in which men negotiated their place in colonial society and both constructed and demonstrated their masculinity. Within gender studies, the first definition of masculinity is the conduct considered appropriate for men within the context of their society and time.[3] It can also be defined as a set of expectations for men often expressed in opposition to the ideals of femininity, although women were also part of the construction of masculinity.[4] In practice, masculinity was not uniform; it varied as boys grew into men, married or not, and on their social position. It was as, gender historian Alexandra Shepard states, "enormously diverse, contingent, and contradictory."[5] The different masculinities that existed in a particular context or period were not separate from one another but rather jostled and came into conflict; there was a tension over men's self-definition, and very often they defined themselves in relation to a definition of manhood or masculinity that was considered "other."[6]

Despite the prevailing literary and moral model of the ideal, there was no one type of man or masculinity in New Spain; rather, men adopted attitudes and conduct appropriate to their social rank and the way that they wished to present themselves to the world.[7] They were constrained by their social status and the conditions imposed on them by racial constructs. As such, there was not one unique male model but rather many masculinities that men deployed and performed as best they could. Gender identity was very much a performance—it was enacted in encounters that occurred on a daily basis as well as in rituals of power and the way that these were deployed to either augment or detract from social position.[8] The colonial experience—not just the conquest of the Aztec empire and other indigenous peoples but also the construction of a new society—meant that male identities were constantly changing and being reinvented within the evolution of social norms and conventions.[9] During the colonial period, indigenous and African men carved out social spaces for themselves, but like other men they had to negotiate their place within a highly hierarchical society. They enacted a dance of power that both imposed their dominant position and demonstrated their submission through body language, speech, and actions.

Masculinity in Mexican History

In 1695 the diarist Antonio de Robles reported on a controversy that highlights the permeability of rank among men and the struggles for status within the performance of masculinity in New Spain. At the end of a celebratory bullfight, as all the dignitaries were leaving and the Count of Santiago was ensconced in his carriage, he made his coachman stop to allow the viceroy's carriage to pass and take the lead. He also extended this courtesy to the next carriage, which conveyed the ladies of the viceregal entourage. But then came the carriage transporting the viceroy's pages—essentially servants—and the count refused to let these men precede him. Both were adamant about their right to pass: the count ordered his coachman to drive over the other carriage, if necessary, and the pages said they would cut off the ears of the mules pulling the count's carriage—perhaps not daring to menace the count himself, they threatened violence to his animals. The men streamed out into the street, drawing their swords and throwing rocks. When he heard of this incident, the viceroy was aghast and called in his officials for a consultation; they agreed that the count had shown contempt for the viceroy's royal authority. The count was therefore punished with exile from Mexico City.[10] He had assumed that his title, lineage, and wealth afforded him priority over servants, but these men were part of the viceregal household and thus absorbed and benefited from their master's rank. Hierarchy was mediated by many different factors.

This episode shows how men had to maneuver the complexities of hierarchy that were by no means straightforward. It reflects skirmishes at the highest echelons, but men in New Spain clashed over precedence and position at all social ranks. Plebeians, as we will see in chapter 4, even fought because one man's dog cut in before another man, thus causing insult. Throughout this book I document battles over chairs and roadways, doors and keys, hats and words, and many other rights that were symbolically charged; all these elements were significant to men in ways that went well beneath the surface. They represented the status of each man within his social milieu, and men fought over these symbolic elements because they were essential to their social position. Hierarchy within male ranks was never so unequivocal that it could not be challenged, for elements such as lineage, race, wealth, and official posts and titles intersected to define individuals in different ways according to the setting and context.[11]

Although the calculations of rank and social precedence were infinite and never entirely settled, status was central to the way that men performed their masculinity. In New Spain, men had a dominant role within gender relations, and their violence toward women has been carefully described and documented. The picture deployed in studies on gender relations reflects only part of the male experience—their authority was not always so clear-cut outside the domestic realm. Rules of precedence were often ambiguous and contested, and men exploited these uncertainties to assert rank.

During the conquest period and the following years, Spanish men were at pains to demonstrate their supremacy over the indigenous population. In the immediate postconquest period, male residents of Mexico City used pomp and pageantry to reinforce their dominance. Celebrations, including the commemoration of the conquest, were marked by militaristic games on horseback; these were an opportunity to show off the men's horsemanship, but ultimately they served a political purpose.[12] As demonstrated in chapters 4 and 5, in New Spain manliness was frequently associated with equestrian skills. Most indigenous men, with the exception of some of their leaders, were not allowed to ride horses in the early years of the colony.[13]

As the conquest period faded from memory, these equestrian celebrations lost some of their significance and disappeared from custom; some officials began to worry that young men were losing their ability to ride horses and thus wage war.[14] In addition, the model of ideal manhood began to diverge from that of the blustering conqueror to one that valued composure and calm. Among other changes, the Holy Office of the Inquisition began to crack down on the expansive masculinity of the conquest period: in 1527, Dominican Friar Domingo Betanzos put eighteen former conquerors on trial for blasphemy.[15]

Curses, profanity, and blasphemous expressions were ways that men acted out their manhood, especially within social settings such as taverns, card games, and cockfights. It was a practice deployed as a form of affirmation of manhood.[16] This change was one of the many ways that men in New Spain were directed toward a different model of manhood as the colony matured. Yet as will be evident throughout this book, even though men in New Spain were violent, they claimed a rationale for their aggression—one that fit into notions of hierarchy but also of honor. Nonetheless, lapsing into violent acts was considered a failure, a loss of self-possession that diminished the individual.[17] In fact, there was considerable pressure on men, especially those who aspired to the upper class, to avoid losing their composure, and thus they often sublimated their struggles for ascendancy into symbolic details that might seem unimportant to us.

From a very young age boys learned that they were part of a hierarchy and had to accept their place within the social structure. This apprenticeship into the pecking order began at home, in their households or in the institutions where boys grew up. Watching older men, they observed how some bent their bodies and removed their hats whereas others stood erect. They became part of a loose-knit community of similarly ranked people in which they could tell jokes, drink, and sing, but this liberty was in stark contrast to the self-control they had to exert when they were in the presence of others higher on the social ladder. Much of the tension over social position and the struggles to assert one's station came out indirectly, as shown in chapter 6, in jokes and allusions as well as veiled insults. Humiliation could arise in many forms: the refusal to doff one's hat, an indirect insinuation about lineage, or a forced haircut. While some young men were learning deference, others absorbed lessons of dominance.

At every level of New Spain's society, from the viceregal court to the indigenous villages, certain men tried to enact a dominant masculinity, and others either fought back or accepted their place. At times, this dynamic led to a feminization of those humiliated, often indigenous men; as shown in chapter 3, the logic of violence toward them was strikingly similar to that used to justify domestic violence. Violence, real and symbolic, was a guiding principle of colonial society. But its equilibrium and the capacity to maintain some semblance of peace meant that much of this violence had to be sublimated. In New Spain, as in many other colonies, there was permissible violence—a correction to an insolent employee or a rude passerby—and this was approved as part of discipline and the maintenance of social structures. Within New Spain, men continually referred to themselves as *quieto* (quiet), *sosegado* (calm), or *pacífico* (peaceful)—all descriptors that seem at odds with the bravado associated with Mexican men. In fact, these were the values espoused not only in individuals but by widely read moral authorities such as don Juan de Escoiquiz.[18]

Thus, for most of the colonial period both officials and the general population kept a lid on violence, with some eruptions at regular intervals, such as during religious festivities that allowed social inversion and rule breaking. This equilibrium began to change toward the late colonial period as the Bourbon Reforms launched the militarization of New Spain; troops of all types proliferated, and with them an expanded sense of permissible violence. Within the documents, confrontations between soldiers of different garrisons as well as with other officials and civilians became ever more frequent. The tensions that preceded the Grito de Dolores (Cry of Dolores, the battle cry for Mexican independence) only exacerbated this quarrelsome atmosphere. For so many years men had channeled their violent emotions and frustrations with symbolic gestures; with the explosion of the war for independence, men could act out their violence openly, and the seeds of the Mexican macho were sown.

There was not one gender model that endured from conquest to independence; rather, as the period of the conquistador gave way to a more settled colony, new models of the masculine were imposed by various authorities. In addition, colonial society was hardly homogeneous; along with many different indigenous peoples, others, such as Africans and Asians (enslaved and free) as well as Spanish migrants, competed for social position within their particular context.[19] Men's experiences thus varied as they moved through cities and villages and when they were in the presence of employers, officials, or simply their friends. They had to negotiate these different settings and deploy the appropriate masculinity. The machinations for influence and dominance of upper-class men in New Spain have long been part of the historical record; they have been discussed mostly in relation to power but rarely in terms of gender.[20]

Honor systems were another value central to ideas of masculinity that meshed quite easily with Nahua notions of bravery and lineage.[21] It also placed significant importance on ancestry and race—which in theory excluded many men. Yet lower-class men of all ethnicities and racial identities claimed honor and rank within their communities. Studies of honor in New Spain and other parts of the Hispanic world provide a framework for the ways that men dealt with insults, corporeal codes of submission and authority, and the violence that pervaded their world.[22] Men regularly referred to their honor as a justification for their actions.

Although men in colonial Mexico understood how to negotiate their social position on a daily basis, the concept of masculinity is a recent one. Men in New Spain described themselves and their manhood in words and expressions of their time. *Macho* was certainly not a word that men would have used to convey their manhood; in fact, it was associated with male animals.[23] The association between the word *macho* and a violent masculinity was a twentieth-century development.[24] Men addressed each other in easy camaraderie as *hombre*, or man, often sprinkling the word into their banter.

Yet *hombre* could also be used to question another man and demean his manhood. It was often used as a challenge; for example, "Come into the street if you are an hombre"; "You would come out one by one if you were hombres"; or "Catch me if you are hombres."[25] Another way that men used *hombre* was to refuse a confrontation because of their superior manhood; for example, "I am too much of an hombre for this nonsense" or "It was not dignified for him to answer because he was too much of an hombre." The challenge could also be turned around, saying to another man, "Now you need to become an hombre."[26] The possibilities for manipulating the word *hombre* to either shore up a personal sense of manhood or tear down that of another person were numerous.[27] In the eighteenth century men began to describe themselves frequently as *hombres de bien*, or respectable men, and, less often but in the same vein, as *hombres de honor*, or honorable men.[28] These were both expressions that corresponded to the new emphasis on order and decorum.[29] *Hombría*, or manliness, would have been the closest in meaning to masculinity, but I found it only once in my sample, in an eighteenth-century document in which don Francisco Arana denounced his friend's lack of hombría de bien, or respectable manliness, for having seduced his daughter.[30]

Methods and Approaches

Although the histories written about New Spain are full of men, those featured in these studies were frequently rich and powerful. It is harder to retrieve the experiences of people whose levels of literacy were low and whose existence was not central to the day's great events. To bridge this gap, I, like other historians, chose to work on court cases in order to explore male interactions as well as their pastimes and pleasures, their frustrations and feelings. Yet even though I use court cases, this book is neither a legal history nor a study of crime. Judicial archives are not a perfect source, but as Arlette Farge notes, they "reveal a fragmented world" in which the people who testify narrate not just the elements of a crime but their ways of socializing, the contours of their daily life, and what seemed acceptable within their worldview.[31]

Historians of Europe have charted a methodology to use criminal archives, delving into the material to find patterns and to reveal codes of behavior. My approach in this book is a derivation of this methodology but more akin to the wonderful explorations of daily life in New Spain written by cultural historian Antonio Rubial García and the social history of Felipe Castro Gutiérrez. Verónica Undurraga Schüler's analysis of the power dynamics of eighteenth-century Chilean men has also influenced my work. Using judicial records as well as diaries, travel accounts, and morality treatises, I re-create the experiences as well as the interactions of men in New Spain in order to gain an appreciation of how men understood their masculinity. The testimonies contained in the Mexican archives are incredibly rich and provide one of the few points of access for nonelite people, but as Kathryn Burns and others warn, they are not unmediated.[32] When facing a criminal conviction either personally or for their family members and friends, witnesses crafted their statements. Nonetheless, the many different testimonies provide a picture of what was acceptable, what was usual, and how people occupied their time at home, at work, and at play.

The Archivo General de la Nación (National Archives of Mexico) contains two important collections of court cases: the Ramo Criminal, which is all-encompassing, and the Tribunal Superior de Justicia del Distrito Federal (Superior Tribunal of Justice of the Federal District), which holds cases from Mexico City and the surrounding areas. Using both of these document series, I focused on Mexico City and nearby villages in order to make the research manageable and to present contrasting pictures of men in a large metropolis and small communities within the area. These collections are vast, and for the purposes of this study I located cases that could shed light on primarily male interactions, such as homicides, beatings, grievances, insults, disrespect, mistreatment, wounds, and whippings. For the section on male youth I examined vagrancy cases in which parents or guardians denounced their own sons and asked for their exile either to military service or the Philippines. In order to discuss male sexuality I built on the main corpus of cases and added some relating to promises of marriage and illicit relationships.

Table 1. Self-Identification and Race

AGGRESSOR	NUMBER	PERCENTAGE	VICTIM	NUMBER	PERCENTAGE
Español	113	19.82	Español	67	11.75
Indio	101	17.71	Indio	171	30
Mestizo	32	5.71	Mestizo	15	2.63
Mulatto	13	2.32	Mulatto	7	1.25
Pardo or Negro	4	0.71	Pardo or Negro	2	0.35
Castizo	4	0.71	Castizo	4	0.71
Chino	3	0.53	Chino	0	0
Lobo	2	0.35	Lobo	0	0
Not specified	298	53.21	Not specified	303	54.10

Sources: Archivo General de la Nación, Ramo Criminal, and Tribunal Superior de Justicia del Distrito Federal.

The sample for this book is composed of 570 cases consisting of all these different types of court proceedings and all contributing to an overall picture of the daily life of men in New Spain. Those involved were not men of the upper echelons but mostly plebeians, as well as some individuals from the middle to upper ranks. Titled nobility appear mostly when their servants got into trouble; as the heads of their households, they sometimes intervened. The vast majority of both victims and aggressors in the cases did not indicate their racial self-identity. Among those who were accused of an aggression, *españoles* (Spaniards) and *indios* (Indians) formed the largest groups, but among the victims, indios represented a much larger total, whereas españoles were considerably less well represented (table 1).

Other racial groups were really negligible in terms of the sample as a whole. The disparity of representation of racial groups is one of the disadvantages of this type of source. Ecclesiastical personnel were also present in my sample, though not in huge numbers. Nevertheless, they populate the court records as witnesses, victims, and aggressive participants in male interactions, ranging from a murder mystery in the monastery of Merced in Mexico City to being the brunt of a campaign of tricks and teasing against the local priest in the Chalco region. Clerics were men like other men, yet slightly apart, but they did mingle with others in the streets and at residences, and they clearly experienced the same passions as other men.

Names in this period were important indicators of rank and class. The poorest people generally had quite simple names, maybe only a first name, whereas the higher-status people often had several last names. For this reason, in this book I don't shorten names after their first mention. I believe that it is important to give the historical actors their full names. There is also a practical reason for this course of action: at times the plebeian actors all had similar names; thus, the more ways to distinguish them, the better. I also use the spelling that was present in the documents even if that seems archaic.

For various reasons, criminal records for the early years of the colony were never produced or were destroyed—seventeenth-century looters conveniently (for them) destroyed the judicial records during a riot. Therefore, my sample begins with a court case in 1542, but the majority of the documentation is from the mid- to late seventeenth and the eighteenth centuries; within all sources most cases were produced in the eighteenth century. Because of these uneven records, this study tends to overemphasize the late colonial period, and I have tried to compensate for this deficiency by using the diaries of several residents of New Spain as well as some travel accounts. Despite some weaknesses, these narratives provide abundant details of men's lives—elements that create a rich and exuberant portrait of male experiences in New Spain. It is one approach, but certainly not the only possible way to discover masculinity in this colonial setting, a task that I hope other scholars will take up in order to fill in the many gaps in our knowledge of men and masculinity in New Spain and colonial Latin America.

Outline of Subsequent Chapters

Starting with the various childhoods of boys, this book is organized thematically; where possible, I indicate the chronological development within the topics. This thematic organization is not always clear-cut, however, and there are several analytic threads that run throughout various chapters. Hierarchy and its operationalization represent the most important of these threads; it makes an appearance first with boys who have to learn their place and act out their submission, then within the work environment and throughout the book, since hierarchy was a constant in men's lives. The imposition of rank on some men sometimes meant the feminization of others—at times with punishments, humiliation, and insults, but also by categorizing the men as having *malicia*, or shiftiness. Their lives intersected with many animals, which sometimes served to define their manhood; horses were particularly important in this role. Violence that was permissible because it was defined as discipline formed an important way for dominant men to make sure that others remained subservient. Clothes and the manner in which men presented themselves to the world is another theme that runs through the book; dress was part of the uniform of a respectable worker, and it demonstrated men's manliness and their social position. But the world of men was not all grimness—friendship and solidarity was vital to their survival in work and beyond. They indulged in many games and much drinking and partying; among friends and neighbors they relaxed, joked, and indulged in banter and tricks. Sometimes this relaxation went too far, jokes fell flat, and companions fought and exchanged insults. There were many such moments of leisure and also of social inversion during festivities in which men let loose and challenged the social order.

Depending on his family of birth, a boy grew up on the street, was educated, or was apprenticed to a master artisan, but all boys had to learn their place within the complicated hierarchy of New Spain. Chapter 2 follows this path. Parents and other family members hoped their sons would live up to their expectations, and boys were socialized to live up to these ideas. When young men rebelled too much, they appeared in the record through their parents' or guardians' denunciations of vagrancy. Although parents cherished their sons, boys went out on the streets and into the workplace at a young age, and they had to mediate dangers both symbolic and very real. Even their play was often a peril—toys themselves or the amusements. Colonial legal statutes defined twenty-five as the age of majority, but most boys had to grow up and support themselves and often a family well before that point.

Chapter 3 moves to a more interior, intimate part of men's lives: their sexuality. Despite Church teachings that promoted rather bland sexual relations between men and women, many men were involved in extramarital affairs or were part of a same-sex couple. People in New Spain were generally fairly tolerant of those who skirted the rules, but they would denounce illegitimate pairs when they were either too flagrant or an annoyance in some other matter. When interviewed, neighbors often defined marriage as cohabitation and acting like a couple, so clearly ecclesiastical instructions were only superficially accepted. This laxity was also apparent when men borrowed from codes of courtship and seduction used to seduce women to make advances to other men.

Work was a central part of most men's identity. Chapter 4 explores how it contributed to men's dignity, for it defined them as productive and respected members of the community. Work was also a place of considerable male interactions, with consequent hazing, nicknames, and joking around, but also discipline and rules. Not all work was entirely voluntary, since mostly indigenous and African men were often sentenced to work in the prisonlike settings of workshops and bakeries. Many men took pride in their work and reacted aggressively when others disparaged their capacities or its quality. Nonetheless, despite the often harsh conditions, jobs were also a place of friendship and strong alliances. Work took men out of the house; consequently, gender historians have noted that in colonial times women were associated with the home and men with the streets.

Chapter 5 delves into the truth of this assertion, but it also shows that a man was defined by his home: he sought refuge in it at night, defined himself by keeping a moral household, defended it when necessary, and attacked other men's front doors to make a point. Control over the home, including possession of its keys, was vital to male identity. Nonetheless, men spent considerable time outside and away from their homes: they went on *paseos* (strolls) that included stops at many taverns as well as walks in parks and along the canals that intersected Mexico City; they went to parties, where they played guitars and sang; and they gambled through various games, horse races, and cockfights. Many men had close contact with the natural world: they rode horses or mules, interacted with pet dogs, and quarreled over pasture rights and woodcutting.

Chapter 6 moves on to the ways that men constructed their manhood and gender identity. They had to dress the part, appropriate to their social rank and ethnicity. But they operated within certain male enclaves. Surrounded by their own group, they had nicknames and developed firm friendships in which they could joke and have fun. Yet this merriment could be turned against others who were not part of the inner sanctum. Tone of voice was vital in teasing and horseplay and could make the difference between wit and insult. But in many cases, slurs and mockery were deliberate strategies of exclusion. Increasingly, toward the end of the colonial period, plebeian men deployed many approaches to show their defiance of the colonial authorities.

Chapter 7 explains how the masculinity of the colonial period was the incubator for what would later be associated with the Mexican macho. In New Spain, men of different ranks conformed to the ideal of emotional control, not necessarily out of choice, but because of social pressure and because it was mandated by the authorities. By force they adapted to their place in the social and political hierarchy, and they had to repress any mutinous thoughts. Nonetheless, insubordination and defiance often lurked under the surface. The eighteenth-century Bourbon Reforms aimed to create a more disciplined society, but the increased drive for order and good conduct meant an even more repressed masculinity for most men. Men often rebelled in minor ways in taverns and social gatherings as well as in situations such as religious festivals, when social inversion allowed for a loosening of the rules. Men who rebelled and rejected the ideals of emotional control served to allow others to live their noncompliance vicariously for much of the colonial period. But as tensions grew and exploded into the war of independence, these men suddenly became valued for many of the traits that had previously made them outsiders. It is to this period and this process that the origins of the Mexican macho can be traced.

Taken together, the chapters provide an exploration of the various masculinities present in New Spain, with an emphasis on the plebeians and middle-ranked men most commonly represented in the documents. Following the trajectories and contours of men's lives allows the discovery of how men performed their masculinity, mediated by the push and pull of hierarchy. Within New Spain, male lives were dominated by dualities: men were defined by their capacity to protect the sanctuary of their home, but they also lived and worked very much in the streets; they had to show deference in the presence of social superiors, but they let loose among friends; and they maneuvered around all types of boundaries and thresholds, lines in the sand visible only to certain men, but they found enjoyment and pleasure in joking, singing with friends, and, in contrast, poking fun at those outside their group. Men also had to negotiate the contradictions between the ideal of emotional composure and the violent anger they often felt. Although the Mexican macho did not exist in the colonial period, characteristics of this archetype lurked under the surface.

CHAPTER 2

Becoming a Man

✝ ON THE EVENING OF MAY 20, 1729, A NINE-YEAR-OLD BOY LAY DEAD in a Mexico City tavern. Like so many child victims, he was in the wrong place at the wrong time. Another young man, Juan Caetano de Uribe, had thrown the rock that hit the boy in the head and killed him.[1] But the rock was meant for another man, a well-known thief, who was robbing Juan's friend. What was such a young boy doing in a tavern? Why was he exposed to such danger? For plebeian boys, growing up happened very much in the streets and in many rough places. It was among these dangers that they learned how to be a man. If masculinity is learned, then boyhood is the training ground. It was during boyhood that Mexican men absorbed these lessons, and childhood was therefore an important phase in the formation of young men and their inculcation with masculine values and conduct.

Despite the importance of this phase, historians have generally taken it for granted. There is a small amount of literature on children in colonial Latin American history, but because it is still pioneering the topic, the focus of most of the work tends to be general or concentrates on topics other than how boys learn masculinity.[2] Despite these limitations, an exploration of the formative influences, and the ways in which boys were conceived of in ideal terms in contrast to how they actually lived their lives, is an important stepping-stone in the delineation of masculinity in colonial Mexico.

Although people in New Spain held general beliefs about boys and defined them both legally and culturally, boys' experiences were distinct: children were born into different ranks and into families that were ethnically distinct, and experiences in Mexico City contrasted with those in smaller communities. The legal system demarcated uniform life stages that were applied evenly in theory, but the reality was quite different. Many poor people did not know their ages, and age-related categories were often applied very inconsistently. At a very young age, boys began to realize their place in society: they had to acquire the skills to discipline their bodies in proper deportment, and they learned from seeing how their fathers exhibited submission to the higher-ups. These lessons of manhood began in boys' early years as they took their place in the world.

Although the etiquette and morals literature presents us with one image of the ideal boy, boys were, in fact, born into very different circumstances in terms of families and homes. Some boys were left in friaries or foundling homes, and others lived within a household in a role akin to servants. Within these settings they went through the difficult stages of adolescence and young adulthood with varying success. If they were lucky, they negotiated the dangers that confronted them in the streets and in their early work lives and found their place in the community. The more fortunate boys were apprenticed and learned a craft, whereas even more privileged young men continued their education beyond the first years of learning. Some even went to a university, but these were a minority; the vast majority of young men in New Spain had little or no exposure to book learning and began contributing to the family economy at very young ages.

Although the saying "boys will be boys" makes boyhood seem unchanging over the course of centuries, attitudes about young men have certainly changed throughout history. The eighteenth century was a period of anxiety about order for New Spain's elites and officials; this meant apprehension about young men as undisciplined, shiftless youth. Young men deemed to be *vagos*, or vagrants, were rounded up and, if eligible, conscripted into the army; if not, they were put to work. At times parental love turned into disappointment, which led to written family denunciations of their own sons as vagos; these petitions provide an insight into the behavior of troubled adolescents and young men who did not live up to social and familial expectations. Vagrancy laws had existed since the early colony, but the intensity of their use by officials and parents increased in the late eighteenth century, with regular roundups of supposed vagrants. The pressure on young men—those without jobs or the appearance of respectability—escalated substantially in the twenty-five years before the wars for independence. As young boys in New Spain slowly became men, they absorbed the lessons of daily life and found their place within this complex society.

What Was a Boy?

Boys have been defined by the culture and the time in which they lived; they were also demarcated by laws, customs, and period ideas derived from medical and scientific practice. In New Spain, male children entered a world that classified them and expected them to behave in certain ways. Boys were born with a distinct advantage: the prevailing belief systems decreed that they were superior because of their sex. The birth of a male child positively reflected on his father; in European thought, it was a sign of the father's strength and vitality.[3] Midwives no longer welcomed boys into the world with war cries (the practice among the Nahuas), but they still treated the umbilical cord with care, burying it so that the vulnerable newborn child would not be afflicted with *mal de ojo*, or the evil eye.[4]

The male child, who was considered innately virtuous because of his sex, was received into the world of righteousness with the ritual of baptism and thus joined the realm of faith and a religious culture.[5] In colonial Mexico boys were also born into a hierarchical framework, and they were largely defined in terms of their families, their households, and the larger society. They took their place within this larger world and remained subservient for a long time. Yet as Cynthia Milton reminds us, they were also individuals who experienced the world in their own manner.[6] During their boyhood they had to negotiate the tensions between what society expected of them and their own dispositions.

The law delimited the period of boyhood by giving this phase a cap, the age of majority, and by demarcating certain life stages. At the same time, there were cultural ideas about how boys were supposed to mature and how they should develop into men. Clearly, in the first stage, a newborn boy was closely tied to whoever was breast-feeding him: in the case of a poor family his mother usually did this, but among the wealthy a wet nurse frequently took over.[7] In New Spain, unlike in Europe, wet nurses usually lived in the family's home, and upper-class babies therefore resided in their family homes even when their mothers did not breast-feed them.[8]

The fact that these babies were nursed by women other than their mothers did not necessarily mean that the babies were not cherished. María de Jesús

Agreda, a widow who was employed to breast-feed a little orphan boy, described him as her *hijito* (little boy), using the same vocabulary and showing the same affection for him as for her biological daughter.[9] Child mortality was a brutal fact for parents in this time; thus wealthy parents celebrated their baby's first year with great relief, sometimes with festivities that marked their pleasure at their child's survival.[10] When children died young, fathers wept openly.[11]

Moral commentators defined the first stage of life for all children as *la infancia*, or infancy. During this period it was normal for boys and girls to interact and play together, and perhaps their gender differences were not so stark for the first few years. The initial period of all children's lives was the mother's responsibility, and children probably lived very much in the domestic world of women.[12] It also fell to the mother to ensure that her child was well nourished and flourishing within the period of infancy—especially before weaning, but infancy was often defined as ending at the age of seven.[13]

It was not only nourishment of the body that fell to the mother to provide, but also moral and intellectual education.[14] Mothers took their role seriously, and toward the end of the eighteenth century their importance in child rearing and the formation of future subjects began to be recognized by thinkers and government officials alike. This acknowledgment also brought critiques of women's role in the early education of males. By the end of the colonial period, some Latin American intellectuals associated "disproportionate" maternal love with the emergence of what they considered a failed masculinity: a tendency to same-sex relationships in the adult male.[15]

Clearly the period of infancy was an important stage for boys; although it centered on the home, once boys were old enough they began to do small chores around the house, such as fetching water.[16] In later stages they might have had a more formal rapport with their female relatives—for example, a young man read to women while they sewed or spun in their *estrado* (a female space in the Mexican home).[17] At the end of the period of infancia, boys began to operate beyond the more feminine realm of the home, but they were still considered very junior within the household and family hierarchy.

Boys were legally defined as minors. The concept of minority was very complex in colonial Latin American law, because many categories of people—such as women, slaves, indigenous people (both men and women), the mentally challenged or mentally ill, invalids, and even criminals—were considered to be minors.[18] Males reached the age of majority at twenty-five; until then they were under their father's authority, or *patria potestad*. The laws about age-relation rights allowed men to gradually have more privileges even while they were still minors. For example, boys could become engaged to marry at age seven, actually marry at fourteen, become a lawyer at eighteen, and serve as a judge at the ripe age of twenty—all while still being considered a minor.[19] Don Rafael Aranvuru, for example, was a professor of medicine at a university at nineteen.[20]

Young men were conscious of their legal status; when Antonio Bocanegra, a resident of Molinos del Rey in Tacubaya, got into trouble and was not able to complete a task set by his father, he claimed to be a man of honor but then demurred and confessed that his main concern was that he was still a minor and under his father's patria potestad.[21] Boys' status as minors could be broken by an act of emancipation or if their fathers committed an unspeakable act. But in effect, all these rules were really meant to control the wealth and possessions that a son received from his family, and they allowed for the safe channeling of wealth from one generation to another.[22]

The law also recognized that young children could not be held responsible for crimes; they could be tried starting at ten years old and be sentenced as adults only after reaching eighteen years of age. Nevertheless, they were deemed to have *uso de razón*, or use of reason, after they reached their seventh birthday.[23] In Mexico City in 1665, Joseph Narvaez, a free mulatto, was accused of wounding a man. Because of his age, sixteen, his confession was halted so that a *curador* (legal defender) could be found for him despite the fact that he was already working in his profession and nominally independent. In this instance, age of minority trumped the circumstances of a young man who was living relatively independently.[24] Judges did not always follow the rules, however. José María Flores, a fourteen-year-old boy from Coyoacán, was fooling around with his friend while climbing a ladder, and this led to a push and the death of the friend. The judge ruled that José María Flores was old enough to know right from wrong and had to be punished.[25]

These two contrasting examples show how laws about age were often applied inconsistently, and childhood as a category did not mean much for poor boys within the legal system. Both young men were lower class and considered inferior racially, but Joseph Narvaez was already an independent worker, whereas José María Flores was an apprentice in an *obraje*—an almost jail-like workshop. Their work situations undoubtedly influenced the officials who presided over their cases. When boys became embroiled in the judicial system, their treatment could be harsh. For instance, while taking testimony from Jacinto, a seven-year-old indigenous boy, the authorities decided that he was lying. They pulled down his pants and whipped him.[26] The implementation of these laws and their practical effect on boys and young men were haphazard. Designed to protect family fortunes, they had little relevance to the vast majority of mostly poor young men in New Spain unless they were charged with a crime.

For most boys age was the factor that was most real and had the greatest effect on their lives. Relative youth was an important element in determining a young boy's place within his family, his household, and his community.[27] Although boys were learning to be men, they had to do so within a context that forced them to constantly reiterate their subservience to their fathers, their masters, or other older male authority figures within their surroundings. The allegiance to older males did not end with childhood; young men continued to be part of a web of relationships in which they had to know their place and demonstrate their loyalty and respect.[28]

Younger boys also had to obey their elder siblings, but, as don Joaquin de Obregón experienced in 1801, it also meant that older sons had to mind their younger brothers and discipline them.[29] Chronicles from this era stressed the hierarchical relationship between father and sons but also described affection and natural love demonstrated in gestures of fondness.[30] Parents, and especially fathers, owed their offspring the care and nurturing that would transform them into respectable adults. Any decent parent provided food, education, an occupation, and a good example; all these ingredients were supposed to allow young men, when they came into their majority, to live properly according to their class and race.[31]

Young boys held such an inferior place within this schema because they were dependents; they owed their lives and their continued well-being to others who were their social superiors. Such bonds did not disappear as the young men aged but rather marked their identities and their modes of being. Even as adults, if they were good sons they continued to show deference and gratitude to those who had raised them. Within Mexican colonial society, people were particularly shocked when they witnessed behavior that was disrespectful and implied a lack of appreciation of parents and their equivalent.[32] Don Juan de Escoiquiz, an influential author on the education of boys, wrote, "After God, there is no greater obligation than to our parents."[33]

Although age determined rank within this very hierarchical society, many plebeian men had only a vague idea how old they were. When a man testified, he was frequently asked to provide his age, but if he was illiterate, poor, and indigenous and did not know his age, the officials would provide a rough guess of his age range.[34] It was probably not the actual age, then, that counted for a boy or a young man in terms of his relationship with older men but rather his relative position with the family or household. The concept of age relationships was flexibly interpreted within social and familial settings.

The period of minority, from birth to twenty-five, is too wide-ranging to allow us to delineate the frameworks that governed the lives of boys in colonial Mexico. Ideas about the stages of life corresponded to a preoccupation derived from classical thinkers about human development.[35] But within the documents there are contradictory hints at what age really meant, undoubtedly because of the differences in life experiences between upper-class and plebeian boys. At times parents complained to the authorities, trying to protect their children who were at the edge of the age of majority. In January 1802, for example, María Victoriana Romero came to the *corregidor* (Spanish administrator) to complain that her son had been involved in an informal horse race through Mexico City's streets—a dangerous but exhilarating exploit that usually occurred after much drinking and boastful competition. Her son's horse threw him, and he hit his head. She wanted the authorities to hold the other young man responsible because he clearly was a bad influence.

Throughout the testimonies this complaint seems to be a clear case of a protective mother trying to ensure that her son was not led astray and hurt badly. María Victoriana Romero's son was already married and worked as a servant, but he was just twenty-five, on the cusp of his majority.[36] Mexican parents were often very protective of their children no matter what age, but the reality was that plebeian children had to engage in dangerous work from a young age. In smaller communities they often began to work with animals when still quite young and sometimes ran into problems. Bernardo José Moctesuma objected in 1790 that when his eleven-year-old son had trouble separating the bulls from the herd, the overseer hit him. As a father, Bernardo José Moctesuma recognized his child's tender age, but the boy was already a worker and had to live up to his employer's expectations.[37] Although the vagueness of our knowledge of colonial ideas regarding age and boyhood are frustrating, it is important to avoid assuming that their ideas about age and maturity were the same as ours.

Adolescence was not recognized as a life stage in Spanish law, nor was it commented on by the moralists who wrote about the proper education and raising of young men. Males were supposed to seamlessly move from boyhood to adulthood with no uncomfortable transitions or pimples. The concept of adolescence, according to Philippe Ariès, began to be mentioned only in the eighteenth century. It was not so much a period of youthful rebellion; rather, as boys achieved the strength of men but were not yet men, they were considered adolescents.[38]

Despite the fact that Mexicans did not contemplate a period equivalent to the teenage years, some young men did act out in ways that we might recognize as typical of adolescence. Parents and neighbors complained about young men's disrespectful attitudes; all-night partying, gambling, and sexual activity; dishonesty; and general lack of work ethic. When Juan Mantilla was eighteen, his mother was in despair that he was lazy and disrespectful. Witnesses reported his propensity to drink, steal, and pay someone else to do his work. Losing hope that she could remedy his waywardness, his mother asked that he be enlisted in the army against his will.[39] At sixteen years of age, José García had already spent some time in jail for seducing a virgin, had robbed his grandmother, and spent much of his time drinking and playing cards.[40]

Parents petitioned for help with wayward teenagers only when their behavior was extreme, so these examples should not be taken as representative of most the period's adolescents. But one of the common threads of all these denunciations of defiant sons was that the young men refused to conform to social expectations, showed little or no respect for their elders, and, in particular, avoided or refused to embrace the next stage of their lives: earning a living. Without having a clear concept of adolescence or a word for this stage, perhaps colonial Mexicans recognized that young men went through a turbulent period in the transition from boyhood to adulthood, but this phase ended when these men took up a profession or work and also when they married. Essentially, when these young men joined the world of adults by acting more like men than boys and by functioning within the framework of manhood, those around them ceased to view them as boys.

Model Boys

How did boys learn to behave in colonial Mexico? Without the pervasive mass media that saturates our lives, boys in earlier periods had role models closer to home, but elite boys were also supposed to absorb the lessons of ideal conduct from religious teachings and etiquette guides. It is hard to know how influential the morals or manners guides were, especially in a population that was largely illiterate, but it is clear that when they grew up, Mexican boys had a strong sense of how they should behave and how the people they interacted with should conduct themselves. These ideas provide a starting point for determining what ideals boys were supposed to aspire to.

Morals and manners experts began publishing guides to raising the perfect child—usually girls, but sometimes boys—as early as the fifteenth century. It was a codification of ideas about proper comportment that did not change much over the years and was imported into New Spain.[41] The guides that targeted male manners describe how boys should regulate their bodies—that is, in what ways they were to show respect and deference physically. For example, they were supposed to hold their bodies straight but keep their heads a little lowered.[42] These books were aimed at an audience of upper-class boys—even they had to show respect and a certain submission within their own social strata (note the lowered head). There were no special sections for plebeian boys, but these youngsters too had to learn a bodily language, albeit one of considerably more deference; undoubtedly they acquired it from watching their fathers, who had to bow before their social superiors (discussed in chapter 6), take off their hats, and speak with restraint and diffidence.[43]

The guides also describe the quiet bodies that boys had to attain: they could not fidget, look around, stare, make faces, run, stomp their feet, or make much noise.[44] "When seated," wrote one author, "keep both feet on the ground equally, do not cross your legs or separate them exaggeratedly, nor should you stretch them out from the chair."[45] Bodily sounds such as loud sneezes and yawns, noisy actions such as spitting and gargling, and behaviors such as talking with a mouth full of food were all similarly inappropriate.[46] Good boys, in addition, were clean boys, with washed faces and hands, spotless teeth, combed hair, unstained clothes, and pleasant smells.[47] Their behavior at the dinner table was beyond reproach: they waited for the blessing and then ate modestly without gluttony, refraining from gnawing on bones, chewing loudly, or banging the table.[48] Such politeness in boys was, of course, an archetype, and it is impossible to know how many boys even tried to realize this ideal of mild, quiet composure or whether such ideas had much sway within plebeian models for manhood.

More important, these guides spelled out the ways in which boys had to learn the rules of deference. They had to be very aware of always positioning themselves so that they yielded to the higher-status person—for example, by walking on the left side rather than the right, stopping to allow the passage of an adult, or strolling a few steps behind a person of respect.[49] It was also vital to know how to greet people of higher status: if on horseback, by dismounting; if seated, by getting up, receiving them, and finding them an appropriate seat. Finally, boys had to learn to remember to doff their hats and perform a deep bow.[50]

Beyond their early years, Mexican boys were out and about, observing male interactions. Don Vicente de la Rua, for example, stated in 1800 that it was his small son who told him about an altercation between a prisoner and an official in Amecameca.[51] Although this young boy did not testify, nor is he even named in the document, it was his observation of the struggle over deference and submission that brought his father into the melee. Clearly the boy had the freedom to roam and was able to monitor adult men's ways.

Plebeian boys learned the rules of deference and submission by observation and experience. There was an implied differential in the kinds of deference that the various classes and ranks of boys, and later men, were supposed to display. Escoiquiz noted that those of high rank should avoid the coarse manners associated with the lower classes, such as exaggerated compliments and inflated ceremony; instead they should maintain a politeness appropriate to their rank in relation to others.[52] Knowing the proper gradation of submission and deference was an important skill for all boys to learn. Those who belonged to the upper classes deciphered the codes of politeness and rudeness in small slights and minor rebuffs as they experienced high society, bureaucracy, and commerce.[53] Plebeian men also had to gauge the proper level of respect, and in fact the stakes were often higher for them: the consequences might be a beating or even worse.

Apart from learning polite ways and respect for hierarchy, boys were inculcated with religion; their lives began with baptism, then it was their parents' duty to raise them in a moral household that operated to the rhythm of Catholic customs and patterns.[54] It was important for parents to guide their children in this process by providing them with an appropriately pious house: one that had no lewd decorations or improper reading materials (such as novels or books of chivalry) and that was peopled with serious, devout residents and guests.[55] In this ideal world, upon waking up boys would pray, clean up their rooms, and go to school. When leaving the house a boy would make the sign of the cross to arm himself with the holy protection of his guardian angel and his namesake saint.[56] These recommendations were clearly directed at boys of the elite; a plebeian boy often lived with his entire family in one room and would not necessarily be able to go to school. But like the privileged boys, those of the lower classes were instilled in religious practice. They did not escape the customs of religious greetings such as "Ave María" and the practice of blessing oneself with the sign of the cross.

Both religious and secular doctrine gave fathers the right to discipline sons who did not conform to these lifestyle guidelines. Spanish colonial law conferred upon fathers the right of patria potestad, or dominion over his household. This dominance was far-ranging and applied to all minors within the household.[57] The right to discipline was not to be taken lightly, for people in New Spain believed that a father's failure to correct children for misbehavior led to incorrigibly bad young men. Harsh punishments such as beatings were considered normal and, in fact, desirable, at least among the Spanish population.[58] Pedro Galindo, a seventeenth-century author of moral guides, reassured parents who worried that they had been too harsh with their children; it was their duty, he told them.[59] Doña Josefa Amar y Borbón wrote that loving your children to an extreme was a defect, not a virtue, and recommended hitting them and giving them penances.[60]

The father's right to discipline within the extended-family household was generally unquestioned. At times, however, fathers went too far even for the standards of the time. Mothers occasionally intervened to prevent their husbands from applying excessive or unjustified punishments.[61] Although there was widespread community support for paternal discipline, when it crossed a certain line, neighbors, community members, and even family refused to endorse it and protected abused children. In 1796 a frustrated father, Juan de los Santos, an indigenous man from the village of Tecomic in the area of Xochimilco, petitioned local officials to force his son, José Alexandro, to return home. He appealed to the local governor, who tried to enforce these paternal rights and extract the son from his godfather's home, where he had taken refuge. Mateo Galicia, the godfather, argued that he was obligated to protect the boy from his father's poor example and bad treatment. Later, when the governor showed up at Mateo Galicia's house, the whole family rejected him in order to protect José Alexandro.[62] It is telling that those who intervened to prevent these cruel punishments were indigenous; their philosophy of child rearing was gentler than that of the Hispanic groups.

In the late eighteenth century some parents or guardians, generally of wealthier and higher status, became desperate over the young men in their families and asked the state for assistance in reforming their characters—but first they had to defend their parenting. In 1754 don Antonio Zedillo and doña María Sánchez Arefansor complained about their son, who in their words was lazy, disobedient, and inclined to scandalous pastimes. Witnesses confirmed that their son behaved badly despite the fact that "they raised and educated him in the fear of God" and with good doctrine, "giving him a good example and wise counsel." His parents and everyone of his lineage were ashamed of his scandalous behavior.[63] In 1806 don Miguel Ramiro Rodríguez complained that his son was incorrigible: dedicated to gambling, and disrespectful and spent more time on the streets than at home. Don Miguel Ramiro Rodríguez had failed as a father, despite disciplining his son with "repeated corrections" and sometimes hitting him; the father had to specify this treatment to show the court that he had not neglected to discipline his child properly.[64]

These parents, and others who similarly complained about their own sons, were at pains to defend themselves from the charge of having been too soft on their boys. Parental attitudes about discipline were not uniform, however; according to Dorothy Tanck de Estrada, many indigenous parents advocated a gentler, loving attitude and found the Hispanic emphasis on corporal punishment unsavory.[65] Because their sons' conduct was so far from the ideal that was presented by morals and manners writers, the parents who denounced them had to justify their ostensible failure as parents. These accusations became more common in the late eighteenth century as residents of New Spain had accepted the Bourbon message of productivity and order.[66] In reality, boys probably rarely lived up to these ideals, and their lives, especially in the lower classes, were much more complicated and precarious than those described by the guides.

The Lives of Boys

The ways that boys experienced the world around them depended a lot on their families. Whether their parents were wealthy and upper class, whether they lived in Mexico City or the smaller communities that surrounded the metropolis, and their ethnicity, race, even language all affected their experiences. After the first years of their lives at home, they began to venture out into the wider world. For some, this meant going into the streets or the fields to make a living; for others, it meant being apprenticed or going to school. Farming families needed their children's labor, so most boys went out to work in the fields or pastures, and few were able to attend school.[67] The vast majority of boys born into poor families faced considerable dangers in their

Figure 1. Sortie du caffé—marchand de viande (Door to the café—meat vendor). A boy goes unnoticed in the streets of Mexico City. Like many poorer boys, he had to learn early to make his way through the urban world. It was also in the streets that boys learned how to perform a masculinity appropriate to their sphere. Theubet de Beauchamp, *Vistas de México y trajes civiles y militares y de sus pobladores entre 1810 y 1827* (n.p.: n.p., 1830), n.p.

everyday lives, whether they were in cities or the countryside.[68] Those orphaned in childhood often ended up in the streets; mistreated and ignored, they took up small errands to try to hide their vagrancy.[69] Many boys lurked about in the streets (fig. 1) trying to find their way and survive.

Some families placed their sons as apprentices so they would learn a trade from a master craftsman and potentially gain status in a guild. One of the most important things a parent could provide for a son was an occupation, whether a profession or a trade. Parents with connections or some means thus negotiated an apprenticeship contract for their sons. Masters charged a fee to take on an apprentice, so not all parents could afford such opportunities for their sons.[70] For families of modest means, such a prospect might represent some social mobility for their children. It was not a given that all apprentices became masters within their craft but, even so, colonial families frequently viewed apprenticeships as a way for young boys to learn important values and to manage the transition from boyhood through adulthood to become productive, respected men.[71] In addition, those admitted to an apprenticeship lived in the master's house and received food and clothing along with instruction in the trade. By signing an apprenticeship contract, parents were essentially agreeing that the master became a quasi-father to their son.[72]

Nevertheless, despite transferring this authority, some parents did not accept that their sons might be abused by the masters. Although apprenticeships were governed by contracts and the rules set out by guild ordinances, in many cases work conditions were not ideal, if not outright abusive.[73] In 1632 Catalina de la Cruz, a free black woman, complained that although she had signed an apprenticeship contract with the shoemaker Alonso Rodríguez, he had not yet taught her eleven-year-old mulatto son any of the craft and had treated him very poorly. She argued that the contract should be rescinded so that her son could follow a new vocation, to become a tailor.[74]

In 1791 María Josefa de la Vega complained formally about the conditions that her son, Juan José Doistua, experienced while apprenticed to the Mexico City master silk weaver don Juan Antonio Delgado. During the year of his apprenticeship Juan José Doistua had been treated cruelly. The day before María Josefa de la Vega's complaint, the master weaver had tied her son to a fig tree and whipped him repeatedly, throwing buckets of cold water on him to revive him when he passed out. He managed to escape by untying himself with his teeth. This punishment was excessive in its cruelty and seems to have been part of an attempt to break the boy's spirit; apparently the master wanted him to cry or admit that the whipping was painful.[75] This incident represents an extreme, and certainly many apprentices were content in their placements, whereas others left their masters just because they did not care for the trade they were learning or perhaps lacked the maturity to embrace working life.

Many of these failed apprentices were later reported as vagos by their parents or other relatives; their rejection of an apprenticeship was just another sign of their lack of maturity and their rejection of the value of honest work advocated by colonial authorities. Because the various crafts tended to be grouped together on a particular street in Mexico City, apprentices were probably able to socialize and share a sense of camaraderie with others their age. Many silversmiths, for example, had their stores on San Francisco Street, and it was there that one of the apprentices, fourteen-year-old Pedro Alcántara, ran into trouble with the neighboring business, a wine shop whose owner did not appreciate having garbage dumped nearby. Pedro Alcántara's experiences show how these young men had to negotiate the street's dangers. Pedro Alcántara was intimidated into not dumping his barrel of refuse and had retreated, but later he tried to sneakily dump it after dark and was hit over the head.

In the aftermath of his injury, the solidarity and sociability between apprentices and master craftsmen was apparent. Numerous apprentices and master craftsmen from other shops all testified regarding the events; they had clearly been keeping an eye on the situation, and they rushed to help the wounded boy when he was discovered.[76] Apprentices' experiences were diverse—some more successful than others—but this training was a period of transition for many young men in which they learned to deal with the dangers of adult life and the world around them.

Hazards lurked in many places. In Mexico City, when two men decided to race their horses through the streets, they trampled two small boys.[77] In the village of Santa María Maxatla (Tlanepantla), several dogs bit eight-year-old José when he was playing behind his aunt's house.[78] In the smaller towns around Mexico City, many boys or young men worked with animals like these dogs. Lucas Phelipe, a boy of either fifteen or sixteen, was responsible for the dogs that bit José. He worked as a shepherd, and three dogs accompanied him everywhere—when he watched over his flock and even at night.[79] In the area surrounding Mexico City, people made a living with agriculture, and young boys began to work early.[80]

In 1749 in a village on the outskirts of Tlanepantla, a conflict between adults descended into violence. The local *teniente* (deputy) was not able to find the man accused of beating a number of people, so he took twelve-year-old Joachim into custody in his place. At the time of the melee, young children had been witnesses to the fight, and some (according to one witness) might even intervened to help break up the brawl. After Joachim had spent two weeks in jail, the local judge recognized that he was too young and childlike to be held responsible for any criminal acts, but the judge still chose to hold him there until his brother presented himself.[81]

In 1773 Juan Manuel's son was herding some cows in the area of Cuautitlan when some of them tore off some cornstalks from the adjoining field. As a result, the farmer who owned the field hit the young man.[82] Young boys were fair game, and it was hard for them to protect themselves; sometimes others tried to defend them. In 1793, on the roads around Tacuba, Miguel Gerónimo ran into a muleteer who was mistreating some boys who were working with him. Miguel Gerónimo confronted the muleteer on this abuse, but unfortunately his words merely provoked the muleteer, who thrashed Miguel Gerónimo quite badly.[83] Young men were often witnesses to brutal beatings, and because they began to work early in their lives, they were exposed to all the perils that existed in everyday life.[84]

Boys in this period were indeed subjected to many dangers, but they also had a sense of fun, and they found their diversions wherever they could. Undoubtedly they were present at many adult male diversions, such as cockfights, bullfights, and gambling. In Claudio Linati's early nineteenth-century picture of a cockfight (fig. 2), a small boy can be seen pressed against the boards on the left. The moralists hinted at the juvenile appetite for adult pastimes and warned against them; for example, Escoiquiz cautioned that young boys should avoid playing cards so that they would not get used to such diversions and be tempted into gambling. In this idealistic vision, boys should refrain from anything that would entice them into bad habits like gluttony, overconsumption of alcohol, and games of chance.[85]

In Mexico City there were many festival times when no one was supposed to work because of their religious nature. Despite their serious content, these events had much to recommend them to children. The processions that marked the major saints' days and festivals such as Corpus Christi featured musicians, dancers, people in costumes or wearing giant heads, giants, dragons, and much more. Actors performed short plays on the elaborately bedecked allegorical carts and along the route, and some guilds constructed altars. Huge audiences lined the processional route, and more activities took place at the cathedral. On these holidays boys had a chance to enjoy the music, the costumes, and all the excitement.[86] The smaller towns also had processions; although they were probably less ostentatious as those in the capital, they still attracted the local population.[87] The day before patron-saint festivals, village organizers set off rockets in the church's atrium. The procession itself had dancers and musicians, and at night the people enjoyed really elaborate firework displays.[88]

When there were no processions, boys could go the Alameda—the largest park in Mexico City at the time, where both the elite and the poor congregated. There children could watch puppet shows and enjoy the big open spaces.[89] These activities, like so many, were outside; the temperate climate allowed people to enjoy excursions and open expanses. The streets were full of people, and boys often played games there such as *moros y cristianos* (Moors and Christians—probably a bit like cowboys and Indians) and

Figure 2. *Pelea de gallos* (Cockfight). Boys crept into such adult diversions; note that one child is hanging onto a pillar, and the head of another (on the left) barely reaches the top of the wall. Claudio Linati, *Trajes, civiles, militares y religiosos de México (1828)* (Mexico City: Universidad Nacional Autónoma de México, 1956), n.p.

gallina ciega (blind man's bluff); sang children's songs; and hunted chickens or turkeys that roamed the streets. Some of the amusements were more elaborate, such as the *juego del volador*, or flying game, in which the boys swung from a large pole, imitating flying (fig. 3). Groups of boys did battle using blowpipes and small fruit as projectiles, but sometimes they went further and used rocks to fight each other.[90]

Some of the most common toys of the period were blowpipes, kites, spinning tops, balls, lassos, swings, wooden swords, horns used to imitate cowherding, rattles, and hoops used to blow soap bubbles.[91] Boys could also satisfy their appetites for sweets at the *baratillo de los muchachos* (kids'

Figure 3. *L'enjambée des géans* (A Mexican game). The *juego del volador*, or flying game, allowed young boys to engage in the thrills and dangers of being airborne. These were just one of the many perilous games that delighted young boys of the period. Claudio Linati, *Trajes, civiles, militares y religiosos de México (1828)* (Mexico City: Universidad Nacional Autónoma de México, 1956), n.p.

market) in the center of Mexico City, where they could buy as many as six-teen candies for half a real.[92] In both cities and smaller communities, boys had considerable freedom and roamed around without much parental over-sight. For example, it did not seem extraordinary if boys were playing outside well into the night, if the moon was full.[93] In villages, children (girls as well as boys) enjoyed simple games such as hopscotch, but they shared a passion for kites with children of the bigger cities.[94]

In Mexico City children took advantage of the buildings' typical flat roofs (*azoteas*), which were accessible and perfect for flying their kites, but this was a dangerous habit because some boys got carried away, forgot where they were, and fell off the side of the roof.[95] When the wind was strong, the sky would fill up with huge painted kites, and sometimes people would place small lanterns on their kites to light up the night. Occasionally there were so many kites soaring in the air that their movements made murmuring sounds similar to soothing music.[96] Undoubtedly, boys in Mexico City and the surrounding communities found their fun where they could, even if at times it was rather wild and dangerous. This liberty may have led some of them to embrace a life of dissolution as they entered adolescence. But for many it was a break from lives that were challenging and austere.

More privileged children went to some type of school; education was by no means standardized at this time. If parents could afford it, most children started their schooling with the *amigas*, women who ran private primary schools that have been compared to nurseries or even a type of day care. Despite a 1601 prohibition against boys attending the amigas' schools, both girls and boys went, usually from the age of three. They received a rudimentary education, learned to memorize the catechism, and were mostly indoctrinated in the discipline that was to go with learning: silence, obedience, and calm—essentially the type of emotional composure that men were supposed to embody later in life.[97] For boys this meant suppressing what was considered their natural inclination to anger and passion.[98]

Whereas the amigas' establishments mingled boys and girls, schools for children ages five to seven were no longer coeducational. Boys who could continue their education generally went to an *escuela pía* (pious school). These schools were a free option, usually run by parishes or municipalities; they were typically located in an ecclesiastical establishment, and the male teaching personnel were religious. For six hours a day boys studied the ubiquitous catechism of Padre Jerónimo de Ripalda and guides to polite behavior. In addition, the young students learned calligraphy, grammar, arithmetic, history, and art.[99]

Even though these schools were free, not all families could forgo the income that their sons could produce by working, so most boys left school around the age of thirteen and began their working lives.[100] They could enter an apprenticeship between the ages of nine and eighteen.[101] Families always had to balance the advantages of more learning with the domestic economy.

Since the early days of colonialism, local governments had paid for schooling in the smaller villages around Mexico City. This instruction was, like that in Mexico City, heavily religious in content and dependent on Ripalda's catechism. Learning basic prayers and Christian doctrine was central but minimal. In Xochimilco, for instance, students were also taught to cross themselves four times in the morning and four times in the afternoon. Every Friday 100 or more students from the local school paraded through the streets reciting the catechism. In several village schools, boys with some talent sang for the church choir, and others learned musical instruments so that they could accompany the Mass.

In addition to providing the very important religious content, village schools were meant to expose young indigenous boys to the Spanish language. Despite this goal, it was not until the eighteenth century that this project began to be put into effect; in the late colonial period teachers began to ask students to repeat prayers in Spanish, and reading materials started to include side-by-side Nahuatl and Spanish texts.[102] Within the various indigenous villages there was considerable resistance to this trend and in Xochimilco the community defended a teacher who had been fired by local officials especially because his replacement did not speak Nahuatl.[103]

Village schools were not homogeneous, however; boys from other racial groups (españoles, mestizos, and mulattoes) could attend if their parents could afford to pay a fee to the teacher. Because these schools were underwritten by local government funds, officials expected boys to attend. In Tacubaya, both the indigenous boys who did not show up for class and their parents were punished, with six lashes for the adults and three for the children.[104] In the village of Totolapa, in the Chalco area, officials would make trips to the school to reprimand the students, apparently on principle.[105] Yet even with such drastic measures, only about 8 percent of the local population of indigenous villages attended some type of school; at sowing and harvest times and during the rainy season, when roads were often impassable, attendance dropped.

Despite the presence of schooling, the vast majority of colonial Mexicans were illiterate. According to Dorothy Tanck de Estrada, because few jobs required literacy skills, there was no stigma attached to this state.[106] Yet the lack of literacy could be used to torment young men. In 1749 Phelipe de la Cruz, an indigenous man, reported that his brother and others teased him cruelly because of his inability to read.[107] Schooling in the villages was not a brick-and-mortar experience—that is, there was not usually a building set aside for this purpose. Rather, instruction happened wherever the teacher set up—at times in his home, in an empty building lot, or even in a storeroom in the church. There was little equipment beyond the readers, which the boys often shared, and because most learned to read but not write, the older and more advanced students used the teacher's table when they were practicing their letters.[108]

Wealthier families might hire a tutor (usually a cleric) to instruct their sons at home or in either a friary or a priest's home. Others paid to send their boys to grammar schools or colleges.[109] For a family with pretensions of gentility, education for the sons was important. In 1798 María Ignacia San Román wrote to her eldest son complaining bitterly that her other son, don Manuel de Obregón, had terrible handwriting and could not pen a proper letter despite his extensive schooling. She worried that this incompetence would harm him when he circulated among the smart set, and she added that his calligraphy nauseated her, perhaps because it reflected badly upon his character.[110]

Among the many religious orders the Jesuits dominated the educational field; the vast majority of boys who were able to continue their schooling beyond the very basic primary education did so with the friars.[111] Those who attended the Jesuit colleges followed a regimented schedule, but on Saturdays, when they were not learning Latin or other important topics, they organized quiz games of general knowledge. Even these amusements had an intellectual affectation: the teams were called the Carthaginians and the Romans. In their free time the boys played dominoes, threw a ball against a wall, or napped. They had to be careful not to seem too relaxed, because if it appeared that they had too much free time, the Jesuits would organize talks and other educational events.[112] Boys also unwound by smoking cigarettes or using snuff, and although these habits were not uncommon among the general population (even among children), they were considered undesirable inclinations in an educational setting.[113] Studying within a college was an experience limited to a small but influential group of boys defined by their privilege and their upper-class status.

Domestic Surroundings

Children were born into certain situations. Some were welcomed into nuclear or extended families that cherished them from birth and set them on the path to success. Others were born on the sly, the result of amorous trysts and considered dishonoring and illegitimate because they were produced out of wedlock. Aristocratic babies were brought into the world in large mansions surrounded by relatives and servants. Yet in the same building another child might be born to an enslaved mother, and despite the auspicious location, he would not be free or have many chances at social advancement. Families and households tended to be large, composed of many branches of the family, and although the norm was that they were headed by a man, a paterfamilias, female-headed households were common.

Children born to a precarious union or to a woman without any partner faced enormous challenges, whereas others had many advantages. Some had had no parents from a young age; orphaned or abandoned, they grew up in institutions or in families other than their own biological ones. The problem of child abandonment was recognized in New Spain soon after the conquest, and in 1529 Fray Pedro de Gante founded one of the first institutions to look after poor boys and especially mestizo children; wealthy residents provided donations to support the orphans.

In the eighteenth century Archbishop Antonio de Lorenzana established an orphanage, Casa de Niños Expósitos de la Ciudad de México (Foundling Home of Mexico City), specifically to make sure that abandoned babies did not die of exposure. There were similar institutions both in Spain and in other parts of Latin America, and before the creation of orphanages, both convents and friaries received abandoned newborns.[114] The Casa staff baptized all the babies they received and named them; they were breast-fed by wet nurses and then placed with foster families. If all went well, these families adopted the children while they were still young, and the children were integrated into their adoptive families.[115] In smaller communities no such institutions existed, but there was a long tradition of *apadrinados* (children of godparents), through which parents could entrust their newborns to others better able to look after them.[116]

Adoption was an unofficial process, with no set bureaucratic procedure, and it was usually accomplished on an informal level. Sometimes parents on their deathbeds could arrange an adoption or at least a custody arrangement. In his will Lorenzo García named Captain Sebastián de Arteaga as his seven-year-old illegitimate son's guardian; the captain swore to take care of the boy's property (of which the captain received 5 percent a year for his own needs) and raise him to be a good and moral subject.[117] Not all arrangements were lucrative; when doña María Rosalia Cabeza de Vaca's husband left her with a ten-month-old son and no money, she was destitute and could not work while caring for her baby, so she decided to transfer custody to don Andrés Mariano Gardua, a wealthy man who would be able to provide for her child both morally and physically.[118] Among indigenous families it was common practice to take in orphans, who were usually simply incorporated into these families.[119] These adoptions were most frequent during periods of stress, such as epidemics and poor harvests.[120]

Yet whatever the reason, the ties of adoption could be very strong. When Juan Antonio Vásquez heard that his adoptive son had been killed, he traveled a great distance to identify him and testify. At the end of his testimony he expressed a sentiment unusual for this type of proceeding: he stated that he wanted to bury José Mariano because he "treated him as if he were his own son and raised him in his house."[121] Wealthier families also followed this practice; Joseph Antonio Arauz y Figueroa was taken in as a baby by doña María Theresa de Figueroa, who gave him her surname and raised him as her own. He considered her to be his mother, and it was only after her death that other family members turned against him and denounced him as a vago.[122] Joseph was not an isolated example of adoptions within New Spain's upper classes. In some instances upper-class women even "adopted" their very own children who had been born out of wedlock through sexual indiscretions.[123]

Foundlings who were not adopted as babies sometimes found homes when they were older. Between the ages of fourteen and sixteen, these male foundlings were often placed with artisans. These assignments were essentially a modified type of apprenticeship, since it was expected that the orphaned boy would eventually learn a craft from an adoptive father.[124] Among more humble families, the use of adopted children for work was frequent; biological children were expected to contribute to the family economy, of course, but in some cases the line between an adopted orphan and a servant became a bit blurred.[125] José Sebastian, a tributary Indian of San Andrés in Xochimilco, was one such orphan. His parents entrusted him to don Pedro Balderrama as a *huérfano de la casa* (orphan of the house), and starting at a very young age he worked from early morning well into the night, suffering physical abuse, insults, and hunger. He wanted to work elsewhere but his putative adoptive parents would not allow him to leave; they kept him there "as a slave."[126]

Still another alternate family for boys was the friary. Although placing babies in a friary was a less common practice than placing them in a convent, some foundlings—mostly mestizos and mulattoes—ended up living among friars. Parents who could not provide adequately for their boys sometimes sent them to live within the friary walls. The boys became servants of the friary, not destined to take its vows, but living there in perpetuity.[127] Destitute parents considered the friary a sanctuary; if their sons died at a young age, some of these parents would leave their bodies at the church of the Friary of San Diego. The friars buried the young boy—with any friar who had died recently, if possible, thus relieving parents of the funeral expenses.[128] Young men from wealthier families also went to live in friaries, often beginning as students and then joining the order by taking their vows.[129] Not all boys took the vows voluntarily. Some friars recounted much later in life that they had been intimidated or even threatened with death if they did not join a monastic order.[130]

Families and households had different living arrangements, ranging from palatial to derelict. The number of people in a household was also variable and not usually limited to a nuclear family. In Mexico City the most prestigious addresses were large multistoried buildings in which aristocratic and/or wealthy families lived in the upper stories along with their retainers and servants. Most urban residents did not enjoy so much living space; many lived in small apartments or simply rooms on the lower floors of such buildings or in tenements. Numerous families slept in one room and shared communal services with the rest of the residents.[131] Some lived in makeshift structures called *jacales* (shanties) in vacant lots or courtyards.[132] Most people dwelled in very crowded accommodations, with as many as twenty-two people living in a room or two.[133]

Although there were many beggars in Mexico City, their number cannot be unambiguously pinpointed, nor is it clear whether there were homeless people for whom these crowded accommodations would have seemed like a welcome respite. In the late eighteenth century, years of poor harvests led to an inundation of women and children begging in the streets, but no information seems to exist about street children. Boys over the age of ten who were found in the streets soliciting alms were put to work on road projects.[134] In the smaller villages surrounding Mexico City, homes were arranged differently, but households were similarly extended. In these smaller communities, people generally resided in a group of small residences arranged around a central patio.[135]

Whether in a biological family or an adopted one, most boys grew up in these busy households and learned to negotiate their place in the world while absorbing the lessons of hierarchy at home. It was within their homes that boys learned how the pecking order worked. Others, less fortunate, learned these skills in the streets.[136] In theory, the head of an extended family and a household was the father or the most senior male. In reality, for many reasons numerous households were led by women.[137] It is impossible to know what the internal workings of these households were unless domestic relations broke down and came to the attention of the courts. Ideally, household members preserved harmony by respecting the ranking within the extended family.

The bonds of family and the need to protect sons and other relatives was clearly a strong impulse for many residents. Josefa de la Encarnación adopted her nephew when he was very young. When another relative abducted him from her home, she spent a year looking for him, and finally, in 1693, she found him working in a Mexico City bakery. Bakeries often functioned almost as jails, so she could not simply take the boy away, but she began to work on getting his release through the courts.[138]

Custody fights reveal how deeply people felt for the children in their lives: they wanted to protect them, and they could not fathom losing them to another. Don Antonio Rodríguez was a devoted grandfather. When his daughter died at a young age, he adamantly wrote to her father-in-law that he wanted guardianship of the two children. Ventura de Taranco y Gortazar, the other grandfather, responded with a refusal, saying that the two children were surrounded by a loving family—grandparents and a devoted aunt—who was able to provide "maternal love."[139] Parents, other relatives, and even fictive kin such as godparents were all willing to fight for the well-being of the children they adored.

This devotion and parental devotion could also be exploited. Don José Sigher de Cardona reported a scam that took advantage of the love he felt for his son. In 1785, in his capacity as mayordomo (administrator) of the Cofradía de Santísima Señora del Rosario (Sodality of the Sainted Virgin of the Rosary), he was collecting donations in a town in the jurisdiction of Coyoacán when a woman rushed in saying that one of his sons had been murdered. Aghast, he ran out of the house, but as he rounded the corner someone hit him in the head with a rock, and he lost consciousness.[140] His heartfelt reaction was counted on by his attacker, who exploited it to lure him outside and attack him. The love of a child thus trumped his common sense. Parents and other fictive kin often went to great lengths to protect their children and ensure their survival.[141]

Living Up to Expectations

By the time they reached adolescence, Mexican boys, whatever their class, ethnicity, or race, were expected to have absorbed the lessons of social etiquette and to have taken their place within both the household and the larger society. They had to negotiate the contrasting pulls of exerting their manhood in an acceptable or unacceptable manner. For a very few this might mean pursuing a university education, but for the majority it represented work, either in a workshop as an apprentice or in some other kind of occupation that usually entailed manual labor. It is clear that many young men made this transition seamlessly into the world of quasi-adults and work, but some resisted it, and some families—only upper-class ones of Spanish descent—denounced their own sons. Although the use of vagrancy laws to discipline unruly plebeians had occurred in the seventeenth century, such petitions by relatives represented an alteration in the mindset of New Spain's residents. Eva Mehl argues convincingly that the parental accusations of vagrancy reflected the Bourbon promotion of the values of order and productivity.[142] Nonetheless, the prosecution of young men for vagrancy added another layer of pressure to conform to ideals of manhood that were decorous and compliant.

These cases contrast with those in which parents and relatives went to great lengths to safeguard children well beyond their vulnerable years. The accused young men had broken with the fundamental rule of Mexican families: respect for and obedience to the patriarch, an attribute central to New Spain's society.[143] These sons also stood out because their rebellious misbehavior was uncommon. Parents considered them not just failures but also a stain on the family honor and a blot on society. These young men generally fell into two groups: those who refused to work, and those who were considered immoral.[144] The petitions lodged by parents of rebellious sons provide an insight into young men who chose a different path from the norm, but perhaps their behavior indicates a reality closer to the norm than the model boys presented earlier in this chapter. Yet these boys are also an extreme, not the typical child but rather one end of the spectrum of adolescent male conduct in the late eighteenth century. If there is such a creature as the typical male teenager, no doubt he existed somewhere between the model child described in etiquette and morals guides and the young man whose parents were so ashamed of him that they tried to get rid of him through exile.

Most of the examples that I found were from the late eighteenth century, when there seems to have been considerable anxiety among government officials and family members about young men, but such denunciations did begin earlier in the period.[145] Many of the complaints were about young men in their early twenties—still below the age of majority under Spanish colonial law, but not what we would consider teenagers.[146] Those who complained about these young men emphasized that their petitions were the culmination of a long period of attempted corrections and failed punishments that did not change the behavior; the young men refused to work, to give up pastimes, and to be serious. They also demonstrated the typical lack of respect that characterized most teenagers but that colonial Mexican society found abhorrent.[147]

Relatives gave examples of conduct they found shocking. Don Egidio Marulanda complained that his son wrote him letters full of insults and taunts.[148] Ignacio Lucena threatened to beat his mother and his sister and used foul language to insult them.[149] Don Joseph Antonio Arauz y Figueroa called his aunt and female cousins *putas* (whores).[150] The vagos denounced by their own families may have been examples of a failure to move on from adolescent behavior and an inability to transition into manhood. When these young men continued to operate in the manner described in the complaints, their actions could have serious consequences for any families they started. The kinds of behavior that their parents catalogued were very consistent with the problems that desperate wives enumerated in mistreatment and ecclesiastical divorce petitions when they tried to divest themselves of deadbeat and violent husbands.[151]

When men did not make the transition into responsible manhood, the consequences for their wives and children were serious, but even before this stage it was a stain on their parents' honor. The majority of the family based cases were brought forward by people with the honorific title *don*. These families believed that their reputations were important and were affected by the conduct of all those associated with them.[152] But they were not members of the highest aristocracy, who were differentiated with titles such as *count* or *duke* and whose sons would not take up apprenticeships but rather would have access to independent wealth in the form of entailed property.

For example, don Miguel Ramiro Rodríguez described how his son's comportment was a blot on his family's reputation and the honorable way that he had lived his own life.[153] Don Simón de Figueroa objected to his adopted nephew sharing his surname and thus sullying their familial reputation.[154] Don Xavier Esteban Hugo de Omerique stated that his son's road to perdition was discrediting him and his family.[155] Don Antonio Zedillo and doña María Sanchez Arefansor wrote that their entire lineage was ashamed of their son.[156] Don Egidio Marulanda asked that his son be sent to Manila to separate him from his noble family.[157]

Honor was an extremely important value for all residents of New Spain, whatever their rank or ethnicity, but this type of blot on familial reputation also brought with it a stain on the patriarch; it was not only the son who was failing but also the father, who had not properly disciplined his son. In addition, fathers were supposed to provide four things to their sons: food, a proper upbringing, an occupation, and a good example. It was a father's obligation to make sure that his son was able to support himself and his family in a fitting manner and suitable to their rank.[158] When sons did not become productive subjects but instead refused to take up a respectable occupation, it reflected badly on the parents, but especially the father, whose manhood was sullied. It was also an economic threat.[159]

Apart from causing reputational damage, a young man's refusal to take up a trade or a profession had very profound economic implications, as did other habits that often went hand in hand with unemployment: excessive drinking and gambling. Doña Joaquina Ortiz despaired at her son's failure to take up an occupation. She had gotten him a job in a store, where he stole a few coins; then he was apprenticed to a silversmith, but he ran away after a month. When his mother began the proceedings to declare him a vago in 1794, he professed that the only occupation that interested him was painting. Unfortunately, when the authorities made some inquiries about placing him in such an apprenticeship, they discovered that he was too old and did not qualify.[160] At fourteen years of age, José García had already escaped from five different apprenticeships. His stepfather denounced him in 1798 as "insubordinate and not wanting to learn any trade."[161] Even though Tómas Torres was not his son, Lorenzo Lagunas placed him with three different masters, but by 1803 the young man had abandoned each career.[162] Sixteen-year-old José María Dávalos admitted that his father had tried to find a way for him to earn a living in many different areas: administering a hacienda, working in a store, and serving as a notary for a priest.[163]

Sometimes the apparent reason a son did not take up an occupation was related to his lifestyle, usually, a combination of vices and addictions. One of the ways that family members and witnesses described this destructive behavior was simply to say that these young men avoided home and were always in the street. Because the street was perceived as opposite to the house (discussed in chapter 4), this became a metaphor for out-of-control young male conduct. Don Miguel Ramiro Rodríguez wrote that his son "could not be controlled; he abandoned the family home and devotes himself to his vices in the streets."[164] One of the witnesses in the proceedings against Pedro

José Oviedo reported that the young man would not come home to his brother's residence for six to eight days at a time, "staying in the streets."[165] José Angel Saldaña, nineteen years old, would spend entire nights partying in fandangos (private house parties that could be very boisterous), not coming home for several days and failing to show up at his job at the Royal Tobacco Manufactory.[166]

These young men refused to work in order to spend time in what many witnesses called vices: gambling, drinking alcohol, going to fandangos, and engaging in trysts with various women.[167] None of these activities was illegal or even viewed with contempt in New Spain, except when people were not able to moderate their habits and when these interfered with their responsibilities. Those who brought charges clearly thought that the young men had crossed the line between diversion and excess. Some of them had begun to steal from their family members or employers in order to support their habits.[168] Others even sold all their clothes for the same reason.[169]

Similarly, some relatives denounced their young men because they had progressed from flirting to full-blown affairs and involvements with women that were not casual. In all of these cases, the young men reported as vagos had failed to become economically productive, were disrespectful, refused to acknowledge their lower rank in the family hierarchy, and engaged in behaviors such as gambling, drinking, and sex that went well beyond the relatively high levels of tolerance typical of New Spain's society. The young men had not lived up to the expectations held by their parents (and the rest of the family) since their birth, and most were sentenced to four to eight years in the Philippines or in one of the armed services.

Conclusion

When did boys become men? Although there were legal and cultural guidelines that were supposed to mark the transition from one stage to another, officials often interpreted these markers as mere suggestions. There was no formal rite of passage that celebrated adulthood. This question, then, would not have had a clear answer in colonial Mexico. Men spent their lives negotiating their manhood in relation to others. At times they may have felt like full-fledged men, such as in the company of friends or when they could impose their will on men of lower status or power. But this manhood was always contingent, for they learned early in life that they were but one part of a hierarchy; even when they passed the magical age of twenty-five, they still had to defer to men and higher-status women who were older, more powerful, and more forceful.

Becoming a man in colonial Mexico was obviously a messy experience, with few well-defined guideposts and many possibilities to go wrong. Despite this lack of clarity about manhood, there were some socially sanctioned markers for it. When men began to earn a living and could support a household, when they began to court and became sexually active, they joined the ranks of men of equal status. The routes that individual boys took from infancy to manhood also depended on their origins: Were they born into a wealthy family of noble lineage, or were they left at the door of a friary?

Being part of a plebeian or indigenous ethnicity meant having to restrain their behavior in the presence of others of higher status. It must have been galling in that period of adolescence, when young men were discovering themselves and their masculinity, to have to rein in their exuberance and wildness. For indigenous, black, mestizo, or mulatto boys, learning this restrained masculinity must have been infuriating as they watched their fathers, uncles, and other community elders act in subservient deference. It became all the more difficult in the late colonial period, when they had the added pressure of possibly being accused of vagrancy and shipped off to the far-flung edges of the empire. Status made access to education or apprenticeships all the more likely, and thus the opportunity to gain a decent standard of living and the trappings of success were more accessible to some boys. Yet it is clear that boys had fun; unlike girls of the period, they enjoyed relative freedom in the streets of Mexico City and other communities and in the parks, fields and countryside. Their youth was tinged with hard lessons, but for a few years they knew the pleasures of roaming the streets and playing.

CHAPTER 3

Sexuality

✦ AS JOSÉ VASQUEZ LAY IN BED SUFFERING FROM AN ILLNESS, MARÍA
Guadalupe Villaseñor, his mistress, came to him. Contrary to all the prevailing norms, she was dressed as a man. Although cross-dressing was common during periods of abandon such as the Carnival, it was uncommon to do so outside this time. In the eyes of José Vasquez's wife, it seemed to demonstrate not only that inappropriate clothing led to a strategy of seduction but that the two had been carried away by blind passion.[1]

According to the moral authorities of the time, sex was not supposed to be a large part of men's lives; at least, if they obeyed all the rules set out by the Catholic Church, that would certainly be the case. Religious teachings limited men to sexual relations with their wives, and even within marriage intimate contact was supposed to be loving but rather unimaginative. The sexual lives of colonial Mexicans generally remained private as long as they did not attract censure; thus historians have tended to know more about prohibited sexual activities that were condemned by both canon and secular law and less about consensual activities that were close to the social norm. It is harder to find noncriminalized consensual sex in the archives, but in fact the sexual desires and pursuits of colonial Mexican men form a type of undercurrent in much of the documentation. Witnesses in many cases indulged in gossip and hinted at improprieties, but these observations were fleeting and often lacked much substance.

Men, young and old, flirted with and pursued women and sometimes men; they engaged in affairs and lived with partners in *amasiato*, a type of quasi-married liaison, and they had sex in all sorts of places other than their beds.[2] Some men began their sexual lives early; at the age of fifteen or sixteen, for example, Augustín Montiel was already living with his *amasia*.[3] Most people, especially in the lower classes, accepted many sensual behaviors that were common practice but not within the official guidelines. The community understanding of acceptable conduct by a couple often showed a healthy disrespect for or ignorance of the rules and a greater tolerance for behavior outside the norm than was reflected by the official discourse. Under the Bourbons, however, the penalties for inappropriate sexual conduct became more severe—deportation or forced enlistment in the army—and complaints about illicit sexual behavior increased in number.[4]

Colonial Mexicans adopted particular ways of being sexual and witnessed the sexual styles of others along a kind of spectrum; just as there were many masculinities, there were many ways for men in New Spain to express their sexual desires. The "gold standard" was procreative: relations between a man and a woman who were married. Premarital and extramarital sexual relations were tolerated up to a certain point. It was expected that when men and women had an engagement or a promise to marry, they might begin to make love, but they would eventually get married, especially if there was a baby on the way. In the lower classes, a man and a woman who lived together as if married were accepted to a great extent and were probably denounced only if they encountered someone of a more conservative bent or they annoyed a neighbor. Those who were denounced had often lived together for many years and even had many children. Don Juan Francisco Gutiérrez had lived with Sebastiana Santibañes, his mulatta servant, for twelve years before the local priest denounced him—probably because they clashed over other matters.[5]

Mexicans were getting into sexual practices that were further from the "gold standard" but still received a certain amount of tolerance. Attitudes toward prostitution, and toward the women and men who were involved in such conduct, varied over time; they were frequently condemned by authorities but rarely reported, and prostitution was mostly tolerated as a necessary evil.

Sexual practices that were criminalized, such as sodomy (defined as male homosexuality in the present), were even further outside the accepted norm, as other authors have shown. Although there were some spectacular arrests and executions, most Mexicans seem to have tolerated these men as long as they were discreet.[6] Accusations of sodomy were rare in the documents that I used for this book, but the few that I encountered indicate the presence of a subculture of men whose sexual practices included same-sex relations. In 1749 the obraje of Panzacola in Coyoacán was rocked by a report of sexual relations between two male workers. Yet even more interesting, because it demonstrates a kind of tolerance, is that another worker, Marcelo Antonio Quintana, reported that ten years earlier, in the same obraje, one of these men had been discovered having sexual relations with a married man. At that time the obraje's solution was to allow the two men to leave once their debts had been paid off.[7]

Although the other workers and their supervisors objected to the men among them engaging in sodomy, they did not report these individuals to any authorities, nor were the offenders persecuted in any other way having to leave their employment. For that reason, in this chapter I integrate same-sex practices into a larger discussion of the more dominant and pervasive culture of sexuality. Sexual practices diverged from the "gold standard" set by the Church in many ways. Within colonial Mexican society, there were numerous ways in which practices became generally accepted. As a result, a type of vocabulary of courtship, seduction, and relationships developed that was used by individuals across the sexual spectrum in New Spain.

Models and Modalities of Daily Life

The Catholic Church was central in enforcing its version of acceptable sexual practices in colonial Mexico. After the Spanish conquest Church officials imposed this new model on the indigenous peoples of central Mexico; there were attitudes and practices among indigenous men, such as the polygyny (polygamy for men) customary among the upper ranks and the easy access to prostitutes, that were prohibited under colonial rule. But despite the Church's preoccupation with what it considered indigenous sexual sins, conduct outside the rules was widespread within New Spain's population. Both men and women paid lip service to the guidelines but constructed their own version of acceptable customs within their community. Although a large percentage of couples married and lived blameless lives, they lived side by side with others who had affairs with men or women, who engaged in shameless flirting, who lived together as if married, and who even practiced sexual acts that were contrary to all the religious teachings. The Church's model of acceptable sexuality is a good place to start, but it does not represent the reality of many residents of New Spain.

The road to permissible sex began with marriage. The formalities started with a promise to marry, called the *esponsales*; it was usually symbolized by an exchange of gifts, but most important was the mutual assurance of a forthcoming wedding. Some promises were furtively made, often as an excuse for some amorous moments, but others were registered solemnly in front of family, friends, and maybe a priest.[8] For the wealthy, this ritual meant spelling out the economic side of a wedding: the dowry that a woman brought to the marriage and the *donas*, or presents, provided by the groom.[9] This exchange of gifts was not just an element of the official path to marriage; as we shall see later in this chapter, it became integral to courtship rituals and the vocabulary of seduction. The public acts of the esponsales and the actual wedding led to more private ones. Once wedded, a couple could legitimately (but not necessarily satisfyingly) engage in sexual acts; the sacrament of marriage did not, however, exempt husbands from worrying about other rules, such as the forbidding of lust.[10] Weddings permitted men and women to consummate their relationships, but it was not license for pleasuring or sexual practices that were contrary to religious doctrine.

According to the Catholic moralists, once a couple was married, sex became a type of obligation between men and women, called the *débito conyugal*, or conjugal debt.[11] These moralists weighed in at length on the private sex life of a married couple, especially in defining how this conjugal debt should be paid. It was supposed to be a mutual, reciprocal obligation in which both parties were willing participants. A husband and wife did not have to ask each other for sex, but once sex was requested, the spouse was required to comply.[12] This obligation led to official complaints from some wives who claimed that their husbands either refused sexual relations or were impotent.[13]

The sixteenth-century Fray Francisco de Osuna wrote that to deny this duty was a mortal sin unless there was some impediment or reasonable excuse. Despite this portrayal of marital relations as a stark obligation, Osuna also wrote that even though men might be more aggressive and shameless in their desire for sex, wives too could make advances. Because women were by nature more timid about such matters, or because they did not want to appear lewd or lecherous, Osuna continued, they were more subtle about their desires, and therefore their husbands should look for signs that their wives wanted sex. Yet men should also understand that their wives would not necessarily want sex when pregnant or when they had recently given birth. Osuna subtly advised men not to hurry the sexual act; they should "wait for their wives in the business of marriage: because some [women] take longer: men should not satisfy themselves first without waiting for their wives."[14]

Moralists urged husbands to restrict their demands for the conjugal debt to reasonable frequencies.[15] Vicente Ferrer, an eighteenth-century Dominican friar and moralist, wrote, "There is no obligation to pay [the conjugal debt] when it is requested with too much frequency, because this is repugnant to decency and health."[16] Asunción Lavrin reports that one wife complained to religious authorities that her husband asked for sex too often—both day and night. Her perception of the débito conyugal was that it had to be proportionate, and her husband's constant demand did not correspond to the social understanding of a proper married sex life, in which daytime sex was both inappropriate and asking for too much.[17]

Moralists provided some exceptions to the obligation: if the husband was sick, repugnant, drunk, or crazy; if the husband was engaged in an adulterous affair; or if the request was for a prohibited sexual act.[18] The conjugal debt could also be denied when one spouse had a sexually transmitted disease or on days when sex was prohibited for religious reasons.[19] Because marital relations were mostly private, their regularity or absence came to light only if one party lodged a complaint. Some wives did indeed complain about their husbands' conduct. María Gertrudis de Sierra caught her husband having an affair and denounced him; she further objected that her husband had sex with her only when he was drunk, and on these occasions he "did not do it with the affection or love that is required, but on the contrary, slapping and pushing her about."[20] Some rationales for refusing the débito conyugal were not as weighty; one wife complained that her husband had bad breath as a reason to avoid sex.[21] Undoubtedly, most couples had relatively tame but pleasing sexual lives within some level of privacy.

Religious teachings provided guidance on the actual mechanics of sexual relations as well. Osuna listed four positions other than the classic missionary one: on their sides, standing up, with the woman seated, and with the woman on her hands and knees so that the man could penetrate her vaginally from behind. The first three were considered not sinful but indicative of disordered desires and thoughts; the last one, however, was a mortal sin. Osuna recommended the missionary position not only because it prevented sin but also because the consensus of thought, at the time, was that it was more likely to lead to conception. Flipping the missionary position over so that the wife was on top was also considered sinful unless her husband was very obese or if he was ill and could not perform the sexual act any other way.[22]

There are some rare insights into sexual relations that did not follow the prescribed model—but again, only if one party complained. In 1790 don Manuel Hermoso reported his wife to the religious authorities for disturbances in their marriage. His wife countered by accusing him of impotence and of being able to consummate their marriage only with prohibited sexual positions. Through her lawyer she claimed that her husband found many excuses to avoid relations, but when they did have sex, she had to get down on her hands and knees so that he could penetrate her from behind—a position she described as being "like brutes" and likened to dogs. In addition, don Manuel Hermoso may have used his finger to stimulate her, but she equated this act to sodomy.[23]

Of course, the intimate relations of a couple were not centered only on sex; kisses and hugs were an integral part of an amorous relationship. Married people were allowed such pleasures, and these tender gestures were encouraged as long as they were done in private and the couple avoided "excessive enjoyment."[24] There was a fine balance between the official sanction of sex within marriage for procreation and the associated pleasures that came with it. Both men and women in colonial Mexico frequently acknowledged that they struggled with this "pull of the flesh," but they were constrained by the official demand that they control such yearnings; men frequently explained away these urges as a product of their "fragility."[25] It is hard to know how many individuals in New Spain actually took these teachings to heart, but certainly many, especially in the lower classes, flouted the rules and lived according to community standards rather than those sanctioned by the Church.

Like so many other situations, a couple who lived "as if man and wife" came to light only in certain circumstances: if a child was born out of wedlock, if the couple was denounced for living in sin, or if a man refused to marry a woman after engaging in premarital sex with her. The consensus among historians is that these quasi-marriages were very common among plebeians; within their own communities they had a sense of the acceptable limits and an informal set of rules that governed such relationships.[26] Upperclass men certainly engaged in all sorts of affairs, and at times brought their mistresses to live in their own homes, but these men did not usually have affairs with upper-class women, whose chastity was highly guarded.[27]

A quasi-marriage was often disclosed when the couple attracted the attention of authorities, perhaps because of some violence between the spouses or because a neighbor had denounced them as living illicitly or in *amancebamiento* (cohabitation).[28] These accusations may seem inconsistent with the idea of tolerance of quasi-marriages, but in most cases they were made only after a couple had lived together many years, sometimes after several children had been born.[29] The language of the witnesses followed a formula—the same set of words returns as if by rote—and this pattern allows us a glimpse of the community standards that defined a couple, whether married or not.[30]

In 1581 two Mexico City mestizos, Juan Torres and Ana Perales were accused of amancebamiento because they "ate and slept together at one table and in one bed."[31] The words are typical: there is always a reference to eating and sleeping together. Amancebamiento was not just about sex—people had flings and other sexual encounters all the time; rather, it was the re-creation of the intimate domestic life of a married couple, who did not just have sexual relations but who also shared meals and other cozy domestic moments. In 1796 Juana Martina testified about her tenants, a Mexico City couple, who had been denounced for living together "as if husband and wife, and in her opinion that meant that they were married." In a twist on the usual formula, she noted that they fought every day.[32]

The interactions of a couple, including fighting, reassured community members that the people involved had a relationship equivalent to marriage. Consequently, witnesses assumed a couple was married because of the familiar way the partners interacted; in 1796 one witness stated that he assumed Norberto de la Trinidad and María Josefa Domínguez were married because of the way she scolded him.[33]

When Fray don Pedro Garduño was caught in an illicit relationship with María Calderón, it was harder to determine what to call this union. One witness noted that the two got drunk together every night; another reported that in the fights between them, the friar told his mistress that "what I give you is for God," to which María Calderón replied that this did not make sense, since he was her lover. The witness reasoned that they were in a quasi-marriage because otherwise Calderón would not fight with a man of God, nor would a cleric beat a woman; the two had terrible brawls, so much so that the whole neighborhood heard, and their room seemed to be shaking.[34]

The domestic life that neighbors perceived in unmarried couples could include less conflict and more familial types of roles. When civic authorities went to arrest don Juan Antonio Castel for his illicit relationship, they found him cooking the family's meal while his amasia, doña María Ignacia Garrote, was upstairs breast-feeding their youngest child.[35] There is no question that religion was an incredibly strong force in the daily lives of colonial Mexicans, but that did not mean they exhibited a slavish obedience to the rules set out by the Catholic Church or an inability to construct their own sense of what constituted couplehood and the role of sexuality within their relationships, formal and informal.[36] Similarly, sexual relationships between both young and old frequently began in ways that were not contemplated by clerics or moralists.

Courtship and Seduction

Young love was not well constrained by the rules in colonial Mexico, and even though the clergy preached against it, many couples began their sexual lives outside marriage. These first steps at love are better documented for relations between men and women, but certainly there were men who discreetly sought male partners. Some partners then tied the knot, but others continued either in quasi-marriages or in casual sexual relationships. Despite constant admonitions from religious authorities, premarital sex was quite common, probably because the community tolerated it within certain guidelines and limits.[37] Although women were supposed to be secluded and protected from the hubbub of daily life, in reality, depending on their socioeconomic status, they circulated within the streets, marketplaces, churches, and many other venues, allowing men various opportunities to charm and seduce them. Not all women were so readily accessible for courting, however; those of the upper classes were more isolated, although Ann Twinam has shown that this seclusion did not protect them from having nonmarital sex.[38] Plebeian men, because of their greater interaction with women, had more liberty than upper-class men for courtship and seduction.[39] Men found occasions to present themselves attractively and then used different strategies to gain women's trust, affection, and desire.

Lower-class men often simply chanced upon their inamoratas in the streets or in the *vecindades* (tenements) where they lived, but generally they tried to get close to the objects of their desire in some way. Some encounters seem incredibly simple: Simón Tlatemanpan testified that he met Josefa Teodora on a street in Milpa Alta and stopped to chat. He reminded her of the good times they had had previously, and they went to her house to have sexual relations.[40] María Dolores Iglesias, a seventeen-year-old Mexico City Morisca (a racial term for African ancestry), related that don Ignacio de Lis walked and chatted with her in the street, and they arranged to have sex.[41] José Ignacio Ocariz met Ricarda Gutiérrez in the street and invited her to drink some pulque, an alcoholic beverage. She accepted and got rather tipsy, after which she did not want to return home. He took her to a friend's house, and they had sex, beginning a six-month relationship.[42] Other men, such as Manuel Lascano, an español, used to hang around Juana Avilez's house and try to catch a glimpse of her from the street.[43]

Young women's guardians recognized the practice of young men lingering about in the streets, and when the guardians were trying to stop a relationship they sometimes attempted to ban certain suitors from the areas near their homes.[44] Two young people, José Heredia and María Hilaria Martínez, lived in the same vecindad and, despite adult objections, felt an attraction. They met under the tenement stairs instead of on the street.[45] Juan Antonio Castel took a room in the same building as the woman he wanted to seduce.[46] All these examples were recorded only because relatives denounced their sexual intimacies. Proximity was crucial to having the chance to seduce, and when people lived close to each other, liaisons were more likely.

Social events in New Spain brought people together: formal occasions at the viceregal court, a fandango in a private house in Mexico City, or a village fiesta. At more popular parties the spaces were small, and people of both sexes got close to each other. When Antonia Gertrudis Maqueda, a mulatta, returned to her home in the neighborhood of Santísima Trinidad in Mexico City in 1701, a party had started. Various men were there, some were playing the guitar and some were dancing. She sat down on a bed next to one of the men, asked for the guitar, and began to play.[47] In 1786, at a lively Mexico City gathering where people were doing a *contradanza*, don José Leandro Ochoa was alarmed to see a young man named Manuelito sitting between two women—his wife and a neighbor—with his hands up their skirts.[48] José María Ramírez, an indigenous youth of seventeen, got into trouble when he went to a fandango in 1801; he innocently began to converse with his friend's wife, but instead of being fun this conversation led to jealousy and blows.[49]

Many religious events had a less holy, more riotous, side that allowed people a certain leeway in their exchanges. Several authors have described the dances and masquerades that accompanied fiestas in Mexico City as well as how the rules were loosened so that it was acceptable to cross-dress.[50] The festivities were probably somewhat tamer in smaller communities, but they did allow for courting. In 1769 Francisca de Lara, a resident of Coyoacán, went to sell fruit in Mixcoac on the occasion of the fiesta of Santo Domingo. Her niece, a *doncella* (chaste maiden) who was eighteen or twenty, came along with her to see and enjoy the celebrations. Early in the afternoon two young men came over and offered the women some pulque. Francisca de Lara stated that she accepted the pulque because she knew one of the youths and did not want to be rude. But she was very much aware that the drinks were really directed at her niece and that the invitation was part of a courtship attempt. When one of the young men returned with more pulque, she refused it, sensing sexual danger for her protégée.[51]

Buying drinks or other treats during fiestas, when it was harder to refuse contact, was a good strategy for men who wanted to begin a courtship. In Mexico City, on the occasion of the fiesta of San Juan, doña Vicenta Peralta went out in a carriage with her two daughters and her son-in-law. Thomás Benegas approached their coach and offered them sweets; they resisted the gift because Thomás Benegas's attention to her unmarried daughter was unwelcome. Out of politeness and perhaps because of the fiesta atmosphere, they relented, but then Benegas returned with a kerchief of fruit and threw it into the carriage (not giving them a chance to decline the offering). They returned it to him.[52] On the occasion of the fiesta of Santa María in Cuautitlan, Josef Mendoza was at a food stall with many women, and he was inviting them all to drink pulque. Previously he had joined in the "fun" of throwing *cascarones* (eggshells filled with flour) at various women.[53] Both fandangos and fiestas were clearly a time of greater freedom, when men and women could engage in banter, get close, drink and eat together, and take the first steps on the road to seduction.

Although these men's actions would not have met the approval of clerics and moralists, in a way they were borrowing from the official discourse on courtship and using a vocabulary of seduction that was accepted within the community. Gift-giving was part of the formalized process of esponsales and thus came to signify a sexual advance. The tokens exchanged by a young couple might include pieces of jewelry or just pieces of cloth.[54] Miguel Fernández gave Ana Lascona a copper reliquary and a kerchief as well as a ring.[55] Cloth and garments had special symbolism for Mexicans and was often part of the rituals of seduction.[56] Many men gave gifts of cloth, but others were more wide-ranging in their offerings. When Juan Antonio Castel was trying to start a relationship with doña María Ignacia Garrote, he sent her a message that he would look after her clothes.[57] When don Juan Pablo Cansino contracted an esponsales with doña Mariana Lozano, he began to clothe her in addition to giving her jewelry in the practice typical of richer Mexicans. After her mother died, he provided her with a heavy black mourning tunic, which she found too hot, so she accepted a lighter version from her cousin. Juan Pablo Cansino was furious; the fact that another man provided clothes for his fiancée was an insult to his honor. He noted that he did not like the idea of other men clothing "his women."[58]

This language of gift-giving and seduction crossed over into same-sex seductions. In 1803 Sergeant Cristóbal Sánchez got into trouble for his generosity with soldiers of lower rank than he was. To various men he gave money to see a play at the Coliseo, advances on their salaries, and many gifts of shirts. Some of his recipients chose to perceive these favors as innocent tokens of his generosity, but others reacted by assuming that Sánchez was a man of irregular dealings and "dishonest thoughts." Sánchez was aware that his gift-giving could arouse suspicion, and he reportedly stated to one recipient that "he [the recipient] should not think that he was giving him money because he wanted something bad but rather that he liked him a lot and saw that he was a nicely shaped man."[59]

It is much harder to know how men might try to seduce other men when such acts were so dangerous. Zeb Tortorici mentions the gift of a piece of blue cloth as part of the dealings between two men who were caught in same-sex acts. In his testimony, one of the men related that he had given the other man a piece of cloth, but as the seriousness of the charges against the two men became clear, he changed his story and said that he had sold the cloth.[60] His denial is revealing because it is a small detail; it was important to deny the gift, I believe, only because such a gift was part of the codes of seduction. Admitting to a gift of cloth in such a situation was tantamount to admitting to consenting to the act of sodomy. Courtship and seduction were fraught with anxiety, but they did follow certain patterns.

Extramarital sex was more or less tolerated, but it was still inhibited because it could have dire consequence for both men and women. Thus putative lovers had to find ways to communicate without alerting parents, guardians, or the authorities to their intentions. Many lovers would make signs at each other, either because it was exciting or maybe to keep their communication secret.[61] María Gertrudis de Sierra caught her husband making signs to his mistress; unfortunately she did not specify what these gestures were.[62] We are left to imagine that they were recognizable as a sexual invitation. Similarly, Antonio de Jesús observed a man signaling to his wife, after which she left with the man.[63] The Spanish man Eugenio Sánchez de Valderrama slit the cleric Diego de Castro's throat simply because he observed him making signs to his sister.[64] Others were more candid about their intentions and openly flirted with their lovers. Neighbors saw Josef Ignacio Morales and Deonicia Rivera cavorting in the streets, but they had exchanged pieces of cloth, so their actions seemed less objectionable.[65]

Kidding around, or *chancear*, was also part of the language of seduction.[66] Estevan José Gutiérrez had begun such light-hearted teasing and fooling with María Josefa Pomposa Meléndez; in fun she told him that his beard was too long, and she took him to the barber to be shaved. From a contemporary viewpoint her actions might seem innocent and irrelevant to courtship, but hair had multiple erotic associations, which the other men in the house understood.[67] Her intervention with a man's hair was a type of signal of her sexual interest.

When don Juan Villanueva had an affair with his servant, Petra Robles, she described how he was playful with her and caressed her. Although the two might have believed they were being discreet, other servants observed the flirtatious conduct. Don José Magallanes was shocked to see his master sitting on Petra Robles's skirts and treating her with affection that did not seem appropriate, especially in the public eye.[68] Remember that even married couples were not supposed to kiss or hug in public. Witnesses also recognized this kind of flirting as a preliminary between two men, who were caught one night having sex in the obraje de Panzacola in Coyoacán.[69]

Words were very important; to woo successfully, men had to use *palabras dulces* (charming words).[70] Men also usually had to make some kind of promise. If they had some education, they often wrote notes or letters to express their affection. They frequently had to recruit allies—friends, relatives, or servants—to carry these messages.[71] Although he was married, Phelipe Jesús sent a note to Isidra Josepha inviting her to a baptism; this invitation was a subterfuge to seduce her.[72] The love letter of Benacio Salvador to doña Felipa Gómez began, "Very esteemed *Negrita* (little black one) of my heart," then stated that he "would not have any pleasure, my esteemed Felipita, until I am once again in your arms so that you can delight me, *nanita*." He signed off as "Your *negrito* who really loves you." As a postscript he added, "I wish that this lucky letter would give a thousand hugs to the angel who will open it."[73]

Unfortunately, it was Felipa's husband, don José Ignacio Valdivieso, who opened the letter, but the sentiments provide an example of the eloquence that colonial Mexican men could employ when inspired by love. Imagine the frustration and humiliation that don José Ignacio Valdivieso felt. Previously he had denounced his wife's affair and had ensured that Benacio Salvador was sent to serve in the army in a far-flung post. But despite his authority as a husband and his influence, he was powerless against this love affair. Reading Benacio Salvador's note confirmed don José Ignacio Valdivieso's lack of power despite his status and wealth; his sense of manhood was damaged, and the only way to attempt to repair it was to once again denounce the two lovers.

Although premarital sex was quite common in colonial Mexico, respectable doncellas would not agree to give up their virginity or their virtue too easily. Sex outside marriage carried the risk of pregnancy, and the loss of virginity tarnished young women for other possible marriages. Although some women embraced these risks, many were conditioned for a life of chastity. In order to break down their resistance, men had to make promises. Most commonly, men (such as Joseph Seferino) would include a promise to marry in their loving words.[74] Without a doubt, many couples began married life in just such scenarios, but these stories did not usually make it into the archives. When a man withdrew his agreement to marry, the woman or her relatives complained, and a record was created. These accounts reveal certain patterns in the promises made by men before the act. Although the most common undertaking was the promise to marry, there were some variants.[75] Men of high status seemed allowed to be vague in their assurances. Many such men seduced women with the ambiguous assurance that they were *caballeros* (gentlemen) or *hombres de bien* (men of honor).[76] Suitors who could not lay claim to this status sometimes promised to make things right in case of a pregnancy, which was a nebulous promise that allowed them some room to wiggle out of their obligations.[77]

Despite women's postsex recourse to these promises, Asunción Lavrin wonders why women agreed to intercourse when it was such a gamble. She concludes that many women agreed to a sexual relationship as a form of rebellion.[78] Doña María Ignacia Garrote fits this model; by the time a neighbor reported her for an illicit relationship, it was four years old and had produced two children. Looking back on the beginning of her romance, she related that when don Juan Antonio Castel approached her, she was "tired of her mother scolding and controlling her" and agreed to a sexual relationship with only the assurance that he was an hombre de bien.[79] Her reasons are eerily similar to those that Kathryn Sloan discovered among young Oaxacan women one century later.[80] A colonial Mexican man clearly knew that he had to at least go through the motions of making a promise when the object of his desire was young and a virgin. He had to play the role of a man whom women would believe and who would become an ideal husband or at least an exciting lover.

The decision to give in to a man's seductive ways was not entirely a logical decision based on whether he was likely to live up to his promise. When women complained about the cads who abandoned them, they seldom mentioned whether the men were handsome or charming, but surely such factors must have swayed them. Barbara Moctezuma thought that her son-in-law was really handsome and warned that his looks could cause problems; her comments represent a very rare instance in the judicial documents.[81]

The erotic was often somewhat hidden just under the surface for colonial Mexicans, but it nevertheless lurked on the edges, along with magic.[82] Some men resorted to various strategies to attract a loved one, including herbs, help from the devil, and the use of images or amulets made from hummingbirds.[83] Others used strategically placed amulets or erotic tattoos on their legs, arms, or chest to catch another person's eyes.[84] Lower-class men, primarily mestizos and mulattoes, often used tattoos of a male goat, a figure associated with diabolism but also with courage and sexual prowess. These tattoos were part of an image of manliness they wished to project; it was supposed to exemplify their sexual abilities as well as other masculine qualities such as horsemanship.[85]

Horses were often central to men's livelihood, and their ability to ride was tied to manliness. Manhood included riding horses; the ability to ride was an integral part of masculine identity.[86] On one level, this connection was related to men's role as soldiers, but there was also a more fundamental erotic association between riding a horse and the sexual act.[87] Whether women found good riders sexy was probably inconsequential to colonial Mexican men; nevertheless, they made such qualities part of their strategies to conquer female hearts. They did, at times, use their horses to get closer to women (fig. 4). Returning from a fiesta in Mixcoac, Mateo de Lara rode his horse with his cousin, an attractive young woman, behind him on the horse's rump—a position that forced her to hug him in order to stay on.[88]

These seductive ways were intertwined; horse tattoos, horsemanship, and magic overlapped and reinforced the self-image of manliness for men in New

Figure 4. Recréation mexicaine (Mexican pastime). This picture shows three seductive strategies: riding together on a horse, having a fighting cock, and playing music. Theubet de Beauchamp, *Vistas de México y trajes civiles y militares y de sus pobladores entre 1810 y 1827* (n.p.: n.p., 1830), n.p.

Spain. These elements were layered into a performance of masculinity that was seductive. The mystical attractions of amulets, tattoos, and good horsemanship might have been augmented by fashion statements. Moralists of an earlier period generally targeted female fashions for their scorn, but they worried that men took fashion too seriously and often deviated into feminized styles.[89] In the sixteenth century Fray Thomas de Trujillo was aghast at men who let their hair grow long and tied it in pigtails and who wore all types of ornamentation; other moralists deplored the use of cuffs and ruffs.[90] When Mexico City erupted in a riot in 1692, some indigenous men taunted the Spanish but also made fun of their clothes. They shouted, "Spanish swine, here are the ships, get going to the draper's store, you sodomites, to buy ribbons and caballeras."[91] This moment of rebellion allowed the normally downtrodden and feminized indigenous men to turn the tables and poke fun at upper-class fashions.

The appeal exerted by colonial men because of their looks is impossible to measure, but some did take trouble with their appearance. Plebeian fashion was probably pretty static and mostly geared to ethnic identity, but these men stood out with their highly colored garments; they dressed much more simply than indigenous men, who wore cotton pants and shirts supplemented with a *tilma*, a blanketlike cape. Mestizo and mulatto men wore variants on Spanish fashion, but gradients of luxury depended on financial and social status. In the eighteenth century the upper classes imitated the latest French fashions with wigs and jackets.[92] There are very few fashion notes in the archives, but the 1801 account of don Manuel Obregón, a military cadet, is an exception. He stole some clothes and jewelry from his brother "in a fit of vanity" to impress some friends he was meeting. The items in question were a scarlet cape (*chipota inglesa*), a hat, and a watch.[93] In this case it was male friends whom the cadet wanted to impress—there were no women present at the meeting. The authorities did express some concern about cross-dressing (except during Carnival), but there are very few reports of transvestites.[94] What was more common was the insult *amujerado*, (effeminate), which men used with one another to emphasize the contrast with their own manliness. But which was more attractive to women: the brash male with violent tendencies (a don Juan character), or the softer version (fig. 5)?

An incident in Cuautitlan in 1778 provides some contradictory evidence. It was during the period of Carnival, when many social restrictions were lifted, that Pablo Guerrero and Josef Mendoza clashed. Guerrero was an aggressive brute: he picked fights, lacked respect, constantly insulted others, and refused to obey local officials and his elders. He was a braggadocio who liked to ride his horse everywhere. In contrast, Josef Mendoza was a painter by trade, a hard worker, and described by his elders as "quiet and peaceful." Pablo Guerrero bullied Josef Mendoza not only physically but also by constantly denigrating his manliness. His insults included *teton* (mama's boy) as well as "amujerado," but mostly he called him Susano. This nickname stuck so much that early in the document Josef Mendoza is referred to as Susano or Josef Susano.[95] Pablo Guerrero's use of this masculinized version of the women's name Susana is a bit mysterious, for that was not even a common name in the period, but it seems to have been part of the campaign of violent and demeaning behavior directed at Josef Mendoza.[96] It is hard to know why Pablo Guerrero engaged in this campaign of bullying the seemingly harmless Josef Mendoza—he may have just rubbed him the wrong way. But one reason Josef Mendoza infuriated Pablo Guerrero so much does become clear.

Figure 5. *Puesto de chia* (Chia drink stand). The young man at this drink stall seems to fit the mold of what Pablo Guerrero called amujerado, or effeminate. He is socializing with others at a festival, perhaps taking advantage of the looser customs of the time. Theubet de Beauchamp, *Vistas de México y trajes civiles y militares y de sus pobladores entre 1810 y 1827* (n.p.: n.p., 1830), n.p.

Despite the fact that Pablo Guerrero was the epitome of certain masculine qualities, the local women all seemed to like Josef Mendoza better.[97]

Colonial Mexican men had to negotiate the fine line between respecting the social strictures of hard work, respect, and orderliness and exuding a masculinity that they thought was attractive. In some contexts Pablo Guerrero's version of masculinity would certainly have been the dominant and more appealing model. Yet even though there was some tolerance for same-sex acts, the sexuality that dominated was between men and women, and most men therefore operated within the confines of this model. Just like Pablo Guerrero, some men used insults such as amujerado to denigrate other men by impugning their sexual identity and consequent manliness.

Manuel Mota was upset with Manuel de la Vega over an unpaid bill for some work. While Manuel de la Vega was working with others on a job site, Manuel Mota came by and not only called him amujerado but also said that "he is like women."[98] Witnesses remarked that despite the severity of the insults, Vega remained calm—a quality that he shared with Josef Mendoza. Some insults were more direct—the term *puto*, or sodomite, was not a common insult but did occur. Among his many other acts of rebellion, Juan Velásquez called one of the officials trying to arrest him a puto.[99]

Men in New Spain had a huge range of insults, so it is not clear why they used these particular terms in these situations. Was there something in the context or the individuals that made the use of insults related to sexual identity and manliness appropriate? There were certainly other insults with sexual connotations, such as *cabrón* and *cornudo* (both referring to cuckolds), which had associations with marriage and the respect that a wife had for her husband. An assertion of accepted sexuality was evidently vital in some situations, and using insults connoting sodomy could invert this need. In a very short but evocative document, Thomas de la Cruz, a twelve-year-old boy, testified that an older man, Phelipe de Santiago, had tried to seduce him. The boy not only defended himself by knifing Phelipe de Santiago, he also asserted a standard sexual identity by declaring that he had an *amistad* (friendship) with a girl, María de Vota.[100] In this context the "amistad" referred to a sexual relationship.[101] It was not enough for the boy to have fought off his attacker with a knife; he also had to emphasize his sexual identity as a person not engaged in same-sex encounters.

The contexts of courtship and seduction varied widely depending on the ethnicity, social rank, and economic status of those involved. It was a dance of veiled messages, sometimes communicated by signals and other times with notes, but men tried to entice the objects of their desire with tempting treats, an alluring physique, or proper conduct. They used a common language of wooing, but the process was fraught with danger regardless of where they were on the spectrum of sexuality.

The Spaces of Sexuality

Privacy was rare for all but the wealthiest of colonial Mexicans, so people had sex in all sorts of locations. But homes were the settings for most lovemaking, whether a couple was in a licit or an illicit relationship. Despite the efforts of fathers who were vigilant of their daughters' virginity and honor, many seductions and first amorous fumblings took place indoors. The sleeping arrangements of colonial Mexicans did not always provide for much separation between unmarried men and women and often allowed for individuals to move around at night, enter homes under cover of darkness, and consummate the desires evoked earlier by the rituals of courtship. Heads of households granted access to their homes to people they trusted, at times including their daughters' fiancés, but allowing someone to enter one's home was risky.[102] Colonial Mexicans engaged in trysts in all sorts of places, finding secret or not-so-secret retreats wherever they could. They also went to certain spaces to meet others and engage in games of seduction; because of these activities, these places became associated with sex—that is, they were transformed into sexualized spaces.

Living quarters for most Mexicans were often crowded. Overflowing residences were typical both in Mexico City and in the surrounding villages because households were composed of immediate family members, other relatives, and servants. With such proximity, it was not always easy to make sure that there was a separation between boys and girls and between young men and women. Nevertheless, Vicente Ferrer admonished parents that they had a "grave" obligation to make sure that after the age of seven, children slept in different rooms in their own beds so that in their curiosity they would not hear, observe, or learn things that might sully their natural purity.[103]

In her study of the history of bedrooms, Michelle Perrot asserts that it was only after the eighteenth century that separate bedrooms for sleeping became a norm. Previously, most residences had one common room that was multifunctional and where various generations all slept. A married couple would usually have a separate bed, but often in the same room. Probably because of these close quarters, people mostly slept with their clothes on.[104] It is striking that in some of the cases of nighttime raids on the residences where couples were suspected of having illicit sex, the individuals were found naked.[105] Only the upper classes had residences with multiple rooms and could therefore afford privacy and separation, but even so there were still illicit encounters between men and women.[106]

Within the honor system that prevailed in colonial Mexico, fathers or other guardians had to preserve the virginity of their daughters or suffer a blow to both their own honor and that of their children. When young men seduced women in the women's own homes, they violated not just the daughters' purity but the trust that had been afforded them as friends and trusted confidants.[107] Don José Arteaga complained in 1793 that his friend, don Francisco Arana, had abused his affection and confidence. He had granted his friend free access to his house in Rivera de San Cosme, a Mexico City neighborhood and a place at the communal table. Don José Arteaga expected that his friend would not "exceed societal limits" and would safeguard don José Arteaga's honor because of the blind faith he had in his friend. In this particular instance, the sleeping arrangements typical of Mexican families were a contributing factor to the seduction. When the neighborhood celebrated the fiesta of the Virgin Nuestra Señora de la Consolación, don José Arteaga hosted many extra guests and friends who had come for the occasion. He explained that he had put his friend in the room where he and his wife usually slept, and everyone else was in another room, while he and his wife bedded down in the main room. Don Francisco Arana sneaked out of the room, and because he had been courting Don José Arteaga's daughter, he was able to slip into her bed and consummate their relationship.[108]

Colonial Mexican men were jealously protective of their homes; protecting the chastity of the women and girls within was just one more reason to adopt such an attitude. Friendship was not the only motivation for allowing men from outside the household to enter the family home. Many businesses operated from homes, and thus employees—or in the case of artisans, apprentices—usually lived with the family. Don Francisco Orgaz owned a draper's store in Mexico City and had living quarters above the shop. He hired don Manuel Caballero, who lived, ate, and slept with the family. But don Manuel Caballero abused this confidence and began to solicit don Francisco Orgaz's daughter; he had gotten as far as a promise of marriage when don Francisco Orgaz discovered the young man's subterfuge, fired him, and kicked him out of the house.[109] These rare glimpses into the implications of sleeping arrangements and the possibilities for seduction were recorded only because they went terribly wrong. Undoubtedly many young couples managed to sneak around at night with more finesse.

It was not just young lovers who took advantage of the sleeping arrangements in Mexican homes to engage in premarital sex. In Coyoacán, María Petra Robles, a chambermaid in the house of don Juan Villanueva, thought she was being very discreet. She slept in the same bed as the kitchen maid in the residence's main room; María Petra Robles would position herself near the door, and when she believed that the other maid was sound asleep, she would sneak out to her master's bedroom.[110] The priest of Tultitlan, in the Tacuba region, accused Marcos Nicolás, the indigenous governor, of making sure that most of the town's men were stuck working in nearby haciendas so that he could have sexual relations with their wives.[111]

Colonial Mexicans denounced sleeping arrangements when they suspected illicit activities. When don Manuel de Santa María y Escobedo was running an errand at the house of doña María Sevallos in 1796, he found the entire household sleeping in the main room. He arrested a lodger, don Joaquín Burgos, who protested his innocence. Don Joaquín Burgos claimed that these were not the regular sleeping arrangements; they had whitewashed the walls in the other rooms and were forced to sleep in another area. In order to preserve their decency, doña María Sevallos and her daughters had placed a folding screen between themselves and don Joaquín Burgos.[112] In 1806 two couples were arrested because all four people were sleeping on the same mat. They denied all wrongdoing and claimed that they were just sleeping.[113] The boundary between decent and indecent sleeping arrangements clearly fluctuated, depending on the situation and the individuals involved.

Homes were not the only places where Mexicans bedded down. Because bakeries and obrajes operated as semiprisons, many workers, both male and female, were not allowed to leave at night. In the obraje de Panzacola, in Coyoacán, workers set up planks to delineate their individual spots (which they called *ranchos*) and then covered themselves with blankets. On a stormy night in 1749, Juan Carmen Thorres placed some ranchos near where Juan Joseph Molino, an indigenous worker, had set up for the night. Juan Joseph Molino stayed up for a while because the bugs were bothering him; then he remembered that he had forgotten to pray, so he blew out the candle and in the darkness said his rosary. Thinking that Juan Joseph Molino was finally asleep, Juan Carmen Thorres began to have sex with Joseph García.[114]

In Mexico City, Thomás Angulo, the doorman of a bakery located in Callejón Amor de Dios, took advantage of his control of the door and the quiet of the night to bring in a woman. He made an assignation with a woman identified only as La Sargenta but known to be of dubious morals. Thomás Angulo, who was originally from Manila, claimed that he had solicited her for sex just the one time; other employees, however, reported that he had been bragging that she came to sleep in the bakery every night and that they were lovers.[115] A couple that was determined enough always found ways to hide their trysts. Don Mariano Padilla and doña Joaquina Balderrama knew that their every move was under scrutiny because they had previously been accused of illicit relations. They generally avoided meeting in their homes and either rented rooms for their liaisons or had sex in hired carriages.[116]

The Mexico City public prison was the setting for a shocking love affair between the head jailer's wife and one of the prisoners. In 1797 Pedro Benavides had just finished his sentence for vagrancy, but he stayed in jail apparently because of illness. Taking advantage of the times that the jailer's wife, doña Gertrudis Contreras, brought him food, Pedro Benavides began to flirt. Soon the two began to go out together, and various prisoners witnessed them kissing and hugging. Pedro Benavides stated that he seduced his jailer's wife simply by taking her out for coffee; they had sex in the jail's mezzanine.[117] For Pedro Benavides this affair carried multiple attractions: the draw of the illicit, the chance to take vengeance on the man who held power over him, and the ability to diminish the jailer's manhood while building up his own.

Although beds and sleeping rooms might have been primarily associated with sexual relations, at least in the minds of officials and religious authorities—in fact, in the minds of many colonial Mexicans—many other spaces were linked with the allure of sex.[118] These were the places people went to engage in courting, where men flirted and made advances and which were redolent with the promise of erotic and sensual pleasures. These spaces often became places associated with sexual acts, a type of shorthand for seduction in the courtship rituals that were common between Mexicans. The preliminaries to seduction often occurred outdoors; colonial Mexicans were fond of going out to *pasear*—literally, to wander about. Men often spent a lot of time going from one tavern to another. They often took their wives or girlfriends with them, but an invitation to pasear was commonly part of the initial flirting phase of a relationship.

Josef María Mota came by María Gertrudis Sota's house in the early evening and took her out to pasear. First they went to the area of Salto del Agua, where they had some *aguardiente* (brandy), and then they headed toward San Antonio Abad. They ended up in an empty room, having sex on the floor. A few days later, they walked around the Lagunilla, a market in Mexico City.[119] Some invitations to pasear were disguised as innocent requests. When the widow María Josefa Carrillo was walking to church, she met some soldiers who said, "Señora Pepa, where are you going? We are off to pasear." Although the words were simple enough, it was in fact a solicitation.[120]

Similarly, the soldier Ignacio Zapata related how some friends came by to invite him to pasear along with two women; they went from one *pulquería* (a tavern where pulque was served) to another and ended up fighting over the women.[121] The mere act of going out to pasear with a woman could be construed as a sexual act. In the village of Tlacotepec, one witness reported the suspicious behavior of Rufino Calixto, an indigenous man, who was observed constantly going out to pasear with Manuela la Vermeja, a woman believed to be his mistress.[122]

To pasear could mean walking about from one pulquería to another, but often these promenades were location-specific. Colonial Mexicans had many places where they went to promenade, but the Alameda stood out for its erotic associations. This park was fairly central, easily accessible, and visited by all classes. It was a public space that also afforded some private spots because it was enclosed by a wall and had benches all around it.[123] The Alameda provided a space for sociability and especially for courtship; colonial Mexican elites went there regularly in impressive carriages, riding on horses and showing off their fashionable attire.[124]

Despite the fact that he was in the novitiate in the friary of San Juan de Dios, don Mariano Ochoa Obscuras invited his lover, Teodocia Venegas, to go to the Alameda.[125] It was also where Mauro Arizaga had a short career as a flasher.[126] But the symbolic association of the Alameda with sexuality was clearest in the accusations made against Sergeant Cristóbal Sánchez for lewdness. Corporal Pedro Ballesteros reported that he had asked Sánchez for help cleaning his jacket, and the next day he asked for an advance on his salary—both of which could be understood, under certain circumstances, by both men and women, as sexual advances. Sexual tension within a couple gave meaning to otherwise innocent acts.[127] Sánchez apparently asked Ballesteros to walk over to the doorway, making sure that their conversation was private, and said "that this night the two of them would go to the Alameda." Ballesteros suddenly realized what was going on and protested fulsomely that Sánchez "should not believe that he was a man of such irregular dealings." Nevertheless, Ballesteros did keep seeing Sánchez, and another night they were going to a play near the Alameda's gates when Sánchez commented that "one night you must give me pleasure."[128]

The theater and the Coliseo also had some erotic associations, probably because many inhibitions were loosened in these places and decorum was forgotten. The Coliseo had entertainment besides plays, such as musical interludes with words considered obscene at the time. There were also female dancers to whom audience members often appealed with expressions such as *mi alma, Dios te guarde* (my soul, God keep you).[129] The women who acted and danced were reputed to be "loose"; as early as 1644 Bishop Juan de Palafox y Mendoza (1600–1659) lamented that Mexican men were being

seduced by theater women.[130] Josefa Ordóñez, New Spain's most famous
courtesan, moved to New Spain to work in the Coliseo as an actress and was
also a theater impresario, among her other activities.[131]

When don Guillermo Brixis y Prado began to regret his affair with an
"indecent dancer" from the Coliseo, he explained how his better sense was
overcome in "this place known for its prostitution." The lure of this class of
women "with their beautifications and brazenness provoke lechery."[132] The
dancer in question, Micaela del Corral, also known as La Zua, was actually
infamous for her many lovers.[133] What the Alameda and the Coliseo had in
common was that both were public places with strong sexual associations.
They became part of the lexicon of seduction because an invitation to either
place functioned as a veiled reference to the erotic.

Whereas public places like parks and theaters suggested sensual pleasures,
other more enclosed and private settings provided a somewhat secluded
space for actual trysts. Colonial Mexicans enthusiastically embraced the pre-
Hispanic tradition of the sweat bath, or *temascal*. But even before the Spanish
conquest people used these baths for furtive encounters, whether men with
women or men with men.[134] In his confessional for indigenous people, Fray
Augustín de Quintana included the question "Have you bathed in a temascal
with men?"[135] His question was ambiguous; it could be directed at either
men or women. Certainly scandals in the temascales continued with a big
uproar when two men, one mulatto and the other indigenous, were caught
having sex in a temascal. This incident led to a whole series of regulations for
temascales that were meant to prevent any more such incidents.[136]

Despite these efforts, temascales continued to be known for clandestine
sex, including same-sex encounters.[137] In 1791 the temascal of Canales,
located in Mexico City, was the subject of an investigation. The midwife doña
María Cartagena recounted that she had brought her patient María del
Castillo to the temascal to recover from the recent birth of her child. This
practice was supposed to be medicinal and therapeutic for the new mother,
but it quickly devolved into a party. The new mother was joined by family
members and friends, both male and female, who all disrobed and began to
drink pulque. The shocked midwife described the women wiggling their
bodies and running around playfully. What was supposed to be a solemn
occasion became a drunken celebration that lasted from ten o'clock in the
morning until the early evening. The scandal was partly explained by the fact
that the new mother was an actress—thus her propensity for such shocking
conduct was assumed.[138]

In another example, Juan de Paez, an indigenous man in Ecatepec, was arrested for his sexual abandon with Martina Andrea; the two were married to others but would bathe in the local temascal in front of both men and women "with public and notorious scandal."[139] Because horses were so common, stables were present all over Mexico City. These dark enclosed places were sometimes a good spot for an assignation. Two soldiers and a woman caused a huge scandal with nearby Mexico City residents when they all went into a stable—a location known to the neighbors as the site of many sins. One of the witnesses reported the group to the authorities, who confronted the group. One of the soldiers replied that "they were going to fuck this woman" and became incensed at being interrupted.[140] When he was on guard at the viceregal palace, the soldier José María Molina confronted two men as they made their way to the stables. He explained that he stopped them because he knew they intended to have sex in the stable. One of the men was known to him as a puto and had previously tried to seduce him.[141]

There were many spaces in Mexico City with erotic associations, but these became even more charged at night. The links between places and these charged overtones were connected to what occurred in them as well as to a Mexican sense of the connection between space and morality.

Sexual Freedom

Even though the ultimate ideal of virtuous, procreative, sexual relations was not lived by many colonial Mexicans, they still mostly aimed for it, on some level. Men and women skirted the rules, yet many of the couples discussed so far in this chapter at least pretended to aspire to be virtuous.[142] When neighbors denounced a pair that was living "in sin" or in quasi-marriages, the accused partners had to justify their conduct and defend themselves during official investigations. They explained, they expounded on all the reasons it had been impossible to marry, they lamented their fragility, and frequently they vowed to put things right and live a better life. They had played a type of game, betting that they would not be caught, but as Lavrin writes, despite their religiosity, colonial Mexicans engaged in a dialogue between official norms and their actual lives. Men and women in New Spain, especially plebeians and manual workers, were relatively free in terms of their sexuality.[143] Some of them did not pretend to try to obey the rules, and they lived with considerable and surprising sexual freedom.

For many Mexicans the night was associated with immorality, sin, and the temptations of parties and lewdness; they tried to distance themselves from this stain by closing their doors tight and staying in their homes. The night tugged at the imagination of colonial Mexicans; they conceived it as the realm of the devil, of lasciviousness and delinquency.[144] Others, of course, reveled in the entertainments available in dark corners, in the houses that remained open, and with others who were like-minded. At night the city streets were mostly quiet, with only the soft whistles of crooks and the cries of revelers to break this silence.[145] It was after dark that plebeians went to the fandangos and other parties mentioned throughout this book, and given the alcoholic drinks and the closeness of bodies, inhibitions were lowered. In 1796 the viceroy, the Count of Revillagigedo (1681–1766) tried to prohibit these nighttime outings at which men and women sang, danced, and ate gluttonously, stimulated by drink and the sensation of freedom from the rules.

Over the years New Spain's governing class attempted, unsuccessfully, to eliminate the houses where people congregated to dance.[146] The raids conducted by the authorities of these gatherings, and also of the homes of couples living in illicit relationships, were usually at night. The Mexico City patrol searched a house near the Puente de Solano in 1790; it was described as "a tenement full of a disorderly crowd of men and women." The officials found a room crammed with plebeians of both sexes and proceeded to make arrests.[147] Those detained clearly did not subscribe to the official view of proper conduct between the sexes. When an official challenged Ignacio Arana for wandering Mexico City's streets at night embracing a woman, he countered the reprimand by stating "that it was no sin to cuddle women."[148]

Others evidently shared this mindset. Joseph María Carrasco and María Gertrudis González were arrested at either two or four in the morning in the doorway of the calle de la Buena Muerte because they were making a ruckus. They had been to a fandango together where Joseph María Carrasco was one of the musicians. María Gertrudis González freely admitted that she had sex with Joseph María Carrasco often but denied being in a quasi-marriage. He did not support her financially and they did not live together. Every once in a while he would invite her to fandangos and then "they would mix." Joseph María Carrasco's account was similar but less graphic; he went on to say that he had no intention of marrying María Gertrudis González because he thought that they would not get along.[149] Neither one tried to disguise the relationship or pretend to subscribe to conventional sexual morality. Others were not quite as explicit in their rejection of formal relationships but plainly had fairly casual dealings. Norberto de la Trinidad went to find María Josefa Domínguez at the tavern where she worked and invited her to have a drink. He was very inebriated, and she was accompanying him to his house when the night watchman caught them.[150] These men and women lived outside the boundaries of the prevailing morality, embracing the night as their space of tolerance.

It was also mostly in the dark that female prostitutes came out to find customers. There were a number of strolls, but places associated with commerce predominated: the various markets, the Parián, the *baratillos* (flea markets), and the Paseo de Jamaica, where people congregated to promenade and to buy small food treats. The area around the Plaza Mayor, including the Viceregal Palace, also became a hot spot for prostitutes at night. There were few sources of light and, in the dark all the porticos and doorways provided cover for illicit sex; in the places where women sold fruit and foodstuffs during the day, couples hid their activities under stalls and in the shacks around the plaza. Prostitutes brought their clients into the empty Viceregal Palace and used the dark corridors, stairs, patios, and alleyways. Around the city they took advantage of the vacant doorways of churches at night and cemeteries (where individuals brought ladders to climb in when the gates were closed).[151] It was probably because of this association between sex and cemeteries that Isabel Chacón thought it relevant to remark on the fact that she had seen Pedro de la Cruz and María del Castillo together in the Cathedral cemetery.[152] Chacón was not actually accusing Castillo of being a prostitute but instead was slandering her for being in a place associated with illicit sex.

Attitudes about prostitution were, in fact, rather surprising in New Spain. Although illicit sex was condemned consistently, the Church viewed prostitutes as a necessary evil who protected honest women from being the victims of seduction and promoted sexuality between men and women. Royal authorities authorized the construction of a bordello in Mexico City in 1538, but there is no evidence that it was ever built.[153] Instead, prostitution seems to have been less formal, often practiced in the streets but also in inns and taverns and at the highest levels of society by courtesans.

In 1678 Diego Rodríguez Carmona reported that he was very disturbed by the solicitations of Leonor del Castillo. He was walking in the callejón de Córdova when he heard Leonor del Castillo calling to him from one of the upstairs windows. She told him that they had business to conduct. He resisted but she insisted, and not wanting to be rude, he went upstairs. There he observed a girl with Leonor del Castillo. He sat down and asked what they wanted. Apparently Castillo was the madam of the girl; she told Diego Rodríguez Carmona, "I was not calling you, it was this little girl" and proceeded to set a price of two pesos. It is not clear whether he took up the offer (and later regretted it), but when Leonor del Castillo left them, she said, "I am going downstairs; negotiate well."[154] This incident occurred in the seventeenth century as attitudes of tolerance were beginning to change, but prostitution did not disappear; rather, it seems to have become more widespread at the end of the colonial period.[155]

At higher levels prostitution was often conducted from homes or businesses. In 1631 Antonio de Ysla, María del Castillo, and her mother all went to the house of Francisco Alvárez in the barrio of Santiago in Mexico City. They confronted Francisco Alvárez, saying that his wife prostituted herself, and by extension accusing him of consent and/or pimping. They asserted that his wife had at least twenty partners of all races. Conversely, the witnesses charged the accusers of being *mujeres de mal vivir*—a synonym for prostitutes.[156] Historian Ana María Atondo Rodríguez lists some of the words used for prostitutes: *mujeres públicas, mancebas, mujeres de mundo, mujeres escandalosas, enamoradas, meretrices, gayas,* putas, *mujeres perdidas,* and *mujeres malas.*[157] The soldier José Reolosa recounted how he and others went out to pasear in 1809. They ended up in a house on the Plaza Juan Carbonero where pulque was sold illegally and that seems to have also been a venue for prostitution. It was crowded with women who went along with the men and seemed unusually agreeable to having sex with the various soldiers.[158]

Finances were often an undercurrent in sexual relationships, whether it was a direct transaction between a prostitute and her client, the daily sum required by spouses and amasias, or the lush dowry provided by wealthy parents. Many wives and amasias depended on their men to give them a daily sum for household sustenance; conversely, these men usually relied on the women to do the domestic chores necessary for daily survival. Manuel Pedraza's testimony shows this arrangement from a male point of view. When he was caught in an illicit relationship in 1779, he explained that his wife had left him, so because he knew Mariana, he began to live with her.[159] In many of the prostitution cases uncovered by Atondo Rodríguez, payment was complex; it involved not just money but services and often political influence.[160]

Sometimes the line between a consensual relationship and a financial arrangement seemed blurred.[161] In 1809 two soldiers, Francisco Aguirre and

Joaquín Cepeda, got into a fight over a woman named Jacinta. Such conflicts were not uncommon in New Spain, but the circumstances were atypical. Francisco Aguirre was talking to Jacinta in a house full of women when Joaquín Cepeda came in and challenged him, saying that Jacinta was his *querida* (beloved) and that he paid her monthly rent; then he began to fling around accusations of pimping.[162]

Arrangements such as these corresponded to the patterns of prostitution uncovered by Atondo Rodríguez. She writes that in the late eighteenth century, prostitutes began to associate primarily with soldiers.[163] One night in 1810 the soldier José Magdaleno got into trouble because he was embracing two women—a mother and her daughter—in public. Another witness related that José Magdaleno went to the women's house at all hours of the night.[164] José Aguilar recounted that he went out to a pulquería one night and met up with a soldier. They were talking when some women came by and began to chat; the soldier signaled to him to wait while he went off with the women.[165] The realities of economic survival meant that many women who were not able to marry or whose husbands were absent had to earn their living by other means. Some chose prostitution, although many women whose morals would have been considered loose and deficient would not have defined themselves as prostitutes. For the men of colonial Mexico, these women were just one other way to find sexual partners.

Sex and Control

Within the honor system that prevailed in colonial Mexico, the chastity and reputation of women was important not just for them but also for the men associated with them. A contradictory double standard operated in which the men who seduced got bragging rights and enhanced their manliness, but the men who were not able to protect and control the virtue of their daughters, wives, and mothers were tarnished. The tension over controlling the sexual lives of these women led to outbursts of jealousy that often descended into violent attacks.[166] In 1679 the diarist Robles reported that one husband, worried over his wife's fidelity, had placed an iron truss on her lower body to prevent her from betraying him.[167] Jealousy also led to conflicts between men who fought over both their conquests and their honor. Ideally, men should have fought over the reputations only of women officially linked to them. But because the types of connections they enjoyed with women varied greatly, so too did their reactions when an amasia or a female friend was slighted or attacked in some way. Men in colonial Mexico had to juggle these competing imperatives: seduce other men's women but try to protect their own. Essentially this attitude meant that for colonial Mexican men, their sexuality included a need to maintain some control over the reputation of women or the women themselves.

As with so many other elements of propriety, the respect owed to upright women could be inverted in order to insult. Assaults against women could at times be indirect attacks on their husbands, lovers, or other family members.[168] In the village of Tisapan in Coyoacán, the shopkeeper don Francisco Ximenes was abusive and used discourteous language with the wives of indigenous men. In his complaint on this matter, Clemente José, an indigenous man, emphasized that offending married women trampled on the respect owed to their husbands.[169] Similarly, Miguel Gerónimo, an *indio principal* (indigenous leader) of Cuautitlan, reported that one of the village officials, Manuel Antonio, came up to him as he was working in his fields and audaciously insulted his honor by mistreating his wife. Manuel Antonio called her "una puta, muy puta" (a whore, really whorish), even though he knew that she was married. This conduct dishonored Miguel Gerónimo.[170]

In Mexico City there were comparable incidents. Don José de Nava was engaged in a running battle with Mariano Licona, the barber who rented the shop below don José Nava's apartment. One day while don José Nava was out, Mariano Licona came up to his residence and called his wife and daughter black whores.[171] Another time, when they were returning from Mass, Mariano Licona insulted them as they were passing his store on the street. Don José Nava asked that Mariano Licona be kicked out of his place of business in order to repair don José Nava's honor. What prompted this battle between tenants is not clear, but Mariano Licona indicated that his upstairs neighbors were interfering with his business and had insulted him by calling him an amujerado because he worked with women's hair. Mariano Licona clearly felt an insult to his manhood, because he responded by asking if don José Nava had the "balls" to come down and confront him. Mariano Licona also threw water and garbage around the doors of his shop so that don José Nava's wife and daughter would not pass by there.[172] Problems between neighbors were probably quite general, but it was easy to indirectly attack men's honor through the women associated with them.

Flirting with a woman and making various attempts at seduction were no less effective in striking out at another man's reputation and dignity. Working women were the easiest targets for such campaigns because they had to go out in public to do their various tasks. Doña Filomena Contreras served in the family business, the café on the calle Espíritu Santo in Mexico City. She was behind the counter in the late afternoon in 1809 when a soldier, don Miguel Preciado Serrano, came in with a friend. They ordered coffee; then, when the hatmaker don Juan Sanone, apparently a rival, came in, don Miguel Preciado Serrano imperiously ordered two glasses of liquor. Don Miguel Preciado Serrano and don Juan Sanone began to argue vociferously, but when doña Filomena Contreras intervened asking for moderation, don Migual Preciado Serrano turned his attention to her. He called her a "*grandissíma* puta" (great big whore) and an *amancebada* (a woman without morals). She threatened to tell her husband about these insults, but it was an empty threat because she worried how her husband would react.

However, this seems to have simply spurred don Miguel Preciado Serrano on. He claimed that his military uniform must be impeding her desire for him, so he left, returned in civilian clothes (on horseback), and proceeded to demand sex, saying that "he would not go to Veracruz before having his way with her." He then kissed and rubbed her and even ripped her shirt. Because her husband was absent when this episode occurred, doña Filomena Contreras relied on servants and clients to defend her, but when the episode came to light, her husband was outraged that don Miguel Preciado Serrano had "damaged his honor and cast doubts among those who might question his wife's chastity."[173] His comments reflect the general theme that men acted against other men by tarnishing or commenting on their wives' chastity. The husbands who complained do not seem to have been terribly concerned about the women's feelings or even their safety; these women were simply intermediaries for their own struggles.

Young men also clashed over their love interests; sometimes they fought over the women they wanted to marry, but in many cases the conflict was simply over those who excited their interests. Their bonds to these women were not the same as for wives, but their feelings were often just as strong. In 1798 the friendship of Juan Gómez and Juan Castillo was tested because of Andrea Cárdenas. Juan Gómez wanted to marry her, so he told his friend and his potential fiancée to stop having any contact with each other. In this testimony he used the word *communicación*, which at the time had sexual overtones. Juan Gómez was suspicious because Juan Castillo and Andrea Cárdenas had previously been lovers. This earlier liaison might have heightened Juan Gómez's sensitivities, because he attacked his friend simply for talking to Andrea Cárdenas in the street. Juan Castillo was standing in the doorway of his home when Andrea Cárdenas passed by. Out of politeness he acknowledged her, and to be courteous she returned the greeting.[174]

Friends even fought over the looks of an inamorata. Don José María del Campo and don Gabriel Bringas were in the billiard rooms at the Coliseo when they started fighting about whether a woman they knew was pretty or not.[175] Feliciana Espinosa (La Escova) aroused the interests of several men and did not operate within the traditional boundaries of sexual morality. When don José Ignacio Espino found out that she was involved with his friend, he avoided going anywhere near her house, but he met her in the plaza when she expressed her need to talk to him. Don José Ignacio Espino decided to visit her residence at night, perhaps trying to avoid any notice of his visit. Five minutes after she let him in, his friend began to insult him from the doorway. In order to avoid a confrontation, he snuck out by a window that had access to the patio.[176]

Tensions over love interests often seem to have been the undercurrent for fights. When two groups of soldiers insulted each other in his *vinatería* (wine shop), Hipólito del Castillo reported that he heard that it was over a woman who was one of the men's mistress.[177] When the parties involved were not free, tensions over women had different implications. Antonio Lucas, the mulatto slave of don Juan de Sobena, was in love with a mulatta slave belonging to don Juan de Lovera, who tried to stop the two from meeting.[178] For many men, sexual relations with a woman meant possessing her; in their jealousy they often expressed this sentiment.[179] But this control was not just about simple possession; it reflected their bond with other men and also their sense of security within the community.

Conclusion

The public lives of colonial Mexican men were full of pressures to conform and to fit into a fairly rigid hierarchical social system. Their private lives were perhaps somewhat less constrained, but rules still crept into the bedroom. Both canon and secular law aimed to channel the sexual drives of all Mexicans into the narrow confines of the acceptable: a married couple engaging in coitus for the purpose of procreation. It is impossible to know how many pairs lived up to this rather constricting ideal, because they do not generally appear in the documents. Certainly, however, men's sexual lives were much more complex and messy, and they were probably reminded of the rules regularly—during confession, at Mass, and at other religious events. Yet Mexicans were fairly tolerant of those who bent the rules (unless they were bad neighbors).

This was just one of the contradictory elements in the sexual lives of colonial Mexicans. Even within the ecclesiastical realm, the religious calendar prohibited sexual acts on certain days but also provided periods of abandon, such as Carnival, when cross-dressing was allowed and people engaged in lewd acts without reprisal. Although it is important to know what the rules on sexuality were, it is equally important to acknowledge that these rules shaped the sexuality of New Spain's men but did not entirely contain it.

The official rules and procedures for courting and seduction provided a type of vocabulary that crossed over into many different contexts and sexualities. The provision of gifts during the esponsales and the notion of a promise to marry became shorthand for skirting the rules about premarital sexual relations and a handy way to signal interest in a woman or another man. Men proceeded from giving gifts to making promises—sometimes to marry, but also vague pledges to do the right thing. Higher-status men had a lower threshold than plebeian men for the acceptance of their undertakings—they could refer to their status as caballeros or hombres de bien. Undoubtedly, the fact that they usually were wealthier made such seductions easier. The attractions of men were various; they could be handsome, well dressed, and good horsemen but also hardworking and a good catch for a woman who wanted a steady companion.

Men and women in New Spain recognized that being in a relationship was not just about sex; eating and drinking together, having children, fighting, and scolding were all elements of the bond between two people. Most couples at least paid lip service to the prevailing norms, but some rejected the rules entirely: they flirted and philandered shamelessly, went to prostitutes, or found men or women with similar inclinations. There were many places in Mexico City and the surrounding towns where illicit liaisons could occur: parks and paseos, rented rooms and inns, temascales and stables, and even the carriages that were so common on the city streets. Despite all the prohibitions that prevailed, men took many liberties, and thus their sexuality was, for some, quite free despite the unfree norms. The rules provided a blueprint for how to rebel and what would be sexy. When the moralists wrote their tomes and denounced fashions and behaviors, they unwittingly provided a primer on alternate forms of sexuality and sexual identity.

CHAPTER 4

Men and Work

✦ MANUEL FELIPE, AN INDIGENOUS MAN FROM THE TLANEPANTLA region, was poor but also proud and sure of himself. One day, as he was working as usual in the hacienda of don Laureano González, the estate's muleteer came over and told him to fill some nets with hay for the animals. Despite his humble position, Manuel Felipe refused; he stated that his *oficio*, or occupation, was to work with the maguey plants, and he had other tasks at hand. Despite the violent beating that the muleteer unleashed upon him, Manuel Felipe stood his ground; he did not look after animals.[1]

For the vast majority of men in New Spain, work defined them at least in part and was a key piece of their identity as men. Having an oficio was expected of men; ideally, with the income from their employment they supported wives, children, and even extended households. Not all men did hard and dirty manual work as Manuel Felipe did; those with education, patronage connections, or simply wealth did not sully their hands, but despite their good fortune they too identified with their posts and titles—essentially their oficios. As such, in addition to being a fundamental part of male identity and a core part of men's experiences on a daily basis, work was also an activity that very frequently brought men together: in workshops, in institutional settings such as factories, or in closed prisonlike locales such as bakeries or obrajes. Outside urban boundaries men's work was often solitary—herding or planting small plots of land—but they were brought together on estates and to do communal work.[2] Work also provided places for men to come

together: the workplace itself, associations such as confraternities, or socializing after hours. Through work men developed alliances, friendships, and
enmities.

Yet even though work was an important part of male identity, it was also
contradictory for many men. Iberian culture had traditionally denigrated
labor, especially jobs considered menial or dirty. Thus elite men or those who
aspired to status often eschewed formal employment, sometimes preferring
to live by their wits. These attitudes began to slowly shift in the eighteenth
century, when Bourbon campaigns to reform the economy extended into
ideas about the dignity of work. Artists and writers embraced new approaches
to employment that praised humble occupations rather than vilifying them;
laziness and sloth became the new reasons for shame. It is hard to determine
what effect these intellectual movements had on the larger population, but it
is not difficult to find examples of Mexican men who were proud of their
oficios. They demanded respect for their efforts and did not always accept a
critique of the results of their toil. Yet many workplaces were simply grim, so
workers escaped into drink, malingering, humor, and pranks. Some men
preferred semiformal employment that allowed them independence from the
hierarchies inherent to most businesses, but this choice left them particularly
vulnerable to the economic vagaries of the day.

Toward the end of the eighteenth century, various pressures led to
increased unemployment and migration into cities at the same time that the
Bourbons were cracking down on vagrants.[3] Plebeian men were caught
between two contradictory forces: on the one hand, they had to appear to be
respectable workers; on the other hand, jobs were scarce, and appearing
upright was difficult. Labor history provides an abundance of material on
various types of work, but these studies do not necessarily address how men
related to their work as men. This chapter explores men's occupations in New
Spain only tangentially and certainly not with any claim to being exhaustive.
Rather, it is an examination of the effect of men's experiences as workers on
their masculinity, the pride they took in their work, the ways work defined
them as men, and the space it provided for male sociability.

Work and Identity

Male associations with the street and the world outside the home were very
much tied to their role as breadwinners. Moralists assumed that husbands

Figure 6. Sereno (Night watchman).
In the eighteenth century, as the
Bourbons installed street lamps and
tried to bring order to New Spain,
they also created this post in order
to protect both the lamps and the
citizens. It was a respectable occupation, with authority and decent
attire. Claudio Linati, *Trajes, civiles,
militares y religiosos de México
(1828)* (Mexico City: Universidad
Nacional Autónoma de México,
1956), n.p.

would have a profession or skills that were lucrative and could provide for
their wives.[4] In fact, within this advice literature, authors counseled women
to consider their future husbands' earning capacity; wise women, they said,
would not marry unless their bridegroom had a profession or job that could
support a family.[5] When witnesses gave statements to the court, a central way
that they identified themselves (along with name, racial identity, marital status, age, and origins) was by trade or profession. Even when a man no longer
practiced an oficio, it remained part of his identity. When José Antonio Roa
testified in 1808, he described himself as a silversmith even though at that
time he was a *sereno*, or night watchman (fig. 6).[6]

In the late eighteenth century, as more men were enlisted in the military,
their identities were tied up with their jobs as soldiers. Whereas other men
identified themselves by their oficios, these men put forth their military identities as their work selves. Don Alexo de Domingo was the sublieutenant of
the regiment of Infantería Provincial of Tlaxcala—a post he explicitly
equated with an oficio.[7] These men were, of course, not part of the colony's

elite, whose identities were mostly tied up with titles of nobility.[8] But even those men who could not aspire to the heights of aristocratic designations could distinguish themselves by the positions they held. These labels could be numerous, such as in the case of don Antonio Columna, who was not only a lieutenant colonel in the Royal Army but also a knight of the order of Santiago, the *alcalde* (provincial magistrate) of the Santa Hermandad (a type of constabulary), and a judge of the royal tribunal for prohibited beverages.[9] Work was part of who these men were, but work was also necessary for purely practical financial reasons.

Ideally Mexican men had an occupation or a profession, but their experiences were much more complex. A large percentage of the lower classes earned very little, especially if they relied on work that was unskilled.[10] Despite this reality, their jobs were an important part of their daily lives. Within the ranks of plebeian men, those with skills had definite economic advantages, so within the plebeian class there were distinct echelons that were partly related to race but perhaps more so to economic status. If a young man's parents did not have the financial means or patronage connections to apprentice him or fund the purchase of tools or a position, he had to compete with a large pool of unemployed or underemployed men who were day laborers. These jobs were the worst, most physically demanding, hazardous, and poorly paid; they started at dawn and ended at dusk, and the workers were at the mercy of their employers, whose rights extended to corporal punishment.[11]

Many jobs were also dangerous; for example, one of the work obligations of the men who served drinks in pulquerías was to break up fights.[12] Toward the end of the eighteenth century, those who frequented the streets, living precariously and with no discernible work identity, were rounded up and either shipped off to the imperial frontiers in the army or sent to the Hospicio de Pobres (the poorhouse). At the end of the colonial period the practical application of this policy—the rounding up of presumed vagabonds to be shipped to the hospicio—had become very unpopular. In 1808 a crowd in Mexico City attacked a soldier, José Ortiz, because it associated him with this process. Ortiz described his assailants as *enfrezados*, or covered only in blankets—the kind of men who were typically the objects of the operation.[13] Because of their poverty, men often pawned their clothes and consequently covered their bodies with either a sheet or a blanket. Men were very much defined by their clothes. The working poor struggled to avoid such a fate and the identity inherently imposed on them.

These men did not have the luxury of worrying whether their jobs affected their status, nor could they be fussy about the company they kept. Wherever unskilled workers labored in Mexico City, they rubbed shoulders with men of all racial designations. In obrajes or workshops, for example, despite the many means used to coerce indigenous and mestizo people into servitude, many workshop owners still needed even more workers, so they also used African or Asian slaves.[14] When don Zirilo Chaves purchased the obraje del Pedregal in Coyoacán, he acquired any slaves associated with the workshop.[15] Quite a few of plebeian men's worksites were small spaces—sometimes these were also where the men and their families lived.[16]

Thus, while plebeian men did sometimes harbor racial animosities, they also socialized, both at work and in leisure times, with people of other racial identities.[17] Some occupations came to be identified with certain racial groups. Bakers, for example, tended to be indigenous, whereas house servants were usually mulattos or enslaved men of African or Asian origins.[18] Within urban populations, Africans were one of the largest groups; slaves performed varied jobs, but in households they were often coachmen or personal attendants. These slaves had a dual function: performing their jobs and enhancing their master or mistress's social status. Some members of the urban elite went even further, surrounding themselves with retinues of armed mulattoes whenever they left their residences.[19] Such men would have been identified with their jobs, not just by the functions they performed but also by the distinctive livery they wore that was associated with the households they served in.

Other African slaves had more freedom within the city. Many worked independently as street peddlers; others were apprenticed to artisans by their masters to learn valuable and lucrative skills. All these men could then work autonomously, remitting a quota to their masters or mistresses regularly.[20] In the seventeenth century, trusted African slaves functioned as muleteers, piloting long mule trains that transported valuable goods from town to town.[21] By the late eighteenth century, men of African descent in Mexico City were more often free than enslaved, and they practiced many different trades, but a great number were artisans.[22] It is hard to generalize about such a large and diverse group. But one element that these men had in common was that any identification they had with work or as vagabonds was very often imposed on them by colonial elites.

From the vantage point of the apex of society, plebeians may have all seemed the same, but within their ranks, those who had skills (such as

artisans) or capital (such as tavern owners or shopkeepers) were a cut above
the day laborer. Artisans had a natural work identity associated with a particular trade and guild. In addition, many guilds were organized into confraternities, which meant that the craftsmen socialized outside the workshop.
These organizations had both ritual significance and practical benefits,
because they served as a type of mutual benefit association.[23] Not all the
guild workers were master craftsmen, of course; there was an internal hierarchy, but they generally lived and worked together in the same workshop-
residence. In addition, specialists were grouped together on particular
streets. Thus their identification with their work had to be strong.

Other workers, such as those of the Royal Mint, also lived in their places
of employment—although in the case of the mint, it was only the upper-
echelon employees who enjoyed this right as a perquisite. In their free time
these mint workers often organized fandangos, and on nights of the full
moon they would go up to the azotea (flat roof) to socialize.[24] Respectable,
well-paid workers could also distinguish themselves from the day laborer by
their proper clothing, and institutions and public workers often imposed a
dress code that cemented this identification as a class above other plebeians,
who were known to walk about covered only in a blanket or a sheet and
allowed their identification as workers.[25] These men knew that their work
gave them not just a roof over their heads, it also distinguished them from
those whose livelihoods were more precarious and provided them with a
means to assert their manhood.

Elite men were in an entirely separate category, but they too identified
with their work—or rather, with their official positions. Bureaucratic
appointments were incredibly hard and expensive to attain, but they provided men with distinctions and income. These men rarely appeared in the
judicial documents that plebeians populated so abundantly, but their struggles to uphold their positions within the hierarchy show up in different docu-
mentary sources such as journals and petitions. Unlike the young men whose
parents denounced them as vagos, these men had absorbed the lessons of
self-discipline and emotional composure and thus generally avoided the violent outbursts recorded in the archives. They asserted themselves in a more
indirect fashion, so instead of coming to blows they inverted the rules of
etiquette.

In one example, the diarist Robles detailed a conflict between Viceroy
Juan de Leyva de la Cerda and the bishop of Puebla, Diego Osorio. Rather
than attacking the viceroy physically, the bishop used the language of

protocol: in 1664, coinciding with the ceremonial viceregal entry, Bishop Osorio undermined the viceroy by coming into Mexico City in a carriage pulled by six mules with bareheaded coachmen.[26] This incident may seem trivial, but at the time it was a clear attack on the viceroy's legitimacy and authority—in effect, his identity. Elite men usually attacked one another using methods that sublimated violence but that, within their own ranks, were just as effective. Alejandro Cañeque documents these skirmishes over precedence and shows how they were essentially an inversion of etiquette designed to weaken other officials. Thus he shows the anguish felt by colonial judges when the viceroy took away their right to use black velvet cushions in church. Their distress was quite real, because they understood that the viceroy's decree rescinding this customary entitlement was an attack on their privileges and even themselves.[27]

This symbolic violence rarely erupted into physical actions; as Andrew Fisher shows, colonial officials considered it a sign of weakness to show emotional distress by acting out with punches or blows.[28] Despite this unwritten rule, there were very rare exceptions. Although the details are murky, it seems that in 1657, when Manuel Mendoza, a royal notary and secular official, went to the archbishop's office, ecclesiastic officials confiscated his sword (an important symbol of manhood), then attacked, punched, insulted, and briefly imprisoned him. Subsequently, in a final insult, these religious men ejected him by the back door next to the stables.[29] This report shows that the tensions between secular and ecclesiastical officials could descend into actual violence, but those investigating the allegations could not find any witnesses to substantiate the claim.

Pride and Work

Despite the centrality of work to male identity, it was also a contradictory and ambiguous association for men who aspired to high status. Within the honor system imported from Iberia, work—especially manual labor or dirty jobs—were incompatible with status. The early Spanish migrants arrived in New Spain with grandiose ideas of nobility; they upgraded their last names, added letters to transform them (e.g., from the humble Caldero to the more exalted Calderón) and also tacked on the honorific title of *don* while still on board the ship.[30] Many of these newly minted hidalgos disdained conventional occupations and manual labor even more so. Sixteenth-century colonial officials tried to legislate away the embarrassment of Spanish men who were identified as vagabonds, sustaining themselves with gambling and thievery, but to little avail.[31]

Thus, in the early colonial period many men of Spanish extraction had equivocal feelings about the traditional notion of work as central to their identities. Their pretensions of nobility were also tied up with ideas derived from the honor system, which made certain occupations incompatible with respectability and status. Spanish nobles lost their rank if they engaged in "low and vulgar offices."[32] Early in the colonial period many men of Spanish descent avoided such humble jobs, but by the eighteenth century some reluctantly found relatively lucrative work, such as in the Royal Mint (fig. 7).

Although the comparatively excellent pay softened the blow of performing manual labor, Castro Gutiérrez notes that the men still considered the jobs at the mint a step down in status. Their pretensions and their insistence on being called by the honorific *don*, despite the institutional convention that only supervisors had that title, led to much derision on the part of other employees. Their fellow workers frequently called these men *gachupines* (a slightly rude slang term for Spaniards).[33]

Despite engaging in humble work, Juan Francisco Granado expressed such a sense of being entitled to respect because of his Iberian roots. Originally from Castile, Juan Francisco Granado worked as a carpenter in the Royal Mint. He complained that his superior, the director don Nicolás Bernardo y Valenzuela, had criticized the quality of his work. When Juan Francisco Granado tried to justify his efforts, the director reprimanded him and hit him with a stick. Juan Francisco Granado was stunned at this treatment, because despite his lowly profession, he was, in his own words, a "white man."[34] He expected better treatment and respect even from a person whose superior status was cemented with the honorific *don*. Apparently his claims to whiteness and Spanish origins were erased by his status in a lowly post within the mint; to his superiors he could not be distinguished from the other workers.

Juan Francisco Granado's claim to respectability might seem rather odd, except that in the seventeenth century Spanish officials began to contest the old ideas about the lack of decorum of manual labor. As part of an effort to transform the Iberian economy and enhance wealth, political thinkers, such as Diego Saavedra Fajardo, reasoned that hard work and even physical toil could be honorable and were preferable to the laziness justified by the traditional honor system.[35] Charlene Villaseñor Black shows how these new

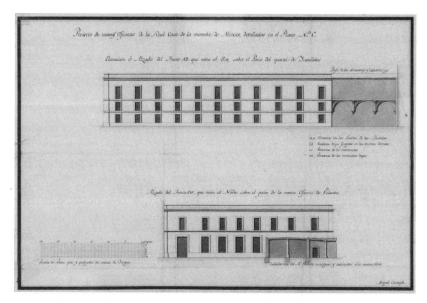

Figure 7. The Casa de Moneda (Royal Mint). The Royal Mint, depicted in 1779 by Miguel Constansó. It was a place of work for many men; jobs there were a source of dignity because the salaries were comparatively high. AGN, Casa de Moneda, vol. 355, exp. 5, fol. 104.

philosophies of manual labor were represented in the paintings of St. Joseph that became pervasive in Spain and Mexico in the latter part of the colonial period.[36] It was perhaps not a coincidence that Juan Francisco Granado, like St. Joseph, was a carpenter. Although it is impossible to know where Juan Francisco Granado picked up his ethos of the respectable worker, albeit a "white" one, but he might have seen paintings of St. Joseph in his carpenter's workshop at church, or he might have belonged to one of the many Josephine confraternities of carpenters.[37]

These representations valorized manual labor in a way that was antithetical to the earlier ideas that vilified such work as base and incompatible with status and honor. But even honor was being rehabilitated and transformed so that it was consistent with a more progressive economic outlook. In a 1786 discourse on honor, Spanish legal author and academic don Antonio Xavier Pérez y López praised artisans for performing the most physical labor; his description echoed the depictions of St. Joseph in his workshop surrounded by family, but most of all it demonstrated that idleness was no longer an acceptable trait for honorable men.[38] These were, of course, intellectual deliberations, but they do seem to have had an impact on the larger society, at least in some instances.

In the late eighteenth century some Mexican men began to consider an insult to their post, or *empleo*, synonymous with an offense to their person or identity, and such complaints began to be included in the archival documentation as an important part of the record. In the village of Santa Bárbara in Cuautlitlan, the indigenous governor don Miguel Aparicio confronted don Luis Alacavale over the imprisonment of one of don Luis Alacavale's servants. Insults among men were not uncommon, as we will see, but in this case don Miguel Aparicio noted that the insults were not just to his person (something quite usual in this society) but also to his post. Undoubtedly don Miguel Aparicio was correct in objecting to this disrespectful attitude toward his position, because, as he stated, the prisoner Miguel Pacheco and his brother also disparaged him.[39]

Officials who were belittled took offense not just personally but also as representatives of royal authority; thus the affront was twofold.[40] In 1785 don Francisco Pastor, a Mexico City alcalde, referred to the municipal ordinances to justify his strong reaction to the disrespect shown to his position; he stated that empleos implicitly conveyed honor, thus those who occupied these posts had to be esteemed and respected. He also asserted that an insult to an official was an offense to royal authority.[41] In 1784 Joseph Ramírez, a minor official in Mexico City, complained that a mulatto man had insulted his "noble oficio" with various rude words and epithets, and he added that these offenses demeaned his authority.[42]

Not fulfilling the duties of one's empleo was also cause for concern and a way to denigrate a fellow official. In 1808 the *portero* (doorman) of the Royal Jail explained that one of the soldiers had neglected his duties by hanging out on the stairs flirting with the female prisoners. The portero portrayed this lapse as an insult to the institution.[43] Another way of expressing this connection to work was to profess one's *amor al servicio*, or devotion to one's duties. Mariano Garcés, a soldier, fought with another soldier, Alexo Rendón, over who would deliver some papers to their commanding officer. Alexo Rendón found Mariano Garcés at a store that doubled as a vinatería (probably having a drink) and demanded the papers. When Mariano Garcés refused, Alexo Rendón insulted him by saying that he "did not seem to know how to fulfill his obligations and had little devotion to his duties."[44]

What all these men had in common was that they considered their jobs to be part of their honor; their reputation as good and diligent workers was part of their persona, inseparable from the reputation they wanted to preserve. Work had always been part of men's lives, but it began to also be part of their identities as men and, as such, made them vulnerable to insults for not living up to their duties.

Dignity and Work

Some men found dignity through their employment; it allowed them to distinguish themselves and to play the role of patriarch within their households. Workplaces often had an internal hierarchy; the guilds, for example, had masters, journeymen, and apprentices. This hierarchy provided Mexican men with a vocabulary that distinguished those who were more successful in the workplace. Outside the guild system, work skill or expertise was the way to internally rank staff members. Royal Mint workers were grouped into two camps: *operarios* (workers), who did the most physical tasks and were the lowest within the ranks, and *empleados* (employees), who were supervisors and considered both "decent" and "trustworthy."[45]

Employers recognized that work titles were synonymous with a vocabulary of respect.[46] In the Royal Tobacco Manufactory, workers were divided into those with experience and skills (*de la profesión*) and those without (*de la calle*, "from the street").[47] The terms used for workers at this lower end of the spectrum were important, because these workers clung to any small amount of status they had—sometimes in opposition to workers who were African slaves. At the lower end of the spectrum of unskilled labor at the Royal Mint, being called an *oficial* was a way to distinguish a free worker from one who was enslaved. Even though the two men were doing the same tasks, this distinction allowed the men "dignity in their work."[48]

As Spanish officials tried to reform both the peninsular and the colonial economies, they needed to reorient attitudes about jobs, and thus they tried to adjust the mindset about work. Writers and artists began to portray work as the route to dignity. Some authors compared laziness to a type of poison and contrasted it to the honesty of manual labor. Even nobles, they wrote, should learn trades.[49] At the same time, the Bourbon campaign to reform work was also gendered: the Count of Campomanes, a Spanish intellectual and an advisor to King Charles III, argued that women (mostly those of the lower class) should enter the workforce and take over weaving, lacework, fan painting, baking, and shopkeeping, jobs previously held by men. This would free these male workers to undertake more strenuous, perhaps more complicated, tasks that were more suited to their manliness and physical strength.[50]

These attitudes were also represented in Mexican writer José Joaquin Fernández de Lizardi's novel, *La Quijotita y su prima* [The Female Quixote and her Cousin], in which the author contrasted two young women and their upbringing. The rational and forward-thinking father encourages his daughter to learn to fix clocks, embroider, and draw; he argues that there is no reason young women should be excluded from oficios that do not require physical strength.[51] Women did not suddenly flood into previously male work enclaves, but some women, especially the respectable poor, began to sell their wares openly even though they encroached upon the guilds' monopolies.[52] They also joined the ranks of factory workers at the newly established Royal Tobacco Manufactory in large numbers.[53]

The official view was that more Mexicans needed to be productive; thus the breaking down of the gender barriers of work, though enlightened, was really part of an economic project. The female encroachment into male work areas highlighted some of the realities that both men and women faced in this process of making work more dignified: the changing gender patterns of work encroached on some men's income, and this in turn infringed on their dignity as men. Work that was dignified was all the more so with a good salary; an income was an unspoken but vital part of men's hold on their family position as patriarch.[54] Moralists assumed that husbands would support their wives.[55] What they never stated openly but implied was that this economic sustenance was also the basis for husbandly authority.

Within the judicial documents, however, various witnesses show the connection between income and patriarchal authority. Within both marriages and informal illicit relationships, women expected their partners to provide the *diario*, a daily sum of money to buy food and other necessities. Men understood that their authority and right to discipline their wives or mistresses was tied to the provision of this money; in the case of an informal relationship, Mexican men explained that because they gave the diario they had rights over these women similar to those they enjoyed over their wives.[56] Likewise, when their husbands did not provide, Mexican women withdrew their obedience. In the words of doña Luisa Ayala, "What is the authority of a husband who does not maintain his wife? Where there is no food, there is no obedience."[57] Leonarda Galindo stated "that any man who does not discharge his marital obligations should not have a wife."[58]

Work and income were thus an important component of marital authority; consequently, well-paid work allowed men to maintain their dignity at home. The Bourbon reformers had unwittingly launched an informal campaign among Mexican women to claim parental authority and challenge their husbands' custody rights over their children. These women argued that they, unlike their husbands, were working and could provide for their children's needs. Some wives basically used their status as workers and breadwinners to undermine their husbands' authority and dignity.[59] They were able to defy the well-established role of patriarch because of their salaries and work.

Despite the entry of many more women to the laboring classes, most workplaces remained highly masculine spaces. Therefore, even though these gendered changes were transforming the connections between work and dignity, the central way that men defined themselves and asserted their self-worth on the job was still by doing good work. Along with developing work skills, young men were toughened up; the workshops and apprenticeships were "classrooms and proving grounds of masculinity."[60] In the workshops of master craftsmen, young men went through a formal apprenticeship, but even in nonguild situations, those new to the job often went through some rite of passage. It could be compared to a type of hazing, but in order to be accepted by the established workforce, these men had to prove their competence and their solidarity with their fellow laborers.

Even when male workers did not belong to a guild, they frequently developed a kind of pseudo guild conscience and expressed their *orgullo de oficio*, or pride, in their trade or occupation.[61] They expressed this sentiment, often with great vehemence, when others criticized their work. Such incidents occurred in many different types of workplaces but most frequently in workshops or factories, where men were brought together by the institutional nature of their occupation. These work locations became central to the construction of the masculinity of the working class; the workshops guided young men into a generally accepted plebeian masculinity.

Because of the hierarchical nature of the workplace, instructions and performance critiques were supposed to be unidirectional. Consequently, when men disrupted this arrangement or objected to criticism or scolding, they challenged the pecking order and the inherent rank and dignity of their supervisors, perhaps deriving some mischievous pleasure in subverting this hierarchical arrangement. Good work was part of a man's reputation, and attacking it was an assault on his dignity. In 1632, when Mathias Bernardino, an indigenous Mexico City bakery worker, went into Pedro de Castañeda's tavern and asked for some wine, he added that "he wanted a just measure." Pedro de Castañeda, a Spanish man, took offense at this implicit critique of his service and stabbed Mathias Bernardino in the face.[62] Also in 1632, Gregorio Lorenzo tried to return some broken pliers to Juan Felipe's store in Mexico City. Each accused the other of dishonesty in his dealings, but ultimately it was the storeowner's reputation that was at stake.[63]

Don Pedro García reacted in this way in 1751 when Miguel Gusmán came into his store in Mexico City and accused him of selling him a tarnished sword and demanding thirty pesos in compensation. He caused a public scandal and smeared don Pedro García's integrity.[64] When the community of San Pedro Azcapotzaltongo (Tacuba) was building a bridge in 1801, Cosme Damián, an indigenous man, warned Justo Flores, a town official, that because of the road's narrowness it would be safer for men to carry the beams than for oxen to drag them. Apparently incensed at this challenge to his authority, Justo Flores insulted Cosme Damián and ordered him imprisoned.[65]

Conflicts also occurred when ranks were more subtle. In 1803 José María Lora and Doroteo Herrezuelo were both working in the Royal Mint. When Doroteo Herrezuelo scolded José María Lora for not filing a piece of metal properly and then reported the poor workmanship to the guards, José María Lora worried that as a result his fellow workers would no longer respect him.[66] Two other cases in the Royal Mint show that tensions could also arise around workplace issues other than job performance, such as whether a fellow worker properly cleaned his work area or brought in water buckets on schedule.[67] These incidents descended into violence easily and quickly when the insulted party tried to repair his dignity by violence.

Work conditions in colonial Mexico were generally quite harsh, and it was understood that supervisors or masters had the right to discipline their employees, not just with scoldings but also with corporal punishments that were frequently very harsh. Even though younger men continued to accept the hierarchy of the workplace, as they gained confidence in their skills they became less deferential and stood up for themselves.[68] Thus, when men who were scolded for their work reacted with violence, it was because they believed that the reproach was unwarranted. They lashed out in many different settings: a Mexico City building site, a rancho construction site in San

Agustín de la Cuevas, a Mexicalcingo hacienda, and a road construction site in Tlanepantla.[69] In each of these settings a worker refused to accept the supervisor's authority and right to correct his work because he considered the reprimand unjust, an attack on not just the quality of his work but also his dignity.

Men were often prickly about their work even in situations where hierarchy was not such an important factor. In the farmland around Tlanepantla, Augustín Antonio Pichardo, an indigenous man, wandered over to a small rancho where José María Robles was working. Augustín Antonio Pichardo greeted his friend with a joking critique; he said, "You must be earning nothing; you should be finished with that job already." These words, though said in a joshing spirit, infuriated José María Robles, and he started insulting Augustín Antonio Pichardo. If events had unfolded according to a common pattern, their fighting words would have led to blows or stabbing, but Augustín Antonio Pichardo understood the dynamics he had unleashed, and he stepped back to try to repair his unfortunate attempt at humor (jokes sometimes failed because the speaker got the tone wrong). He joined José María Robles and helped him with his tasks among the maguey plants. Augustín Antonio Pichardo knew that working together as companions would diffuse the ugliness that had marked their greetings.

All seemed well, and the act of helping appeared to have smoothed things over, but then José María Robles's brother Leandro joined them and unexpectedly remarked, "*Carajo* [prick], who offended you?", using the very strong expression *mentar* (swearing, usually with a reference to mothers). His words broke the peace by attacking José María Robles's masculinity. José María Robles turned on Augustín Antonio Pichardo, who, in a rage, threatened to eat José María Robles's soul; this time, no acts of cooperation could save the men from descending into fatal violence.[70] These dynamics are instructive mostly because of Augustín Antonio Pichardo's self-conscious step back from his words; but language, especially the language of insults and male self-respect, was important. Augustín Antonio Pichardo understood that the implied criticism in his flippant salutation had offended his friend, and he tried very hard to repair the damage to José María Robles's dignity through shared work.

Because most of these incidents occurred in the late eighteenth century, it is tempting to attribute these men's prickliness about their jobs to the Bourbon rebranding of work as dignified. Certainly some workers in this period were quick to defend themselves from what they considered to be undue criticism, but was this sensitivity really the product of the Bourbon attempt at a reengineering of the male work ethos? In her study of the Royal Tobacco Manufactory, Susan Deans-Smith notes that supervisors reported that on most days, those who worked there came to blows.[71] The tobacco workers were not particularly well paid, nor did they seem particularly invested in their jobs. Workers at the Royal Mint, in contrast, were well compensated and found their employment a source of dignity. In their campaign to rebrand work, the Bourbons neglected this element: it was hard to find dignity in a job while still struggling to keep afloat. Without the judicial documents from earlier periods of colonial Mexican history, it is impossible to answer definitively, but these incidents demonstrate that workers considered well-compensated work to be not only part of their identity but also a source of dignity.

Working Conditions, Discipline, and Respect

Although some workers might have embraced the dignity of work under the Bourbon rebranding efforts, the campaign to change the workplace did not eliminate the very real hierarchies that were part and parcel of the job environment. The power of guilds was waning in the eighteenth century, but the influence of guild ways of organizing work and the hierarchies within the guilds seem to have persisted and influenced even workplaces that were not part of the guild system—notably, both the Royal Mint and the Royal Tobacco Manufactory.[72] This pecking order made it permissible for employers and their proxies to hit their workers in the spirit of a paternalistic correction, just like the custom in the guild workshops. Workers had to embrace this subordination with an attitude of humility, doffing their hats and speaking with soft voices. They addressed the man in charge with reverence, always calling him señor (sir) or el amo (the master).[73]

Guilds endorsed a paternalistic culture in which masters were expected to discipline apprentices just as fathers punished sons; this discipline, however, often mutated into abuse and cruelty.[74] This culture meant that men learned a masculinity that alternated between deference and violence. Although men sometimes lashed out when unjustly criticized, they had to accept their subordination to masters and supervisors because of their dependence on the availability of work.[75] Workers put up with some level of violence, but they had a sense of justice, and despite all the power allotted to one group, they expected to be treated with a certain amount of respect; they had an "imagined moral code of work."[76] Perhaps because the right to punish was framed within a type of paternalism, it was part of the informal notions of traditions and customs. When workers complained of disrespect and masters' violence, these bosses had undoubtedly crossed some imaginary line that was not written down anywhere.

The prevailing attitudes allowed employers to use physical force as punishment because they were, in effect, masters, and as such they needed to keep discipline among their workers, even if it meant being unfair or going too far. In 1744 Cristóbal Santiago, an indigenous man and worker on the Hacienda San Antonio Pantano in Azcapotzalco, complained that one day around noon he drank some water because he was thirsty and hot. Simply because of his action, the *mayordomo* (foreman) beat him so cruelly with a stick that he was injured and could not function. When asked to account for his actions, Santiago's supervisor accused the worker of laziness, ill will, insubordination, and incitement of the other workers to defiance.[77]

Similarly, two other indigenous men, Joseph Gabriel and Joseph Miguel, hacienda workers in the Xochimilco area in 1797, reported that they paused in their duties for a moment because in the heat of the day the sun's warmth was tiring them. The captain of their work gang came over and proceeded to beat and kick them. Although they continued to work, some days later the administrator called them over and whipped them, adding the humiliation of making them bare their buttocks in the presence of other men. The excessive nature of this punishment may have been related to the workers' complaints about an unreasonably long workday, a lack of time to rest, and insufficient time to eat their midday meal.[78] But these incidents also shed some light on the delicate balance between what workers believed their labor conditions should be and how supervisors and employers reacted when workers asserted such rights.

There may have been a larger dynamic at work in these incidents as well. Not all supervisors testified about their rationale for lashing out against these men, so unfortunately it has to be pieced together. Perhaps the right of supervisors and employers to deploy violent punishments was so widely accepted by those investigating and recording the complaints that no one thought to ask them for a justification. Such violence against lower-class men, especially those considered inferior because of their race, was not unusual in New Spain. But, as we saw earlier, elite men and particularly officials prided themselves on their reserve and their emotional control. Within New Spain the

prevailing norm that men ascribed to—no matter what their status or background—was composure. So when men in charge lost their self-control and
lashed out against men who were expected to treat them with respect, they
were breaching this convention.

In 1724 the Tacuba teniente Miguel de Villalobos wrote that the local
alcalde had reacted to the alleged malicia of some indigenous people and lost
his self-control. Malicia (shiftiness or slyness) was often used to discredit
women when they accused men of raping them. It was also a quality that the
elite associated with plebeians, who they thought were inherently dishonest
and lazy. In this example, however, it was used to demean and feminize this
man. Villalobos argued that the alcalde's conduct was of great concern
because "it would cause the indigenous people to lose respect for His
Majesty's justice officials."[79] The violent punishment meted out to Juan
Pasqual, an indigenous man from the village of San Miguel Yla in the
Tlanepantla region, was sanctioned in 1793 because the worker had "the
temerity to hit his master" (actually, the fourteen-year-old son of his master).[80] This logic is perilously close to the rationale often used in colonial
Mexico to justify the murder of wives: if women defended themselves when
they were beaten, their husbands often justified their own fatal violence by
this breach of the conduct expected within a hierarchical situation.[81]

What did the men who suffered the violent punishments do to provoke
such a strong reaction that made their supervisors lose their composure? The
answer, I believe, is that respect was more fluid in practice than in theory;
although it was supposed to be unidirectional, it was part of a range of attitudes. Those at the bottom of the social ladder had to behave in a submissive
manner, but, as in many traditional societies, they were able to gain certain
rights through the power of custom and tradition, and these also had to be
acknowledged.[82] Plebeian men were not without power, and even though
they had to act in a deferential manner, they did not accept punishments that
crossed certain lines.

When workers asserted their customary right to drink water or take a
break, perhaps they were stretching the boundaries of custom and pushing the
buttons of their supervisors. It was a clash of different masculinities as well as
different cultures of respect within a range of such behaviors. Salvador
Antonio, a hacienda mayordomo in Tacuba, provides some clues to the dynamics of such situations. In 1796 when he saw Antonio Florencio, an indigenous
worker, talking to a woman when he was supposed to be working, he went over
to scold him because he believed that the worker was maliciando (slyly

shirking work) and probably trying to steal some corn. Salvador Antonio thought that Antonio Florencio was not only stretching the boundaries of his customary rights but also being insolent; therefore, cloaked in his authority, Salvador Antonio asserted his power to punish. In the evaluation of the merits of Antonio Florencio's complaint, the municipal magistrate did not deny that the plaintiff had been wounded but stated that "he had provoked it." Both the mayordomo and the worker expected respect: the official simply because of his position, and the worker because he had certain customary rights. Antonio Florencio felt so strongly about these traditional rights that he left the jurisdiction to try to find an official who would take his complaint seriously and treat him with the respect that he did not find in Tacuba.[83]

Plebeians insisted on the recognition of their customary rights, which were vital to their survival. When Domingo Ramos, an indigenous man from Coaspusalco (Tacuba) ran out of food at home, he went to the edge of don Lucas Domínguez's wheat field and collected some of the green shoots to feed his family. A hacienda supervisor grabbed him and took him to the mayordomo, who beat him and put him in jail.[84] In the countryside, indigenous people maintained their claim to residual plants—those left behind in the harvest or at the edge of a field—partly because they sometimes depended on such scraps and partly because it counterweighed some of the abuse they suffered on a daily basis.[85]

Men at the lower end of the work spectrum did not have much choice when it came to jobs, but at least they could leave at the end of the day. In bakeries and obrajes, however, many workers were also prisoners or enslaved. Either they were sentenced to work in these places because of some minor crime or, more often, they accepted an advance on their salaries and were not able to leave because they could not pay off their debt.[86] In 1631 Francisco de la Cruz and Joan Felipe, two indigenous workers from the barrio of Santa María la Redonda in Mexico City, complained about the conditions in Alonso Bueno's bakery. They had refused the simple task of putting wood in the oven, and their employer's reaction was to beat them severely. Perhaps because they needed medical assistance, they were able to present their complaint.[87] The workers were not allowed to go out, even to eat and even on feast days, which were normally holidays.

Many such workers depended on their families to bring them meals.[88] In 1806 Severino Pérez, along with his wife and brother-in-law, delivered food to his son in the bakery of the Puente de la Aduana.[89] When workers were allowed to leave or perhaps slipped out, sometimes they came back with

Figure 8. La vinatería à Mexico—La marchande de souliers à Mexico (Mexico City winery and shoe saleswoman). Men spent a great deal of leisure time drinking in different kinds of establishments. Drink was a social lubricant and a way to relate to other men by offering and receiving beverages. Note that the drinkers are portrayed as plebeian and raggedy—a comment on the lower-class affinity for alcohol and perhaps the bad influence of the nearly nude man on the semirespectable worker. In addition, the women in the background—smoking, no less—are selling shoes and thus cutting into the shoemakers' guild business. Theubet de Beauchamp. *Vistas de México y trajes civiles y militares y de sus pobladores entre 1810 y 1827* (n.p.: n.p., 1830), n.p.

alcoholic drinks. Drinking establishments were ubiquitous in Mexico City and the surrounding villages, and men migrated to these spots with friends (fig. 8). Drunkenness was a serious problem in many workplaces. Drinking on the job made workers more volatile and sensitive; perhaps it made them feel braver, more of a man.

Two friends who both worked in the Aceituna Bakery in Mexico City got into a fight when inebriated. Through the fog of alcohol, Manuel González, a mestizo, decided that his friend's position as oven master made him conceited.[90] Francisco Xavier Navarra, an indigenous man, complained to the authorities when he believed that his employer had gone too far in exercising this right to punish employees. Francisco Xavier Navarra lived in the bakery where both he and his wife worked; one day he left the premises to dispose of some garbage and took the opportunity to buy some pulque. He continued to drink when he returned, and despite his request for a break, his master and supervisor grabbed him by the hair, lifted him up, beat and insulted him, and finally imprisoned him because he did not want to work.[91] His complaint did not result in any sanctions against the bakery owner because such conduct was considered part of the paternalistic supervision that masters owed their workers.[92]

Agustín Flores, an indigenous cacique and baker, contested this paternalistic attitude in Tacubaya in 1727. When the bakery owner refused to pay him, he took some bread and then reported the abuse, showing the scars left from his master's beatings. The bakery owner countered that Agustín Flores actually owed him work—an indebtedness common in bakeries—and asked for his arrest.[93] The prisonlike conditions in obrajes and bakeries often included locked doors.[94] José Antonio Orejuela, an indigenous man, reported that after a fight in 1785 with his son-in-law, he suddenly found himself working in the obraje Puríssima in Coyoacán without really knowing the conditions of his service.[95] His experience was not extraordinary, Justice officials often sent plebeians to work in obrajes without really solid reasons; this was one of many strategies to ensure that these worst-of-all jobs were filled.

In this way plebeian men supported the colonial economy; their labor provided at low cost allowed these enterprises to flourish. Not many men wanted to work in either bakeries or obrajes.[96] Jobs such as these were so bad that only desperate people took them on voluntarily, and employers usually had to find ways to tie their employees to the jobs with debt or prison sentences or by using slaves. Elsa Malvido reports that one man, probably the owner of an obraje, adopted eighteen children to use them as a workforce.[97] Some obrajes employed children as young as nine or ten.[98] Even in workplaces that had much better and less coercive conditions, work discipline was important and was increasingly promoted by Bourbon officials. The progressive thinkers of the day advocated for a more orderly and productive workforce, but this meant curtailing many of the traditional customs common among laborers and brought considerable strife to all areas of employment.

Informal Workers

Work options were quite grim for many men. *Jornaleros*, or daily laborers, had to depend on finding work from day to day; they were often journeymen doing manual labor that was arduous and dangerous. Others worked independently, growing food on plots of land at the edge of Mexico City and selling it in market stalls or on the streets—in a sense opting out of labor arrangements that were disadvantageous to them. They existed on the edge of the formal labor market; traditionally, historians have emphasized their vulnerability and the low status they usually occupied. But as men they sometimes also gained, in terms of their identities, a certain freedom from the kind of bowing and scraping typical of so many jobs, even if this freedom came at a very high cost.

Within these activities, which were hardly lucrative, there was considerable competition. Simón de los Santos, an indigenous man, lived with his wife in a jacal (shanty) near the Alameda—the ritzy park where so many upper-class men and women promenaded. He worked as a porter carrying heavy loads for a small fee. In 1726, when he was kneeling down to pray the orations, Chimal, a rival porter, told him that he was trespassing on his family's turf and proceeded to knife him.[99] These men's livelihoods were tenuous at best; they worked hard for a very small wage, but to them it was worth protecting. In smaller communities, indigenous men often tried to avoid employment on haciendas, and if they had their own land they could sometimes make a living and remain independent. Cutting wood and making charcoal for sale in Mexico City was another common source of income in the countryside. It was not just arduous work; competition for control of the woods and their products was intense. In addition, when charcoal workers missed work, they went hungry.[100]

Muleteers were, at times, semi-independent workers. Like the charcoal producers, they spent a great deal of their time away from towns and cities, dealing with the vicissitudes of muddy roads, heat so strong they had to travel at night, and the responsibility for valuable cargo as well as the animals themselves. A good mule was worth more than oxen or even a riding horse; at the top of the range, such an animal was valued at about seventy pesos in the late eighteenth century. If the muleteers lost a mule, its value was deducted from their compensation; therefore if a mule died en route, the muleteers had to cut out its brand as proof of death.[101] Sometimes even with this proof, the owners of mules demanded compensation for missing animals; in 1754 a proprietress claimed sixteen pesos from Michaela Francisca's son for a mule that died in his care.[102]

It was undoubtedly for this reason that Domingo Cabañas, a pardo (black) muleteer, was so concerned in 1754 when the mayordomo of the

Hacienda de San Nicolás confiscated five of his mules, alleging that they had damaged the estate's wheat crops.[103] Another muleteer, Nicolás de Santiago, was still furious three years after an incident in which three of his mules had disappeared.[104] Muleteers also ran into trouble with one another while on the road. Antonio de Fuentes, a Spanish muleteer, was taking a load of charcoal on his master's mules in the area of Tlanepantla and ran into two other muleteers as they were both reaching a bridge made of beams. According to Antonio de Fuentes, because these men were indigenous they should have shown him some respect, but instead they disparaged him by urging their mules forward so that they trampled on his animals. He pleaded with the muleteers, but they just insulted him and then attacked him. The other men argued that in fact it was a tiff over precedence: Whose mules would pass over the bridge first?[105] These men all appealed to judicial officials to repair the damage to their livelihood and reputation, but clearly their work took them far from any potential intervention, and ideally they had to be tough enough to protect themselves and their mules.

All these workers had to protect the assets that allowed them to remain relatively independent from a more institutional type of employment. Mules for some men, and territory for others, were tangible sources of income. Men whose livelihoods were not part of the traditional employment patterns had to jealously guard the tools of their trade. Because the tools used by the charcoal producers were relatively light and portable, these men seem to have been particularly vulnerable. In 1782 the men of the village of San Miguel Topilejo (Xochimilco) petitioned to have their axes and sickles returned. They were in conflict with the forest guardians of the Hacienda Xoco; when the men went into the woods, claimed by both the estate and the community, to cut trees, the guardians arrived and confiscated their tools.[106] Without their equipment they were deprived of an important source of income and independence. In 1791 some indigenous men from San Mateo Xoloc in the area of Tepozotlán (Cuautitlan) managed to cut wood for charcoal without the benefit of axes; they improvised with pieces of metal and took only branches left by the forest guardians. Nevertheless, the administrator of the Hacienda de Xuchimanga caught up with them on the road and confiscated their wood and tools.[107] These incidents were part of a larger struggle to control a resource: the woods. But for these men whose livelihood was tenuous, their tools were a source not just of income but also of independence from the abusive work practices of the hacienda.

Sometimes skilled workers were not part of a guild workshop, so despite their inherent advantages they had to find transient work. Isidro Castro, a *castizo* (a person of mixed racial ancestry) blacksmith, wandered into José Ignacio Espinosa's shop in 1809. He asked for work, and José Ignacio Espinosa, a Spanish man, told him to make a key. Isidro Castro began to work with the material provided, but at midday he wanted to go out and eat. José Ignacio Espinosa and his family were all eating, probably in sight of Isidro Castro, but José Ignacio Espinosa refused him permission to leave. Isidro Castro was not beholden to José Ignacio Espinosa except for the small amount of money promised to make the key, so he was angry at this attempt to control his movements. He told José Ignacio Espinosa that "he might be an official in his house but not in the street" and insulted him.[108] Isidro Castro's words seem to encapsulate the ethos of the men who refused the institutional setting of either workshop or factory, but the context also demonstrates the precarious nature of their existence. His resistance could be seen as a precocious assertion of labor rights, but it might also represent a refusal to accept the subservient masculinity that colonial society had assigned to him.

Plebeian Mexicans often preferred the informal economy—they avoided the abusive conditions so common to formal institutions and remained outside the formal labor market. Because they often had only oral agreements regarding their jobs and were paid daily in cash, such informal workers often operated in ways that left little documentation. Their employment was governed more by custom and traditional rights than by any written rules or practices. Historian R. Douglas Cope notes that the colonial elites found this independence rather disturbing; instead of recognizing it as a rational choice for these men, they viewed it as insolence and laziness.[109] In the eighteenth century officials moved from distaste toward these men to the action of rounding them up as vagrants.[110]

Informal workers also seemed to refuse the costume of the respectable worker, shocking the elites by wrapping sheets and blankets around their bodies for some flimsy semblance of decency. Even lesser elites, such as the indigenous governor of Ixtapaluca, was frustrated by the lack of control he exerted over a musical family, the Escuelas. Because their services were so much in demand for religious ceremonies and events, these musicians picked their venues and often arrived late. They did not show the humility that the governor believed musicians and commoners ought to display.[111]

The tension over whose work was important was an ongoing cause of conflicts. In 1729 the administrator of the Jesuit hacienda San Miguel

(Tepozotlán) begged local indigenous officials to release some of his *gañanes* (farmhands) to work on the estate; instead they insisted on working in the community fields.[112] Throughout the colonial period, officials used minor infractions to force them to work in obrajes or bakeries. By the late eighteenth century, with the renewed emphasis on vagrancy laws, the authorities had a new institution in which they could confine the working poor: the Hospicio de Pobres.[113]

Friendships on the Job

Workplaces generally brought a lot of men into contact, often in small crowded places. Naturally these men frequently developed friendships while on the job, and these attachments were a vital part of masculine sociability. They made employers and supervisors uncomfortable, however, because they were an element that was out of their control. In a sense male camaraderie provided workers with a break from the discipline and regulation that prevailed in most workplaces. It also often extended beyond the walls of the work environment: these friends wandered about the city, hanging out to watch a procession or a ceremony, having a drink, or stopping for a game of chance or billiards.[114]

Drinking could bring men together, allowing them to socialize—sometimes even crossing the boundaries of rank—and could promote social harmony.[115] Drinking was a major part of these workplace friendships, but it was also a huge impediment to a labor force with serious, regular work habits. In the Royal Tobacco Manufactory, supervisors blamed the workers' inebriation over the weekend for rampant absenteeism on Monday—a colonial version of the San Lunes (Saint Monday, referring to the many saints' days on which there was no work).[116] But aside from the effect on truancy, friendships on the job meant that the men had allies.[117] Cope believes that by the seventeenth century, plebeians in New Spain had developed their own subculture.[118] It is possible that these alliances were part of this value system. Beyond having a drink together, friends on the job had each other's backs and would cover for one another. For this reason, when providing a character reference in a work context, witnesses would often state as a positive attribute that "he did not hang around with friends."[119]

Part of the culture of friendship in these masculine settings was joking or fooling around; it was a way to leaven harsh conditions and to build ties of solidarity. Plebeian men often gave each other nicknames that might seem rude or aggressive but that created a sense of familiarity between men and helped to foster the plebeian subculture.[120] These aspects of male sociability are discussed in more detail in chapter 6. All this joshing usually built camaraderie, but it sometimes fell flat. Two young men, José María Flores and José María Rivera, were working in Coyoacán in 1802; Flores was standing at the base of a ladder while Rivera was working at its top. They were chatting and playing around when Flores went too far, Rivera pushed him; Flores got mad and knifed him fatally.[121] These types of scenarios were common—friends messing about when one lost control and the easy jocularity turned into violence.

In many cases, confounded witnesses and participants would testify about their friendship despite violent confrontations.[122] They expressed their friendship in a number of ways. When commenting on two fellow bakery workers, Francisco Xavier Navarro recounted that the two friends always found an alcove where they could eat together and had shared their morning snack on the day of the murder.[123] In Xochimilco, Francisco Ramírez described his sense of companionship with his fellow worker: they were equally workers and friends, and they would lend each other the tools of their carpentry trade.[124] Friendships started at work but spilled outside into the many and widespread diversions of Mexican street life. At the end of the long workday, some friends went to eat an evening meal together; others got into a small launch and tried to rob a *chinampa* (raised agricultural beds in water); and still others played simple little games such as jacks.[125] Friendship often made these men embark on destructive, dangerous paths, but they did so with a companion. The male bonding that occurred at times within the workplace undoubtedly made some rather vile labor conditions tolerable; the companionship helped alleviate some of the hardships of the job.

Conclusion

Most men in New Spain spent a great deal of each day making a living, so to a great extent work dominated their lives. As a result their jobs became a key part of their identity as men. For those who had the good fortune to learn a trade or gain a lucrative bureaucratic position, pride in their occupation or their post probably came easily. But, even men whose jobs were less desirable and more onerous took some satisfaction in doing good work. Workers found a kind of dignity in their occupations by taking some pride, by defending themselves when corrected and criticized, and by upholding their reputations and their ranks within the workplace. In the eighteenth century Bourbon officials tried to reframe ideas and attitudes about employment; they wanted to foster a culture of disciplined laborers whose sobriety and thrift promoted greater productivity. At the same time, artists promoted not only a sense of the dignity of manual labor but also a change in the gender divisions within trades, allowing women to make a living using skills previously contained within the guild system and actively recruiting women into some factory situations.

These changes coincided with the tumultuous late eighteenth century, when many residents were enjoying boom times but others were increasingly marginalized. The greater emphasis on work discipline and productivity occurred simultaneously with the implementation of new poor laws, the creation of the Hospicio de Pobres, and a vigorous enforcement of vagrancy rules. Thus working men had greater incentives than ever to appear to be respectable workers, but without any real improvements in their working conditions. They still faced hierarchical environments in which their employers could use violence to punish them and where they were expected to show abject deference when doing often dangerous and hard jobs. Work was a huge part of most men's lives, but they also needed refuges within their work. No doubt the companionship they found at work allowed them to survive such difficult situations, transcended the boundaries of the workplace, and moved (as so many activities in New Spain did) into the streets.

CHAPTER 5

Men and Their World

~✍

✣ JUAN TERÁN SCHEDULED A SPECIAL RACE OF THE HORSES FARDI, Rabón Chisqueño, and Ruis, to be held on May 9, 1802, if the conditions and footing were good in the flatlands outside Mexico City. The race attracted a multitude of spectators whose excitement was undoubtedly heightened by the riders' colorful outfits, the many bets, and the fact that the horses were neck and neck until the very end. The event included so many appealing elements: horses, speed, competition, gambling, and maybe some refreshments, including alcohol.[1] Such diversions punctuated men's lives and, typical of many of their experiences, brought them outdoors and in contact with nature; they went about cities and villages, in parks and taverns, gambling and singing; their domain was equally the house, the streets, and the countryside.

Mexican men could circulate in the world quite freely—particularly in comparison with women. Their occupations usually took them out of the house; even those artisans whose homes were frequently the same as their workshops spilled jobs out into the streets. This external orientation meant that men engaged with the world around them in so many ways: work and play, devotion and transgressions, pleasures and dangers, controlling and being controlled. On the surface it seemed that men's lives in New Spain were entirely free, but in fact they were constantly negotiating boundaries within their surroundings. Some of these limits were tangible—for example, the threshold between the home and the street, or the sentry posts around cities—but others were more elusive, unspoken rules based on societal norms of race and class. Although gender historians have characterized men as being of the street, their experiences were more complex, for both home and street tugged at a man's sense of self.

Men of the elite were separated from plebeians not just by their occupations, which kept them in mansions and other institutional buildings, but also when they circulated throughout the city, for they rode on horses or in carriages that kept them at a distance from the street's sights and smells. Yet despite the fact that men spent a lot of time in the street, the home defined men's morality and their ability to act as paterfamilias. The home was considered a sanctuary, and violating the precinct of a residence was an attack on the masculine qualities of the head of household. The home was also an important contrast to the street; it derived some of its traits simply by being in opposition to the street's dangers and pleasures. As such, the space on the edge of a home, the threshold and the area around a residence's facade, presented issues of control. In order to maintain their hierarchical status, Mexican men tried to restrict access to both their homes and their streets. At times they blocked the way on public thoroughfares or set up informal sentry posts in the countryside on the *camino real* (royal road). When they imposed these unofficial checkpoints, they enforced their superior status within plebeian ranks but also made it very difficult for other men to circulate.

Yet despite these many dangers, as men moved around the streets they engaged in many diversions: they visited taverns, danced and sang in fandangos, played cards and other games, and went to cockfights and horseraces. Officials tried to control or stop many of these plebeian diversions, but with only moderate success. The amusements of the wealthy were often simply a more refined version of plebeian ones; elites drank wine rather than pulque, sat in the good seats at the theater and did not throw food at the actors, and danced elegantly in *saraos* (soirées) rather than engaging in prohibited sensual dances at fandangos.[2] Men, much more than women, came into contact with the natural world, both in cities and in the countryside: they rode horses or mules (depending on their status), worked with dogs or had canine companions, herded and protected their livestock, and collected wood and other resources from the forests and swamps. In all their interactions with the natural world and within their communities, Mexican men had to contend with unseen boundaries and had to negotiate their dealings within other spaces.

The Home—*Recogimiento*

Mexican men circulated through many spaces; in fact, their sphere of movement was extensive as they lived, worked, and played outside their homes. Because of the nature of their experiences and the period commentary, gender historians have tended to describe the home in New Spain as a feminine space whereas the streets and the countryside have been classified as masculine.[3] Sixteenth-century moralist Martín de Córdoba expressed the prevailing thinking this way: "The functions of the man and the woman are divided. The husband obtains sustenance outside the house; and the woman does so inside the home."[4] This binary division of responsibilities has led scholars to emphasize male association exclusively with spaces outside the house. But the home actually had very potent significance for men: it was their refuge and also the source of their authority as men.

Doña Josefa Amar y Borbón, an eighteenth-century Spanish writer, captured some of this sentiment when she urged wives to make their residences into a restful oasis for their husbands after their long days outside dealing with worldly and tiresome business.[5] Historians of Europe have explored men's connection to the home in ways that can inform men's experiences in New Spain. John Tosh argues that the home in Victorian England was an essential part of male identity. Establishing a home and a family as well as safeguarding it were central defining elements of masculinity. Men, he argues, developed a sense of domesticity—"a profound attachment: a state of mind as well as a physical orientation," which he argues, emerged only in the nineteenth century.[6] Architectural historian Witold Rybczynski emphasizes the emotional content of domesticity; it is "a set of felt emotions"—not one unique sentiment but rather many, all intertwined with "family, intimacy, and a devotion to home."[7] It is embodied in the family residence, which became the receptacle for all these emotions.

The home did have profound significance for men in earlier periods, albeit perhaps in a different way than for women. Studies of domesticity have mostly centered on Britain, so it is hard to conclude whether such a material culture and the set of emotions associated with the home had emerged in eighteenth-century New Spain. I argue that despite the fact that work and entertainment took men out of the house for long periods, the home had a strong emotional pull for Mexican men. They derived many attributes—such as their authority and moral stature— from a well-run home, and the home was therefore a beacon to which they returned.

In Latin American gender studies, the concept and significance of the home has often been associated with enclosure, or *recogimiento*. Because of the trajectory of gender history, the study of this concept has mostly been associated with women and the house or other institutions that were used to limit their movement. Perhaps because of this connection, recogimiento, or staying within the walls of the home, was often equated with female virtue.[8] In reality, homes were a core part of Mexican men's identity as moral men and as figures of authority.[9] Without a residence a married man could not have a household; he could not play the role of paterfamilias, nor did he have a refuge from the streets. Although a great part of men's lives was spent in the streets, the marketplace, the countryside, and various offices or workshops, for Mexican men the home had an "emotional power."[10] The home also could serve as a type of barometer for men's masculinity: when they were able to protect it, when others respected it, and when they ensured the well-being and moral conduct of those within it.

Women regularly used the term *recogimiento* as a synonym for moral purity; they particularly invoked it when their homes were invaded and they were assaulted. The vocabulary that colonial Mexicans recognized in terms of morality, therefore, was very much associated with this term. When the *ronda* (patrols) picked up José Antonio Guevara, an eighteen-year-old castizo, in a house of ill repute in a bad neighborhood, he needed to rehabilitate himself because he risked being punished as a vagrant. José Antonio Guevara presented two witnesses in his favor who both claimed that he was an hombre de bien with blameless and well-regulated habits, and both insisted that he was *recogido* (at home with his family, or moral). His supervisor from the cigar factory even emphasized that he was "muy [very] recogido."[11]

It was more common, however, for men to emphasize their presence in the home, especially when colonial Mexicans believed it was an inappropriate time to be out in the streets. Don Blas Martínez de la Vega, complaining about his wayward stepson in 1799, wrote that the culprit "entered his recogimiento"—in other words, his house.[12] The home was supposed to be a refuge, a safe place where all Mexicans could retreat at the end of a work day—a haven where they could unwind among family members and friends, sheltered from the travails of the world.[13]

Men often painted a picture of cozy home life that was interrupted and violated by intruders. Domingo Antonio, an indigenous man from the village of Santa María Cuautepec (Tacuba), was at home with his wife amusing himself and darning his pants.[14] In Milpa Alta, Manuel Cayetano and his brother, both indigenous men, were eating their dinner in the house of Juan Maquilhuacatl.[15] In Mexico City, in the company of a friend and his wife, Juan Nuñez was having a late meal in his store.[16] Manuel de Arenas, a castizo, was praying with his family behind closed doors.[17]

All these men emphasized the domestic nature of their pursuits and the presence of their family members, perhaps to remind officials that they were also paterfamilias. Work was often carried out within the home, so there was not a neat division between the private space of home and the public one of work. The Mexico City pharmacist don Juan Leandro Romero, originally from Spain, equated insults he received from an angry creditor in his business to being assaulted in his home. He asserted that it would be natural for a man to defend himself when "insulted in his own home."[18] The line between business and home was often blurred, especially since many merchants and artisans lived and worked in the same space. Some homes were particularly vulnerable; for example, jacales (shanties) and *accesorias* (street-facing commercial spaces).[19]

Men, like women, were affronted when others breached the sanctuary of the home uninvited, but men had the added responsibility of protecting their wives, daughters, and mothers. Being able to control access to their homes was a way to perform their masculinity. Etiquette standards of the times emphasized that visitors to another's home should be diffident and respectful.[20] Although the rules in these manners guides were directed at the elite, plebeians also understood the need to respect the boundaries of the home, but they could invert these rules to attack and insult others. These customs were meant for interactions between social equals; they did not apply when entering the home of a person lower on the social hierarchy.

Many home intrusions occurred later in the day and even more frequently at night.[21] In numerous cases Mexican men reported that officials or other men broke down their doors when they and their families were asleep.[22] In 1767 Joseph Ignacio, an indigenous man from Totoltepeque (Coyoacán), complained that officials came to his house at midnight, a time that was "nocturnal and domestic," and violated "private and domestic" spaces.[23] When men complained about these late-night invasions, they were at pains to emphasize that they were recogido, or at home with their families.[24] They also had to have been *quieto y sosegado* (quiet and peaceful) or *quieto y seguro* (quiet and secure).[25] At night, or after the prayers of the evening, people expected to be safe in their houses; they shut their doors and assumed that the resulting enclosure would provide protection. Shut doors were supposed to protect colonial Mexicans from the night's perils and were also were associated with high moral standards and the rejection of nocturnal rowdy and sensual activities.[26] It was a way of asserting morality. Consequently, when others broke down doors and disturbed quiet family times, it was an affront not just to one's safety but also one's reputation. For men it also meant that they could not ensure the sanctity of their homes, and thus their manhood was jeopardized.

There were additional ways to add insult to injury besides breaching the protection of the home. In larger homes, the most interior and private spaces connoted the qualities of morality and honor. Thus, going into the inner sanctum was not common and was considered an additional violation. When intruders pushed their way into a home when the husband was absent, it was an additional wrong, for it meant that the husband's masculinity was not sufficient to protect his wife. Leonicio Antonio Samudio, an español from San Juan Ystayopan (Xochimilco), complained in 1749 that some indigenous men thrust their way into his house when he was absent and insulted his wife even though she tried to appease them.[27] His denials are instructive because they show the importance, within the etiquette of the day, of respecting the boundaries of a home. Don Andrés Suárez Peredo Vivero (an aristocrat with multiple titles) reported that his house been intruded on over a debt for some dishes in 1804, and because he was absent the merchant insulted his wife and caused a scandal.[28] He seemed particularly upset that his lineages and titles as well as his wife's did not protect their home from violations when they owed money.

These forms of rudeness were remarkably consistent during the period under study—cultural values often changed slowly. Wealthy people lived in houses with many floors; the superior levels were reserved for the owners and were their inner sanctum. It was rude to go to these upper floors without an invitation, and even when one was asked, it had to be done according to the rules of politeness. In Mexico City in 1632 a Spanish cooper climbed up to the top floor and the residence of Captain Román de Cuellar when he was absent. The cooper was very angry and used heated words that, according to the captain, should never be uttered in front of a lady of stature.[29]

In 1748 in the area around Tlanepantla, two estates squabbled over pasture rights and livestock. Most of the confrontations between estates occurred in the countryside, but in this case don Juan de Jandite had the temerity to go the manor house, and "with great boldness he and his companions went into the most interior rooms of the hacienda home."[30] José Valentín Tlatic, an indigenous man from San Gregorio (Xochimilco), explained that he killed José Barrera when this man drunkenly came into his house in 1799 and went into the oratory—a type of informal chapel that many people had in their houses—and grabbed a candle that Tlatic was burning in honor of the Santos Reyes (Three Wise Men).[31] Some men also actually entered houses on horseback, which was an inherently provocative act.[32] Horses, as we will see later in this chapter, were a natural and frequent presence in the lives of most men, but they also had many symbolic connotations for the men who rode them, bonded with them, and used them to express their masculinity. They were associated with the conquest and could be used to intimidate or injure people on foot, much as police horses are used today to control crowds.

Control and Keys

The sanctity of the home was also code for control: if other men could come into a man's residence without invitation and with impunity, it was not only insulting but also degrading to masculine identity. Thus it was very important to be able to have command over access to and movement in and out of the home. It was partly for this reason that husbands were so anxious about whether and when their wives left the home.[33] For poorer Mexican men this control was harder to achieve; unlike wealthy Mexicans, whose upper-floor apartments were shielded by armies of servants, or even men like the viceroy, whose palace was guarded by soldiers, these men often had flimsy dwellings. Pedro Mendes faced such challenges; he lived in a Mexico City tenement with walls full of holes. In 1683 his neighbors complained that he came into their rooms through these holes, but he countered that he went into their rooms because his wife was ill and they were making too much noise.[34]

For more well-off men, who lived in apartments within the larger multi-dwelling buildings typical of colonial Mexican cities, their control over access was sometimes denied because they did not have a key to the building's front door. Don José Gutiérrez had been living in a building on the Calle del Coliseo in Mexico City for seven years. When he took on the lease, one of the conditions was that he would have a key to the front door because his job as a court official meant that he sometimes had to go out at night, when that door would normally be locked. A new owner took over in 1803, and when he changed the locks he refused to give don José Gutiérrez a replacement key. His reasoning was that even in tenements it was not customary for those who lived in the apartments to have a key to the building's front door because such a practice could make all the tenants vulnerable if one person forgot to lock the door at night.[35]

Another conflict over keys arose in a more commercial setting. Don Andrés Noriega took over the lease of a store in Mexico City; in 1809 he was remodeling and wanted to be able to use the door at the back of the property that opened onto the building's patio. He had an apartment in the main building and did not want to have to leave his store by its front door, walk in the street, and enter through the building's front door. He believed that going through the back door directly onto the patio was safer; he stated that "my interest is to be able to sleep restfully and without having to worry about my goods."[36] In this case, the building owner refused him a key to the door that led to the patio.

Denying tenants a key was linked to control, but doors held a particularly symbolic importance in colonial Mexican society: they were associated with morality.[37] Thus the motives for refusal may have been partly about ensuring the building's reputation. Don José Careaga, a master silversmith, expressed this dual concern over morality and doors in his complaint about don Joaquín Beltrán, a glazier who had sublet his upper apartments in don José Careaga's building. Much to don José Careaga's dismay, don Joaquín Beltrán left the building's front door open at night, and people were constantly coming and going. This practice endangered don José Careaga's business, not only because it might be robbed but also because his reputation had suffered. His customers believed that he was allowing gambling on the premises or even running games himself, and they took their commissions elsewhere.[38] Control over the front door of a building and access to keys were part of ensuring the integrity of a household, its honesty, and its security. If the home was to be a sanctuary, the owner had to be able to regulate who could enter its doors.

On the Edge: The Threshold

Because the house was such an important aspect of male identity, it was not just when other men invaded the domestic realm that men took offense. Other parts of the house were also significant, especially the door and the threshold. Historian Deborah Kanter writes, "Walls, doorways, and windows held great symbolic importance as elements that divided a house from the outside. If an outsider breached or assaulted these boundaries in any way, residents were deeply troubled."[39] The division between outside and inside was therefore an important boundary for men; as the paterfamilias a man had to guard against intruders and ensure the appropriateness of those who came into their household. The door was the border between the street and the building, the home and the outside world.

Consequently, as the point of entry the threshold became a vital strategic location and was loaded with symbolism.[40] Both the doorway and the area in front of the house in the street were part of the space associated with a home; in addition, these spaces were connected to those who lived inside the house. The threshold's meaning was variable.[41] It could be a space of sociability where men and women stood, watched the street, and chatted with those who went by. Alternately, it was a vantage point from which men controlled the street. Finally, for those on the outside, it was the ideal place to insult the residents of a building or a home. The threshold was, as Verónica Undurraga Schüler demonstrates for eighteenth-century Chile, highly charged with the family's honor; but even more so, the area up to eight varas (twenty-one to twenty-eight feet) from the doorway was also considered symbolically part of the home and representative of the paterfamilias's honor. Just walking in front of a rival's house could be construed as an insult.[42] Robert Muchembled identifies a "safety zone" in front of the house marked at times by something tangible like a hedge but more frequently by invisible boundaries known to those in the area.[43] In all these aspects Mexican men engaged with the street—their domain. But it is the threshold that highlights the tension between inside and out, between home and the world.

In colonial Mexico, as in many other parts of the world, people liked to stand in their doorways. In gender studies this habit has been commented on mostly for women whose enclosure made it hard to dawdle in the street; by staying within the doorway they reconciled their presence at the edge of the street.[44] In fact, men were just as inclined to linger in their doorways, for it was an excellent way to spy on one another and to act as a sentinel. Don Joaquín Espejo, a master silversmith, was able to give testimony about events in the street twenty days earlier because he was at his shop's door.[45] Merchants of many kinds were often at their business entrances for various reasons. Pedro Aguado was at the door watching as workers unloaded some boxes of soap while on the same street Juan Fernández Barrera was standing at the entrance of his honey stand.[46] Juan Castillo was standing at the door of his Mexico City home when an acquaintance walked by; he greeted him politely.[47]

These were urban men, all residents of Mexico City, but being in doorways was also a common habit in the smaller communities. In San Miguel de Charo Matalsingo (Coyoacán), Isidro de la Cruz was seated in the doorway of a friend's house when he was joined by his friend's wife.[48] Polito Ortiz, an indigenous man and a servant in the Hacienda Blanca in the area around Tlanepantla, reported that he was standing in the door of his father's pulquería when Lucas Hernández wounded him.[49] All these examples are simply a sampling of the many instances when men reported that they were at their doors.[50]

Not all men were so passive when they stood at their doors; in some cases they treated the threshold as a type of last stand. In Coyoacán in 1787 a power struggle between the corregidor and Ignacio Negrete played out on the threshold of Ignacio Negrete's house. The corregidor sent his *alguacil* (bailiff or court clerk) to fetch Ignacio Negrete to the Casas Reales (municipal buildings). When the alguacil arrived, he found Ignacio Negrete standing on his threshold. He asked Ignacio Negrete to accompany him, but Ignacio Negrete refused, insolently saying, "I do not want to go, I am not some mulatto who pays tributes" and "I will not go even if devils come to get me." The alguacil reiterated the corregidor's demand for Ignacio Negrete's attendance at the Casas Reales, and Ignacio Negrete stated, "I have already told you that I won't, so go to hell." The alguacil tried to shame Ignacio Negrete, calling him insolent and saying, "Be quiet, man, this is just talk." Negrete's response was to wound the official with his sword.

A witness recounted the story with a slightly different emphasis. Like the other bystanders he related the fact that Ignacio Negrete was standing at his threshold, but he added the detail that Ignacio Negrete was leaning on his sword. This posture was much more aggressive and gives the impression that he was taking a stand at the boundary of his house. The alguacil was also more aggressive in this tale; he had come to take Ignacio Negrete to the Casas Reales on horseback.[51] Thus the two men seem to have recognized the threshold as a type of battlefield, where aggression is permitted. They both used very aggressive body language: one used a horse to intimidate and show superiority, and the other stood with his sword in his hand. When men stood, sat, or even hung around near the doors of their houses or businesses, they were in part mingling with the people in the streets, but they were also acting as a type of sentinel.

The actions of the men who lingered in doorways were not benign; the threshold was an ideal location to comment on those who passed by, and at times these remarks could turn into cutting observations or even insults. No doubt many of these slights fell on deaf ears, but some men did react forcefully. The coachman of the Count of Alamos was standing at the door of his master's house in Mexico City one day in 1783. He said some disparaging words to a soldier, don Juan Alcalá Olmos, and cursed, saying that things would go badly for him. Who knows how many times the coachman had acted in such a way? He felt protected by the status of his employer and, by extension, the Count's threshold, and he even taunted don Juan Alcalá Olmos with this fact. On this day, however, the soldier reacted with vehemence; don Juan Alcalá Olmos later explained that the coachman's words were indeed very insolent, but he also expected to be able to walk down a public street without being harangued. His remarks highlight the tension that existed between houses and streets and the central role of thresholds in this dynamic. Don Juan Alcalá Olmos reacted aggressively, pushing the coachman into an interior corridor and hitting him several times. Because don Juan Alcalá Olmos had breached the sanctity of his house, the Count of Alamos made sure that he was punished.[52] It was not very common for men to insult others from the doorway (women were more prone to such behavior), which may explain the soldier's strong reaction. But insults around the threshold and bridging the gap between house and street were more customary.

In colonial Mexico men attacked the doors of other men more frequently by hammering very loudly on them, usually at night. By doing so they used the noise of the banging as well as insults and confrontational words at night, a time that was strategic because good people were recogidos in their homes but also because it was quiet and the neighbors could hear. Consequently, even though it was the middle of the night, the attackers had an audience. Mexican men had an expression for this practice: *golpear a una casa*— literally, hitting a house, but in reality they were assaulting those inside a residence by pounding on the door.[53] In some sense these men were mimicking the way that officials frequently arrested people—this procedure was practical because people were more likely to be home in the middle of the night, but they were also more vulnerable.[54]

When men went out to golpear a una casa, however, even though they borrowed some of the elements of nighttime arrests, they did not usually invade the house; rather, they were challenging the residents to come out.[55] The priest don Domingo González de Ocampo was visiting Mexico City and stayed out so late that he was locked out of the inn where he was residing. He was about to sleep on a bench when his friend don Manuel came by and invited him to golpear a una casa. They walked over to the area around the Puente Quebrada (a landmark in Mexico City), and sometime between midnight and one o'clock don Manuel banged loudly on the door of an accesoria. Inside, a brother and a sister, her husband, the mother, and a cousin were chatting amiably when they heard the great racket of don Manuel and don Domingo González de Ocampo banging on and pushing their door. One witness reported that don Manuel was saying, "Come out, Ignacio!" and "Come out, pigs!"[56] It was common practice for men to insult other men by calling them animals, such as dogs, pigs, monkeys, and even salamanders; calling a man an animal was a way to marginalize him, to make him smaller and less of a man. The three men eventually came out to find two men with their swords unsheathed; this was not a duel in the formal, ritualized manner of the elites, but it was clearly a *desafío*, or challenge, a practice that was present in colonial Mexico.

The antagonists in these nocturnal challenges did not always give a reason for their actions: a perceived slight or an incautious word, perhaps, but these details were often lost. When two former employees went to bang on the door of Francisco Sambrano's cigar store and residence at about two o'clock in the morning, they did explain that they were trying to recover some wages owed to them. Otherwise they followed the pattern described above, banging and pushing the door and loudly shouting provocative words. They challenged Sambrano "to come out if he was a man" and told him that "they would squeeze him like an orange," as well as other pejorative expressions that were not specified.[57] Why they referred to an orange is mysterious, but they clearly wanted to use an affront to his manhood to force him out of the security of his home. Sambrano then had to decide whether he should choose safety and a slur on his honor and manhood or a likely beating.

On a February night around eleven o'clock, a young lothario named don Juan Vigil pounded on the Hernández family's accesoria door. His actions provide a variation on the normal pattern of such incidents. Instead of challenging the men inside to a fight, he tried to show that he was not afraid. He had seduced a virgin named Anita, one of the women who lived inside, then cut off his association with her and blamed her brother-in-law for intimidating him. Earlier that evening, she flirted with him at a dance and told him that, unlike him, she was not afraid. After he left the dance, he went to golpear a una casa, probably more to prove to Anita that he was not intimidated by her male relatives than to test the courage of those inside, because on hearing noise on the other side of the door, he left. The Hernández men understood the insult, however, and the next day they beat him up, ripping his clothes and forcing him cover his nakedness with a borrowed cape.[58]

These various incidents were manly challenges that used the threshold and the night as sites because of practicality, but also because of symbolism. These episodes also show how the space in front of houses mediated the domestic associations of the interior and the rowdy connotations of the street. Because of its liminal qualities, the area in front of the house and around the door was the location of many conflicts.

The direction of insults was more frequently from the street to the house, usually but not always directed at the door—the most obvious target and symbol of the house. This practice had roots in Spain, where "house-scorning" involved "burning, breaking, or otherwise defacing the door of someone's house."[59] Deborah Kanter reports an incident in which a man acted out his revenge by constantly dirtying his enemy's door with mud, throwing stones at the door and onto the patio, and climbing onto the walls and mocking him.[60]

One of the strategies to sully another person's space was to dirty or defile it in some manner. Don Francisco Ponze had lived with his family on the calle de Chiconautla in Mexico City for thirty-one years without problems. In 1801 he reported that a family of tenants, who lived at the back of a house called the Once Mil Vírgenes (11,000 Virgins), had windows that looked out over his backyard and had a grudge against him. They expressed their animus by pouring a huge jar of liquid excrement onto the clean laundry drying in the sun in his yard. On another occasion they repeated this act with a pot of cooked beans. Don Francisco Ponze argued that these acts were insulting and demonstrated a "depraved disposition to offend my family." Don Francisco Ponze was outraged at the attack on his family, but he contrasted his emotional control to the insolence and rudeness of his neighbors. He noted that despite being blinded by anger, he used the courts rather than a physical act to respond to his aggravating neighbors. Thus his manliness consisted not of physical aggression or a passive-aggressive act such as the slinging of substances, but of rationally and coldly securing his neighbors' eviction.[61]

Men could use bodily fluids to show disrespect or to mark territory—it was an external manifestation of their manliness. It was not always directed at a residence but could also happen in areas associated with certain men. Toward the end of the eighteenth century there was often tension between soldiers of different regiments but also between the military personnel and other officials. In 1798 a soldier wandered into a storeroom in the Church of the Santísima; the watchman, Basilio Antonio, asked the soldier what he was doing inside the room. The soldier answered that he needed to pee, and when Basilio pointed out how inappropriate this action was, the soldier tried to hit him with a stick and replied that he was a soldier and would shit wherever he felt like it, and he proceeded to do just that.[62] Excrement was a particularly apt way to defile and insult because of its associations with impurity, but it could also be used to mark boundaries. Such practices were not common in colonial Mexico, but historians of England and France reported similar ones.[63] Using bodily fluids was a way to show contempt, but it could also be used to infiltrate another man's space or home.[64] It was a way to literally sully another person's honor, and it might have tied into scatological humor in the retelling. Tales of such feats among men in a tavern must have been much funnier to them because of the use of excrement, and thus such an event augmented a man's standing among his peers.

Controlling the Streets

Mexican men not only spent a lot of time in the streets, they were inherently associated with the streets. Plebeian men, especially, performed many basic tasks outside their homes, including their work and many social activities.[65] Yet even when a man was in the streets, his home remained an important reference point, and the area in front of the house was often a place of contention.[66] The strife over the liminal zone in front of a residence could be directed at the residents, or vice versa.

In 1786 a local Spanish official in the town of Tlayacapa (Chalco) used the occasion of the procession on Holy Wednesday honoring Nuestra Señora de los Dolores to make demands of an indigenous official named Marcelo.[67] These events punctuated the religious calendar but also brought people together in celebration (fig. 9). The procession passed by Marcelo's house as well as the residences of many other important citizens. As was customary for such events, people came out on the streets to watch, and the teniente don

Figure 9. Indiens les jours de fête à Mexico (Feast day for indigenous people in Mexico). Processions and festivities brought out many colonial Mexicans not just as participants but also as an audience. These events were a source of entertainment even as they depicted the hierarchical relations of New Spain. Theubet de Beauchamp, *Vistas de México y trajes civiles y militares y de sus pobladores entre 1810 y 1827* (n.p.: n.p., 1830), n.p.

Antonio Arizaga decided that he and his family should have some chairs to watch the procession in comfort. Even though other residents offered him seats, the teniente went to Marcelo's residence and demanded some chairs.[68] Marcelo refused, stating that it was not customary practice to offer seating. Don Antonio Arizaga's request may seem innocent, but it was in fact designed to reinforce the power differential between Spanish and indigenous officials. It was also an insult to Marcelo in front of his house, where he should have been sheltered from such affronts. The right to sit, as well as the actual seating for ritual occasions, was highly regulated and part of an elaborate etiquette.[69]

Chairs played an important role within the performance of power. At public ceremonies in New Spain, only the highest officials (the viceroy, bishops, and judges were allowed to sit on chairs. Less august personages might sit on benches. Thus chairs were part of what Cañeque calls the "semiotics of power."[70] By demanding chairs from the indigenous governor in front of his house, don Antonio Arizaga was humiliating him, but Marcelo's refusal inverted the insult. Don Antonio Arizaga waited until the procession had passed by, then attacked the governor and his sons and insulted him before taking him to prison.[71] The request for chairs was calculated to be rude, to reinforce hierarchy, but it also, in a strange way, called into question the control over the space in front of the indigenous official's house. Generally it was the house's residents who tried to control the street in front, so this incident must have been confusing and alarming.

Some men in New Spain believed that they should also control the street or sometimes even the thoroughfare. In a sense they may have been mimicking the practice of *garitas*—a type of urban checkpoint where officials collected tariffs on goods entering the city. Taxes are never popular, and thus the garitas and the *embarcaderos* (landing stages) where goods flowed into Mexico City by canoe were points of tension and conflict. In 1766 the people of Mexicalcingo came to the defense of the indigenous man Juan Esteban when Mariano Antonio de Soto wounded him. This incident became a larger issue because it was related to the fees they paid to don Andrés Canto (Mariano Antonio de Soto's employer) when they transported goods in their boats to Mexico City. Don Andrés Canto controlled access to the point at which they passed from one lake to another. At Mexicalzingo there was an important dike keeping the higher waters of Lake Xochimilco at bay, and it is probably this point in the system that don Andrés Canto controlled. The petitioners called this place a garita (although it is unlikely that it was an official customhouse).[72] They used this particular incident to draw attention to ongoing abuses: don Andrés Canto and his guards frequently mistreated them, insulting them and hitting them, even those of higher status within the community.[73]

In 1796 officials at the Santo Tomás sluice gate in the area of Xochimilco cut the hair of don Hilario Antonio Cabrera, an indigenous ex-governor who complained about the various mistreatments he suffered at the hands of these quasi-officials and stressed that "these youths are not customs agents and have no other duty than to collect fees and to make sure that the transit of canoes is orderly."[74] The dislike that many Mexicans felt for these checkpoints and sentinels and those who oversaw them came to a head in 1799, when Pedro Morales, the guard at the garita de la Piedad, caught an indigenous merchant trying to evade the normal procedures and duties for a load of fruit. As he was passing by, the militia soldier Mariano Calado, rather than taking the side of the official, sympathized with the merchant and began to beat the garita guard, saying, "Here is one of those starving thieves!" Some men passing by on horseback chimed in, "Hit him! Hit him!" [75] Clearly everyone's sympathies were with the scofflaw rather than the official trying to collect duties. The men who controlled these access points in the lakes often took on the authority of customs officials and could be abusive. This type of control of public thoroughfares had an economic logic and was a daily reality for Mexicans whose livelihood depended on moving goods between Mexico City and its hinterland.

Although the garitas were, logically, primarily designed to collect funds and tax the movement of goods, the animosity that many Mexicans felt toward them was also related to the ill-treatment they received when they had to negotiate their way through these checkpoints. The guards at the garitas may have used their power to abuse and intimidate people who for a short interval were within their area of control. It was, perhaps, this feeling of power that led some Mexican men to impose an informal kind of garita in the street in front of their residences.

In Coyoacán in 1807 José Julián Romero, an español, was seated with his family in the doorway of his house at around seven o'clock in the evening. José Isidro, an indigenous man from the barrio San Gerónimo in the community of San Angel, walked by the front of the Romero residence with a group of people. José Isidro had been acting as a tour guide for some visiting relatives from Calimaya, and they had previously gone to visit the shrines of the Virgin of Guadalupe and Nuestra Señora de los Remedios. According to the visitors, they acknowledged the Romeros in a polite manner. They had their hats in their hands when they greeted them by saying, *"Buenas noches de Dios"* (a godly good night) to each of the Romeros. Instead of simply returning the salutation, one of the Romeros answered sarcastically, "Go ahead, señoritos (young sirs," but then another one called them carajos (pricks), and a brawl ensued. [76] During the clash someone hit José Isidro on the head—an injury that eventually caused his death.

The Romeros' testimony paints a different picture, accusing José Isidro of drunkenness, stating that the party of tourists was rude, and accusing them of causing one of the Romero women to drop her baby. In the statements given by those who were attacked, the witnesses expressed considerable consternation at the fact that the Romeros effectively blocked free passage in front of their home, even though this was the camino real and thus a public road. The Romeros' logic is mysterious: strangers walking in front of their house do not seem to pose a strong enough threat to warrant such violence. Their actions and those of the visiting outsiders do, however, indicate that passing by another man's house had to be negotiated.

Conflicts also occurred between people who were traveling on the camino real and those with farms or estates along the way. The area around Tultitlan was particularly dangerous for travelers on the camino real. The workers of the Rancho del Tesoro regularly abducted passersby and forced them to either pay a toll or work on the estate. Those who knew of this practice avoided this stretch of the camino real, but there were still many complaints from those who could not avoid it. Sebastián Fernández, an indigenous man, was delivering mail for the owner of the Hacienda San Martín when he was grabbed off the camino real by workers of the Rancho del Tesoro. He argued with his captors that he needed to take the letters in his possession to Mexico City, but like so many others he was put to work forcibly, and he lost the mail.[77]

Not all the incidents were so clearly about control, but they demonstrate a tension between those passing through and those whose livelihoods depended on the area around the camino real. One morning in 1807, when José Vincente Medina, a castizo, was grazing the hacienda's sheep in fields in the area of San Augustín de las Cuebas (Coyoacán), a traveler's dogs barked and chased his sheep. The traveler, Manuel Mendoza, an indigenous man from Coyoacán, was taking his candles to sell in the village of Ajusco. He was in the company of another man, his twelve-year-old nephew, and four dogs that were either very small or very fierce, depending on the witness. Manuel Mendoza was worried about being robbed of his candles, which represented his livelihood, and thus he traveled with others and with dogs to protect his wares. He must have chosen the dogs for their capacity to protect him and perhaps to enhance his image as a man. He did not understand the shepherd's distress when his dogs chased the animals; according to him, they were acting according to their natural instinct.[78] Both men wanted to protect their livelihoods, and it was their proximity along the camino real that brought them into contact and highlighted the tension between those on the road and those on the side of the road.

This tension was also apparent when an indigenous man from Mixcoac, Manuel Antonio, was walking along the camino real innocently (or so he thought) and took a few stalks of corn. Astounded at this transgression, the *milpero* (farmer) from the hacienda of Padre García grabbed him, punched him seven times, and left him unconscious. The other fieldworkers came over and beat him some more, then they jailed him in Coyoacán. According to his brother, Manuel Antonio was not really a thief; he only took the five or six stalks of corn to quench his thirst by chewing on them for the plant's fluid.[79] Their different views of this act show the disparity between the views of those in transit and the views of those who produced the food in the countryside. But it also highlights the fact that the camino real brought different groups together in ways that were not always peaceful.[80]

The camino real was the site for many struggles over resources and the right of transit. In Tlanepantla in 1749 two families fought over access to land. Josefa María, an indigenous woman, reported that her brother and husband had taken a stand forcefully telling a man named Ignacio, "Do not pass through here, for it is not a road."[81] Similarly, in San Augustín de la Cuevas, not far outside Mexico City, Nicolás Antonio owned arable land that bordered on the camino real and that he farmed annually. During the rainy season the proximity of his lands to the camino real became a problem. When the road became extremely muddy, people chose to walk on his land rather than on the road. In 1752 he erected a fence to prevent transit through his fields. Nearby residents complained that his fence actually blocked the road and obstructed the public road, once even preventing a priest from delivering the last rites to a dying man.[82]

Evidently, the boundaries of roads were in contention. A similar conflict arose in 1753 when the don Julián Campos y Cervantes, the owner of the Rancho del Tesoro, sent his workers and a team of twelve oxen to plow the camino real. The owner of the neighboring hacienda was incensed and went there with his men to stop the work, which resulted in a battle between the two groups.[83] Streets and thoroughfares brought people together but also led to problems over control; although men had considerable liberty of movement, there were many invisible boundaries that they had to negotiate. For men in New Spain these encounters were always colored by hierarchical relations, and controlling the space of the road or the camino real was therefore an obvious way to demonstrate both power and masculinity.

The Streets and Leisure

Being in the streets presented many challenges for Mexican men, but it was also there that they had the most amusements. These were the spaces in which male friendships flourished; plebeian men often recounted how two men would spend time together night and day, often taking all their meals together.[84] Mexico City's pleasant climate made life outdoors a welcome contrast to homes that were often poorly ventilated and crowded. In addition, urban dwellers could choose from a large number of open-air venues and recreations.[85] Some destinations were well established, such as the various paseos, the promenades of the elegant in refined outdoor surroundings.

Although plebeians of all ethnicities went to the same parks and canals that attracted fashionable wealthy Mexicans, they also engaged in much more informal promenades: walking from one drinking establishment to another, going to various sporting events, and singing and playing music. Instead of going to balls, they attended fandangos. Many of these activities occurred during the day or early evening; after dark only the boldest braved the unlit and quiet city. Because nighttime was punctuated by the sound of barking dogs, revelers, and the calls of prostitutes, few respectable Mexicans were outdoors then.[86] Some Mexicans simply took their entertainment off the street and went indoors, at times breaking the various laws of curfew— hiding out in taverns drinking and playing cards in vinaterías after hours, organizing house parties, or going to houses of ill repute.[87] There was a variety of entertainment, from the most elaborate to the simplest.

Strolling in beautiful surroundings was an important diversion for many Mexicans in the colonial period. Because the activity was out in the open, it provided a veneer of respectability and was really part of the courtship rituals for young men and women. These places were a framework in which men and women displayed themselves, trying to enhance their masculinity or their feminine attractiveness. The wealthy could afford to go into the countryside to find bucolic areas with orchards, gardens, and olive groves. They traveled to their country homes; San Augustín de las Cuevas was a popular site, but there were other such destinations in Coyoacán, Mixcoac, and Tacubaya.[88] There the affluent could relax, away from the hustle and bustle of the city, in orchards and peaceful gardens complete with fountains.[89] These excursions were very pleasant but perhaps tinged with sensual pleasure; consequently, in the seventeenth century the archbishop declared such pastimes to be scandalous.[90] Not everyone could afford these outings, but plebeians of different ethnicities did travel for curiosity as well as for work. The tourists from Calimaya, discussed earlier in this chapter, are an example of indigenous people who visited some sites of interest in the area around Mexico City. Travel was not easy, especially for those without the means to hire a carriage, and so most colonial Mexicans found their amusements closer to home.

Figure 10. Promenade en canot à Mexico (Boat ride in Mexico City). Mexicans enjoyed boat rides in the various canals that were a leisure destination. Apart from music and flirting, they could partake in food and drink along the shore. Theubet de Beauchamp, Vistas de México y trajes civiles y militares y de sus pobladores entre 1810 y 1827 (n.p.: n.p., 1830), n.p.

In Mexico City early in the colonial period, one of the most important excursions was to the canal de Jamaica, one of the canals that crossed the city. Residents walked or rode in carriages along the edges or went on the water in canoes—some of them large enough to accommodate dancing (fig. 10). The canal attracted many people who sang, played music, and ate. All along the edges there were food stands selling hot chocolate, atole (a hot drink thickened with ground corn), and tamales.[91] In the eighteenth century a concern over disorder during Carnival led Spanish officials to encourage residents to spend quieter, more reflective time at the paseo de Jamaica. But just to be sure that those attending the paseo did not commit any sins, they posted guards to guarantee that everyone went home by nine o'clock at night.[92]

At the end of the sixteenth century the Spanish administration built a new place for recreation: a park called the Alameda. It was located on what was then the edge of town and provided trees, water features, and an air of tranquility; its internal paths were wide enough to accommodate carriages, litters, and riders. Like the canal de Jamaica, it became a site for the wealthy to show off, to meet one another, and to enjoy sweets and fresh drinks.[93] By the end of the eighteenth century it had become very popular, attracting crowds of 5,000–6,000 on holidays.[94] The places that men and women went to meet changed over the colonial period, but attitudes and their conduct in these surroundings did not change substantially, perhaps because the very formal nature of these parks. Only when rules were loosened did men begin to exert a more exuberant and forceful masculinity.

The Alameda was part of a repertoire of places for the flaneur, a man who loitered around the city. In 1797 José Antonio Ortuño, a twenty-two-year-old Spanish man who quit his position as a cashier in a store, described his day playing hooky: at three in the afternoon he left his job in a huff, began to wander around the city, and swung by the Coliseo, but the show had just finished so he went and passed the time in the Alameda.[95] His wanderings reflect the kind of movements and activities of a young Spanish man of middle rank; plebeian men followed different patterns.

Chapultepec Park was another escape relatively close to Mexico City, but it was far enough that most residents had to go via carriage or horse, so it was usually a daylong excursion.[96] The Italian traveler Giovanni Gemelli Carreri described the crowd at Chapultepec as a "considerable turnout of ladies and gentlemen." Most were in large carriages, but there were also people on horseback and on foot. Men and women flirted and engaged in hot embraces.[97] In 1801 don Manuel Obregón went to meet a group of male friends in Chapultepec Park. He wanted to look his best. Trying to make them envious of his sartorial splendor, he stole a scarlet cape, a hat, and a gold watch from his brother's room.[98] Although there were no specific rules excluding certain groups from these venues, the venues were harder to reach, and clearly those who went to these paseos were usually showing off the kind of finery that was not affordable for the vast majority of Mexicans. In the eighteenth century wealthier Mexican men began to adopt French fashion that was showier, more colorful, and in strong contrast to their previous penchant for black attire. The way that men expressed their masculinity through clothes began to change, but it was out of reach for those without means.

Plebeian Mexican men were no less likely to stroll about the city, but their trajectories were quite different. One Saturday in 1796, after being paid for the week, Joseph Ignacio Terán, a Spanish tailor working in a factory, went out onto Mexico City's streets. He met a friend, and they drank some *revuelto* (a mixed drink) at the vinatería at the corner of San Agustín, then they went to the calle de Ortega to a *figón* (a cheap restaurant) to have an afternoon snack. There they drank some pulque. At that point Joseph Ignacio Terán was ready to go home, but his friend invited him to a dance, so they set off to find the party.[99]

Juan Puente, a Mexico City blacksmith, described some of his wanderings in 1801. On Saturday, at a little after five o'clock in the afternoon, he went out to a job for a carriage maker. Along the way he met his friend Antonio Rivera; they stopped to talk, and Antonio Rivera said that he was going to his niece's house on the calle de Santa Clara. He also wanted to swing by his former job in the *tocinería* (pork-processing plant) of Santa Catarina Martir to get his last pay. Deciding to skip his job, Juan Puente tagged along, and after they had stopped by Antonio Rivera's former workplace, they went into the vinatería of San Fermín, where Juan Puente invited Antonio Rivera to have a drink. They continued on their way but got distracted when they saw the vinatería de la Santísima, where they paused and had some aguardiente in the company of several friends. They might have continued in this meandering fashion a lot longer if not for Antonio Rivera's apparent penchant for theft (he had been fired from his job for stealing ham). Antonio Rivera stole a glass from the vinatería, and when the owner asked the men to return it, Antonio Rivera denied having it. The owner jumped over the counter, searched everyone, and found the glass hidden in Rivera's pants. After the vinatería owner hit Antonio Rivera a couple of times, Juan Puente took Rivera home, where they ate bread and drank a bit more aguardiente.[100] Plebeian men stopped to drink either aguardiente or pulque with great frequency, perhaps assisted by the ubiquitous presence of drinking establishments in Mexico City.

Men in smaller communities were no less inclined to stop for a drink, although their beverage of choice tended to be pulque. Drinking establishments were less formal in villages, often consisting of a home where pulque was prepared and sold. In Tacubaya don Miguel de Castro, an indio principal, recounted that in 1757 Cristóbal de Santa Ana and his wife, also indios principales, came to his home at about ten o'clock one night and asked for some pulque. They took their drinks onto the patio and then later into the oratory.[101]

Women often sold pulque as a sideline in their homes. In Coyoacán in 1785 Rafael Nava wanted to buy some pulque at Catalina Josefa's house. Because she was all out of the drink, he and some friends rioted, throwing stones at her door.[102] Even on the edges of Mexico City, where streets were not so orderly or formal, men expected to be able to find pulque in homes. This assumption led to a major clash between some soldiers who, in the middle of a night in 1799, wanted to find a drinking establishment in Santa Fe. They wandered over to the jacales, where the workers in the Royal Gunpowder Factory lived, and demanded pulque even though the sleepy residents kept telling them that their homes were not pulquerías.[103] This may also indicate the type of masculinity that soldiers began to embody in the late eighteenth century.

In both small towns and Mexico City, drinking establishments, whether formal or not, were supposed to close at around ten o'clock. When customers became inebriated, closing time was sometimes difficult to impose. In San Augustín de las Cuevas (Coyoacán), María Nicolasa operated her house as a pulquería. One night in 1805, Ignacio el Cuate and others were still drinking and playing the guitar at eleven o'clock, leading to a conflict between the residents and the patrons.[104] Not all drinking occurred in establishments, however. The various religious festivals were also often a reason for great merriment, some of which was alcohol-based. In the town of Cuautla Amilpas, Pedro Raymundo, a Spanish man, explained that for the town's fiesta people of all races and *calidades* (race and reputation) celebrated in the governor's house, where they ate and drank a great deal, all getting drunk together.[105] Alcohol consumption among Mexican men did lead to many brawls, and even worse, along with much merriment.

Despite efforts on the part of eighteenth-century colonial authorities to make taverns dreary places of little appeal, the men who frequented drinking establishments enjoyed not just the spirits they imbibed but also the company of other men and making music. These drinking establishments were important sites for male socializing.[106] Singing and playing musical instruments was very much part of masculine culture in taverns, homes, and in the streets. In the schools for indigenous children, boys often learned to play various instruments so they could perform in liturgical settings. As adults some became professional musicians, going from one village to another and performing for festivals and in churches. The Escuela family of Santísima Istapaluca (Chalco), for example, formed a group of eight musicians and singers.[107]

In Mexico City some boys sang in the Cathedral, and if they were talented as adults, they became permanent members of the choir.[108] The line between sacred and secular music was often very unclear; composers and choirmasters frequently used popular music forms or themes taken from daily life, such as playing cards, in church services.[109] Music pervaded the everyday experiences of Mexicans, but it was particularly associated with the private dance parties called fandangos. In Mexico City blacks, mulattoes, and mestizos organized dances in private homes, and those who attended frolicked and sang until morning.[110] A couple danced together at the fandangos, which was a novelty because previously most dances were more formal and people danced in patterns not face-to-face or as pairs. It was in this setting that couple dancing emerged in Mexico. Fandangos were part of the street culture of the night—the allure of the forbidden, and both the events and the dances were condemned by colonial authorities. In addition, in the late eighteenth century Mexicans began to organize dance schools, where people could learn the new dances. Men usually learned to dance with other men in these venues.[111] In this informal atmosphere men let loose their inhibitions with each other and with women; they could express a masculinity that was expansive, entertaining, and seductive.

On many of these occasions men played either the guitar or the vihuela (an early form of the guitar) and often sang popular songs.[112] Some of the songs are known to historians because several more devout individuals denounced the songs and the accompanying dances to the Inquisition because of the lewd and blasphemous lyrics and the lascivious movements. Singing could be a way to assert one's masculinity, especially if the words were bawdy. Rude songs also made spaces like pulquerías, vinaterías, and fandangos part of the masculine range of spaces, Loud singing could be a masculine way to claim and dominate spaces; it made a man the focal point of social gatherings, and sometimes men competed for this attention.[113]

At about seven o'clock on an evening in 1804 in the vinatería de Villamil in Mexico City, a black man was playing a tune called the "Son de Justicia" (Song of Justice) on a vihuela when Juan García took the instrument from him and began to play another popular tune, the "Son de Jarabe." Soldiers from different regiments were present, and so many were dancing that when a civilian stepped on a grenadier's foot, a minor skirmish ensued.[114] Also in 1804, in a Cuautla fandango, two men attempted to perform the song "Bamba Poblana."[115] Song lyrics could cause controversy not just for religious reasons but also when they seemed to be directed at a person—satirical songs used humor and mockery to insult both officials and neighbors.

Music and dance moved from the streets to house parties or fandangos to avoid detection, but Mexican men moved relatively freely between these settings, continuing to drink, make music, and make merry. In many of the

Figure 11. Playing cards. Cards confiscated from a tavern. Playing cards were a royal monopoly. In addition, gambling was allowed only under certain circumstances. Nonetheless, many colonial Mexicans flouted these rules. AGN, Ramo Criminal, vol. 613, fol. 213v, Cuautla Amilpas, 1754.

places that men circulated, they also gambled or played various games. Playing cards were a Spanish import; they became a fixture in Mexican society from the early days after the conquest (fig. 11). Not all of these amusements were sanctioned; the Catholic Church frowned upon gambling and games of chance.[116] In Chalco in 1801 Tomás José Baustista, an indigenous man, lost his position as church notary because local officials considered his predilection for playing games such as *rayuela* (hopscotch) and cards to be a bad example for other men and a public scandal.[117]

But the colonial government had a monopoly on playing cards and even tried to tap into the human taste for gambling by setting up an official

Figure 12. Le monté (Three-card monte). Gambling was ubiquitous; here men were playing three-card monte in the streets. Notice how the game brought together men of different stations and forms of dress. Claudio Linati, Trajes, civiles, militares y religiosos de México (1828) (Mexico City: Universidad Nacional Autónoma de México, 1956), n.p.

lottery.[118] Men often played various card games in pulquerías, in vinaterías, or at private parties, but there were many different types of diversions—even in the street (fig. 12). Men frequently combined drinking and gambling—whoever lost paid for the alcohol.[119]

In a San Miguel (Azcapotzalco) pulquería in 1789, Juan del Carmen was socializing with friends when the pulquero invited him to play rayuela.[120] Along with the card games came accusations of cheating and being poor losers who often tried to pull rank by asserting their higher social status. At a party in a Mexico City house in 1796, many men, including soldiers and priests, were playing three-card monte. When a second lieutenant found that the dealer had hidden a card, he and others began to ask for their money back.[121] In a home in Amecameca in 1800, José Antonio Posos had been playing a card game called *rento* with friends that they had made into a drinking game: like many other Mexicans, they bet for aguardiente. When all the friends were leaving, his uncle, perhaps asserting the hierarchical right of being older, refused to give him back his deck of cards.[122]

Many of these games, such as checkers, seem rather innocent, but under some circumstances games were forbidden.[123] The line between forbidden and permitted enjoyments was not always clear; in the village of San Luis (Tacuba) the governor conducted a raid on the house of Manuel de los Santos while he was having a party. Santos argued that the governor's actions were unwarranted because it was a quiet gathering and definitely not a fandango. Officials in Tacuba upheld the governor's actions, stating that he had a duty to guard against excesses, games of chance, drunkenness, and other activities harmful to indigenous people's morality, and for which they were falsely notorious in this area.[124] For Mexican officials at all ranks, these diversions were difficult to manage; the officials had to negotiate the line between control and allowing plebeian men to let off steam. If officials restricted entertainments too much, they risked strong reactions such as minor riots, yet they could not allow the masculine assertion of spatial control to get out of hand.

Flowing from this dilemma, some entertainments in colonial Mexico City, at least, were formalized. One venue for male entertainment was the Plaza de Gallos, or Cockfight Plaza; bouts were held all year except July to September, when the roosters molted and got new feathers and could not fight. The audiences were very diverse, from clerics and nobles to artisans and other workers.[125] Men brought their roosters to fight and would bet on the various matches while plaza officials guarded against various forms of cheating. Cockfighting was a source of revenue, because those who attended had to pay for entry.[126]

Cockfights were one of many cruel diversions. Another entertainment that was called *correr el gallo*: a rooster is buried up to its head and then a man, either blindfolded or on horseback, cuts off the animal's head.[127] This was a means by which men asserted their masculine prowess, and according to Steve Stern because the animals involved were "feminized" and thus performed the role of allowing men to "refortify" their manhood.[128] Without a more detailed analysis of this practice, it would be easy to fill in the gaps with assumptions. However, it does seem telling that they chose to sacrifice male birds in this dramatic way rather than simply killing chickens for dinner.

Horses were a huge presence in men's lives; apart from their practical use in work and transportation, horses were used by men for fun and especially to go fast. Under some circumstances colonial Mexicans became addicted to speed and thrills. Although formal racetracks were not established until much later, men did organize horse races in open areas on the edges of Mexico City.[129] Certain men were not content with the role of spectator,

Figure 13. *Récreation mexicain* (Mexican activity). In the countryside and on the edges of Mexico City, men's work brought them into close contact with the natural world. One way these men defined their manhood was by dominating animals such as the bull, and another way was by the excellence of their horsemanship. Theubet de Beauchamp. *Vistas de México y trajes civiles y militares y de sus pobladores entre 1810 y 1827* (n.p.: n.p., 1830), n.p.

however, and they engaged in informal races in the city that were no doubt exhilarating because of the speed and danger as well as a way to prove their manhood. In 1795 José Justo Tamayo, a mulatto, was passing through the Plaza de San Pablo on horseback when another man charged by at full speed. José Justo Tamayo felt challenged by this racing stranger and urged his mount into a gallop; soon the two were racing through the neighborhood streets and forcing pedestrians to jump out of the way.[130]

Young men also challenged each other to races and feats of horsemanship (fig. 13). In 1802, seeing that his friend had tied up two horses outside the Pulquería de la Alamedita, Mariano Aniceto Cedillo, a mestizo man, challenged his drinking buddy to a race for who would pay for the aguardiente. They each chose a horse and raced from the closest bridge to the bridge of San Gerónimo.[131] Also in 1802, coachmen José María Díaz and Francisco Bigueras raced their mule-driven carriages from behind the Casa de Moneda to the calle de la Merced. At one point they locked wheels—they were alone on an empty street and could not resist the lure of even greater competition.[132]

The countryside provided an even better setting when young men wanted to show off their horsemanship. When a group of four muleteers were returning to their villages after delivering goods to Mexico City, two young men riding horses galloped ahead. Both were flaunting their skills as horsemen, and they challenged each other to *colear*, or to pull the horse's tail. This practice dated back to the early days of *charrería* (a Mexican form of cowboys) and usually entailed pulling the tail of a cow to make her behave.[133] Clearly these two young men had adapted a practice employed by cowboys with cattle in order to make their competition more exciting and perhaps emulating the masculinity of charrería.

Galloping cross-country, the español Ramón Velásquez reached over and pulled the tail of Mariano José's horse. Perhaps they had both played at this pulling of tails many times, but on this occasion the action unbalanced the galloping horse, and it fell along with the rider.[134] The thrill of racing and feats of horsemanship came with a heavy price at times. Nonetheless, men in New Spain, especially plebeian men, had the relative freedom of being in the streets and the countryside and seem to have loved to engage in such dangerous but exhilarating behavior.

The Natural World

Since men circulated in New Spain more than women did, not only did they come into greater contact with many animals, they often made their living using animals or collecting resources from the mountain outside their villages.[135] Animals were a big presence in Mexico City, especially dogs, mules, and horses. Outside cities men worked with animals both as livestock and as part of a team: oxen for ploughing, horses and mules for transportation, and dogs to herd sheep. At times residents considered animals a nuisance—for example, the Mexico City dogs that invaded churches during Mass or barked during siesta time; the viceroy even had to order dogs out of convents.[136] More frequently animals were allies for men, sometimes even an extension of their very beings.[137] Social anthropologists have recently begun to study this phenomenon, which they call cobeing; it is the sense between humans and animals that as they work together, they are no longer separate entities but rather bond and influence each other.[138]

Some animals, such as horses, were symbolically associated with European might and the conquest and played a role in many rituals. When the new viceroy was welcomed into Mexico City, one of the many rituals that symbolized his power was the gift of a horse.[139] This gesture backfired in 1697 when the viceroy mounted the horse and it promptly dumped him; to make matters worse, his wig fell off.[140] The traveler Giovanni Gemelli Carreri, who witnessed this loss of face, noted that the viceroy was a man of letters; so too were the bureaucrats who had to ride horses later that year in the paseo del pendón, an important celebration of the conquest. No doubt the bureaucrats' lack of equestrian skills contrasted very highly with those of the Spanish men who, shortly after the conquest, would ride out in an *alarde*, a group of horsemen that would show off its horsemanship around the newly conquered Tenochtitlan. The bureaucrats' lack of skills also contrasted with the skills of the many plebeian men who made their living as cowboys or in other equine-related professions.[141] This contrast between bureaucrats and men who were innately comfortable in the saddle and with horses might have caused a profound unease on the part of high officials who could not understand the sense of cobeing between plebeian men and their horses.[142]

The connection between horsemanship and manliness was reiterated early in the colony: in a 1577 *cédula* (edict) the king ordered the residents of New Spain to cease using carriages for transportation because the young men were losing their ability to ride horses. Horsemanship was a necessary part of defending the kingdom, but it was also essential to Spanish male identity and honor.[143] Despite such strong reasons for riding horses, the viceroy refused to ride in the next procession, in a fit of pique or perhaps self-preservation, and hid in the viceregal palace.[144] The shame that the viceroy and other men of letters might have felt when they could not sit on a spirited horse was also related to what horses meant within the culture: they were, in the words of Américo Paredes, a "symbol of masculinity."[145] Their discomfort contrasted with the comfort of the many Mexican men who felt so at ease on horseback that in many testimonies they did not even mention that they were mounted during the events they described.[146]

In the countryside, as we saw earlier in this chapter, men often rode into houses. They also used their horses to intimidate unruly workers, pushing the large heavy animal up against them, and sometimes even trampling them under the horses' hooves.[147] Even equestrian equipment such as bridles and spurs were part of elite men's repertoire for disciplining plebeians. Equestrian skills were a source of pride and manliness, so horses became part of many men's lives and even an accessory to their manhood and status.

Dogs were also omnipresent. After the conquest European dogs mostly replaced the indigenous dogs, even becoming welcome additions in Native communities.[148] They were used for protection and herding but sometimes got out of control. Like horses, they were also sometimes used aggressively.[149] When don Augustín de los Rios of Chalco was wandering home one night in 1776, he came upon two friends who were fooling around just outside a store. Ignacio Selis had grabbed his friend don Luis Albares by the kerchief around his neck, and they were play fighting. As don Augustín de los Rios watched in amusement, his dog began to bark and grabbed Ignacio Selis's cape. Apparently misunderstanding the interactions between the two friends, the dog seems to have been trying to defend his master, so when Ignacio Selis began to attack the dog in self-defense, don Augustín de los Rios shielded the animal.[150] In 1780 Carlos Ximénez, a Spanish man living in Tolyahuaclo (Xochimilco), used a fierce dog to intimidate and attack the indigenous man Juan Ignacio when he arrived at Ximénez's house delivering the corn that he had transported in his canoe.[151]

Many Mexicans had dogs that were companion animals, and some dog owners even organized baptisms, weddings, and funerals for their canine companions.[152] José María Morales was walking with his friends and his dog in Mexico City on New Year's Eve in 1795. José María Morales and his friends crossed a bridge, followed by another group of revelers. But as the second group stepped onto the bridge, José María Morales's dog slipped in front of Pedro Albarado. Pedro Albarado was insulted that the dog "cut him off" and responded by kicking the dog into the canal.[153] He interpreted the dog's rudeness as associated with its owner, so Pedro Albarado's attack on the dog was, in turn, equivalent to attacking José María Morales. The dog was a stand-in for and extension of its owner.

In incidents when dogs behaved inappropriately, even with hostility, it is possible to discern the relationship between men and their dogs. In many ways dogs could become men's allies: herding, protecting, and providing companionship. In a twist on this alliance, in 1790 the men of a Mexico City tenement used their dog to humiliate and harass a higher-class gachupin who was slumming in their neighborhood. The dog jumped on his back, grabbed his cape, and bit it; one witness described the dog's actions as *torear*, like the actions of a bullfighter.[154] The dog's exploits clearly amused the tenement residents, who mocked the dog's victim and refused to assist him. This represents just one more episode in the relationship between men and their canine companions, of dogs as extensions of male identity.

Outside cities men quarreled over their control of natural resources. Historians have a long tradition of studying conflicts over land and water in colonial Mexico, but men also struggled to keep control over the pasturing of livestock, which has not been studied as extensively. In the areas around many neighboring communities (such as Chalco, Tacuba, Coyoacán, and Mexicalzingo), estates moved their livestock around to different parts of the *monte* (scrubland, sometimes in the mountains) to graze. Tensions over the movement of the animals led to clashes between the competing interests of the workers and owners when they perceived that the animals caused damage to the land. Don Thomas Ortiz, a hacienda administrator, would patrol the mountains around Tultitlan (Tacuba), and to prevent damage to his lands he would round up the offending animals and take them to a corral controlled by local officials. In 1748 he was especially offended when he found sheep from the neighboring Hacienda Blanca, because he believed that the administrator and workers from this estate allowed their livestock to wander on purpose. His actions, though perhaps following the rules, led to an armed confrontation with the administrator and workers of the Hacienda Blanca.[155]

The intrusion of animals onto others' lands or cultivated fields could have a real economic impact, but their movements were also part of the struggle between men to survive and to ensure respect for their property. In Theoloyuca (Cuautitlan) in 1773, Bernardino, an indigenous boy, was driving an ox along a road next to a field of corn when the animal reached over and grabbed a few stalks, breaking off their tips. The farmer, an indigenous cacique named Antonio Colin, hit the boy's head and knocked him off the mule he was riding.[156] These incursions had to be prevented for very practical reasons. In addition, if they were left unchecked, this reflected poorly on the man's ability to control his resources, including the ability to protect his house. As a result, men of all ethnicities in the countryside fought over minor intrusions of animals onto their lands.[157]

The men who had herds of livestock were clearly wealthy, but residents of the villages around Mexico City had smaller numbers of animals that were an important part of their domestic economy. Just like the large landholders, indigenous farmers were also angered over wandering livestock and the loss of such valuable assets. The animals sometimes came to symbolize the larger community tensions. In Xochimilco in 1749 these conflicts blew up into a loud confrontation over a pig. It all started when a pig belonging to Nicolás de García strayed into the amaranth plants belonging to Pascual Antonio Vásquez. When informed of his pig's movements, Nicolás de García was dismissive and insulting. Gravely offended, the Vásquez family killed the offending pig, and then, following the pattern of attacks at the front of houses, they went to the García home, threw the dead pig through the door into the house, and began to insult all those inside.[158] The pig was a proxy for the frustration that the Vásquez family felt about Nicolás de García's behavior.

Animals were sometimes used as substitutes in conflicts between neighbors, so they often suffered the consequences of their owners' blunders. In a hacienda in the Xochimilco region, Francisco Ortega and his brother turned up one day in 1786 and began to poke a bull with their swords. The bull's destiny was to be eaten at the festival of the saint Santiago, but as Matias de Santiago, the indigenous worker in charge of the bull, stated, after the bull was slaughtered, its skin would be used for leather.[159] This random cruelty went without any explanation, but the Ortega brothers seem to have chosen to provoke an animal belonging to an important estate—perhaps it was a small revenge.

Residents of the countryside often used resources that they found in the mountain. Sometimes they could collect foodstuffs, but more commonly men made a living cutting down trees for charcoal for the voracious Mexico City market. The local haciendas, however, frequently regulated their access to the woods and charged a usage fee to the charcoal collectors. Joseph González, who rented the Rancho de Nuestra Señora de Montserrat in the Coyoacán area, made a deal with the local indigenous residents for grazing rights for his goats in exchange for their right to produce charcoal on his lands.[160] There was often tension between landowners and the charcoal workers, who entered their property and might overstep their traditional rights, taking more coal than allowed or even taking other resources. Don Manuel González, for example, accused a local couple of using the pretext of making charcoal to take other goods.[161] In 1747 some Cuajimalpa men killed Matheo de la Cruz because he had previously stolen charcoal from them.[162]

The right to collect wood and from where were frequently contested. In 1782 the forest guards of the Hacienda Xoco prevented the indigenous men of San Miguel Topilejo (Xochimilco) from cutting wood; both the hacienda and the village asserted that the woods belonged to them.[163] Hacienda workers often confronted charcoal collectors, accusing them of not paying for the wood they had collected from areas belonging to the estate. Some indigenous men of Tepozotlan, for instance, petitioned in 1791 to clarify their rights to the woods that the hacienda owner, don Martín Romero, was contesting. Romero's workers confiscated the charcoal produced by the people of San Mateo Xoloc.[164]

Francisco Antonio, an indigenous man from Santa María in Cuautepec (Tacuba), was accosted by the mayordomo of Joseph Pacheco's hacienda when he was on his way to sell his charcoal. The mayordomo confronted him, saying that he still owed money for the right to collect wood on the hacienda lands.[165] In effect, the hacienda agents acted to control the movement of charcoal from the monte to the market while ensuring that the hacienda collected some revenue. The actions of the hacienda agents were often quite aggressive and in many ways resembled those of the garita guards or many of the other men who controlled streets and roads in colonial Mexico.

Conclusion

Men's lives were punctuated with boundaries. They had to negotiate the dual influence of the home, where they drew on their role as paterfamilias, and the street, in which they could find fun and challenges. Their world was not in one place, nor was it entirely defined by either house or street. Many parts of their lives and worlds were very serious—for example, the protection of their households was a matter of grave concern. Perhaps because men so frequently had to defend their residences, their streets or their places in the neighborhood, these roles led to clashes that were practical but also aimed at defending their manliness and their place in local society. It is not surprising, then, that when they left behind domestic concerns and were out in the streets with their friends, they let loose: gambling, drinking, dancing, and making music.

Men's existence in New Spain was thus very much marked by dualities: house and street, order and disorder, licit and illicit. These two halves of their lives were not clear-cut; men moved from one type of experience to another fluidly, crossing boundaries and thresholds without restraint. Even as they tried to control their domestic environment with keys, doors, and acting as sentinels of the thoroughfare, they chafed at this duty. When men escaped their domestic settings, their fun was exuberant and high-spirited. For those on the edge of Mexico City or in the surrounding communities, the countryside provided men with a livelihood as well as an escape into another area of expertise. Men excelled at horsemanship—a skill that defined manliness and was seductive—but they were also at home with dogs, cattle, and many other domesticated animals. Even while homes pulled at men and provided them with a respectable masculinity, these other parts of their world endowed them with a more expansive manhood.

CHAPTER 6

Men and Men

✛ DURING THE 1746 FESTIVAL OF CORPUS CHRISTI IN COYOACÁN, A
mestizo man named Thomás Antonio had the temerity to challenge the
authority of a priest and called him a "cuckold monk and a jerk." The cleric
tried to use his authority to prevent Thomás Antonio from selling rosaries
and other religious objects.[1] Religious celebrations had overtones of solem-
nity, but they were also moments of pleasure when some people broke free
from conventions. On a daily basis, colonial Mexican men like Thomás
Antonio had to negotiate the divide between submissive respect and merry
camaraderie. From a very early age they had to find their way in masculine
groups where they worked and socialized. In all these settings the various
rankings of individuals were performed in acts of either deference and submission or dominance and authority.

Throughout this book this squabbling for rank has been an undercurrent
that flavored the interactions between men as they grew up, in their homes
and on the streets, at work and in their love lives. This chapter explores the
rapport between men of similar social standing and across class lines. There
were two obvious sides to this masculine world: one consisted of friendly fun
with people of a similar rank, and the other was the much tenser negotiation
of rank, either high or low but also with many gray areas where the negotiation of precise rank was difficult. These two aspects represent what James
Scott calls the hidden and public transcripts; when among men of a similar
class, a man could relax, but in the company of other classes he had to adopt

an attitude of either dominance or submission.[2] This vying for rank might appear quite grim, but among friends men forged strong bonds punctuated with great fun and ribaldry.

Evidence of male friendship and wit has often been found in various societies (but primarily England) through personal letters, memoirs, and jest books (pamphlets of jokes).[3] But in Mexico it is harder to find traces of the camaraderie and humor of poorer men, who were unlikely to write down their thoughts and recollections; these have to be inferred from documents that had other intentions, such as the judicial documents at the center of this book. Yet friendship was extremely important for plebeian men who depended on one another for support and solidarity.[4] It was within these moments of levity and among their own that men could unwind and be themselves. They usually negotiated the hierarchical differences that were ever present by adopting attitudes of deference. Men of superior rank frequently enforced these social gradations with verbal or physical violence; they broke with the prevailing ideal of composure, especially when dealing with someone they considered inferior. These two aspects of the interactions of men were the dual sides of male life: within one's own group and with others. Although the conflicts and strategies of domination that men used to maintain their position often overshadowed the times of repose and entertainment, all of these were equally important parts of men's lives.

The Construction of Male Identities

Identity was complex in colonial settings; the melding of different races and cultures challenged European notions of society and led to the creation of byzantine categorizations of racial mixtures. Colonial ideas about race necessarily intersected with conceptions of hierarchy, since by virtue of their success the conquerors placed themselves at the top of these schemata. But as historians have shown, the neat straightforward model that would have all Spaniards at the top of such rankings was a much more complicated reality for New Spain.[5] Despite considerable scholarly interest in this topic, historians have concentrated on race as the central foundation for identity with little attention to gender as part of male identity. Certainly the two intersected, and it would be impossible to outline masculine identity in New Spain without also taking into account the fundamental importance of race. Masculinity had certain external attributes, however, and these provided a rough guide to how men defined themselves as men, along with the many other ways they had to define themselves, including honor systems.

The elements that became markers for manhood were both tangible and intangible but were easily recognized by others within the community. Clothes were an obvious defining feature of gender; for men, certain items stood out as central to the definition of manliness, but modes of dress were also a way of placing men within the proper social context.[6] Moral authorities had always associated what people wore with their inner being and integrity, but in the colonial context they also defined men by race. Individuals were expected to wear dress appropriate to their ethnicity. Indigenous men were supposed to wear simple clothes such as cotton shirts and trousers that showed not just their race but their humility; when they began to adopt Hispanic styles, they were blurring their identity and provoked much unease.[7]

Diego Nicolás, an indigenous man, presented himself as respectable because he was dressed "under the shelter and cover of his blanket," thus embracing an acceptable indigenous outfit.[8] In a sense, indigenous men who started to adopt European fashions were also demonstrating their wealth and respectability; such conduct was an important way to express honor and masculinity that transcended racial categorizations. Honor and manliness were tied to being able to earn a living and support a family and allowed men greater social freedom and thus status.[9] Indigenous men who were community leaders, prosperous, or simply powerful probably took on elements of Hispanic fashion to emphasize their manliness.

In the later colonial period the adoption of horses—previously off-limits to indigenous men—might also have been a means to assert and construct manhood. Don Antonio Abad y Galicia, the principal cacique of San Salvador el Monte in the area of Xochimilco, was extremely solicitous of his horse, going so far as to launch a judicial complaint against a young man who set off the customary fireworks on Christmas Eve and frightened the horse.[10] Don Antonio Abad y Galicia's motivations may seem, on the surface, to be a simple concern for the animal, but his complaint allowed him to emphasize that he possessed a horse (that attribute of masculine qualities) and that he was wealthy. The horse was a fashion statement as well as a mode of transportation, and it completed the picture of a powerful, wealthy, and honorable man. It was an accessory. But don Antonio Abad y Galicia was also blurring the lines of racial identity in order to emphasize his gender identity as a powerful man. He was seeking to avoid the type of humiliation meted out to the officials of Amecameca; José Ambas had challenged their authority by saying that they wore serapes—blankets often used as capes by indigenous men.[11] It was an indirect way to impugn their manhood, but it also made the connection between racial identity and dress and the right to respect and authority.

Fashion changed slowly in the Hispanic world, but the sober attire of seventeenth-century gentlemen, when black was the color of choice, gave way to more exuberance in the eighteenth century, when French style began to penetrate male consciousness and clothing was somewhat feminized.[12] As Bourbon officials tried to bring order to their colony, they emphasized the externals and tried to impose a dress code of respectability: a 1778 decree instructed all poor Spanish, indigenous, mulatto, mestizo, and casta men to wear cotton pants and shirts along with a cape, a tilma, or a *frezada* (blanket) when in public. The official push to force men to clothe themselves decently was often difficult, given the prevailing problem that some men gambled away their garments and ended up clad primarily (or sometimes only) in blankets or sheets (fig. 14).[13]

These dress codes were part of an attempt at social reengineering: forcing men to adopt the uniform of a productive worker might make them better subjects. Perhaps men whose form of dress scandalized officials and elites were, like men who resisted formal jobs, defying the conformity desired by Bourbon reformers. Workers in many areas—the Royal Mint, the Royal Tobacco Manufactory, and night watchmen—had to be decently attired in the increasingly standardized outfit of five garments.[14] Perhaps without even consciously trying, the Bourbons were attempting to create an alternate gender identity through dress that tied in with the emphasis on the good worker. At the same time, it became more acceptable to show one's wealth through fashion, and in the late colonial period Mexican men increasingly wore such extravagant accessories as diamond buttons and jeweled hat pins.[15]

These changes were part of a redefinition of male identity through clothes, in which one kind of masculinity was being associated with prosperity and respectability. Clothes defined men through shared cultural codes and conventions; they became a bodily metaphor that supported a man's identity.[16] Don Egidio Marulanda understood this connection when he argued that his wayward son should not "be sheltered by the jacket" of the military uniform.[17] He knew how such clothes would redefine his child. Stripping a man of his clothes or rousting him from bed in a state of undress was acutely humiliating because it divested him of his protective layer and rank. Men

Figure 14. *Marchand de biscuit enveloppé dans un drap de lit* (Biscuit merchant wearing a sheet). Men of the lower classes often covered themselves with only a sheet or a blanket. This attire marked them as lacking in rank and respectability. Claudio Linati, *Trajes, civiles, militares y religiosos de México (1828)* (Mexico City: Universidad Nacional Autónoma de México, 1956), n.p.

spoke of the mortifying experience of "not having anything more than a shirt to cover my flesh."[18] Even more frequently they spoke of how, during confrontations, their victimization included the assailant destroying their clothes.[19]

Attacking clothes to insult and unman could be more calculated. While don Manuel López called don José Antonlin Robledo by various epithets, he grabbed his cape and ripped it off his shoulder—an action that was equal to the words.[20] When don José Vigil abandoned don Mariano Hernández's sister after seducing her, don Mariano Hernández lured don José Vigil into his home in 1808, beat him, and forced him to leave the building nude.[21] These acts of vengeance show how men understood clothes as identity. Thus part of an attack on another man frequently included the use of clothes as a way to attack his masculinity.

Clothes could impart many messages; at times men adopted styles that seemed feminized and thus immoral. But clothes were also part of a vocabulary of rank and power, as amply demonstrated by the dress of a rich landowner (fig. 15). The hierarchical aspect of dress reinforced male identity because it accentuated men's power, status, and honor. Wealthy men, especially those with political aspirations, had to dress extravagantly, with many layers of lavish trappings as well as shoes with red heels and, of course, wigs. In the seventeenth century one of the most telling elements of powerful male dress was the elaborate white collar, often in contrast to black clothing.[22] Although these collars disappeared from common usage in the eighteenth century, many men adopted the kerchief, which was, in a sense, a less refined version of neckwear.[23] As with other pieces of clothing, men often grabbed or destroyed the kerchief, but it could also serve other purposes.[24] On an evening in 1776 two friends, don Luis Albares and Ignacio Selis, grasped each other's kerchiefs and engaged in a mock fight, much to the amusement of all those present.[25]

Swords were also an important and distinguishing element of masculine attire; for men of the middle and upper classes, no outfit was complete without a sword.[26] Swords conveyed authority to supervisors and to officials, both civil and military.[27] Lower-class men, in contrast, carried knives even though there were numerous laws prohibiting them from this practice.[28] There was an implicit class difference in the weapons that men carried: swords were for the upper classes, whereas knives denoted a lower status.[29] Officials regularly confiscated knives, unlike swords, and thus their depictions abound in the judicial documents. All these elements of dress were accessories that defined men as men as well as in terms of rank and often race. They provided easy codes to distinguish who was a fellow within class and ethnic parameters.

Hats, however, were the piece of clothing most tied up with male hierarchy. At the highest levels of society, officials followed strict guidelines on when they wore their hats or removed them; their hats were actually symbolic of the way they represented and channeled the king's power.[30] Outside the higher social ranks, it was not so much the appearance of hats that was important as how and when they were doffed in greeting to another male. According to Isabel Cruz de Amenábar, men removed their hats in greeting but not when they entered a house.[31] The use of hats as salutation was, as Cañeque terms it, a shared "vocabulary and grammar of gestured signs."[32]

Hats were also something without which respectable men normally did not leave the house.[33] Don Antonio Gaona, an officer of the grenadiers,

Figure 15. Hacendado
(Landowner). A wealthy
landowner in the dress
appropriate to his rank
complete with a sword,
wearing his hat. His rid-
ing attire includes fierce-
looking spurs that men
sometimes used to disci-
pline those of lower rank.
Claudio Linati, *Trajes,
civiles, militares y religiosos de México (1828)*
(Mexico City: Universi-
dad Nacional Autónoma
de México, 1956), n.p.

recounted how he went into the barracks to remove his cap (associated with his uniform) to put on his hat for the trip home.[34] Men's hats became a hall-mark, a distinctive emblem for which they were known.[35] Men of lower rank, often but not always indigenous, emphatically emphasized that they had removed their hats politely. Gregorio Antonio, a town official in Naucalpan, reported that he had his hat in his hand when he greeted Francisco Sandoval; this wording was repeated so often that it was a clear shorthand for respect and submission.[36] Royal Mint workers had to address their superiors with humility and with their hats in their hands. This was just one part of "a ritual of submission" that occurred on a daily basis.[37] These ritualized gestures undoubtedly became the kind of "mask" that lower-rank men used in the presence of social superiors.[38]

Conversely, when men pointedly did not doff their hats, they showed their contempt for those they were supposed to respect, and this became the opposing shorthand for insolence. In 1757 don Phelipe Fernández de Solis ran into don Francisco Leyte with whom he was locked in a power struggle. The latter not only did not take off his hat in greeting but actually pushed it down on his head.[39] Insolence by hat was even more pronounced in the case of Vicente el Page, a vendor in the plaza, who not only kept his hat firmly on his head in the presence of the market administrator in 1800 but adopted a swagger with a cigar in his mouth. When ordered to doff his hat, he replied that in the matter of his hat he took orders from no one.[40] This association of power, etiquette, and hats was not unique. In 1808, on the occasion of a royalist procession, when those attending were shouting, "Long live the king!", an indigenous man, Angel José Nuncial, refused to remove his hat. Another indigenous man, José de la Merced Mendoza, reprimanded him by pointing out that by not removing his hat he was insulting the monarch.[41] Perhaps because hats played such an important role in this vocabulary of respect, when men attacked each other they very often grabbed them, took them, or simply damaged them.[42]

Apart from clothes and accessories, men also expressed different forms of identity and masculinity with their bodies. There were many ways to hold oneself, straight and haughty or bowing and submissive, and men had to adopt the body language appropriate to their station. One of the defining characteristics for men was the depth of their voices. According to a sixteenth-century medical treatise, a deep voice went with a strong man of large appetites, whereas a high, fluty voice was associated with a man of high intellect but timidity.[43] The documents do not tell us about voice, but witnesses frequently mentioned tone. It was important to strike the right tone of voice within a particular context.[44] Clearly, men of higher status could use a tone that conveyed authority, but when hacienda worker Carlos José spoke "with a haughty tone" or when don Vicente Salazar used a "tone of defiance," it was not acceptable.[45] When Mateo Francisco Sacatengo, an indigenous man, spoke "with a haughty voice" and in his own language, the officials who were present censured him.[46] Men of the same class sometimes used tones of jocularity and sarcasm, which were equally infuriating. When one of his creditors confronted don Juan Leandro Romero in his pharmacy, he not only spoke with dripping sarcasm but augmented the effect by keeping his finger in his cheek.[47] People transformed terms of respect such as *vuestra merced* (your lordship) and señorito (young sir) into vaguely insulting ones simply by using a sarcastic tone.[48] Men clearly used their voices and pitch to accentuate their rank as well as (indirectly) their manliness. The changeable quality of voices seems to have caused some anxiety among colonial Mexicans.

Hair, a very different body part, equally triggered distress. Even though long tresses were fashionable, they could be construed as a feminizing aspect for men. Hair seems to have been contradictory in its connection to masculinity; it is not clear whether, despite the moralist condemnations, the general population believed that long hair was effeminate. Beards were frequently linked with manliness; in fact, chin hair was associated with semen.[49] Yet in daily life, colonial Mexican men don't seem to have been concerned with beards.[50] Robles, however, suggestively noted that when a government official was fired, part of his degeneration into madness was to let his beard grow.[51]

Nevertheless, hair was one of the preeminent markers of ethnic identity and other qualities.[52] Before the conquest, male hairstyles denoted age, military achievements, and profession. Postcolonization, indigenous men alternatively adopted more Europeanized styles in order to pass as either mestizos or Spaniards.[53] They also kept the traditional *balcarrotas*—a style in which they grew their hair out on both sides of the face.[54] Many men, probably indigenous but possibly not always, wore their hair in a braid.[55] Castro Gutiérrez comments on a Royal Mint worker who had braided his hair, which was considered presumptuous or vain in this period.[56]

Early on in the colony, head shaving was a common way of punishing indigenous men—a practice which that continued Nahua conventions. This procedure came to an end because of a reversal of official policy and also, more likely, because indigenous men began to wear their hair short or even voluntarily shave their heads, which thus negated the symbolic effects of the punishment.[57] Nonetheless, hair continued to be part of the punishment equation. Men grabbed and pulled each other's hair when they fought.[58]

In 1739 officials in the town of San Vicente Chicoloapan in Cuautepec enacted this approach on a larger scale. After Sunday Mass, guards who had been posted at the church doors grabbed certain men (described by the Nahuatl term *macehual*, or commoner) and cut off their long balcarrotas. Those affected were all indigenous; a group lodged an official complaint, explaining that when they were working in the fields they tied their hair back, which provided them with protection from harsh weather.[59] They objected that because they could no longer tie their hair, they could not see to work. Don Andrés Antonio, one of the minor officials implicated, reported that higher officials stated that the long-haired men looked like *chichimecs*— a derogatory term for northern peoples considered by the Nahuas to be barbarians, but also a way to say "sons of bitches."[60] The words used in this court case are particularly interesting; the officials associated the longer hair of the macehuales with the unconquered Chichimecs, thus suggesting that they were rebellious. Perhaps these men were simply asserting a masculinity that was too strong for their station in the social rankings.

The association between punishing and cutting hair persisted in other ways. In a few instances, when people were struggling to impose their authority on recalcitrant individuals, they cut the hair of noncompliant indigenous men. Bartolo Antonio García, an indigenous man from Juchitepec, cut Miguel Reyes's braid in 1789; Reyes had promised to marry his daughter in order to seduce her and had then reneged.[61] The guards at the locks of Santo Tomás found don Hilario Antonio Cabrera drunk and insolent when they demanded their fee; in retaliation they cut his balcarrotas with some scissors in 1796.[62] It seems that cutting the hair of indigenous men who did not toe the line remained part of a vocabulary of punishment. Nevertheless, it provides a thought-provoking example of the multiple connections among hair, identity, and masculinity.

Camaraderie

In a society where rank and social dominance were so important, men could more easily relax among people of their own station. Perhaps because of this constraint, identity was vital. But among members of the same class, men developed staunch friendships and amused themselves. Men spent a lot of time with other men at work and in the streets; they developed strong bonds with others that carried over from formal to informal situations. Friends were important allies, but they populated the settings where men could let loose.[63] Companionship became a type of space in which men could unwind and enjoy one another's company. It was where they could operate within what Scott calls "hidden transcripts."[64] The Royal Mint was such a social space; workers there joked around by throwing pieces of silver at each other, they shared food and drink, and the older workers teased the new men by giving them nicknames that bordered on rude.[65] It is hard to capture such an ephemeral quality, especially among those who did not write down their impressions, but within the judicial documents there are small hints of the ways in which men acted out their camaraderie.[66] These clues include stories of failed jokes, attitudes, and laughter, but only in a general way. What is lacking in most accounts are detailed renderings of the words and postures of those involved, so the picture of this sociability has to be pieced together with these fragments.

Because friends were trusted allies, they entered spaces that were off-limits to strangers. Essentially, they became part of a literal and figurative inside group. Men described friendships by the closeness and constancy of their dealings; they spoke of *estrechez y familiar trato* (closeness and affable dealings) and *estrecha amistad* (intimate friendship).[67] They hung around together all the time, went to each other's homes, and ate together whenever possible.[68] Some of their pastimes were quite innocent, such as playing checkers, walking around in the city parks, or going to see the fireworks during a festival.[69] Occasionally young men pushed the boundaries of this harmless amusement—for example, when young friends rambled about the streets of Coyoacán wearing masks and making music with two violinists.[70] Men shared experiences that therefore cemented their friendships. In many cases, these encounters occurred in *fondas* (restaurants), vinaterías and pulquerías, since drinking and eating were the lubricants of male camaraderie.[71] Within plebeian groups men had many nicknames for each other, which in the judicial context were termed aliases.[72] Many of these nicknames associated men with their occupations, but others were playful, such as *el pescadito* (the little fish), and several referred to physical appearance, such as *ermosura* (beauty) or *el sueño* (the dream), and still more of these names referred to race or origins (table 2).

These names provide a glimpse into the plebeian masculine culture; none of the men had any honorific, so they must have been lower or middle class.[73] It is quite possible that the nicknames were utilitarian in purpose, since many people had similar names and some did not even have a surname to distinguish themselves from others.[74] But there were also obvious playful elements among these names. Pedro Alcántara Hueynexco, with a very clearly indigenous last name, had the ironic nickname of gachupín, whereas while a Spaniard, Manuel Castillo, was called El Incas, referring to the Andean indigenous people.[75] There was a long tradition of nicknames in New Spain; the Nahuas had many types of monikers, including such amusing labels as Tochnenemi, or "He hops like a rabbit." The Nahuas also referred to place of origin and animals in their nicknames.[76] In anthropological

Table 2. Nicknames and Aliases

		ANIMALS		
Date	Actual Name	Nickname	Definition	Race
1744	Juan Sánchez	El Pollo	chicken	not specified
1781	Miguel López	El Lora	parrot	mestizo
1790	José Cristóbal Cordero	El Tordo	thrush or dappled, like a horse	mestizo
1808	Ignacio Sarza	El Nagual	animal shape shifter	not specified
1810	Mariano Salazar	El Pescadito	little fish	español

		PHYSICAL APPEARANCES		
Date	Actual Name	Nickname	Definition	Race
1749	Miguel López	Pulido	polished	español
1801	Tomás José Bautista	Cabezas	big-headed	indio
1803	Manuel Guerrero	El Cabezón	the big head	not specified
1808	Agustín	Bigote	mustache	mestizo
1808	Vicente Ruiz	Ermosura	beauty	not specified
1809	Bartolo Sánchez	El Sueño	the dream	indio

		OCCUPATION		
Date	Actual Name	Nickname	Definition	Race
1744	Phelipe Jacinto	El Sastre	tailor	not specified
1749	Miguel	El Zapatero	cobbler	español
1765	Antonio Francisco	El Panadero	baker	indio
1785	Eduardo Mendoza	El Monedero	Mint worker or purse	español
1800	Vicente	El Page	page	not specified
1804	Juan Antonio Gómez	El Curtidor	tanner	español
1804	Miguel	El Varillero	barrel maker	not specified
1806	Enrique Caballero	El Monero	probably a mint worker	not specified
1808	José Monroy	El Matador	killer, bullfighter	español
1809	Pedro Sánchez	El Mercillero	probably a haberdasher	not specified

		ORIGINS		
Date	Actual Name	Nickname	Definition	Race
1726	Juan Caetano de Uribe	Gachupín	slang for Spaniard	mestizo
1742	Juan Joseph Molina	Cholula	a Mexican city	mestizo
1800	José Ambas	El Suizo	Swiss	not specified
1801	Manuel Marcos	Mestizo	racial mixture	not specified
1804	Manuel Marcos	El Poblano	from Puebla	indio
1808	Manuel Castillo	El Incas	Andean indigenous	español
1810	Pedro Alcántara Hueynexco	Gachupín	slang for Spaniard	not specified

		RELATIONSHIP		
Date	Actual Name	Nickname	Definition	Race
1801	Cosme Avila	El Coate	close friend	not specified
1805	Ignacio Mondragon	El Coate	close friend	not specified

		UNDETERMINED MEANING		
Date	Actual Name	Nickname	Definition	Race
1726	Sebastian Fabian	El Coscusero	indeterminable	indio
1775	José de la Trinidad Vargas	Regino	possibly royal	mestizo
1775	Josef Mendoza	Susano	possibly feminizing	mestizo
1790	Isidro	Tlatenpa	indeterminable	indio
1796	José	El Pipilioy	indeterminable	not specified
1797	José Torres	Bandola	musical instrument	español
1799	Mariano Estévez	Calado	soaked	not specified
1801	Diego Martín	El Xico	indeterminable	mestizo
1803	Vicente Sánchez	El Julio	month of July	not specified
1803	Ignacio Rivera	El Talanco	indeterminable	indio
1804	José María Guzman	El Barvas	indeterminable	indio
1808	José Herrera	Montes de Oca	possibly a place	not specified
1810	Marcos	Pilatos	possibly a reference to Pontius Pilate	not specified

Sources: Archivo General de la Nación, Ramo Criminal, and Tribunal Superior Judicial del Distrito Federal.

studies, scholars point to the playfulness of nicknames—often provoking laughter and fun—as well as their potential hostility.[77] It is not possible to glean such insights from archival material, but it does seem that the nicknames created a sense of familiarity and social cohesion.[78] When men who could identify with one another got together in these settings among equals, they loosened up and had fun.

In groups of peers, Mexicans could not help themselves; they mocked each other, joked, and played tricks. Even clerics, who were supposed to provide an example of seriousness, were so prone to such antics that their higher authorities tried to control them with rules for when they attended Mass. They were not allowed to chat, send each other notes, read, or "make jokes, pranks, or signs that would make the faithful laugh."[79] A rival of the cleri don Manuel Portillo went around teasing and making fun of others, not just in the streets but also in public paseos.[80] Even when jailed, Fray Jacinto Miranda could not resist clowning about; he would appear at the prison bars with other inmates, and when a religious procession passed by that included brothers from his friary, "he gestured and provoked much hilarity."[81]

Many men described their friendships as punctuated with humor; they used words such as *chanza* (jokes), *mofar* (mocking) or *hacer burla* (making fun) to describe the way they related to one another. Two indigenous men, Antonio de los Ángeles Barrado and Sebastián Fabian (alias El Coscusero) had a falling out in 1726 over a bet on a game of hopscotch; this argument left everyone puzzled, since previously "they always joked about."[82] Within such an informal mood, men joked and would also mimic fighting for fun. One evening in 1776, while relaxing outside Ignacio Selis's store in Chalco, Selis and don Luis Albares began play fighting. It was, they stated, because of their very close friendship that they could engage in this type of joking around.[83] Similarly, when José Arrequin and José Barantes, two longtime friends, were at a wake that was also a fandango in Cuautla in 1804, they were clowning about, play fighting with a stick when someone suggested that they dance the *bamba poblana* with knives. Although a witness described their actions as a joke, it did not end well.[84] In 1805 don Juan López Cancelada described a relaxed scene in which he was joking and having fun with his employee; this atmosphere was shattered when don Lorenzo Peláez entered and began to insult Cancelada.[85] Still, among friends and people of similar status, they could let go of the ceremonialism and dignity that marked much of their lives.

Even within the salons of the wealthy, joking between men of equal rank was common. In these settings, however, it seems to have been covering up barely disguised hostility. At the same time, by adopting a tone of jocularity, men could often dismiss words that offended as a "failed" joke.[86] In the gatherings of the wealthy, men still joked around, but their humor seems to have had a bit more of an edge to it. On the feast day of San Francisco in 1765, Vicente Villalba described going to the house of Francisco Téllez, where there was a gathering for this occasion. Vicente Villalba began a conversation with don Nicolás Pebedilla and "began to joke around." Unfortunately the content of these jokes was not recorded, but clearly they had some kind of significance or double meaning, because don Nicolás Pebedilla became irate, punched Vicente Villalba, and challenged him to a fight outside.[87] In social circles in which emotional control was so important and so much tension was sublimated into squabbles over etiquette and precedence, such a violent outburst was remarkable. Vicente Villalba testified that there was previous bad blood between the two men. Why then were they joking? Perhaps these jokes were a type of witty repartee with veiled insults—just the way to make an enemy lose face and composure but which could be explained away as "failed" jokes.

The strategy of explaining away controversial or semioffensive comments as jokes was also attempted in other situations. At a gathering in the house of don Antonio Arvide in 1790, the conversation turned to a mutual friend who had been jailed. Angered by the comments, don Luis Uriarte began to insult another guest, Fray Joseph de la Concepción. When challenged, however, he dismissed his words as *pura* chanza (just joking).[88] Although these episodes led to confrontation and thus the failure to maintain the emotional composure required of men of status, they do show that witty repartee and jokes were part of the regular communication when higher-status men relaxed together. Humor seems to have been a type of social lubricant that eased tensions or just made everyone relax, but it had to hit the right note.

Friends of similar status could take some liberties with one another, especially within a group of friends, but the tomfoolery that was so common to these gatherings depended on everyone getting the joke. The tone men used in conversation could be interpreted in many ways. When one man misunderstood another's tone, he reacted in anger, whatever his social status. When some acrobats put on a show in Jilotepec in 1808, among those present were the village's upper crust, who were enjoying the acrobats' antics and tricks. Such shows were part of the many entertainments common in New Spain, but Juan Pedro Viqueira Albán reports that these performers often veered into social satire.[89] Thus, the show in Jilotepec probably had a certain edge to it. Late at night, at about eleven o'clock, one of the acrobats began to pass around a plate for coins. When he tried to give the plate to one audience member, the latter declined loudly, declaring "that he would not take it because Andrade was present and would arrest him." Don Ignacio Andrade was indeed in one of the front rows, and he was an officer of the Acordada, a type of police force. Don Ignacio Andrade joined the fun and replied "as if he were Molina," referring to an official of lower rank, the person who actually made the arrests. So far the statements had been jocular, and the audience was laughing.

Then a person at the back shouted, "Andrade is not the alguacil, but he is an informant for the Acordada." The local priest had spoken these words and had used the very offensive term *soplón*, or snitch. Undoubtedly he believed that he was simply joining the fun, and he was comfortable doing so because he and don Ignacio Andrade were very close friends. Witnesses described their friendship as "total familiarity and trust" and the relationship as close. Don Ignacio Andrade exploded with his own rudeness, calling the speaker a "son of such-and-such," but then he was taken aback when he turned around to see his friend. Andrade seemed to take the words in stride at the show's conclusion, making peace, but his anger soon returned. He could not forgive his friend.

Audience members were puzzled by don Ignacio Andrade's strong reaction; they concluded that he had misunderstood the priest's tone. One witness, Laureano Peña, maintained that the priest had "spoken [not] in an offensive tone but rather one of jocularity, with a soft voice." He also noted that it was to be expected to tease and have fun at an acrobatic show.[90] When two friends met in a field and Augustín Antonio made a joking remark about the work, his humorous teasing was misconstrued, leading to conflicts.[91] Jokes could fail if not universally understood or if the tone was wrong.

The sociability of men also created spaces of inversionary humor that were generated in celebrations that allowed men and women in New Spain to unwind. As seen previously, men played musical instruments, sang, and danced at the numerous private fandangos that punctuated their social lives. Many of these events, both religious and secular, took place at night, when their nature became more subversive—in fact, Scott Taylor argues that many festivals took on the rowdy and undisciplined character of the night.[92] Even seemingly innocuous customs, such as setting up an altar in one's doorway to share with other residents, provoked the wrath of Bishop Francisco Fabián y Fuero (1719–1801) because, he argued, they were an excuse to go out a night.[93] Nonetheless, this practice and nocturnal visits were extremely common in New Spain.[94]

Although people were ostensibly out to share in pious veneration, many men could not resist using these occasions to poke fun at others, particularly through satire. On the occasion of an altar to honor the Virgin of Guadalupe in Xochimilco in 1796, don Miguel Xavier Padilla was in a friend's house when he heard singing outside. When he heard his name in the lyrics, he rushed outside to find a group of men with whom he had fought on many occasions; they were singing a satirical song about him.[95] Using songs was perhaps a way to soften the blow, especially since humor allowed everyone an escape. Some satirical songs were more pointed in their critiques, especially toward the end of the colonial period. Christmas Eve was a time of great celebration in New Spain, but like other festivals, it was open to unruliness, with the added circumstance of being held at night.

In 1803 Tacubaya officials worried about a bad track record of unrest, so they assigned many officials to keep the order. There were altars in the main plaza as well as on many side streets, and residents came out to visit them and to partake in the festivities. A group of young men, armed with vihuelas and guitars, began to sing a "dishonest" ditty about a military officer from Veracruz. The officials on duty intervened and caused a major riot, including a jail breakout.[96] Humor was never terribly far from resistance, either within personal relationships or in the larger sphere. While the viceregal palace was still smoldering after the 1692 riot, someone attached a *pasquín* (lampoon) on the main door that stated, "This corral is for rent for local roosters and Castilian hens." [97] The undercurrent of this joke was a clear feminization of Spanish men and an assertion of the masculine prowess of native-born men.

Pulling Rank

In contrast to the settings where men could relax among people of similar status, when they were in mixed-status company they had to be on guard to maintain their proper position and to behave appropriately. The teniente don Miguel de Villalobos expressed this concern in a 1724 letter to the viceroy in which he described a fellow official's conduct as potentially causing indigenous people to lose respect for the royal justice officials.[98] Even in groups of men who by all accounts were within the same hierarchical group, there were very small gradations of rank that were fiercely defended. This kind of jockeying for position occurred at all levels of society; the lower classes accepted the categories imposed on them and created new categorizations so that they could assert their own superiority.[99] Part of this process involved the creation of groups of insiders who could then affirm their identities and social value by excluding others through many types of insults, digs, and the enforcement of ritual submission.[100]

The struggle to assert masculinity was entangled with all these other jostlings for position; how could an individual assert his manliness if racial categories forced him into submissive and deferential behavior? In many ways the colonial project was predicated on disqualifying men of the subject races from holding positions of responsibility, except at the lowest levels of the bureaucracy, and it did so in part by portraying them as lesser men, "unfit" and effeminate.[101] On a more daily basis men maintained their own rank by putting others in their place and diminishing their manliness.

One of the more subtle ways to assert their position as part of an inside group with greater claims on rank was to use humor—often teasing and putdowns. Witnesses also spoke of mofar and hacer burla, reflecting a more hostile dynamic. These jokes were often insults disguised as humor, but sometimes they were overt slurs. Undurraga Schüler describes how men in eighteenth-century Chile would imitate others in a humorous manner in order to make them the butt of the joke. She recounts another incident in which a hairdresser became the target of nasty teasing that associated his profession with effeminacy because he had to enter spaces associated with his female clients.[102] Similarly, in Mexico City in 1804, when don José de Naba and his family clashed with their downstairs neighbor, a barber, they labeled him effeminate because "he was always with women." Both parties in this dispute also used racial categorizations to try to defame and insult, calling each other *mulatto* and *negro* and contesting these classifications.[103] At the Royal Mint in 1809 a worker named don José Leal accused a guard of using *bachillerías*, or pretentious prattle, and implied that because they were of similar rank, this conduct was disrespectful.[104]

At higher echelons of society, racial slurs were more subtle but still aimed at enforcing a code of insiders and outsiders. Don Antonio Aricoechea experienced this dynamic in 1767 when he went to the Coliseo to see a play. As the audience was milling about before the performance's beginning, a Mexico City merchant identified only as don F. Mora loudly proclaimed to a group of his friends, "There goes the man who is married to the Chinaman's daughter." Undoubtedly his circle of friends had a good giggle, but his words were insulting not just to don Antonio Aricoechea but also to the extended family, which lodged a complaint in order to defend its Christian Spanish lineage and its status as insiders.[105] Those insulted in this way used what Iván Jurado Revaliente calls "family memory" to shore up their claim to respectability and insider status through genealogy.[106]

Using gradations of race to keep a man in his (inferior) place was just as much a tactic within indigenous village society. In Chalco in 1801 members of the indigenous community, and especially those who held official positions, blocked Tomás José Bautista from holding a post. They used many tactics, all revolving around racial identity. They asserted that he was not indio but rather mulatto, or that he was associating with coyotes (another racial designation). Tomás José Bautista's allies retorted that his main antagonist was not an indio principal but rather a macehual reverting to Nahuatl.[107] The lines of belonging were drawn and enforced in many different ways, but they always detracted from a man's capacity to belong to the dominant inside group.

These verbal skirmishes were assertions of power at the same time that they diminished the manliness of others; the two processes were intimately connected. Influential men at all social levels could thumb their noses at rules and sometimes even laws. In Coyoacán in 1785 Antonio Orejuela struck an indigenous man, Manuel José Lara, with a shovel, for which he was briefly jailed. But his influence in that community was such that he was soon released and went about taunting and teasing Manuel José Lara.[108] In the same way, in San Juan Yxtayopan (Xochimilco), despite being accused of murder in 1809, José Cabello was present in the community and made a point of mocking and jeering the parents of the man he had allegedly killed. He was a commanding force within the village and asserted his influence by boasting and swaggering about town.[109] The power dynamics within these small communities revolved around subtle differences of status that were about small differences of rank rather than race. Although violence was always one way to prove oneself as a man, more artful uses of language and the politics of inclusion were often as effective.

Battles for control also occurred between different factions in communities that used mockery and derision to diminish the authority of ostensibly powerful figures such as the local priest. In the village of Chimalguacan Atenco (Chalco), José Manuel Luna, one of the village governors, disliked the priest and openly insulted him with racial slurs such as *meco otomite*, (unrefined indigenous) and *cura otomita sin calzones* (pantsless unrefined priest) as well as *cura vaquero* (cowboy priest). Calling him an Otomí was a way to tap into the Nahua belief that the Otomís were an unsophisticated inferior group. While the priest was saying Mass, José Manuel Luna would pointedly elbow those with him and chortle. After Mass, he would hold court on a bench outside the church, and those who had attended would come out and kiss his hand in a mocking imitation of a common practice with clerics.

But José Manuel Luna's greatest feat of derision was a huge prank played on the priest. In 1802 word came that a man was on his deathbed in the nearby community of La Magdalena. Normally the parish priest would attend the sick man, but those who came with this news could not contain their amusement; one of them had to keep hiding his mouth to conceal his laughter. Suspecting some kind of deception, the priest sent a fellow cleric to La Magdalena to give the last rites to Bentura del Carmen. When he reached Bentura del Carmen's house, he went to the patient and asked him what ailed him. Bentura del Carmen then told the cleric that he was heartbroken that he had missed Mass that day—it was all a hoax. In reality José Manuel Luna had whipped up anger at the priest, and the focal point of their antagonism was that at Eastertime the priest had refused to bless the palm branches purchased by the community.[110] Clearly José Manuel Luna's conduct was just one part of a battle for control of the power dynamics of the village; his use of humor was a veiled way to insult and diminish any respect that the priest could expect because of his position, and it also weakened his masculine presence.

New Spain's men derived authority from their posts by the ways that they presented themselves to the world with regalia, swords, and hats. But when their identity was tied into their external appearance every time they went out in public, they risked being devalued in terms of their masculinity when people jeered at them or mocked them. At the end of the colonial period, as tension began to grow within New Spain, there was also an increased presence of various regiments with their own uniforms. These men, however, were also targets for the anger and hostility that many felt toward the regime. As a result some soldiers or officials became very sensitive to teasing. Lieutenant don Juan de Zabaleta was overseeing guard duty at the Coliseo in Mexico City when he thought he heard a person in the crowd mimicking the soldiers as they sounded off. Hoping that he was wrong, he repeated the exercise, but once again he heard the voice. He understood this echoing of the soldiers' calls as a mofar and an insult to his person. He scanned the assembled people and decided that a man dressed only in a sheet was the offender;

he picked a person who was clearly poor and probably defenseless, and he beat him with the back of his sword.[111]

It seems an overreaction for a well-armed soldier to beat a defenseless man, but if officials did not assert their power effectively, they could be the victims of such abuse.[112] Pedro Morales, one of the guards who watched over goods coming in and out of Mexico City at the garitas caught a man trying to slip by without paying the required fees. He began to arrest the culprit, but people in the area, including a soldier, the grenadier Mariano Estevez, began to jeer at Pedro Morales, calling him a *ladrón hambriente* (a ravenous thief).[113] Night watchmen were often disliked because they guarded the street lamps (a Bourbon imposition). One of them, José Mariano Almaras, ran into problems one evening when a band of ruffians began to tease him and threatened to pelt him with stones.[114] On the cusp of independence, men could no longer count on the trappings of authority to shore up their masculinity; danger and challenges lurked everywhere.

Gestures, Words, and Insults

With so many ways to express polite modalities, it was very easy to upend these selfsame systems to transform them into offenses. Insults were not limited to words; men used many gestures in order to show their disdain and to be rude. There were also gestures that signaled a man's intention to fight, such as taking out his sword or knife or throwing off his cape.[115] Wealthy men often used their horses to intimidate or even attack others, but they also used equine fixtures such as the reins or (more frequently) spurs in their disciplining of insolent inferiors.[116] Felipe Postigo faced a charge of disrespecting a cleric in 1779 even though the priest used his horse to trample him. Felipe Postigo grabbed the reins and defended himself, thus inverting the discipline and the social hierarchy.[117]

Although many insulting words and actions happened in the heat of the moment, some seem to have been more scripted. Men's reputations were important for their economic well-being; their characters allowed them credit and employment. Don Pedro Cunqueirio Bernárdez, the owner of a Mexico City store, complained in 1760 that don Manuel Moreno Chacón called him an *estafador*, or swindler. Beyond being hurtful, he explained, the insult harmed his honor and the good opinion of his potential customers despite the "serenity and good faith as well as purity with which he had conducted his business."[118] Within neighborhoods, the "local morality" enforced ways of being; members of a community or a barrio implemented social norms with informal means such as gossip, hostile stares, and insulting nicknames.[119] When these more subtle methods did not work and when confrontations flared up between men, all the area's people became the target of insults.

The settings for the offenses were varied; they ranged from workplaces, tenements, homes, and streets to social gatherings such as cockfights, taverns, and pulquerías. The offensive words in my sample were uttered in places that all had ready-made audiences—even homes, which were usually populated by many and open to the outside. Insults were more common in places where people interacted every day and lived in close proximity, but these locations also provided a setting and an audience for the offending words or gestures and thus amplified the power of the insult.[120] In many of the court cases, even while men complained that another man had insulted them, they shied away from using the actual words. Instead, they resorted to euphemisms—for example, that they had been called *un tal* (a such-and-such) or the less effective *hijo de* (son of) un tal. Frequently, however, witnesses to these conflicts provided the actual words, thus showing how much they savored the insults.

The words and gestures that men used with one another were important, so complainants and bystanders mentioned them (even if in euphemism) to provide a sense of the incident. In the 570 cases that I read for this book, I collected 235 insults, but some terms were repeated constantly (e.g., carajo, 27 times) whereas others were anomalies. The glossary provides an explanation for 56 words that were presented as insulting within the cases. Many were only used once, and some seem quite mysterious, such as *pichachado* and *revoltijo*. These might have been expressions that were particular to the people involved or the setting. Others, such as those that denoted race or origins, were words that in other contexts were not insulting, but if they attacked a person's self-identity they were offensive.[121]

Name-calling that referenced religion was uncommon but very serious because the practice of Judaism and all non-Catholic religions were punishable by the Holy Office of the Inquisition.[122] The most surprising of this category of insults was the references to *poblanos*, or those from Puebla. It was the only region of New Spain to be singled out, possibly because its city fathers made a point of distinguishing it as sanctified as a result of its angelical associations. Frances Ramos shows that this holier-than-thou attitude attracted derision and satirical mockery.[123] The insulting terms used in New Spain fell into four loose categories: animal, personal qualities, identity (including race, religion, and origins), and sexuality. The appendix provides a breakdown of the racial identities (when explicit) of the individuals involved. The most common insults were: *perro*, ladrón, *pícaro*, cabrón, carajo, *pendejo*, and cornudo (see glossary). Slurs strategically attacked the values held dear by most men, and they varied according to place and time.

These words could be offensive to anyone, but they were most effective with the appropriate target. Insults that impugned a man's character were most commonly used against men considered hombres de bien.[124] Among Mexican men, the most common type of insults was leveled at the individual's personal qualities, but most especially at their honesty; ladrón was among the most used of words.[125] Between workers, however, soplón was one of the worst insults because it implied a lack of solidarity.[126] Indigenous men were most frequently called perro, but it was also directed at other groups including Spaniards; it was also a slur used by indigenous men.[127]

Margo DeMello links the practice of using offensive expressions that refer to animals with marginalized groups; references to wild animals, according to Marta Madero, were intended to suggest a connection to the devil and also to lewdness.[128] It is also possible that calling someone a dog suggested that he had a servile, dishonorable nature, and it may even have been a roundabout way of putting him in a category of subjugation.[129]

Historians have tended to comment on insults of a sexual nature because the honor system privileged male control of women. As a result, they developed a rich vocabulary of sexual insults.[130] The words used to insult fall into categories that were associated with core values of masculinity, but over time some became rather generic and divorced from their original meanings.[131] They also depended on the way they were delivered—the physicality of delivery, in terms of looks and body.[132] Words alone could not convey how insults worked in colonial Mexican society; it was a performance that depended not just on the choice of epithet but its delivery and audience.

These moments of offense contrasted with the prevailing values of quietness and reserve that were always at the forefront of societal expectations. Diarists Gregorio de Guijo and Robles made much of incidents in which men of distinction raised their voices in displeasure.[133] Those complaining continually referred to the "raised" or "altered" voices with which the abuse was said. This feature was undoubtedly made in order to emphasize the good character of those affronted, but it underlines how raised voices attracted attention and an audience.[134] In addition, in many instances insulting words were strung together in groups, resulting in a kind of compound effect. These insult groupings allowed the speaker to declare many slurs all at once; building on one another, they all evoked the residents' fundamental fears.[135] Most of the insults collected for this book were stated along with others in a type of grouping.

Apart from using words that insulted, colonial Mexicans devised all sorts of inventive expressions to communicate their contempt. These expressions can be clustered around some prevailing themes. Just like the slurs, insults about sex were common; some referred to *cuernos*, or horns, and were a reference to a lack of control over wives and girlfriends. Men told each other that they would "cut their horns," "pay you with a horn," or "tighten their horns."[136] Somewhat related to this kind of insult were the many references to mothers; for example, swearing at another's man's mother, including an insulting expression, or denying his mother.[137] Some of these expressions would not be out of place in contemporary Mexico. The witnesses also made reference of mentar or *moler*—words used to explain insulting behavior.[138]

They also mentioned body parts—in particular, testicles, referred to either as *cojones* (balls) or *huevos* (eggs)—threatening to cut them off or boasting of having more of them.[139] Some men also vowed to cut off ears and cut out the intestines, although these were not as vivid or common.[140] With dramatic flourish some men pledged "to drink the blood" of their opponents.[141] Other men articulated their anger and disrespect by undertaking to defecate on either their rivals or symbolic elements such as their uniforms.[142] Perhaps the most malevolent expressions, however, included wishing a man's damnation: asking the devil to take him or simply his soul.[143] All these expressions were simply extensions of the typical invectives and were part of masculine posturing.

The physicality of insulting conduct was also really obvious to witnesses. Actions around hats and capes were part of a vocabulary of rudeness, but there were also other ways of using gestures to show contempt or aggression. Pierre Bourdieu notes that men had to read one another, and body posture was often "a sign pregnant with a meaning that the opponent has to grasp."[144] William B. Taylor explores these moments of tension as part of a complex of belligerence and insults—all part of the bravado that was part of male habits.[145] Some bodily gestures were more subtle than attacks on clothes; they were less of an insult and more of a warning of violence.

Weapons were central to several of these bodily attitudes. Swords were a core part of a gentleman's attire, and thus these weapons became integral to this vocabulary. Witnesses noted with concern when a man kept his hand on his sword, carried a weapon openly, or had unsheathed his sword.[146] In the seventeenth century many witnesses spoke of "nude swords" with distraught apprehension. Although weapons were an important accessory, there were other ways to deploy this body language of insult and threat. Bystanders noted clenching one's hand into a fist, turning one's back on another, and thumping a table repeatedly.[147] Other scenarios seem to have been more particular to the context, such as refusing to stop smoking in front of a social superior or eating a pomegranate and spitting out the seeds at another man.[148] These gestures were at times accompanied by verbal insults but on other occasions seem to have been evocative enough to be used alone. The gravity of these actions is obvious because they often led to serious acts of violence and also because people noted and remembered these small details. The degree of offense, however, is harder to gauge because it depended to a great extent on whether men used these gestures with someone of similar or higher rank.

Desafiar: Challenges and Manhood

In all their interactions, Mexican men had to walk the tightrope of acceptable behavior; this was particularly important when they were in the presence of those of a different rank and they could not expect any leeway for gaffes. Nevertheless, their reputations and sense of manhood were likewise crucial in protecting both themselves and their families. Thus, at times men reacted strongly to any challenge to their masculinity and to insults directed at their partners. Because of the daily small challenges to men's identity and virility, men's reactions became part of who they were. The documents reveal the struggle that men of the higher ranks felt between keeping control and lashing out often with contrasting accounts of which party had actually kept his composure.[149]

When they did resort to violence, clearly lacking serenity, they often justified their actions by framing them as punishment for recalcitrant inferiors.[150] Part of this reasoning was a feminization of lower-class men, whose actions of self-defense were construed as improper aggression. In other parts of the world, upper-class masculine aggression was frequently channeled into the formalized ritual of the duel.[151] Such ritualized confrontations were not generally part of colonial culture (they appeared in

Latin America in the nineteenth century), but men did participate in desafíos, or challenges. In strict terms, any such challenges were prohibited by law, but despite many reiterations of laws against desafíos, they kept happening.[152] Although they lacked a written code of rules, desafíos could lead to pitched battles from which some participants came out bruised, wounded, or even dead.

The lack of formality in violent confrontations did not mean that men had no sense of what a challenge was. But without written protocols, historians have to pull together hints on the informal guidelines for desafíos within New Spain's culture of masculinity. Residents of New Spain understood and described these actions as *echar valentías*, or throwing boasts of bravery, and they also described some men as *valentón*, or boastful.[153] These men did not embrace the ideal of hombres de bien; they were rebellious.[154]

There were different and much more subtle ways to challenge another's manhood, but such men used direct statements. When some former workers attacked their employer's door at night in 1752, one of their loud statements was to "open the door and come out into the street if you are men."[155] The militia soldier Thomas López reacted very strongly at the Cockfight Plaza in 1780 when not given satisfaction; as he was being taken away, he shouted that "he would teach them to be men." Later, in prison, he backed down from his statements and declared himself to be an hombre de bien.[156] The pattern seems to be that men challenged others to be men and to come out into the street as a sign of their manliness.[157]

Yet this type of declarative challenge was used in many circumstances—it could easily be adapted to different contexts.[158] Atanasio Ramos was a poor Spaniard, working as a servant. In 1808, in his frustration over the lack of respect he received, he bellowed out to the saddle makers who did not provide the goods he needed "that if you are men you will come out one by one." In his later statement Atanasio Ramos clarified that the saddle maker, in his emotional composure, had suggested that their social positions were so widely separated that the worker was not worth his time or attention.[159] These expressions implied an inherent manliness that was contrary to the prevailing social norms; its antithesis can be glimpsed in the ways that others described these "real men": "impudent and insolent," "provocative and bold," and finally, "an insolent boy, drunkard, provocative, boastful, cheeky, and not respectful of either his mother or his social superiors."[160] These men grappled with the opposing ideals of the restrained male and the virile attitudes that simmered under the surface of social norms.

This type of behavior questioned the prevailing standards of equanimity but was not entirely foreign—it could easily be inserted into the period's honor system, in which it was vital to answer any insults or slights both for oneself and for the household. In New Spain, men reacted strongly and with violent challenges when they perceived a lack of respect. Because of the hierarchical nature of the society, contempt for individuals considered socially inferior was ordinary. Yet these rankings were constantly contested and conflicted frequently with ideas of manhood. Employers complained regularly, for example, of workers who were "provocative" and "haughty."[161] Because these lines of respect were so blurry, men felt the need to address perceived injustices. The Spanish tailor Francisco Ambrosio de Urbina prowled around the Royal Hospital in 1729 trying to reach a patient in a desafío. The details are a little vague, but it seems that a previous confrontation left his rival wounded. Yet despite this outcome, Francisco Ambrosio de Urbina's rage continued in the form of his vigil and continued desafío.[162]

There were so many small details of everyday conduct that would normally be acceptable but that on this day seemed insulting or wrong for some reason. Residents of New Spain had a sense of the routine greetings and actions that were appropriate—these became a type of code that, when defectively enacted, caused offense.[163] Something as seemingly innocent as drinking together—an activity that seems to have been the leitmotif men's lives—could turn into a conflict over apparent discourtesy. Alejandro Rayón, an aguardiente maker in Tlalmanalco, recounted in 1806 with an air of surprise that a soldier, José Enciso, had wounded him over refusing to accept a second drink.[164] Again the lack of details are frustrating, but as Sandra Gayol remarks in her study of café society in Buenos Aires, the refusal of a drink, even a second one, could be a rejection of the type of equality implied by drinking together. The act of drinking was akin to a scoreboard that defined inclusion and exclusion; it was understood to be reciprocal and inclusive.[165] These incidents of explosive violence and vengeance were not very common in the documents. Nonetheless, men did take offense, usually not at some minor detail but with fundamental challenges to their authority or identity.

Colonial Mexican men were more incensed by disrespect toward women than by an attack on their own identity; it engaged both their sense of chivalry and their honor.[166] Mostly their anger was directed at men who insulted their wives, daughters, or mothers, but mistreatment of an elderly woman was evidently part of the revulsion that bystanders in 1791 felt at a very drunk Dionicio Antonio Romero, an indigenous resident of Mexico City. As

Dionicio Antonio Romero was trying to find Francisca Brigida Herrera, who had rejected him, an *anciana* (elderly woman) tried to calm him down. Instead of responding to her attention, he pushed her to the ground and kicked her. Shocked at this conduct, the neighbors all intervened and stopped him.[167]

Stranger attacks were not all that common; more frequently men lashed out at women they knew because of their attachment to a neighbor or a coworker. Women were often present at the sites of aggressive encounters or were at home when an angry customer came to complain, so they bore the brunt of a physical attack or, more often, a verbal one.[168] It was a core part of the honor system that men should be able to control their wives, daughters, and mothers as well as to protect them. Other men sometimes offended a rival through the women in their lives.[169] Most often they would discredit the woman's chastity, calling her a puta, or whore.[170] When men insulted the wives, daughters, or mothers of their rivals, it is not clear whether this was simply an angry utterance or they were actually targeting the man involved. Nevertheless, it was an indirect manner to provoke an adversary and to question his masculinity.

Conclusion

Men in New Spain had to negotiate many contradictions. Although the social ideal of emotional composure exerted a strong influence, they also needed to maintain rank as well as a sense of honor and masculinity. These inconsistencies meant that they had to make quick decisions about their reactions and attitudes and negotiate interactions with their social group and with others. On some level it seems that their daily lives were bifurcated into tense negotiations over place and position and relaxing times of fun and joking around with like-minded friends of similar rank. Undoubtedly these social worlds and the related experiences were not so neatly divided. Yet, the pull to belong and to either be part of an inside group or snub those not included were patterns that permeated all social levels. Power dynamics and the struggle to maintain status occurred at all ranks and using many different strategies such as humor, pranks, teasing, and more overt insults.

The pull of belonging and the advantage of being part of a group of friends and allies meant that social identity was central to male interactions. To negotiate social place, all men had to wear figurative uniforms—their externals had to match with their ethnicity and rank. Yet there were so many different forms of belonging that social identity crossed through many categories: race, masculinity, honor, and hierarchy, which became a complex brew of symbols and signs. When they were with others of similar social standing, men could be at ease; they engaged in friendly teasing and jokes; they drank, danced, and sang; they competed in card games or feats of bravery; they could relax and be themselves. It was in these moments of respite among their peers that men could let go of the emotional composure that was demanded of them.

Toward the end of the colonial period, as tension was mounting between royalists and the emerging backers of the national cause, the factional divisions began to slip as people—especially men of the lower classes—started to utter the insults that were usually kept private. As the hidden transcripts of many different factions surfaced, men used challenges and insults as part of a newer, embryonic masculine identity—one that was harnessed for the violence of the wars of independence.

CHAPTER 7

The Seeds of Macho

✦ ISIDRO DE LA CRUZ, AN INDIGENOUS WORKER ON THE HACIENDA OF
Zacapendo, was also known as El Hortelano, or the gardener. Despite this
rather innocuous nickname, Isidro de la Cruz incarnated the antithesis of
the ideal man in New Spain. He had a violent, hair-trigger temper; in 1748
officials arrested him first for attacking an elderly woman who had an altercation with Isidro's amasia and then for beating and wounding Pablo Miguel.
Years earlier he had killed a man for putting horses in the wrong pasture and
had assaulted another man for making a sarcastic remark about his mare. He
was an excellent rider, so natural in the saddle that in his testimony he
neglected to mention that he was on horseback when he made the attacks.
Like the early conquistadors and elite Spanish men, he used his horse to
intimidate; one witness described an elderly woman waving her shawl in his
horse's face to force its retreat. In his justifications for his many acts of
aggression, Isidro de la Cruz argued that he simply reacted to insults to his
manhood; these affronts included words, disobedience, interfering with "his
woman," and attitudes.[1]

Unlike many of the court cases that I used for this book, this document
provides a bit of Isidro de la Cruz's history and details some of his life trajectory. Isidro de la Cruz's violent tendencies had clearly not surfaced in 1748—
he had a violent past, and his predisposition for aggression was always just
under the surface. He could not have been further from the ideal New Spain
man—the emotionally composed, serenely peaceful subject. Of course, not

many men in this book entirely conformed to this ideal, but they used it in their testimony to justify their actions. Isidro de la Cruz did not; he did not apologize for his violence but simply explained it.

Isidro de la Cruz could be used as an outlier in a mostly controlled society or as a precursor to the men who later embodied the stereotypical Mexican macho. In fact, because of his innate violence Isidro de la Cruz spent much of his life in sanctuary in the local monastery and had become its gardener. He had to isolate himself from society because he did not fit in. Nonetheless, Isidro de la Cruz was not alone in defying the model of the peaceable nonviolent subject, and toward the end of the colonial period these outliers began to assert their nonconformity in many acts of rebellion that culminated in acts of sedition and the insurgence that led to Mexican independence.

Mutinous thoughts and actions were often present just below the surface of peaceful day-to-day interactions for much of the colonial period in New Spain. Despite the rules that promoted moderation, residents drank, gambled, and partied; they came together to watch entertainment such as acrobats or cockfights; they paraded their finery in the paseos of the Alameda and the Canal de Jamaica. Men found ways of expressing their masculinity in their identity as workers, as providers for their families and amasias, with tattoos, with their skill as riders, and with livestock. They inhabited their spaces as urban dwellers, as paterfamilias, and bon vivants in the streets of Mexico City and the many other smaller communities in the region. All the while they performed the role assigned to them within colonial society: they acted out their dominance by swaggering about with their swords at their hips or demonstrated their submission by doffing their hats in the habitual ritual of deference.

Behind the conventions of obedience, however, lurked insubordinate attitudes that were of constant concern for local officials. The authorities often suspected that indigenous men hid a "rebellious temperament" beneath "pretend humility."[2] There were occasions such as Carnival and other celebrations that allowed people to let off steam and engage in social inversion. During these periods people broke the rules of good conduct; they stayed out late, drank copious amounts, danced and flirted, and at times sang satirical, rebellious songs as the young men in Tacubaya did on Christmas Eve.

On a more regular basis, there were always men who did not conform entirely to the controlled, deferential masculinity that most men were forced to adopt. Miguel López, alias Lora, refused this type of masculinity; officials in Ayotzingo (Chalco) described him as having a "daring temperament" and lacking the respectful attitudes that plebeians were supposed to display, particularly to officials carrying an official staff of office. When ordered to present himself to the municipal buildings, he first refused and then came with his hat firmly on his head and armed with tools that doubled as weapons.[3] Like many men described in this book, Miguel López reminded everyone of the possibility of resistance. Eric Van Young argues that such outsiders played an important role in the social equilibrium of New Spain's society. Up to a certain point, their "social deviancy" was condoned and allowed the other residents to live vicariously through their bad acts. At the same time, by denouncing these outliers, the majority could—even while perhaps enjoying the thrill of rebellion—demonstrate their conformity to the regime.[4]

Boys and young men learned early to balance their aspirations with the imperative to fit into the social hierarchy. They adapted to the social ranking based on age and authority within their own families and households, and they continued to adjust to this classification within places of employment, such as the workshops and factories where plebeian men labored. The hierarchical structure that was inculcated in them from a young age was normal for them by the time they reached adulthood, even if they chafed at the many acts of submission and the humiliation that were their lot.

Apprentices also had an internal pecking order and used their comparatively higher status to tease, bully, and apply rude nicknames to the newer boys in the workshop. These workshops and factories were the training grounds for masculinity, where young men learned fortitude as well as their place. In these same locations young men were inducted into a rich world of friendships and entertainments; their friendships extended from the workplace into taverns and games, dances and drinking, and philandering. They had affectionate pastimes, and they ate with their best friends: the men who would support them in times of trouble. Plebeian men found pleasure where they could; they loved a good laugh and did not mind turning political struggles into a prank. As children they watched the puppet shows of the Alameda and other hidden corners, and as adults they went to the Coliseo to view nonsensical farces and seductive dancers such as La Zua. With their buddies they went to pulquerías to play cards or to a fonda to eat a good stew. They found satisfaction in all these elements of daily life, so within the constraints of the social hierarchy they were able to accept their place and the masculinity that they had to incarnate.

Emotionally composed men who were serene and peaceful were a rather convenient model subject for a colonial régime. Inga Clendinnen, in her seminal article on Aztec warriors, points out this contradiction: even while Aztec society lauded its combatants for their ferocity, it asked them to resume a poised stillness in civilian life. Clendinnen asks how men could reconcile the pull of both standards.[5] Because moral and political authorities advocated for emotional composure, men had to sublimate their anger and frustration on a daily basis; they could not lash out, so they used symbolic actions to express their emotions. It was for this reason that men fought over whose carriage could go first, who could pass by their houses, and many more of the incidents documented in this book.

This sublimation of violence and its eruption in so many other venues, such as humor and the social inversion of festivities, allowed colonial authorities to keep a lid on the violence and maintain a relatively peaceful kingdom. The balance worked within New Spain for centuries; during that period, society controlled masculine violence to some degree. New Spain was a society with many structures and regulations that channeled people into certain behaviors and promoted conformity. The rules were undoubtedly stifling, particularly when wealthy residents or local officials forced obedience and deference. Plebeians, however, often flouted these rules and paid lip service to conformity.

The tension between obedience and resistance was always just below the surface, but it appeared in the frustration of officials reissuing laws and regulations that no one obeyed, such as the law against carrying knives. Because knives were such an integral part of plebeian masculinity and also frequently vital for men's occupations and daily tasks, men simply ignored the law. As with the many rules that governed their sexual lives, residents of New Spain chose to believe that a man and a woman who lived together, ate at the same table, and slept in the same bed were equivalent to a married couple. Although same-sex seductions and sexual acts provoked dismay and discomfort, community members often looked the other way. The tolerance for breaking rules and being nonconformist, as well as the many occasions when residents of New Spain could let loose celebrating or poking fun at the conventions, no doubt allowed for a certain social equilibrium.

Yet as the eighteenth-century Bourbon Reforms tried to rein in what Spanish thinkers perceived as the anarchy of colonial domains, these reforms began to alter this balance. As the Bourbons brought in street lights and tavern reform that infuriated the residents, they also created all sorts of new military units. Tension grew between different groups of soldiers as well as between soldiers and other types of officials and civilians. When the coachman of the Count of Alamos insulted the soldier don Juan Alcalá Olmos in 1783, were these generic slurs, or did they betray some resentment against all these military men who swarmed the street? Soldiers too were sensitive, as seen in the example of Lieutenant don Juan de Zabaleta. Fearing that he was being mocked by a member of the crowd outside the Coliseo, don Juan de Zabaleta beat up a poor man to make his point.

These are just two examples from the many that populate this book. The essential point is the way that the Bourbon Reforms and the policies of cracking down on disorder hemmed in many kinds of masculinity. Although laws against vagrancy had existed since the early days of the colony, the Bourbons began to repurpose these laws in 1783 to punish those who did not fit in. Those rounded up in these sweeps often included plebeian men who refused to conform to the ideals of the productive, orderly subject, but the sweeps also targeted men whose only crime was looking for work. Men who migrated to Mexico City from other parts of the colony because of economic pressures were prime victims. But many others were also targeted in this plan: university students who skipped class, men caught in illicit sexual relations, anyone who vandalized the new public works, those who seemed disruptive, men who harassed women, and finally, those with few clothes who seemed dirty and unkempt.[6] With these measures and many others in the late colonial period, the Bourbon Reforms and the mentality that they produced caused a shift in the social equilibrium of New Spain and prompted the emergence of masculinities that were not compatible with colonialism.

Despite the incredible pressure that existed on New Spain's men to conform, there were always those who refused. This resistance manifested itself in many small ways, but by the late eighteenth century a rebellious temperament began to be associated with political opposition. Although this kind of resistance was not new, it began to be associated with a masculinity that challenged the status quo. In 1790 officials in Xochimilco became concerned with the activities of Isidro Giménez. In line with their crackdown on misfits, they deemed him a vagrant without any discernible occupation. But, more important, they believed that he was sowing the seeds of revolt among the indigenous population. His crime was that he took the legal cases of indigenous residents to Mexico City courts and presented writs on their behalf. He considered himself a "representative" of the people.[7] Men like Isidro Giménez often became part of the insurrection in its early days; they were primed for resistance to the colonial state.[8]

But many of those who joined the ranks of the insurgents were not quite as noble in their goals; others, such as don Ignacio Sánchez and Chito Villagrán, could easily have been denounced as vagrants.[9] These were men whose brand of masculinity was increasingly unacceptable within New Spain, and after 1810 they found a favorable reception within the ranks of the rebels. Much of the conduct found distasteful or reprehensible under colonial rule, however, became useful for the insurgents, and they also inverted the direction of insults. Both the insurgents and their supporters frequently used the insult perro to describe Spaniards; this tendency reversed the colonial propensity to attack the dignity of indigenous men with this slur.

They also used sexual insults in new ways, for example, the term *alcahuete*, or pimp, became associated with royalists. The kind of language that had been unacceptable in polite society became more commonly used by residents to voice their grievances and criticize the regime.[10] The frustrations of plebeian men also came out in other forms: they confiscated the clothes and jewelry of royalists, paraded around in their new finery, and found ways to diminish the honor and manhood of their former social superiors.[11] The ways that rebels insulted and debased Spaniards was derived from the culture of masculinity that had developed over three centuries of colonialism. It was within the language of domination and deference that they found ways to avenge their long submission.

Let us return to the man at the beginning of this chapter. Isidro de la Cruz represents the contradictions of this project; he is both an archetypical macho and not typical at all. His story highlights all the difficulties and complications of trying to pinpoint where this model of the Mexican macho comes from and whether New Spain's social and gender history can provide any clarity to this question. Although the concept of macho did not exist in the colonial period, there are signposts for the origins of the macho throughout this book. But the macho lurked under the surface and was not necessarily typical of New Spain's men. In his study of gender Stern elaborates on this contradictory problem: the violence of *descarga* (explosive violence) ventings among colonial Mexican men seems to confirm every nasty stereotype and all the anecdotal evidence that leaps to mind, according to his statistical analysis, but although they were present, these outbursts were not typical of New Spain's men.[12] It is worth returning to the notion that there were many masculinities present in this period, and in some ways they reflected the colonial process. There was a precarious balance to power relations in New Spain. The hierarchy was constantly reinforced by sumptuous events such as religious processions and the viceregal entrances; the masses were entertained by fireworks, bullfights, and the paseos along the canal banks. All these elements were part of the public face of a colonial society in which everyone had his place and respected his social superiors. Yet there were tensions under the surface, a jockeying for power that occurred at all levels of society. It was, in fact, a precarious balance that could be overturned easily.

Even though the hierarchy was being reinforced by means of celebrations, men and women in New Spain let loose at them. They hijacked religious events and made them into popular festivities in which people cross-dressed, partied, and sang rude satirical songs. Colonial Mexican masculinities, I believe, reflected this fragile balance: although they were taught very young to be deferential, young men also had to eventually assert their manhood. It must have been hard for lower-class men to find the balance between performing their masculinity and not provoking their social superiors. The many experiences and incidents that punctuated men's lives described throughout this book show this tension and men's dual worlds. The realm of men was divided not just between house and street but also between inside groups and outsiders. Men's sphere was peppered with boundaries and lines that were both visible and invisible. Even as they walked through the city or the countryside, sentinels watched; sometimes they could pass through, but on other occasions it meant a toll or a fight. This duality of mobility and obstruction was reflected in social divisions.

In all these tensions and conflicts, under the seeming equilibrium of colonial society, the masculinity that would later incarnate the Mexican macho was being incubated. After Hidalgo's call to arms, deference and submission were no longer the order of the day, and macho behavior was applauded. The violence associated with the macho had always been present, but it was tamped down, controlled, and suppressed. When the insurgency started, men like Isidro de la Cruz were supremely useful, and their type of masculinity was valued and rewarded. They continued to have important roles in the many wars and revolutions of the nineteenth and twentieth centuries. There were many types of masculinities in those periods, as there are today. But although the masculinity associated with the macho was present but hidden in the colonial period, it was with independence that the shackles of control and colonial paternalism gave way and the masculinity of the macho came of age.

Appendix

Insults by Category

These tables are based on the 570 documents in my corpus and the 235 times I recorded insults. Each table shows how often an insult was recorded as well as the racial designations (if known) of the person who spoke and the recipient. The patterns in these tables provide a sense of how race was associated with certain ethnicities.

Animal Insults: Speaker

	ESPAÑOL	INDIO	MESTIZO	MULATTO	NEGRO	CASTIZO	NONE
Ajolote	0	0	0	0	0	0	2
Cochino	3	1	0	0	0	0	1
Oveja	0	0	0	0	0	0	1
Mono	0	0	0	0	0	0	2
Perro	2	7	1	1	1	2	12

Animal Insults: Recipient

	ESPAÑOL	INDIO	MESTIZO	MULATTO	NEGRO	CASTIZO	NONE
Ajolote	0	0	0	0	0	0	2
Cochino	1	1	0	0	0	0	3
Oveja	1	0	0	0	0	0	0
Mono	0	0	0	0	0	0	2
Perro	4	11	0	1	1	1	8

Personal Qualities: Speaker

	ESPAÑOL	INDIO	MESTIZO	MULATTO	NEGRO	CASTIZO	NONE
Alquilado	0	0	0	0	0	0	2
Aparejado	1	0	1	0	0	0	0
Arrastrado	0	0	0	0	0	0	1
Bárbaro	2	0	1	0	0	0	0
Bellaco	1	0	0	0	0	0	1
Borrachón	0	0	0	0	0	0	1
Chalan	0	1	0	0	0	0	0
Chicharronero	1	0	0	0	0	0	0
Chivato	0	2	0	0	0	0	3
Chupahueso	2	0	0	0	0	0	0
Collón	0	0	0	0	0	0	1
Deslenguado	0	0	0	0	0	0	1
Droguero	0	0	0	0	0	0	2
Encubridor	0	0	0	0	0	0	1
Engreído	0	0	0	0	0	0	1
Estafador	0	0	0	0	0	0	3
Faramajero	0	0	0	0	0	0	1
Graduado de mierda	0	0	0	0	0	0	1
Hijo de puta	0	3	1	0	0	0	3
Indigno	1	0	0	0	0	0	6
Ingrato	1	0	0	0	0	0	0
Ladrón[*]	3	4	1	1	3	0	12
Mal criado	1	0	0	0	0	0	0
Montonero	0	0	1	0	0	0	0
Pícaro	5	1	0	0	1	0	9[†]
Revoltijo	0	0	0	0	0	0	1
Salteador	1	0	0	0	0	0	0
Soplón	2	1	1	0	0	0	1
Tonto	0	0	0	0	0	0	1
Topador	0	0	0	0	0	0	1
Tramposo	0	1	0	0	0	0	1
Tuerto	1	0	0	0	0	0	0

[*]There were also two instances that fall outside the racial categories in this table: one person referred to as chino, or Asian, and one francés, or Frenchman.

[†]Includes one example of a chino.

Personal Qualities: Recipient

	ESPAÑOL	INDIO	MESTIZO	MULATTO	NEGRO	CASTIZO	NONE
Alquilado	1	0	0	0	0	0	1
Aparejado	0	0	0	0	0	1	1
Arrastrado	0	0	0	0	0	0	1
Bárbaro	1	1	0	0	0	0	1
Bellaco	0	0	0	0	0	0	2
Borrachón	0	0	0	0	0	0	1
Chalan	1	0	0	0	0	0	0
Chicharronero	1	0	0	0	0	0	0
Chivato	1	0	0	0	0	0	4
Chupahueso	0	1	0	0	0	0	1
Collón	0	0	0	0	0	0	1
Deslenguado	0	0	0	0	0	0	1
Droguero	0	0	0	0	0	0	2
Encubridor	0	0	0	0	0	0	1
Engreído	0	1	0	0	0	0	0
Estafador	0	0	0	0	0	0	3
Faramajero	1	0	0	0	0	0	0
Graduado de mierda	0	0	0	0	0	0	1
Hijo de puta	2	3	0	0	0	0	2
Indigno	1	1	0	0	0	0	3
Ingrato	0	0	0	0	0	0	1[*]
Ladrón	4	3	0	0	1	1	10
Mal criado	0	1	0	0	0	0	0
Montonero	0	1	0	0	0	0	0
Pícaro	4	1	1	0	0	0	8[†]
Revoltijo	0	0	0	0	0	0	1
Salteador	0	0	0	0	0	0	1
Soplón	1	1	0	0	0	0	3
Tonto	0	0	1	0	0	0	0
Topador	1	0	0	0	0	0	0
Tramposo	0	1	0	0	0	0	1
Tuerto	1	0	0	0	0	0	0

[*]Includes one recipient who was described as francés.

[†]Includes one recipient who was described as francés.

Race, Religion, and Origins: Speaker

	ESPAÑOL	INDIO	MESTIZO	MULATTO	NEGRO	CASTIZO	NONE
Gachupín	0	0	0	0	0	0	1
Judío	0	0	0	0	0	0	2
Meco	0	0	0	0	0	0	2
Meco otomite	0	0	0	0	0	0	1
Mulatto	1	1	0	0	0	0	0
Negro	0	1	0	0	0	0	1
Portugués	1	0	0	0	0	0	0

Race, Religion, and Origins: Recipient

	ESPAÑOL	INDIO	MESTIZO	MULATTO	NEGRO	CASTIZO	NONE
Gachupín	0	0	0	0	0	0	1
Judío	0	0	0	0	0	0	2
Meco	0	1	0	0	0	0	1
Meco otomite	0	0	0	0	0	0	1
Mulatto	0	0	0	0	0	0	2
Negro	0	0	0	0	0	0	2
Portugués	0	0	0	0	0	0	1

Sex: Speaker

	ESPAÑOL	INDIO	MESTIZO	MULATTO	NEGRO	CASTIZO	NONE
Alcahuete	0	2	0	0	0	0	4
Amujerado	0	1	0	0	0	0	1
Cabrón	2	1	0	0	0	0	7
Carajo	7	2	3	0	0	0	15
Consentidor	0	0	0	0	0	0	1
Cornudo	5	6	2	0	0	0	5
Jodido	0	0	0	0	0	0	1
Pendejo	1	1	2	0	0	1	7
Puñetero	1	0	0	0	0	0	1
Tetón	0	0	0	0	0	0	1

Sex: Recipient

	ESPAÑOL	INDIO	MESTIZO	MULATO	NEGRO	CASTIZO	NONE
Alcahuete	1	2	0	0	0	0	2
Amujerado	0	0	0	0	0	0	1
Cabrón	5	1	0	0	0	0	4
Carajo	5	9	1	1	0	1	11
Consentidor	0	1	0	0	0	0	0
Cornudo	3	2	3	0	0	1	9
Jodido	1	0	0	0	0	0	0
Pendejo	2	4	1	1	0	0	4
Puñetero	0	0	1	0	0	0	1
Tetón	0	0	0	0	0	0	1

Glossary of Insults

ajolote: An aquatic salamander found in the lakes around Mexico City; derived from the Nahua word *axolotl*.

alcahuete: A procurer or pimp; a person who covers up a lie or an indecent action.

alquilado: A hired hand; in many of the contexts in which it was used in this period, it seems to be an accusation of being a type of mercenary.

amujerado: Effeminate; feminine, womanly.

aparejado: Fit or suitable; considered an insult when combined with another word, such as *carajo*.

arrastrado: Miserable or wretched; someone who grovels and is a brownnoser.

bárbaro: A barbarian; an uncouth person.

bellaco: A scoundrel.

borrachón: A drunk.

cabrón: A cuckold, literally, but over time this word has taken on the connotation of a hard man without scruples.

carajo: The expletive *damn*, as in "I don't give a damn" or "Damn you." It was often combined with other expressions, and men described other men as carajo. Also could be slang term for the penis and scrotum.

chalán: A sharp operator with dubious integrity; a lowly employee.

chicharronero: A person who makes *chicharrón*, or pork rinds; used in conjunction with *poblano*, a person from Puebla, a city that in the colonial period was known for its huge pork-processing industry.

chivato: An informant or a squealer, a variant of *soplón*.

chupa hueso: Someone who sucks on bones, possibly emphasizing either poverty or uncouthness.

cochino: Pig; variants included *puerco* and *bazofia*, or pig swill. In one instance, the combination *puerco cochino* provided extra emphasis.

collón: A coward.

consentidor: A person who spoils another; someone who is too permissive and thus allows dishonesty.

cornudo: Cuckold, in reference to having horns; like cabrón, this insult lost meaning over time and became more generic, without so much sting.

culo de afuera: Having an anus outside the body.

deslenguado: Foul-mouthed.

droguero: A person known for cheating and paying debts slowly.

encubridor: An accessory to a crime.

engreído: Conceited; not knowing one's place.

estafador: A swindler; someone who cheats using tricks and deceptive words.

faramajero: Possibly a variant on *faramalla*; thus, a person who lies or is otherwise engaged in deception.

gachupín: A slang term for a Spaniard that was considered derogatory.

graduado de mierda: A shitty graduate.

hijo de puta: Son of a whore. Because this was a very rude expression, witnesses often used the euphemism *hijo de un tal*, son of a such-and-such.

indigno: Unworthy, shameful.

ingrato: Ungrateful.

jodido: Messed up, awkward, or annoying.

Judío: A Jew; colonial laws prohibited all religions except Catholicism, so it was dangerous to be called a Jew.

ladrón: A thief; a very common insult implying dishonesty and dishonorable conduct.

mal criado: Ill-mannered; a person whose behavior demonstrated a lack of status.

Meco: A shortened version of the name Chichimeco, an indigenous group of northern Mexico denigrated as violent and unsophisticated. In one instance, the name was used in the combination Meco Otomite for another indigenous group, the Otomis, who were from central Mexico but were considered by the Aztecs and other peoples of the Mexico Basin to be less refined and dissolute.

mono: A monkey.

montonero: In contemporary usage, an urban guerrilla, but this was clearly not the meaning in the colonial context. It was used in conjunction with *pendejo* and referred to a person who was also being insulted as a poblano, a person from Puebla. The term seems to refer to a lower-class, uncouth person, but the definition is vague.

mulatto: A racial categorization, usually a person with one Caucasian parent and one African parent; an insult only when used with people who did not consider themselves to be of that racial identity.

Negro: Black or African. Like the previous example, it was an insult only when said to a person who did not self-identify as African.

oveja: Sheep; those who followed blindly and were not "manly" enough to make their own decisions.

perro: Dog; used in conjunction with other words, such as *perro indio*, *perro caballo* (horse) and *perro mulato*. In one instance, the word *escuintle* was used; this is a derivation of the Nahua word for dog, *itzcuintli*. Another variant was *perrazo*, a large dog.

pícaro: A rogue or rascal.

pichachado: Derived perhaps from *picacho*, or peak; the implication is that it refers to a person who speaks ill of women.

pendejo: A jerk.

portugués: From Portugal; in this period the implication was that the person was Jewish.

puñetero: Pitiable; also, one who masturbates.

puto: A sodomite or, in our terms, homosexual; at the time the concept of homosexuality did not exist, but people did understand that some men were inclined to have sex with other men, called *pecado nefando* (abominable sin).

revoltijo: Messed up; not a reliable person.

salteador: A highwayman; thus a variant on *ladrón*. It refers to someone who would rob people in the countryside.

soplón: A squealer or an informant, very similar to *chivato*.

tetón: A mama's boy.

tonto: Stupid.

topador: Usually used for animals, someone who butts heads.

tramposo: Deceitful, someone who uses ruses to defraud others of money.

tuerto: A person with one eye; also, someone crooked.

Notes

Preface

1. Archivo General de la Nación, Mexico (hereafter AGN), Ramo Criminal, vol. 139, exp. 9, fols. 139v–165v, Malinalco, 1799.

Chapter 1

1. Steve Stern, *The Secret History of Gender: Women, Men, and Power in Late Colonial Mexico* (Chapel Hill: University of North Carolina Press, 1995). Stern addresses this stereotype and the pattern of violence that he calls *descarga*. By and large he discredits the predominance of the stereotype in the late colonial period.
2. Américo Paredes, *Folklore and Culture on the Texas-Mexican Border*, trans. Richard Bauman (Austin: University of Texas Press, 1993), 215. Macho is one of the most studied stereotypes of Mexican national character.
3. Robert McKee Irwin, *Mexican Masculinities* (Minneapolis: University of Minnesota Press, 2003), xvii–xviii.
4. R. W. Connell, *Masculinities* (Berkeley: University of California Press, 1995), 22, 38, 44; Judith Halberstam, *Female Masculinity* (Durham, NC: Duke University Press, 1998), 46; see also María Elena Martínez, "Sex and the Colonial Archive: The Case of 'Mariano' Aguilera," *Hispanic American Historical Review* 96, no. 3 (2016): 421–43.
5. Alexandra Shepard, *Meanings of Manhood in Early Modern England* (Oxford, UK: Oxford University Press, 2005), 1.
6. Ibid., 5, 8.
7. Stern, *Secret History*, 157, refers to "ranked masculinity." For styles of masculinity in a later period in Mexican history, see James Garza, "Dominance and Submission in Don Porfirio's Belle Époque: The Case of Luis and Piedad," in *Masculinity and Sexuality in Modern Mexico*, ed. Víctor M. Macías-González and Anne Rubenstein (Albuquerque: University of New Mexico Press, 2012), 79–100.

8. Martha S. Santos, *Cleansing Honor with Blood: Masculinity, Violence, and Power in the Backlands of Northeast Brazil, 1845-1889* (Stanford, CA: Stanford University Press, 2012), 3.

9. Mrinalini Sinha, *Colonial Masculinity: The "Manly Englishman" and the "Effeminate Bengali" in the Late Nineteenth Century* (Manchester, UK: Manchester University Press, 1995), 2. Masculinity in colonial India was a process that emerged from the imposition of British rule and ways on Indians.

10. Antonio de Robles, *Diario de sucesos notables (1665-1703)* (Mexico City: Porrua, 1946), 3:131-32.

11. Kimberlé Williams Crenshaw, "The Structural and Political Dimensions of Intersectional Oppression," in *Intersectionality: A Foundations and Frontiers Reader*, ed. Patrick R. Grzanka (Boulder, CO: Westview Press, 2014), 16-22; see also Connell, *Masculinities*, 76.

12. Marión Juliette Valeri Du Bron, "El Caballo en la sociedad virreinal Novohispano de los siglos XVI y XVII: La caballería del Dios Marte," in *La Gesta del caballo en la historia de México*, ed. Miguel Ángel J. Márquez Ruiz (Mexico City: Universidad Nacional Autónoma de México, 2010), 74; Pilar Gonzalbo Aizpuru, *Vivir en Nueva España: Orden y desorden en la vida cotidiana* (Mexico City: El Colegio de México, 2009), 51.

13. Catherine Héau Lambert, "El caballo en el imaginario colectivo mexicano," in *La Gesta del caballo en la historia de México*, ed. Miguel Ángel J. Márquez Ruiz (Mexico City: Universidad Nacional Autónoma de México, 2010), 283.

14. Antonio Rubial García, *Monjas, cortesanas y plebeyos: La vida cotidiana en la época de Sor Juana* (Mexico City: Taurus, 2005), 75, 77; John Frederick Schwaller, "La Identidad sexual: Familia y mentalidades a fines del siglo XVI," in *Familias novohispanas: Siglos XVI al XIX*, ed. Pilar Gonzalbo Aizpuru (Mexico City: El Colegio de México, 1991), 68.

15. Javier Villa-Flores, *Dangerous Speech: A Social History of Blasphemy in Colonial Mexico* (Tucson: University of Arizona Press, 2006), 46.

16. Ibid., 38-40.

17. Andrew B. Fisher, "Keeping and Losing One's Head: Composure and Emotional Outbursts as Political Performance in Late-Colonial Mexico," in *Emotions and Daily Life in Colonial Mexico*, ed. Javier Villa-Flores and Sonya Lipsett-Rivera (Albuquerque: University of New Mexico Press, 2014), 168-97.

18. Don Juan de Escoiquiz, *Tratado de las Obligaciones del Hombre* (Madrid: Real, 1803). Though originally written for the Spanish court, this book was reprinted many times and is available in many Mexican collections.

19. Tatiana Seijas, *Asian Slaves in Colonial Mexico: From Chinos to Indians* (New York: Cambridge University Press, 2014). This is the first comprehensive study of Asian slavery in New Spain.

20. Alejandro Cañeque, *The King's Living Image: The Culture and Politics of Viceregal Power in Colonial Mexico* (New York: Routledge, 2004). This excellent study is a

good example of a particularly nuanced and insightful analysis of the subtle struggle for power at the highest ranks.

21. The name *Nahua* is a modern invention, but it provides a convenient and accurate term for the peoples who spoke Nahuatl and shared many cultural practices. They were generally present in central Mexico.

22. Osvaldo Pardo, *Honor and Personhood in Early Modern Mexico* (Ann Arbor: University of Michigan Press, 2015); Verónica Undurraga Schüler, *Los Rostros del Honor: Normas culturales y estrategias de promoción social en Chile colonial, siglo XVIII* (Santiago: Direccíon de Bibliotecas, Archivos y Museos [DIBAM], 2012); Lyman Johnson, "Dangerous Words, Provocative Gestures, and Violent Acts: The Disputed Hierarchies of Plebeian Life in Colonial Buenos Aires," in *The Faces of Honor: Sex, Shame, and Violence in Colonial Latin America*, ed. Lyman Johnson and Sonya Lipsett-Rivera (Albuquerque: University of New Mexico Press, 1998), 127–51; Sonya Lipsett-Rivera, *Gender and the Negotiation of Daily Life, 1750–1856* (Lincoln: University of Nebraska Press, 2012); Stern, *Secret History*; Scott K. Taylor, *Honor and Violence in Golden Age Spain* (New Haven, CT: Yale University Press, 2008); Nicholas A. Robins, *Of Love and Loathing: Marital Life, Strife, and Intimacy in the Colonial Andes, 1750–1825* (Lincoln: University of Nebraska Press, 2015).

23. The eighteenth-century *Diccionario de Autoridades* defined *macho* as an "animal of the male sex[;] virile," http://web.frl.es/DA.html. Several references confirm this usage: AGN, Criminal, vol. 50, fols. 7–13, Xochimilco, 1779; AGN–Tribunal Superior de Justicia del Distrito Federal (hereafter AGN-TSJDF), Colonial Alcalde del Crimen, Criminal, box 47A, exp. 15, Mexico City, 1751; AGN, Criminal, vol. 236, fol. 52, Coyoacán, 1767; AGN-TSJDF, Colonial Corregidores (Coyoacán), Criminal, box 28B, exp. 59, Mexico City, 1749.

24. Paredes, *Folklore*, 217, 221–22; Irwin, *Mexican Masculinities*, 47; Jeffrey M. Pilcher, "The Gay Caballero: Machismo, Homosexuality, and the Nation in Golden Age Film," in *Masculinity and Sexuality in Modern Mexico*, ed. Víctor M. Macías-González and Anne Rubenstein (Albuquerque: University of New Mexico Press, 2012), 217; Matthew C. Gutmann, *The Meanings of Macho: Being a Man in Mexico City* (Berkeley: University of California Press, 1996), 226; Víctor M. Macías-González and Anne Rubenstein, eds., introduction to *Masculinity and Sexuality in Modern Mexico* (Albuquerque: University of New Mexico Press, 2012), 13–14.

25. AGN, Criminal, vol. 660, fols. 160–83, Mexico City, 1752; AGN, Criminal, vol. 266, fols. 97–110, Tultitlan-Tacuba, 1760; AGN-TSJDF, Colonial Juzgados Especiales, Auditor de Guerra, box 19, exp. 176, Mexico City, 1808; AGN, Criminal, vol. 129, fols. 1–133, Mexico City, 1799.

26. AGN-TSJDF, Colonial Juzgados Especiales, Auditor de Guerra, box 20, exp. 192, Mexico City, 1810; AGN-TSJDF, Colonial Alcaldes Ordinarios, Criminal, box 35A, exp. 2, Mexico City, 1784; AGN, Criminal, vol. 560, fols. 231–55, Mexico, 1749.

27. AGN, Criminal, vol. 723, fols. 2–21, Mexico City, 1777; AGN-TSJDF, Colonial Corregidores, Teniente General de Xochimilco, Criminal, box 31A, exp. 41,

Xochimilco, 1779; AGN, Criminal, vol. 76, fols. 1–194, Tacuba, 1803; AGN, Criminal, vol. 84, fols. 169–80, Mexico City, 1809; AGN-TSJDF, Colonial Corregidores (Coyoacán), Criminal, box 28B, exp. 78, Mexico City, 1768; AGN-TSJDF, Colonial Alcaldes Ordinarios, Criminal, box 33A, exp. 34, Mexico City, 1804.

28. AGN, Criminal, vol. 131, fols. 127–45, Tacubaya, 1760; AGN, Criminal, vol. 723, fols. 22–35, Mexico City, 1780; AGN, Criminal, vol. 176, fols. 79–87, Tlanepantla, 1787; AGN, Criminal, vol. 402, fols. 17–34, Mexico City, 1801; AGN-TSJDF, Colonial Corregidores, Criminal, box 17B, exp. 112, Mexico City, 1803; AGN-TSJDF, Colonial Alcaldes Ordinarios, Criminal, box 35B, exp. 80, Mexico City, 1803; AGN, Criminal, vol. 405, fols. 370–471, Mexico City, 1805; AGN-TSJDF, Colonial Juzgados Especiales, Auditor de Guerra, box 20, exp. 192, Mexico City, 1810.

29. Verónica Undurraga Schüler, "Fronteras sociales y sus intersticios: Usos y abusos de las categorías 'caballeros,' 'dones' y 'españoles' en Santiago de Chile, siglo XVIII," in *América colonial: Denominaciones, clasificaciones e identidades* (Santiago: RIL, 2010), 306. Undurraga Schüler argues that in Chile men began to refer to themselves as *caballeros*, or gentlemen, because the honorific *don* was too common to be distinctive.

30. AGN-TSJDF, Colonial Alcaldes Ordinarios, Criminal, box 33A, exp. 1, Mexico City, 1793.

31. Arlette Farge, *The Allure of the Archives*, trans. Thomas Scott-Railton (New Haven, CT: Yale University Press, 2013), 79.

32. Kathryn Burns, *Into the Archive: Writing and Power in Colonial Peru* (Durham, NC: Duke University Press, 2010), 133, 135.

Chapter 2

1. AGN-TSJDF, Colonial, section 4A, Hojas sueltas (loose-leaf), box 106, exp. 140, Mexico City, 1726. There were other types of dangers for boys. Robles, *Diario*, reports on one man who strangled eleven boys before he was caught (1:193) and another who accidentally killed a toddler with his gun (2:219).

2. Bianca Premo, *Children of the Father King: Youth, Authority, and Legal Minority in Colonial Lima* (Chapel Hill: University of North Carolina Press, 2005); Cynthia Milton, "Wandering Waifs and Abandoned Babes: The Limits and Uses of Juvenile Welfare in Eighteenth-Century Quito," *Colonial Latin American Review* 13, no. 1 (June 2004: 103–28; Tobias Hecht, ed., *Minor Omissions: Children in Latin American History and Society* (Madison: University of Wisconsin Press, 2002); Ondina E. González and Bianca Premo, eds., *Raising an Empire: Children in Early Modern Iberia and Colonial Latin America* (Albuquerque: University of New Mexico Press, 2007).

3. Martín de Cordóba, *Jardín de las nobles doncellas* (N.p.: n.p., 1542), chap. 9; Rebecca Earle, *The Body of the Conquistador: Food, Race, and the Colonial*

Experience in Spanish America, 1492–1700 (Cambridge, UK: Cambridge University Press, 2012), 9, 26. Earle explains ideas derived from Galenic medicine and how the balance of humors within a person affected not only health but also personality and appearance.

4. Antonio Rubial García, *La plaza, el palacio y el convento: La ciudad de México en el siglo XVII* (Mexico City: Consejo Nacional para la Cultura y el Arte, 1998), 104. He writes that all ethnicities shared this belief.

5. Don Juan Elías Gómez de Terán, *Infancia ilustrada y niñez instruida en todo género de virtudes Christianas, Morales, y Políticas, que conducen a la Santa Educación y buena crianza de los niños* (Madrid: Antonio Marin, 1735), 7–8.

6. Milton, "Wandering Waifs," 104.

7. Despite the urgings of moral authorities, many mothers used wet nurses instead of breast-feeding their children themselves. Juan de la Cerda, *Libro intitulado vida política de todos los estados de mugeres: En el qual dan muy provechosos y Christianos documentos y avisos, para criarse y conservarse debidamente las mugeres en sus estados* (Alcalá de Henares, Spain: Juan Gracián, 1599), 1; Pedro Galindo, *Parte segunda del directorio de Penitentes, y practica de una buena y prudente confesión* (Madrid: Antonio de Zafra, 1680), 156; Padre Matías Sánchez, *El Padre de familias: Brevemente instruido en sus muchas obligaciones de padre* (Madrid: n.p., 1786), 174–76, 185; Don Manuel Rossell, *La educación conforme a los principios de la religión christiana, leyes y costumbres, de la nación española en tres libros dirigidos a los padres de familia* (Madrid: Real, 1786), 64–65; Premo, *Children*, 52–54; Claudia Rosas Lauro, "El derecho de nacer y crecer: Los niños en la Ilustración; Perú, siglo XVIII," in *Historia de la infancia en América Latina*, ed. Pablo Rodríguez Jiménez and María Emma Manarelli (Bogotá: Universidad Externado de Colombia, 2007), 221. Rosas Lauro notes that in upper-class families, children were looked after by slaves and servants and came into contact with women of all ethnicities and classes; thus they were inculcated with many of the ideas of popular culture.

8. Gonzalbo Aizpuru, *Vivir*, 115.

9. AGN, Criminal, vol. 346, fols. 169–169v, Mexico, 1790.

10. Gonzalbo Aizpuru, *Vivir*, 115. On the high rate of child mortality in New Spain, see Dorothy Tanck de Estrada, "Muerte precoz: Los niños en el siglo XVIII," in *Historia de la vida cotidiana en México*, vol. 3, *El siglo XVIII: Entre tradición y cambio*, ed. Pilar Gonzalbo Aizpuru (Mexico City: El Colegio de México, 2005), 216–17. On how residents of Lima, Peru, grieved their babies' deaths, see Premo, *Children*, 49.

11. Robles, *Diario*, 1:270.

12. Rossell, *La educación*; Laura Shelton, *For Tranquility and Order: Family and Community on Mexico's Northern Frontier, 1800–1850* (Tucson: University of Arizona Press, 2010), 119; Rosas Lauro, "El derecho," 220.

13. Sánchez, *El Padre*, 176–77; Rossell, *La educación*, 52–53; Shelton, *For Tranquility*, 118, 120. Shelton notes that after the seventh birthday this care was supposed to

be taken over by fathers and religious personnel, especially in regard to teaching morality.

14. Sánchez, *El Padre*, 174–76, 192–93; Rossell, *La educación*, 51–53.
15. Rosas Lauro, "El derecho," 226.
16. AGN, Criminal, vol. 134, fol. 84v, Mexico City, 1801. Sebastiana María relates how she sent her young son to fetch water at eight o'clock in the morning, but he was scared because of a man who seemed to be sleeping in the road. It turned out that the man was dead.
17. Rosalva Loreto López, "Familial Religiosity and Images in the Home: Eighteenth-Century Puebla de los Angeles, Mexico," *Journal of Family History* 22, no. 1(1997): 32.
18. Silvia M. Arrom, *The Women of Mexico City, 1790–1857* (Stanford, CA: Stanford University Press, 1985), 58.
19. Premo, *Children*, 22–27.
20. AGN, Criminal, vol. 564, fols. 25v–27v, Mexico City, 1801. Robles, *Diario*, 2:232, records that in 1691 don Agustín Franco became rector of the Royal University at age nineteen; he had received his doctorate two years earlier.
21. AGN-TSJDF, Colonial, section 4A, Hojas sueltas, box 107, Tacubaya, 1757.
22. Premo, *Children*, 22–27; Philippe Ariès, *Centuries of Childhood: A Social History of Family Life*, trans. Rober Baldiek (New York: Alfred A. Knopf, 1961), 26. Ariès asserts that people considered childhood to be over when an individual was no longer a dependent.
23. Premo, *Children*, 22, 30, 111; Pilar Gonzalbo Aizpuru, *Familia y Orden Colonial* (Mexico City: El Colegio de México, 1998), 81.
24. AGN-TSJDF, Colonial Alcaldes Ordinarios, Criminal, box 31A, exp. 53, Mexico City, 1665.
25. AGN, Criminal vol. 154, fols. 175–203, Coyoacán, 1802.
26. AGN-TSJDF, Colonial Corregidores, Marquesado del Valle, Criminal, box 30B, exp. 105, San Pedro Cuajimalpa, 1747.
27. Shelton, *For Tranquility*, 117.
28. Deborah Kanter, *Hijos del Pueblo: Gender, Family, and Community in Rural Mexico, 1730–1850* (Austin: University of Texas Press, 2008), 55, 58.
29. AGN, Criminal, vol. 564, fol. 50, Mexico, 1801. Don Joaquín's mother wrote a letter explaining everything he had to do to make sure his younger brother flourished away from home. Don Joaquín's legal defender later used this letter to justify don Joaquín's actions in punishing his younger sibling for stealing from him.
30. Christina Ruiz Martínez, "La moderación como prototipo de santidad: Una imagen de la niñez," in *De la santidad a la perversión o de porqué no cumplía la ley de Dios en la sociedad novohispano*, ed. Sergio Ortega (Mexico City: Grijalbo, 1986), 52.

31. Sánchez, *El Padre*, 25–26. Kanter, *Hijos*, 59, notes that parent-child relations were supposed to be reciprocal.

32. Kanter, *Hijos*, 58.

33. Escoiquiz, *Tratado*, 91.

34. For example, in Tacuba in 1726, Bernardino Antonio testified. He did not know his age, but the officials estimated that he was about fourteen or fifteen years old. AGN, Criminal, vol. 730, fol. 375, Azcapotzalco, 1726. Premo, *Children*, 117, comments on the vagueness of ages.

35. Gonzalbo Aizpuru, *Vivir*, 108.

36. AGN-TSJDF, Colonial Corregidores, Criminal, box 17B, exp. 100, fols. 1–7v, Mexico City, 1802. In another case, Robles, *Diario*, 3:141, reports that a young boy was killed when a carriage ran him over.

37. AGN, Criminal, vol. 266, fols. 146–152v, Tacuba, 1790.

38. Ariès, *Centuries*, 29–30.

39. AGN, Criminal, vol. 675, fols. 23–31, Mexico City, 1794.

40. AGN-TSJDF, Colonial Corregidores, Criminal, box 17B, exp. 114, fols. 1–34, Mexico City, 1807.

41. Victor Macías-González, "Hombres de mundo: La masculinidad, el consume, y los manuales de urbanidad y buenas maneras," in *Orden social e identidad de género, México, siglos XIX y XX*, ed. María Teresa Fernández Aceves, Carmen Ramos Escandón, and Susie Porter (Guadalajara: CIESAS, 2006), 267–97; Valentina Torres Septién, "Notas sobre urbanidad y buenas maneras de Erasmo al Manual de Carreño," in *Historia de la educación y enseñanza de la* historia, ed. Pilar Gonzalbo Aizpuru (Mexico City: El Colegio de México, 1998), 89–111.

42. Anonymous, *Reglas de la buena crianza civil y christiana: Utilísimas para todos y singularmente para los que cuiden de la educación de los Niños, a quienes las deberían explicar, inspirándoles insensiblemente su práctica en todas ocurrencias* (Puebla, Mexico: Don Pedro de la Rosa, 1802), 8–9; Escoiquiz, *Tratado*, 112–14.

43. For example, Miguel López (alias Lora), a mestizo, in 1781 in the village of Ayotzingo, defied his *teniente* (deputy) in many ways, but he did so symbolically by refusing to take off his hat. AGN, Criminal, vol. 142, fols. 234–48, Ayotzingo), 1781. In another case, Joseph Mancera demonstrated his deference by asking questions literally "with his hat in his hands"—an expression found numerous times in the documents to indicate an attitude of respect. AGN-TSJDF, Colonial Corregidores, Teniente General de Xochimilco, Criminal, box 31A, exp. 36A, Xochimilco, 1766.

44. Anonymous, *Reglas*, 8–9; Escoiquiz, *Tratado*, 112–14, 137–39.

45. Anonymous, *Reglas*, 9–10.

46. Escoiquiz, *Tratado*, 134–37.

47. Ibid., 109–12; Anonymous, *Reglas*, 10–11; Padre Gerónimo de Rosales, *Catón Christiano y catecismo de la doctrina christiana para la educación y nueva*

crianza de los niños y muy provechosos para personas de todos estados (Mexico City: Nueva de la Biblioteca Mexicana 1761), 73.

48. Gómez de Terán, *Infancia ilustrada*, 450; Rosales, *Catón Christiano*, 58–59, 67; Escoiquiz, *Tratado*, 34–35.

49. Anonymous, *Reglas*, 11–13, 15–16.

50. Ibid., 70–71; Escoiquiz, *Tratado*, 114–16; Rosales, *Catón Christiano*, 55.

51. AGN, Criminal, vol. 719, fol. 16v, Amecameca, 1800.

52. Escoiquiz, *Tratado*, 139–42. Rosales, *Catón Christiano*, 53, recommends avoiding much contact with the lower classes, showing the appropriate respect, and keeping to one's own social stratum.

53. For a masterful description of these subtle slights, see Cañeque, *King's Living Image*.

54. Rosalvo Loreto López, "Familial Religiosity and Images in the Home: Eighteenth-Century Puebla de Los Angeles, Mexico," *Journal of Family History* 22, no. 1 (1997): 27. Mexican children absorbed many of the lessons of Catholicism from the religious images that were present in all the rooms of their houses, along with practices such as sayings, which were the norm in polite conversation. In addition, their daily lives were punctuated by the periodic ringing of nearby church bells, which reminded them of their religious duties.

55. Rossell, *La educación*, 56–57, 109; Cerda, *Libro intitulado*, 41, 44.

56. Rosales, *Catón Christiano*, 52–54.

57. Premo, *Children*, 23–24.

58. Kanter, *Hijos*, 56. People were suspicious of single mothers because no one believed that they could punish their children adequately.

59. Galindo, *Parte segunda*, 398–400.

60. Doña Josefa Amar y Borbón, *Discurso sobre la educación física y moral de las mugeres* (Madrid: D. Benito Cano, 1790), 117, 119.

61. Lipsett-Rivera, *Gender*, 183.

62. AGN, Criminal, vol. 155, fols. 311–314v, Xochimilco, 1796.

63. AGN, Criminal, vol. 675, fols. 75–103, Mexico City, 1754; these parents were also safeguarding their own reputations. Shelton, *For Tranquility*, 120, notes, "Good child rearing was a signifier of Mexican culture and public order. Good parents had moral children."

64. AGN, Criminal, vol. 415, fols. 1–14, Mexico City, 1807.

65. Tanck de Estrada, "Muerte precoz," 225, points to the Nahua tradition of the *huehuetlatolli*, or talks of the elders, as a reason for embracing a gentler manner of setting children on the right path. See also Dorothy Tanck de Estrada, *Pueblos de Indios y educación en el México colonial, 1750–1821* (Mexico City: El Colegio de México, 1999), 392. The parents in Santa Cruz Atoyac in Coyoacán praised their teacher for instructing "our children lovingly while maintaining great tranquility and peace."

66. Eva Mehl, *Forced Migration in the Spanish Pacific World. From Mexico to the Philippines, 1765–1811* (Cambridge, UK: Cambridge University Press, 2016), 197–201.

67. Kanter, *Hijos*, 56.

68. On the dangers faced by many boys, particularly the poor, see Milton, "Wandering Waifs," 104.

69. Rubial García, *La plaza*, 99.

70. Manuel Carrera Stampa, *Los gremios mexicanos: La organización gremial en Nueva España, 1521–1861* (Mexico City: Iberoamericana, 1954), 33; Seijas, *Asian Slaves*, 129.

71. Carrera Stampa, *Los gremios*, 25–35; Lyman L. Johnson, "The Role of Apprenticeship in Colonial Buenos Aires," *Revista de historia de América* 103 (1987): 8–10; Lyman L. Johnson. *Workshop of Revolution: Plebeian Buenos Aires and the Atlantic World, 1776–1810* (Durham, NC: Duke University Press, 2011), 52.

72. Sonia Pérez Toledo, *Los Hijos del trabajo: Los artesanos de la ciudad de México, 1780–1853* (Mexico City: El Colegio de México, 1996), 60; Carrera Stampa, *Los gremios*, 34.

73. Johnson, "Role of Apprenticeship," 13. Masters insulted nonwhite apprentices with racial epithets.

74. AGN-TSJDF, Colonial Alcaldes Ordinarios, Criminal, box 4A, exp. 7, Mexico City, 1632.

75. AGN-TSJDF, Colonial Corregidores, Criminal, box 16B, exp. 87, Mexico City, 1791. To a certain extent the master confirmed this story by stating that he found Juan José disrespectful and wanted to get him to toe the line. He was upset that Juan José simply laughed when reprimanded. Parents did defend their sons. Robles, *Diario*, 3:280, reports that a man called Villaseca wanted to whip a young boy but the child's father objected, hit him with a stick a little too vigorously killing him.

76. AGN, Criminal, vol. 446, fols. 114–20, Mexico City, 1784–1785.

77. AGN-TSJDF, Colonial Corregidores, Criminal, box 16B, exp. 109, Mexico City, 1795. Robles, *Diario*, records that after the public entrance of the viceroy, that night a boy was hit by a horse rider in the plaza of Santa Catarina (3:243–44) and another boy was killed by a carriage (3:141). Tanck de Estrada, "Muerte precoz," 223, cites a decree that recognized the dangers posed to boys on the streets by horses and carriages.

78. AGN, Criminal, vol. 177, fols. 401–407v, Tlanepantla, 1780.

79. Ibid.

80. AGN, Criminal, vol. 266, fols. 146–152v, Tacuba, 1790.

81. AGN, Criminal, vol. 176, fols. 179–83, Pueblo de Calcoaya, Tlanepantla, 1749.

82. AGN, Criminal, vol. 265, fol. 146, Cuautitlan, 1773.

83. AGN, Criminal, vol. 265, fol. 30, Tacuba, 1793.

84. AGN, Criminal, vol. 232, fols. 396–99, Tacubaya, 1633; AGN, Criminal, vol. 715, fol. 14, Mexico City, 1779; AGN, Criminal, vol. 232, fols. 243–307, Coyoacán, 1806; AGN-TSJDF, Colonial, section 4A, Hojas sueltas, box 107, México 1749; AGN-TSJDF, Colonial Alcaldes Ordinarios, Criminal, box 31A, exp. 53, Mexico City, 1665; Carlos Eduardo Jaramillo, "Los guerreros invisibles: El papel de los niños en los conflictos civiles del siglo XIX en Colombia," in *Historia de la infancia en América Latina*, ed. Pablo Rodríguez Jiménez and María Emma Manarelli (Bogotá: Universidad Externado de Colombia, 2007), 233, 234. Jaramillo notes that when armed conflicts erupted in colonial Latin America, young boys were usually recruited into the armies. In fact, Simón Bolívar began his soldiering at the age of fourteen.

85. Escoiquiz, *Tratado*, 37–40. Ariès, *Centuries*, 81–82, notes that many moral authorities denounced children's games but that most people paid no attention to these authorities. By the eighteenth century, society believed that child's play was healthy.

86. Linda Curcio-Nagy, *The Great Festivals of Colonial Mexico City: Performing Power and Identity* (Albuquerque: University of New Mexico Press, 2004), 28–29; Carolyn Dean, "Sketches of Childhood: Children in Colonial Andean Art and Society," in *Minor Omissions; Children in Latin American History and Society*, ed. Tobias Hecht (Madison: University of Wisconsin Press, 2002), 21–51. Dean uses paintings of the Corpus Christi procession in Cuzco, Peru, to show how boys participated in such events.

87. AGN, Criminal, vol. 2, fols. 276–311, Tlayacapa, 1786.

88. Tanck de Estrada, *Pueblos*, 301–3.

89. Rubial García, *Monjas*, 73. Puppets had a long history in Mexico. Introduced by the Spanish, both missionaries and conquerors used them to communicate with the indigenous population. By the eighteenth century puppeteers were plying their craft in many spaces, such as private houses, alleys, and parks, and some went to cities and smaller communities all over Mexico. Yolanda Jurado Rojas, "Puppet Theater in Eighteenth-Century Mexico," *Americas* 67, no. 3 (January 2011): 315–29. Puppet theaters of poor reputation congregated in the calle de Venero (now Mesones). Noële Vidal, "'El pequeño teatro del mundo': Les marionettes et l'histoire du Mexique," *Revue d'histoire moderne et contemporaine* 32 (January–March 1985): 99–113.

90. Rubial García, *Monjas*, 71; Tanck de Estrada, "Muerte precoz," 224; Francisco de Ajofrín, *Diario del viaje que hizo a la American española en el siglo XVIII* (México City: Instituto Cultural Hispano, 1964), 1:88; Juan de Viera, "Breve Compendiossa narración de la ciudad de México, corte y cabeza de toda la América septentrional," in *La Ciudad de México en el siglo XVIII (1690–1780): Tres crónicas*, ed. Antonio Rubial García (Mexico City: Consejo Nacional para la Cultura y las Artes, 1990), 282. On *sacemis*, regular rock fights between indigenous people in the pueblos and on the haciendas, see Dana Velasco Murillo, "The Creation of

Indigenous Leadership in a Spanish Town: Zacatecas, Mexico, 1609–1752," *Ethnohistory* 56, no. 4 (Fall 2009): 673.

91. Ajofrín, *Diario del viaje*, 84; Tanck de Estrada, "Muerte precoz," 223–24. Some of the toys were imitations of adult tools. Ariès, *Centuries*, 68.

92. Viera, "Breve Compendiossa," 213.

93. AGN, Criminal, vol. 129, fol. 4, Mexico City, 1799. In Jilotepec there was a gathering where children and adults flew their kites. AGN, Clero Regular y Secular, vol. 28, exp. 1, fols. 1–29, Jilotepec, 1794.

94. Kanter, *Hijos*, 56.

95. Rubial García, *Monjas*, 68. See also Robles, *Diario*, 3:133, 3:227, for an incident in which a boy playing in the Sagrario tower fell to his death.

96. Rubial García, *Monjas*, 71. On government efforts to stop this practice and its fatal consequences, see Tanck de Estrada, "Muerte precoz," 222–23. When a boy died in this manner, he was buried with his kite. Boys who died were often buried with a toy.

97. Angela T. Thompson, "Children and Schooling in Guanajuato, Mexico, 1790–1840," *SECOLAS Annals* 23 (March 1992): 37; Gonzalbo Aizpuru, *Vivir*, 119; Arrom, *Women*, 17–18; Pilar Gonzalbo Aizpuru and Anne Staples, eds., *Historia de la educación en la época colonial: La educación de los criollos y la vida urbana* (Mexico City: El Colegio de México, 1990), 39; Viera, "Breve Compendiossa," 245. Even the poor in New Spain tried to secure some education for their offspring. Ajofrín, *Diario del viaje*, 82–83.

98. Escoiquiz, *Tratado*, 54–55.

99. Thompson, "Children and Schooling," 38; Gonzalbo Aizpuru, *Vivir*, 120–21.

100. Thompson, "Children and Schooling," 39.

101. Carrera Stampa, *Los gremios*, 25–26. Jorge González Angulo Aguirre, *Artesanado y ciudad a finales del siglo XVIII* (Mexico City: Secretaría de Educación Pública, 1983), 178, reports that boys could begin at age eight but that most started at ten. Johnson, *Workshop*, 54, writes that in Argentina boys left home as early as seven years of age for their apprenticeships.

102. Tanck de Estrada, *Pueblos*, 339–40, 412–13, 430, 433, 407. Padre Ripalda's catechism was published with large print, as a kind of reader, in 1784, but some schools also used a Nahuatl-language catechism written by Father Bartolomé Castaño.

103. Ibid., 390. Most indigenous villages wanted a teacher who spoke their language (340).

104. Ibid., 390, 395.

105. AGN, Criminal, vol. 274, fol. 282v, Chalco, 1795.

106. Tanck de Estrada, *Pueblos*, 398, 406, 438.

107. AGN-TSJDF, Corregidores, Criminal, box 16B, exp. 74, Mexico City, 1749.

108. Tanck de Estrada, *Pueblos*, 400–401, 406.

109. Gonzalbo Aizpuru, *Vivir*, 121; Thompson, "Children and Schooling," 42.

110. AGN, Criminal, vol. 564, fol. 50, Mexico City, 1801. I thank Laura Shelton for her insight on the connection between bad penmanship and character.
111. Gonzalbo Aizpuru, *Vivir*, 120.
112. Rubial García, *Monjas*, 203–4.
113. Tanck de Estrada, "Muerte precoz," 227. On the ubiquity of smoking in New Spain, see Ajofrín, *Diario del viaje*, 78–79.
114. Angélica Jiménez Martínez, "¿Somos de la basura? El mito fundador de la casa de niños expósitos de la ciudad de México (1767)," *Revista de historia de América* 139 (2008): 170–71, 176. Between 1777 and 1786 the majority of abandoned babies at this new institution were españoles (50 percent), followed by mestizos (45 percent), *castas* (37 percent), and indigenous (15 percent). See also Pilar Gonzalbo Aizpuru, "La Casa de niños expósitos de la ciudad de México: Una fundación del siglo XVIII," *Historia Mexicana* 31, no. 3 (1982): 410.
115. Gonzalbo Aizpuru, "La Casa," 422–23.
116. Elsa Malvido, "El abandono de los hijos: Una forma de control del tamaño de la familia y del trabajo indígena; Tula (1683–1730)," *Historia mexicana* 26 (1980): 544.
117. AGN-TSJDF, Colonial, section 4A, Hojas sueltas, box 106, exp. 44, Mexico City, 1679.
118. AGN-TSJDF, Colonial Alcaldes Ordinarios, box 26B, exp. 50, Mexico City, 1802.
119. Kanter, *Hijos*, 61–62.
120. Malvido, "El abandono," 539, 542. The incidence of abandonment was highest in May, June, and July, before the harvests; if the crops failed, the rate spiked again in December and January.
121. AGN, Criminal, vol. 134, fol. 83v, Mexico City, 1801.
122. AGN, Criminal, vol. 560, fols. 369–79, Mexico City, 1753. In a similar case, doña Rafaela Patiño adopted and raised a young girl, María Mauricia Tapia, who died after marrying and giving birth to a son. Doña Rafaela then tried to gain custody of this son, saying that her adopted daughter had wished it so. AGN-TSJDF, Colonial Juzgados Especiales, Libros y Expedientes Sueltos, box 100, exp. 6, Mexico City, 1803. See also AGN-TSJDF, Colonial Alcaldes Ordinarios, Criminal, box 23B, exp. 55, Mexico City, 1790. Don Juan José Deza y Villoa asserted that while very ill, don Pablo Ruiz de Aranda had transferred custody of his eight-year-old son to him. He was required to certify this "donation."
123. Muriel Nazzari, "An Urgent Need to Conceal: The System of Honor and Shame in Colonial Brazil," in *The Faces of Honor: Sex, Shame, and Violence in Colonial Latin America*, ed. Lyman L. Johnson and Sonya Lipsett-Rivera (Albuquerque: University of New Mexico Press, 1998), 101–26; Ann Twinam, *Public Lives, Private Secrets: Gender, Honor, Sexuality, and Illegitimacy in Colonial Latin America* (Stanford, CA: Stanford University Press, 1999).
124. Gonzalbo Aizpuru, "La Casa," 424.

125. Shelton, *For Tranquility*, 128–33. Malvido, "El abandono," 552, makes a clear connection between adoption and work. She shows that most children were adopted by higher-status families, who often did so to provide a workforce for their workshops.

126. AGN-TSJDF, Colonial Alcalde Mayor de Xochimilco, Criminal, box 32B, exp. 47, Xochimilco, 1795.

127. Rubial García, *Monjas*, 199; Premo, *Children*, 82.

128. Rubial García, *Monjas*, 198.

129. Gonzalbo Aizpuru, *Vivir*, 121.

130. Bernard Lavallé, "Miedo reverencial versus justo miedo: Presiones familiares y vocación religiosa en Lima (1650–1700)," in *El miedo en el Perú, siglos XVI al XX*, ed. Claudia Rosas Lauro (Lima: Pontificia Universidad Católica del Perú, 2005), 94; Premo, *Children*, 63. On sons reported as vagos by their parents for their refusal to take vows, see Beatriz Cáceres Menéndez and Robert Patch, "'Gente de mal vivir': Families and Incorrigible Sons in New Spain, 1721–1729," *Revista de Indias* 66, no. 237 (June 2006): 376.

131. María Dolores Morales and María Gayón, "Viviendas, casas y usos de suelo en la ciudad de México, 1848–1881," in *Casas, vivienda y hogares en la historia de México*, ed. Rosalva Loreto López (Mexico City: El Colegio de México, 2001), 345.

132. Pilar Gonzalbo Aizpuru, "Familias y viviendas en la capital del Virreinato," in *Casas, vivienda y hogares en la historia de México*, ed. Rosalva Loreto López (Mexico City: El Colegio de México, 2001), 82–83. People constructed *jacales* in vacant lots and courtyards in the more central part of Mexico City.

133. Guadalupe de la Torre V., Sonia Lombardo de Ruiz, and Jorge González Angulo A., "La vivienda en una zona al suroeste de la Plaza Mayor de la ciudad de México (1753–1811)," in *Casas, vivienda y hogares en la historia de México*, ed. Rosalva Loreto López (Mexico City: El Colegio de México, 2001), 120.

134. Silvia M. Arrom, *Containing the Poor: The Mexico City Poor House, 1774–1871* (Durham, NC: Duke University Press, 2000), 25.

135. Caterina Pizzigoni, *The Life Within: Local Indigenous Society in Mexico's Toluca Valley, 1650–1800* (Stanford, CA: Stanford University Press, 2012), 25–27.

136. Pilar Gonzalbo Aizpuru, "Los primeros siglos de la Nueva España," in *Historia de la educación en la ciudad de México*, ed. Pilar Gonzalbo Aizpuru and Anne Staples (Mexico City: El Colegio de México, 2012), 98–99.

137. Elizabeth Anne Kuznesof, "Gender Ideology, Race, and Female-Headed Households in Urban Mexico, 1750–1850," in *State and Society in Spanish America during the Age of Revolution*, ed. Victor M. Uribe-Uran (Wilmington, DE: Scholarly Resources Books, 2001), 161. In the late eighteenth century, 24 to 36 percent of Mexico City's households were female-headed.

138. AGN-TSJDF, Colonial, section 4A, Hojas sueltas, box 106, exp. 73, México, 1692–1693.

139. AGN-TSJDF, Colonial Alcaldes Ordinarios, Criminal, box 28A, exp. 24, fols. 1–11v, Mexico City, 1809.

140. AGN-TSJDF, Colonial Libros y Expedientes Diversos, Hojas sueltas, box 96, exp. 33, Coyoacán, 1785. Premo, *Children*, 188, states that parents began to express their love for their children more openly in the court documents after the middle of the eighteenth century.

141. Milton, "Wandering Waifs," 104.

142. Mehl, *Forced Migration*, 197–200. See also Stephanie Mawson, "Unruly Plebeians and the *Forzado* System: Convict Transportation between New Spain and the Philippines during the Seventeenth Century," *Revista de Indias* 73, no. 259 (2013): 693–730.

143. Peter N. Stearns, "Obedience and Emotion: A Challenge in the Emotional History of Childhood," *Journal of Social History* 47, no. 3 (2014): 603.

144. Cáceres Menéndez and Patch, "Gente de mal vivir," 365, 368–75.

145. Milton, "Wandering Waifs," 107; Premo, *Children*, 194. I found a few cases earlier in the eighteenth century: AGN, Criminal, vol. 622, fols. 119–26, Mexico City, 1757; AGN, Criminal, vol. 560, fols. 369–79, Mexico City, 1753; AGN-TSJDF, Colonial Corregidores, Criminal, box 16B, exp. 70, Mexico City, 1744; AGN, Criminal, vol. 560, fols. 231–55, Mexico, 1749; AGN, Criminal, vol. 675, fols. 75–103, Mexico City, 1754.

146. Robert Muchembled, *A History of Violence: From the End of the Middle Ages to the Present*, trans. Jean Birrell (Cambridge, UK: Polity Press, 2012), 17. Young men in their twenties were the most likely to be violent and to commit murder.

147. Cáceres Menéndez and Patch, "Gente de mal vivir," 377; Shelton, *For Tranquility*, 123, 126.

148. AGN, Criminal, vol. 473, fols. 383–89, Mexico City, 1797.

149. AGN-TSJDF, Colonial Libros y Expedientes Diversos, Hojas sueltas, box 96, exp. 3, Mexico City, 1792.

150. AGN, Criminal, vol. 560, fols. 369–79, Mexico City, 1753.

151. Lipsett-Rivera, *Gender*.

152. Cáceres Menéndez and Patch, "Gente de mal vivir," 365–66.

153. AGN, Criminal, vol. 415, fols. 1–14, Mexico City, 1807.

154. AGN, Criminal, vol. 560, fols. 369–79, Mexico City, 1753.

155. AGN, Criminal, vol. 560, fols. 231–55, Mexico City, 1749.

156. AGN, Criminal, vol. 675, fols. 75–103, Mexico City, 1754.

157. AGN, Criminal, vol. 473, fols. 383–89, Mexico City, 1797.

158. Sánchez, *El Padre*, 25–26.

159. Cáceres Menéndez and Patch, "Gente de mal vivir," 382.

160. AGN, Criminal, vol. 675, fols. 23–31, Mexico City, 1794.

161. AGN, Criminal, vol. 556, fols. 177–79, Mexico City, 1798.

162. AGN-TSJDF, Colonial Corregidores, Criminal, box 17B, exp. 115, Mexico City, 1803.

163. AGN-TSJDF, Colonial Alcaldes Ordinarios, box 31B, exp. 93, Mexico City, 1729.
164. AGN, Criminal, vol. 415, fols. 1–14, Mexico City, 1807.
165. AGN-TSJDF, Colonial Corregidores, Criminal, box 17A, exp. 14, Mexico City, 1797.
166. AGN, Criminal, vol. 715, fols. 397–404, Mexico City, 1796.
167. AGN, Criminal, vol. 556, fols. 61–74, Mexico City, 1798; AGN, Criminal, vol. 675, fols. 75–103, Mexico City, 1754; AGN, Criminal, vol. 675, fols. 129–140, Mexico City, 1797; AGN-TSJDF, Colonial Alcaldes Ordinarios, box 31B, exp. 112, Mexico City, 1775; AGN, Criminal, vol. 609, fols. 287–306, Mexico City, 1797; AGN-TSJDF, Colonial Corregidores, Criminal, box 17B, exp. 114, fols. 1–34, Mexico City, 1807; AGN-TSJDF, Colonial Alcaldes Ordinarios, box 32A, exp. 68, Mexico City, 1791; AGN-TSJDF, Colonial Alcaldes Ordinarios, box 32A, exp. 38, Mexico City, 1790. See also Cáceres Menéndez and Patch, "Gente de mal vivir," 380.
168. AGN Criminal, vol. 675, fols. 23–31, Mexico City, 1794; AGN, Criminal, vol. 556, fols. 54–60, Mexico City, 1798; AGN, Criminal, vol. 560, fols. 369–79, Mexico City, 1753; AGN-TSJDF, Colonial Corregidores, Criminal, box 17B, exp. 115, Mexico City, 1803; AGN, Criminal, vol. 622, fols. 119–26, Mexico City, 1757. In addition, two young men were said to hang out with petty thieves (*macutenos*). AGN, Criminal, vol. 675, fols. 129–40, Mexico City, 1797; AGN, Criminal, vol. 560, fols. 369–79, Mexico City, 1753.
169. AGN-TSJDF, Colonial Alcaldes Ordinarios, box 31B, exp. 112, Mexico City, 1775; AGN, Criminal, vol. 675, fols. 129–40, Mexico City, 1797; AGN, Criminal, vol. 675, fols. 75–103, Mexico City, 1754; AGN, Criminal, vol. 560, fols. 231–55, Mexico, 1749. Selling clothes was a frequent way to raise money, but it left many poorer Mexicans in states of nudity that many eighteenth-century elites found disturbing. Norman Martín, "La desnudez en la Nueva España del siglo XVIII," *Anuario de Estudios Americanos* 29 (1972): 261–94.

Chapter 3

1. AGN-TSJDF, Colonial Alcaldes Ordinarios, Criminal, box 35B, exp. 82, Mexico City, 1804. Robles, *Diario*, 3:132, recounts the extraordinary sight of a mulatta dressed as a man who fought a bull in the 1695 bullfights. It is, of course, possible that more people cross-dressed in New Spain than is possible to gauge in the documents. Unless they were denounced or commented on, their choices went unrecorded. For an interesting case of a transgender man, see María Elena Martínez, "Sex and the Colonial Archive: The Case of 'Mariano' Aguilera," *Hispanic American Historical Review* 96, no. 3 (2016): 421–43.
2. Margarita R. Ochoa, "'Por faltar a sus obligaciones': Matrimonio, género y autoridad entre la población indígena de la ciudad de México colonial, siglos XVIII y XIX," in *Los Indios y las ciudades de la Nueva España*, ed. Felipe Castro Gutiérrez

(Mexico City, Universidad Nacional Autónoma de México, 2010), 365. She uses the term *seudomatrimonio*.

3. AGN, Criminal, vol. 411, fols. 20–24, Mexico City, 1805.

4. Mehl, *Forced Migration*, 167.

5. AGN, Criminal, vol. 708, fols. 1–511, Chalco, 1757.

6. Serge Gruzinski, "The Ashes of Desire: Homosexuality in Mid-Seventeenth-Century New Spain," trans. Ignacio López-Calvo, in *Infamous Desire: Male Homosexuality in Colonial Latin America*, ed. Pete Sigal (Chicago: University of Chicago Press, 2003), 210. He argues that homosexuals formed a type of subculture in New Spain and were afforded a certain amount of tolerance. See also Rafael Carrasco, *Inquisición y represión sexual en Valencia: Historia de los sodomitas (1565–1785)* (Barcelona: Laertes, 1985), 134. Zeb Tortorici, "Sins against Nature: Sex and Archives in New Spain (1530–1821)," unpublished manuscript, notes that it is difficult to assess levels of tolerance for sodomites.

7. AGN-TSJDF, Colonial Corregidores (Coyoacán), Criminal, box 29A, exp. 86, Mexico City, 1749. Tortorici, "Sins," mentions a 1710 denunciation of sodomy in an obraje in Coyoacán. Robles, *Diario*, 1:137, 2:130, mentions sodomitical acts in the obraje of Juan de Avila in Mixcoac and executions. For reports on executions for sodomy, including of a man who had lived as a sodomite since the age of seven, see Gregorio M. de Guijo, *Diario, 1648–1664*, vol. 1, ed. Manuel Romero de Terreros (Mexico City: Porrua, 1952), 105–7, 139–40.

8. Twinam, *Public Lives*, 38, remarks these could range in form from a quick promise to a ceremony in which the couple exchanged gifts or even a written contract. See also Nicole Von Germeten, *Violent Delights, Violent Ends: Sex, Race and Honor in Colonial Cartagena de India* (Albuquerque: University of New Mexico Press, 2013), 193; and Renato Barahona, *Sex Crimes, Honour, and the Law in Early Modern Spain: Viscaya, 1528–1735* (Toronto, ON: University of Toronto Press, 2003), 19.

9. Gonzalbo Aizpuru, *Vivir*, 288; Asunción Lavrin, ed., "Sexuality in Colonial Mexico: A Church Dilemma," in *Sexuality and Marriage in Colonial Latin America* (Lincoln: University of Nebraska Press, 1989), 61; Guillermo F. Margadant, "La Familia en el derecho Novohispano," in *Familias novohispanas: Siglos XVI al XIX*, ed. Pilar Gonzalbo Aizpuru (Mexico City: El Colegio de México, 1991), 28; Rubial García, *La plaza*, 75. The esponsales were not obligatory, but if they occurred they were an impediment to contracting marriage with another person.

10. People learned these rules when they studied the catechism in school, through the weekly sermons preached by their priests, and during the sacrament of confession. Asunción Lavrin, "La sexualidad y las normas de la moral sexual," in *Historia de la vida cotidiana en México*, vol. 2, *La ciudad barroca*, ed. Antonio Rubial García (Mexico City: El Colegio de México, 2005), 494, 496–97; Lavrin, "Sexuality," 47–92; Gonzalbo Aizpuru, *Vivir*, 283.

11. Lavrin, "La sexualidad," 497. Few judicial documents mention the débito conyugal, but in 1786 the archbishop ordered Josef María Martínez and his wife, Anna Gertrudis, to confess their sexual sins (incest) so that Josef could regain his right to ask for and receive the debito conyugal. AGN, Criminal, vol. 641, fols. 64–70, Ecatepec, 1786.

12. Anonymous, *Breve instrucción a los Christianos casadas y útiles advertencias a los que pretenden serlo* (Puebla, Mexico: Don Pedro de la Rosa, 1790), xlvi–xlvii; Vicente Ferrer, *Suma Moral para examen de curas y confesores en que a la luz del sol de las escuelas Santo Thomás, se desvanecen los perniciosos extremos de laxedad y rigor* (Valencia, Spain: Joseph Thomas Lucas, 1736), 187.

13. Linda Curcio-Nagy, "Magic, Sexuality, and the Manila Galleon Trade," paper presented at the annual meeting of the Rocky Mountain Council on Latin American Studies, Santa Fe, New Mexico, 2016.

14. Fray Francisco de Osuna, *Norte de los estados en que se da regla de bivir a los mancebos: Y a los casados; y a los viudos; y a todos los continentes; y se tratan muy por estenso los remedios del desastrado casamiento; enseñando que tal a de ser la vida del cristiano casado* (Seville: n.p., 1531), 70v–71v; Ferrer, *Suma Moral*, 187. In contrast, Martín de Cordóba, *Jardín de las nobles doncellas* (N.p.: n.p., 1542), pt. 2, chapt 4, condemned women who had any carnal appetites, including for sex.

15. Rubial García, *La plaza*, 78.

16. Ferrer, *Suma Mora*, 187. There were two important Dominican friars named Vicente Ferrer, one a logician and missionary who lived during the fourteenth and fifteenth centuries, was active in Spain and France, and was canonized in 1455. The other, from the eighteenth century, worked in New Spain, and probably took his name from the former. The work of the second one is more important for my study.

17. Lavrin, "Sexuality," 75. Ferrer, *Suma Moral*, 187, agreed that a spouse should not ask for sex too often.

18. Ferrer, *Suma Moral*, 186–89; Fray Augustín de Quintana, *Confesionario en lengua Mixe Con una construcción de las Oraciones Christiana y un Compendio de Voces Mixes para enseñarse a pronunciar dichas lenguas* (Puebla, Mexico: Viuda de Miguel de Ortega, 1773), 48–49.

19. Lavrin, "La sexualidad," 74.

20. AGN-TSJDF, Colonial Alcaldes Ordinarios, Criminal, box 33A, exp. 18, Mexico City, 1797.

21. Teresa Lozano Armendares, "Las sinrazones del corazón," in *Amor e historia: La expresión de los afectos en el mundo de ayer*, ed. Pilar Gonzalbo Aizpuru (Mexico City: El Colegio de México, 2013), 100.

22. Osuna, *Norte*, 71v, 73. Lavrin, "La sexualidad," 497, states that the religious authorities regulated acceptable sexual positions.

23. AGN, Bienes Nacionales, vol. 292, exp. 23, Mexico City, 1790; Tortorici, *Sins*.

24. Lavrin, "Sexuality," 73; Lavrin, "La sexualidad," 497; Osuna, *Norte*, 71, also recommended kissing and hugging between spouses. For the claim that passionate love had no place in marriage, according to Church authorities, see Guiomar Dueñas-Vargas, *Of Love and Other Passions: Elites, Politics, and Family in Bogotá, Colombia, 1778-1870* (Albuquerque: University of New Mexico Press, 2015), 2, 20.

25. Lavrin, "Sexuality," 49, 61; Twinam, *Public Lives*, 62.

26. Lavrin, "Sexuality," 62 ("consensual marriages"); Lavrin, "La sexualidad," 490; Schwaller, "La Identidad," 71; Gonzalbo Aizpuru, *Vivir*, 283; Margadant, "La Familia," 27; Lipsett-Rivera, *Gender*, 173-74, 182; Ochoa, "'Por faltar,'" 365 ("*seudomatrimonio*"); Teresa Lozano Armendares, *No codiciaras la mujer ajena: El adulterio en las comunidades domésticas Novohispanas ciudad de México, siglo XVIII* (Mexico City: Universidad Nacional Autónoma de México, 2005), 67, 70; Dueñas-Vargas, *Of Love*, 37.

27. Lavrin, "La sexualidad," 494; Schwaller, "La Identidad," 68. Twinam, *Public Lives*, 107, likens these relationships to the medieval practice in Spain of *barraganía* (concubinage with a legal contract setting out the conditions), except that unlike that custom, these relationships were not formalized by a notarized contract.

28. Lipsett-Rivera, *Gender*, 173-74, 241, 243.

29. Gonzalbo Aizpuru, *Vivir*, 287; Lavrin, "La sexualidad," 498.

30. Herman L. Bennett, *Colonial Blackness: A History of Afro-Mexico* (Bloomington: Indiana University Press, 2009), 41, 48; Barahona, *Sex Crimes*, 95-96.

31. AGN, Criminal, vol. 641, fols. 278-83, Mexico City, 1581. For similar wording, see AGN, Criminal, vol. 641, fols. 288-98, Mexico City, 1581; AGN, Criminal, vol. 703, fols. 85-98, Mexico City, 1586; AGN, Clero Regular y Secular, vol. 197, exp. 1, fols. 1-9, Mexico City, 1651; and AGN, Criminal, vol. 149, fols. 271-347, Tlacotepec, 1774.

32. AGN, Criminal, vol. 725, fols. 2-54, Mexico City, 1796; AGN-TSJDF, Colonial Corregidores, Teniente General de Xochimilco, Criminal, box 31A, exp. 41, Xochimilco, 1779; AGN-TSJDF, Colonial Corregidores, Marquesado del Valle, box 30A, exp. 29, Coyoacán, 1748. Another variation was if the man was jealous over the woman. See AGN, Criminal, vol. 624, fols. 214-305, Mexico City, 1778.

33. AGN-TSJDF, Colonial Corregidores, Criminal, box 17A, exp. 11, Mexico City, 1796. For a case in which a female servant is assumed to be in a sexual relationship with her employer because she manages the household finances, see AGN, Criminal, vol. 708, fols. 1-511, Chalco, 1757.

34. AGN, Clero Regular y Secular, vol. 201, exp. 2, fols. 29-62, Mexico City, 1788.

35. AGN-TSJDF, Colonial Alcaldes Ordinarios, Criminal, box 31B, exp. 115, Mexico City, 1776.

36. Lavrin, "La sexualidad," 499; Schwaller, "La Identidad," 71.

37. Schwaller, "La Identidad sexual," 59-72.

38. Twinam, *Public Lives*, 62.

39. Gonzalbo Aizpuru, *Vivir*.

40. AGN, Criminal, vol. 235, fols. 69–78, Milpa Alta, 1778.
41. AGN-TSJDF, Colonial Corregidores, Criminal, box 17A, exp. 2, Mexico City, 1796.
42. AGN-TSJDF, Colonial Corregidores, Criminal, box 16B, exp. 106, Mexico City, 1795.
43. AGN, Criminal, vol. 641, fols. 71–79, Mexico City, 1785; Von Germeten, *Violent Delights*, 22.
44. AGN-TSJDF, Colonial Alcaldes Ordinarios, Civil, box 27B, exp. 54, Mexico City, 1806. Don Ignacio López y Zeballos, the uncle of doña Mariana Lozano, asked that don Juan Pablo Cansino leave his niece alone and if possible to avoid even walking on her street.
45. AGN, Criminal, vol. 565, fols. 70–117, Mexico City, 1793.
46. AGN-TSJDF, Colonial Alcaldes Ordinarios, Criminal, box 31B, exp.115, Mexico City, 1776. Bennett, *Colonial Blackness*, 41, reports that Juan Francisco Blanco began an illicit relationship with a woman named Francisca after she began coming to his house to wash his clothes.
47. AGN, Criminal, vol. 703, fols. 428–32, Mexico City, 1701. One witness stated that nothing indecent had happened, but the situation was suspicious enough that her husband had accused her of adultery. Rubial García, *Monjas*, 164–65, writes that blacks, mulattoes, and mestizos organized nighttime dances in houses, where people got together to sing obscene songs and dance lasciviously until the morning.
48. AGN, Clero Regular y Secular, vol. 641, fols. 40–63, Mexico City, 1786. Manuelito was later reported to have contracted gonorrhea.
49. AGN-TSJDF, Colonial Alcaldes Ordinarios, Criminal, box 35B, exp. 70, fols. 1–7, Mexico City, 1800.
50. Rubial García, *La plaza*, 58; Robles, *Diario*, 1:29, 1:72, 1:87, 1:112–13, 1:158, 1:205–6, 2:224–25, 3:129; Hipólito Villarroel, *Enfermedades políticas que padece la capital de esta Nueva España en casi todos los cuerpos de que se compone y remedios qu se le deben aplicar para su curación si se requiere que sear útil al rey y al público.* (1785–1787; repr., Mexico City: Planeta, 2002), 23–24.
51. AGN-TSJDF, Colonial Corregidores (Coyoacán), Criminal, box 28B, exp. 81, Mexico City, 1769.
52. AGN-TSJDF, Colonial Alcaldes Ordinarios, Criminal, box 32A, exp. 41, Mexico City, 1790.
53. AGN, Criminal, vol. 677, fols. 243–273v, Cuautitlan, 1778. On throwing such eggshells during Carnival, see Rubial García, *La plaza*, 62. See also Juan Pedro Viqueira Albán, *Propriety and Permissiveness in Bourbon Mexico*, trans. Sonya Lipsett-Rivera and Sergio Rivera Ayala (Wilmington, DE: Scholarly Resources, 1999), 109–10.
54. Sonya Lipsett-Rivera, "The Intersection of Rape and Marriage in Late-Colonial and Early-National Mexico," *Colonial Latin American Historical Review* 6, no. 4 (November 1997): 559–90; Lipsett-Rivera, *Gender*, 222–24.

55. AGN, Criminal, vol. 667, fols. 184–93, Mexico City, 1793; AGN-TSJDF, Colonial Alcaldes Ordinarios, Criminal, box 32B, exp. 95, Mexico City, 1792.

56. Lipsett-Rivera, *Gender*, 221–27.

57. AGN-TSJDF, Colonial Alcaldes Ordinarios, Criminal, box 31B, exp. 115, Mexico City, 1776.

58. AGN-TSJDF, Colonial Alcaldes Ordinarios, Civil, box 27B, exp. 54, Mexico City, 1806.

59. The original reads "no pensase que se los daba para lo quisiera por cosa mala sino porque lo quería mucho y contemplaba que era un hombre formado." AGN-TSJDF, Colonial Juzgados Especiales, Auditor de Guerra, box 13A, exp. 117, fols. 17v–19v, Mexico City, 1803.

60. Zeb Tortorici, "'Heran Todos Putos': Sodomitical Subcultures and Disordered Desire in Early Colonial Mexico," *Ethnohistory* 54, no. 1 (Winter 2007): 37–38.

61. Gonzalbo Aizpuru, *Vivir*, 288.

62. AGN-TSJDF, Colonial Alcaldes Ordinarios, Criminal, box 33A, exp. 18, Mexico City, 1797.

63. AGN, Criminal, vol. 222, fols. 159–83, Chalco, 1807.

64. Robles, *Diario*, 3:111.

65. AGN-TSJDF, Colonial Alcaldes Ordinarios, Criminal, box 32B, exp. 95, Mexico City, 1792.

66. Taylor, *Honor and Violence*, 113; Quintana, *Confesionario*, 59–61.

67. AGN, Criminal, vol. 573, fols. 136–54, Mexico City, 1805. On the symbolism of hair, see Lipsett-Rivera, *Gender*, 151–57, 233–48.

68. AGN-TSJDF, Colonial Corregidores (Coyoacán), Criminal, box 28B, exp. 102, Mexico City, 1789.

69. AGN-TSJDF, Colonial Corregidores (Coyoacán), Criminal, box 29A, exp. 86, Mexico City, 1749.

70. AGN-TSJDF Colonial Alcaldes Ordinarios, Criminal, box 31B, exp. 105, Mexico City, 1763; AGN-TSJDF Colonial Alcaldes Ordinarios, Criminal, box 31B, exp. 115, Mexico City, 1776.

71. Twinam, *Public Lives*, 74; Lavrin, "Sexuality," 59–60; Tortorici, *Sins*, 89. Letter writing among young people was discouraged by some because it led to secret affairs. Father Gaspar de Astete, *Tratado del buen govierno de la familia y estado de las viudas y doncellas* (Burgos, Spain: Juan Baptista Varedio, 1603), 170–71. Juan Antonio Castel sent a message through a servant offering a relationship. AGN-TSJDF, Colonial Alcaldes Ordinarios, Criminal, box 31B, exp. 115, Mexico City, 1776.

72. AGN, Criminal, vol. 131, fols. 149–53, Mexico City, 1763.

73. AGN, Criminal, vol. 475, fols. 37–49, Mexico City, 1801; AGN-TSJDF, Colonial Alcaldes Ordinarios, Criminal, box 33A, exp. 26, Mexico City, 1801. For a series of love letters that all begin with *Mi alma* (My soul), see AGN, Clero Regular y Secular, vol. 145, exp. 9, fols. 230–77, Mexico City, 1784. When a relationship

soured, the letters exchanged between the lovers became a bone of contention. AGN-TSJDF, Colonial Alcaldes Ordinarios, Civil, box 27B, exp. 54, Mexico City, 1806.

74. AGN, Criminal, vol. 119, fols. 320–42, Actopan, 1791.

75. AGN-TSJDF, Colonial Alcaldes Ordinarios, Criminal, box 32B, exp. 95, Mexico City, 1792; AGN-TSJDF, Colonial Alcaldes Ordinarios, Criminal, box 32A, exp. 21, Mexico City, 1785; AGN-TSJDF, Colonial Alcaldes Ordinarios, Criminal, box 31B, exp. 105, Mexico City, 1763; AGN-TSJDF, Colonial Corregidores, Criminal, box 17A, exp. 2, Mexico City, 1796.

76. AGN-TSJDF, Colonial Alcaldes Ordinarios, Criminal, box 31B, exp. 105, Mexico City, 1763; AGN-TSJDF, Colonial Alcaldes Ordinarios, Criminal, box 31B, exp. 115, Mexico City, 1776; AGN-TSJDF, Colonial Corregidores (Coyoacán), Criminal, box 28B, exp. 102, Mexico City, 1789; AGN, Clero Regular y Secular, vol. 641, fols. 40–63, Mexico City, 1786.

77. AGN-TSJDF, Colonial Alcaldes Ordinarios, Criminal, box 31B, exp. 115, Mexico City, 1776; AGN-TSJDF, Colonial Corregidores, Criminal, box 16B, exp. 106, Mexico City, 1795.

78. Lavrin, "Sexuality," 47–92.

79. AGN-TSJDF, Colonial Alcaldes Ordinarios, Criminal, box 31B, exp. 115, Mexico City, 1776.

80. Kathryn A. Sloan, *Runaway Daughters: Seduction, Elopement, and Honor in Nineteenth-Century Mexico* (Albuquerque: University of New Mexico Press, 2008).

81. AGN, Criminal, vol. 364, fols. 1–40, Mexico City, 1803.

82. Noemí Quezada, *Sexualidad, amor y erotismo: México prehispánico y México colonial* (Mexico City: Universidad Nacional Autónoma de México, 1996), 233–34.

83. Joan Cameron Bristol, *Christians, Blasphemers, and Witches: Afro-Mexican Ritual Practice in the Seventeenth Century* (Albuquerque: University of New Mexico Press, 2007), 167; Noemí Quezada, *Amor, magia amorosa entre los aztecas: Supervivencia en el México colonial* (Mexico City: Universidad Nacional Autónoma de México, 1975), 101–2.

84. Quezada, *Sexualidad*, 102.

85. Rubial García, *Monjas*, 155. Quezada, *Sexualidad*, 238, notes that it was desirable for men to be good riders in order to be attractive to women.

86. Paredes, *Folklore*, 215; Schwaller, "La Identidad," 68.

87. Schwaller, "La Identidad," 67, writes that the elites in New Spain found it difficult to circulate in the cities that did not have cobblestones, and thus they usually chose to use carriages. In 1577 the king promulgated a decree prohibiting residents of Mexico City and other cities from traveling in coaches and carriages because "the young of the country were losing their ability to ride horses." Eventually the loss of this ability could lead to the loss of the colonies

because men would not be able to defend the territories. Herón Pérez Martínez, "El caballo y la mujer en el refranero mexicano," *Relaciones* 26, no. 104 (Fall 2005): 182–83.

88. AGN-TSJDF, Colonial Corregidores (Coyoacán), Criminal, box 28B, exp. 81, Mexico City, 1769. In another instance, the fact that Marcos Nicolás took a woman with him on his horse's rump was considered an indication of their sexual liaison. AGN, Criminal, vol. 111, fols. 168–235, Mexico City, 1777. See also Lozano Armendares, *No codiciaras*, 84.

89. Federico Garza Carvajal, *Butterflies Will Burn: Prosecuting Sodomites in Early Modern Spain and Mexico* (Austin: University of Texas Press, 2003), 18, 62–63, 66, 68.

90. Fray Thomas de Trujillo, *Libro Llamado Reprobación de Trajes, Con un Tratado de Lymosnas* (Navarre: n.p., 1563), 94v. Garza Carvajal, *Butterflies*, 66, refers to Fray Pedro de León.

91. Rubial García, *Monjas*, 56.

92. Rubial García, *La plaza*, 97. Artisans, mulattoes, and freed slaves tended to imitate Spanish forms of dress. Rubial García, *Monjas*, 56.

93. AGN, Criminal, vol. 564, fols. 19–143, Mexico City, 1801.

94. Galindo, *Parte segunda*, 241; Osuna, 132; Gruzinski, "Ashes of Desire"; Martínez, "Sex and the Colonial Archive." For a case in which a mulatto dressed as a woman was whipped, see Rubial García, *La plaza*, 73.

95. AGN, Criminal, vol. 677, fols. 243–273v, Cuautitlan, 1778.

96. Peter Boyd-Bowman, "Los nombres de pila en México desde 1540 hasta 1950," *Nueva Revista de Filología Hispánica* 19 (1970): 48. In this exhaustive study of Mexican baptismal names from 1540 to 1950, Boyd-Bowman did not encounter the male name of Susano once, and he found its female version only in 1952. Lidia Becker, a historical linguistics expert, found three instances of the name Susano in eleventh-century Spain publications (personal communication).

97. Robert McKee Irwin, *Mexican Masculinities* (Minneapolis: University of Minnesota Press, 2003), 47. Before the twentieth century, Mexicans appreciated the hombre de bien over the macho.

98. AGN-TSJDF, Colonial Alcaldes Ordinarios, Criminal, box 35b, exp. 80, Mexico City, 1803.

99. AGN-TSJDF, Colonial Alcaldes Ordinarios, Criminal, box 35A, exp. 18, Mexico City, 1785; AGN, Criminal, vol. 490, fols. 2–32, Mexico City, 1804; Pete Sigal, ed., "Gendered Power, the Hybrid and Homosexual Desire in Late Colonial Yucatan," in *Infamous Desire: Male Homosexuality in Colonial Latin America* (Chicago: University of Chicago Press, 2003), 104. The term *puto* referred to an effeminate male who was anally penetrated.

100. AGN-TSJDF, Colonial, Hojas sueltas, section 4A, box 106, exp. 129, Mexico City, 1722. Tortorici, *Sins*, mentions that nonconsensual anal sex occurred more often between an older man and a youth.

101. Ana María Atondo Rodríguez, *El amor venal y la condición femenina en el México colonial* (Mexico City: Instituto Nacional de Antropología e Historia, 1992), 108.

102. Gonzalbo Aizpuru, *Vivir*, 289. Tortorici, *Sins*, 82–83, writes that the places of sexual encounters were often chosen for privacy, but not always. See also AGN-TSJDF, Colonial Alcaldes Ordinarios, Criminal, box 31B, exp. 115, Mexico City, 1776, in which doña María Ignacia Garrote explains that her mother gave her seducer access to the family home.

103. Ferrer, *Suma Moral*, 417. French moralists similarly recommended a separate sleeping space for a married couple, keeping children out of the conjugal bed. Michelle Perrot, *Historia de las alcobas*, trans. Ernesto Junquera (Mexico City: Fondo de Cultura Económica, 2011), 54.

104. Perrot, *Historia de las alcobas*, 47, 48, 49, 53.

105. AGN-TSJDF, Colonial Alcaldes Ordinarios, Criminal, box 31B, exp. 81, Mexico City, 1696; AGN-TSJDF, Colonial Alcaldes Ordinarios, Criminal, box 31B, exp. 106, Mexico City, 1763; AGN-TSJDF, Colonial Alcaldes Ordinarios, Criminal, box 35A, exp. 38, fols. 1–20, Mexico City, 1791. Bennett, *Colonial Blackness*, 25, reports that in a 1569 raid of the home of the free mulatto, Jusepe de la Cruz, he was found nude with a woman named Melchora.

106. Twinam, *Public Lives*, 78.

107. Lozano Armendares, "Las sinrazones," 93, 101.

108. AGN-TSJDF, Colonial Alcaldes Ordinarios, Criminal, box 33A, exp. 1, Mexico City, 1793. See also AGN-TSJDF, Colonial Alcaldes Ordinarios, Criminal, box 34A, exp. 8, Mexico City, 1810.

109. AGN, Criminal, vol. 455, fols. 198–219, Mexico City, 1783. In another case, don Vicente Ortiz complained that he contracted an esponsales with his employer's daughter and was consequently fired and kicked out of the house. AGN-TSJDF, Colonial Corregidores, Civil, box 13B, exp. 90, Mexico City, 1791. See also AGN, Criminal, vol. 556, fols. 61–74, Mexico City, 1798.

110. AGN-TSJDF, Colonial Corregidores (Coyoacán), Criminal, box 28B, exp. 102, Mexico City, 1789.

111. AGN, Criminal, vol. 111, fols. 168–235, Mexico City, 1777; AGN, Criminal, vol. 252, fols. 399–406, Chalco, 1802.

112. AGN-TSJDF, Colonial Corregidores, Criminal, box 16B, exp. 92, Mexico City, 1791.

113. AGN, Criminal, vol. 411, fols. 25–55, Mexico City, 1806.

114. AGN-TSJDF, Colonial Corregidores (Coyoacan), Criminal, box 29A, exp. 86, Mexico City, 1749.

115. AGN-TSJDF, Colonial Corregidores, Criminal, box 17B, exp. 96, Mexico City, 1802.

116. AGN, Criminal, vol. 495, fols. 130–48, Mexico City, 1807. They also said that they communicated in the streets.

117. AGN, Criminal, vol. 367, fols. 385–456, Mexico City, 1797.

118. Viqueira Albán, *Propriety*, 100, notes that courtship between men and women took place in the streets.

119. AGN-TSJDF, Colonial Alcaldes Ordinarios, Criminal, box 32A, exp. 21, Mexico City, 1785. In another case, the relationship between don Alonso Alvárez Cordero and his servant was confirmed in the minds of witnesses because he expressed jealousy over her and took her out to pasear. AGN, Criminal, vol. 624, fols. 214–305, Mexico City, 1778.

120. AGN-TSJDF, Colonial Alcaldes Ordinarios, Criminal, box 35A, exp. 34, fols. 1–35, Mexico City, 1790.

121. AGN, Criminal, vol. 407, fols. 209–27, Mexico City, 1809.

122. AGN, Criminal, vol. 149, fols. 271–347, Tlacotepec, 1774.

123. Viqueira Alban, *Propriety*, 171; León Cázares, "A cielo abierto," 27. The paths were wide enough to allow the passage of carriages, litters, and riders.

124. Viqueira Alban, *Propriety*, 173–74. León Cázares, "A cielo abierto," 27, notes that it became a site for gallantry, preening of fashionable attire, duels, and love.

125. AGN-TSJDF, Colonial Alcaldes Ordinarios, Criminal, box 33A, exp. 26, Mexico City, 1801.

126. AGN, Criminal, vol. 595, fols. 29–40, Mexico City, 1805. For another example of such behavior, see Mehl, *Forced Migration*, 204.

127. Lipsett-Rivera, *Gender*, 225–26.

128. AGN-TSJDF, Colonial Juzgados Especiales, Auditor de Guerra, box 13A, exp. 117, Mexico City, 1803.

129. Rubial García, *La plaza*, 113.

130. Atondo Rodríguez, *El amor*, 241–42.

131. Ibid., 246–47.

132. AGN, Criminal, vol. 458, fols. 82–212, Mexico City, 1795.

133. Atondo Rodríguez, *El amor*, 265.

134. Patricio Hidalgo Nuchera, "Los 'malos usos' y la reglamentación de los temascales públicos mexicanos (1686–1691)," *Anuario de Estudios Americanos* 69, no. 1 (January–June 2012): 92–93.

135. Quintana, *Confesionario*, 59–61.

136. Hidalgo Nuchera, "Los 'malos usos,'" 94, 105.

137. Lee Penyak, "Criminal Sexuality in Central Mexico, 1750–1850," PhD dissertation, University of Connecticut, Mansfield, 1993, 250; Tortorici, "Heran Todos Putos," 35–67; Víctor M. Macías-González, "The Bathhouse and Male Homosexuality in Porfirian Mexico," in *Masculinity and Sexuality in Modern Mexico*, ed. Víctor M. Macías-González and Anne Rubenstein (Albuquerque: University of New Mexico Press, 2012).

138. AGN-TSJDF, Colonial Alcaldes Ordinarios, Criminal, box 32B, exp. 81, Mexico City, 1791.

139. AGN, Criminal, vol. 91, fols. 57–90, Ecatepec, 1759; see also AGN, Criminal, vol. 50, fols. 354–57, Xochimilco, 1782.

140. AGN-TSJDF, Colonial Alcaldes Ordinarios, Criminal, box 35A, exp. 34, Mexico City, 1790.

141. AGN, Criminal, vol. 490, fols. 2–32, Mexico City, 1804. In Puebla, according to Archbishop Francisco Fabían y Fuero, the keeper of the bell tower charged people a fee to go into the bell tower, where they committed indecent acts—probably sex—and drank pulque. Francisco Fabián y Fuero, *Colección de providencias diocesanas del Obispado de Puebla de los Ángeles* (Puebla, Mexico: Real Seminario Palafoxiana, 1770), 225–26.

142. *Virtuous* meant not engaging in illicit relations. Twinam, *Public Lives*, 83, defines illicit relations as those begun without the promise of marriage.

143. Lavrin, "La sexualidad," 497, 499; Quezada, *Sexualidad*, 239, 247.

144. Fabián y Fuero, *Colección*, 451–52, stated in one of his edicts that the night was "when the Prince of Darkness exerts his maximum power." See also Lipsett-Rivera, *Gender*, 130–33. Mehl, *Forced Migration*, 164, writes that infractions were considered more serious if the offenders were caught at night.

145. Rubial García, *La plaza*, 42.

146. Atondo Rodríguez, *El amor*, 235–36.

147. AGN-TSJDF, Colonial Alcaldes Ordinarios, box 23B, exp. 70, Mexico City, 1790.

148. AGN, Clero Regular y Secular, vol. 57, exp. 2, fols. 148–56, Mexico City, 1796.

149. AGN-TSJDF, Colonial Corregidores, Criminal, box 16B, exp. 85, Mexico City, 1791.

150. AGN-TSJDF, Colonial Corregidores, Criminal, box 17A, exp. 11, Mexico City, 1796.

151. Atondo Rodríguez, *El amor*, 232–34.

152. AGN-TSJDF, Colonial Alcaldes Ordinarios, Criminal, box 31B, exp. 62, Mexico City, 1696.

153. Atondo Rodríguez, *El amor*, 27, 38, 41, 44. On the Church's position on prostitution, see also Sergio Ortega Noriega, "Teología novohispano sobre el matrimonio y comportamientos sexuales, 1519–1570," 19–46, in *De la santidad a la perversión o de porqué no cumplía la ley de Dios en la sociedad novohispano* (Mexico City: Grijalbo, 1986), 37. Official attitudes did condemn pimping and procuring. Thus it was insulting to be called a *lenon* (pimp) or an *alcahuete* (procurer). AGN-TSJDF, Colonial Alcaldes Ordinarios, Criminal, box 33B, exp. 53, fols. 1–4, Mexico City, 1809.

154. AGN-TSJDF, Colonial Corregidores, Criminal, box 16B, exp. 53, Mexico City, 1678.

155. Atondo Rodríguez, *El amor*, 42, 273.

156. AGN-TSJDF, Colonial Alcaldes Ordinarios, Criminal, box 31A, exp. 12, Mexico City, 1631.

157. Atondo Rodríguez, *El amor*, 139.

158. AGN, Criminal, vol. 407, fols. 209–27, Mexico City, 1809.

159. AGN, Criminal, vol. 715, fols. 81–94, Mexico City, 1779.

160. Atondo Rodríguez, *El amor*, 111. Von Germeten, *Violent Delights*, 91, remarks that sex was part of public rivalries.

161. Ochoa, "Por faltar," 360, reports that a man who was caught in an illicit relationship argued that her husband could not support her financially, but he could. See also AGN, Criminal, vol. 556, fols. 75–98, Mexico City, 1798.

162. AGN, Criminal, vol. 408, fols. 346–67, Mexico City, 1809.

163. Atondo Rodríguez, *El amor*, 82, 97, 273, 276, calls this type of prostitution "domestic procuring." See also Marcela Suárez Escobar, *Sexualidad y norma sobre lo prohibido: La ciudad de México y las postrimerías del virreinato* (Mexico City: Universidad Autónoma Metropolitana, 1999), 195.

164. AGN, Criminal, vol. 421, fols. 25–39, Mexico City, 1810.

165. AGN, Criminal, vol. 88, fols. 242–68, Mexico City, 1810.

166. Sonya Lipsett-Rivera, "'If I Can't Have Her, No One Else Can': Jealousy and Violence in Mexico," in *Emotions and Daily Life in Colonial Mexico*, ed. Javier Villa-Flores and Sonya Lipsett-Rivera (Albuquerque: University of New Mexico Press, 2014), 66–86.

167. Robles, *Diario*, 1:265.

168. Susan Socolow, "Women and Crime: Buenos Aires, 1757–1797," *Journal of Latin American Studies* 12, no. 1 (February 1980): 45–46.

169. AGN-TSJDF, Colonial Corregidores (Coyoacán), Criminal, box 29A, exp. 2, Coyoacán, 1808.

170. AGN, Criminal, vol. 630, fols. 281–286v, Cuautitlan, 1760. José Leal, a worker in the Royal Mint, complained of the treatment given to the wife of one of his fellow workers. He argued that as a married woman she was owed "much honor." AGN, Criminal, vol. 718, fols. 269–77, Mexico City, 1809.

171. For a discussion of this insult and its implications, see Sonya Lipsett-Rivera, "Scandal at the Church: José de Alfaro Accuses Doña Theresa Bravo and Others of Insulting and Beating His *Castiza* Wife, Josefa Cadena (Mexico, 1782)," in *Colonial Lives. Documents on Latin American History, 1550–1850*, ed. Richard Boyer and Geoffrey Spurling (New York: Oxford University Press, 2000), 216–23.

172. AGN-TSJDF, Colonial Corregidores (Coyoacán), Criminal, box 28B, exp. 117, Mexico City, 1804.

173. AGN-TSJDF, Colonial Juzgados Especiales, Auditor de Guerra, box 20, exp. 185, Mexico City, 1809; see also AGN, Criminal, vol. 481, fols. 2–15, Mexico City, 1798.

174. AGN-TSJDF, Colonial Alcaldes Ordinarios, Criminal, box 35B, exp. 63, Mexico City, 1798; AGN-TSJDF, Colonial Alcaldes Ordinarios, Criminal, box 33B, exp. 52, Mexico City, 1809. Joseph Narvaez, a free mulatto, wounded Melchor de los Reyes for talking to a woman he knew in a doorway. AGN-TSJDF, Colonial Alcaldes Ordinarios, Criminal, box 31A, exp. 53, Mexico City, 1665.

175. AGN, Criminal, vol. 571, fols. 294–302, Mexico City; 1794; AGN, Criminal, vol. 412, fols. 24–56, Mexico City, 1805.

176. AGN, Criminal, vol. 362, fols. 235–81, Mexico City, 1802.

177. AGN, Criminal, vol. 694, fols. 71–176, Mexico City, 1803.

178. AGN, Criminal, vol. 678, fols. 82–90v, Mexico City, 1722; Von Germeten, *Violent Delights*, 54, 70.

179. Lipsett-Rivera, "'If I Can't Have Her,'" 66–86.

Chapter 4

1. AGN, Criminal, vol. 177, fol. 468, Tlalnepantla, 1748.

2. There were often tensions around participation or nonparticipation in these communal projects, especially around irrigation. AGN, Criminal, vol. 1, fols. 423–66, Chalco, 1801; AGN, Criminal, vol. 630, fols. 198–207, Cuautitlan, 1740; AGN, Criminal, vol. 232, fols. 222–42, Coyoacán 1809; AGN, Criminal, vol. 649, fols. 279–282v, Cuautitlan, 1792; AGN, Criminal, vol. 267, fols. 206–7, Cuautitlan, 1729.

3. Mehl, *Forced Migration*, 162–64.

4. Córdoba, *Jardín*, pt. 2, chap. 3; Escobar, *Sexualidad*, 199; Santos, *Cleansing Honor*, 118.

5. Anonymous, *Breve instrucción*, xi; Pedro Galindo, *Excelencias de la castidad y virginidad* (Madrid: Matheo de Espinosa y Arteaga, 1681), 5v.

6. AGN, Criminal, vol. 538, fol. 108v, Mexico City, 1808.

7. AGN, Criminal, vol. 399, fol. 142, Amecameca, 1800.

8. Mark Burkholder, "Honor and Honors in Colonial Spanish America," in *The Faces of Honor: Sex, Shame, and Violence in Colonial Latin America*, ed. Lyman Johnson and Sonya Lipsett-Rivera (Albuquerque: University of New Mexico Press, 1998), 27–28.

9. AGN, Criminal, vol. 134, fols. 80–110, Mexico City, 1801.

10. Viqueira Albán, *Propriety*, 97, writes that at end of the colonial period, Mexico City's population was 137,000, of which about four-fifths (about 110,000) was plebeian, and about 15,000 lived from begging or other less respectable occupations.

11. R. Douglas Cope, "Los ámbitos laborales urbano," in *Historia de la vida cotidiana en México*, vol. 2, *La ciudad barroca*, ed. Antonio Rubial García (Mexico City: El Colegio de México, 2005), 412; R. Douglas Cope, *The Limits of Racial Domination: Plebeian Society in Colonial Mexico City, 1660–1720* (Madison: University of Wisconsin Press, 1994), 87.

12. AGN, Criminal, vol. 159, fols. 73–93, Chalco, 1808.

13. AGN, Criminal, vol. 496, fols. 159–202, Mexico City, 1808. One of the witnesses in this proceeding was another soldier who was in charge of rounding up the poor; he reported having been attacked by a group of men earlier in the year.

14. Frank Trey Proctor III, "Afro-Mexican Slave Labor in the Obrajes de Paños of New Spain, Seventeenth and Eighteenth Centuries," *Americas* 60, no. 1 (2003): 35;

Richard Greenleaf, "The Obraje in the Late Mexican Colony," *Americas* 23, no. 3 (1967): 227–50; Seijas, *Asian Slaves*, 110.

15. AGN-TSJDF, Corregidores Coyoacán, Criminal, box 28B, exp. 19, Coyoacán, 1722.

16. Cope, "Los ámbitos," 416; Cope, *Limits*, 90.

17. Herman L. Bennett, *Africans in Colonial Mexico: Absolutism, Christianity, and Afro-Creole Consciousness, 1570–1640* (Bloomington: Indiana University Press, 2003), 20–21; Felipe Castro Gutiérrez, *Historia Social de la Real Casa de Moneda de México* (Mexico City: Universidad Nacional Autónoma de México, 2012), 140–41.

18. Cope, *Limits*, 88–89; Bennett, *Africans*, 18, 20–21. Because slaves had traditionally been domestic servants, there seems to have been a continued tradition for free black or mulattos to work in domestic service. Ben Vinson III, "From Dawn till Dusk: Black Labor in Late Colonial Mexico," in *Black Mexico: Race and Society from Colonial to Modern Times*, ed. Ben Vinson III and Matthew Restall (Albuquerque: University of New Mexico Press, 2009), 110. See also Seijas, *Asian Slaves*, 119; and Pilar López Bejarano, "Dinámicas mestizas: Tejiendo en torno a la jerarquía, al trabajo y al honor; Nueva Granada, siglo XVIII," *Nuevo Mundo*, February 17, 2008, http://nuevomundo.revues.org/19263.

19. Cope, *Limits*, 95–96; Bennett, *Africans*, 18; López Bejarano, "Dinámicas mestizas," 14.

20. Cope, *Limits*, 96–97.

21. Clara Elena Suárez Argüello, "Los arrieros novohispanos," in *Trabajo y sociedad en la historia de México: Siglos XVI-XVIII*, ed. Gloria Artís Espriu (Mexico City: CIESAS, 1992), 98–99.

22. Vinson, "From Dawn," 106, 110.

23. Felipe Castro Gutiérrez, "Salud, enfermedad y socorro mutuo en la Real Casa de Moneda de México," *Historia Social* 63, no. 1 (2009): 3–17; Pérez Toledo, *Los Hijos*, 53, 57, 65–66, 69–70. Workers at the Royal Tobacco Manufactory and the Royal Mint also had a mutual benefit society called La Concordia, which provided limited sick pay and funeral insurance. Susan Deans-Smith, "The Working Poor and the Eighteenth-Century Colonial State: Gender, Public Order, and Work Discipline," in *Rituals of Rule, Rituals of Resistance: Public Celebrations and Popular Culture in Mexico*, ed. William Beezley, William French, and Cheryl Martin (Wilmington, DE: Scholarly Resources, 1994), 51; Castro Gutiérrez, *Historia Social*, 170.

24. Castro Gutiérrez, *Historia Social*, 155, 159.

25. Deans-Smith, "Working Poor," 51–52. Martín, "La desnudez," 279, notes that guarda faroleros, Royal Mint employees, and Royal Tobacco Manufactory workers all had to present themselves for work in decent garb.

26. Robles, *Diario*, 1:28. Cañeque, *King's Living Image*, 94, writes about the political consequences of this symbolic confrontation.

27. Cañeque, *King's Living Image*, 119, 123.
28. Fisher, "Keeping and Losing," 168–97.
29. AGN, Criminal, vol. 624, fols. 129–213, Mexico City, 1657.
30. Norman Martín, *Los Vagabundos en la Nueva España, siglo XVI* (Mexico City: Jus, 1957), 7.
31. Ibid., 64–66, 107–9, 115.
32. Burkholder, "Honor and Honors," 19–20; López Bejarano, "Dinámicas mestizas," 10. Taylor, *Honor and Violence*, 111, notes that Spanish men's reputations in the Golden Age were linked to their trades and any offices they held.
33. Castro Gutiérrez, *Historia Social*, 128, 140.
34. AGN, Criminal, vol. 602, fols. 48–56, Mexico City, 1732; AGN, Criminal, vol. 730, fol. 375, Azcapotzalco, 1726. There was a similar dynamic among some muleteers. A plaintiff believed that the indigenous workers owed him respect because of his Spanish background, even though they were all doing the same work. AGN, Criminal, vol. 177, fols. 348–56, Tlanepantla, 1739.
35. Charlene Villaseñor Black, *Creating the Cult of St. Joseph: Art and Gender in the Spanish Empire* (Princeton, NJ: Princeton University Press, 2006), 121–22, 131; López Bejarano, "Dinámicas mestizas," 13.
36. Villaseñor Black, *Creating the Cult*, 117, 119.
37. Ibid., 117, 130.
38. Don Antonio Xavier Pérez y López, *Discurso sobre la Honra y deshonra legal*, 2nd ed. (Madrid: Real, 1786), 16–18.
39. AGN, Criminal, vol. 265, fols. 190–192v, Cuautitlan, 1779. For other insults or disrespect to a man's empleo, see AGN, Criminal, vol. 565, fols. 260–305, Mexico City, 1794; AGN, Criminal, vol. 272, fols. 200–220v, Chalco, 1780; AGN-TSJDF, Colonial Alcaldes Ordinarios, Criminal, box 35A, exp. 15, Mexico City, 1785; and Taylor, *Honor and Violence*, 128.
40. Respect for royal authority, especially on the part of plebeians, was very important. Thus many witnesses talk about the need to protect this inherent respect and to quash conduct that was insulting or irreverent to royal authority and its representatives. AGN, Criminal, vol. 266, fols. 154–159v, Tlanepantla, 1724; AGN, Criminal, vol. 165, fols. 224–242, Escapusalco, 1641; AGN, Criminal, vol. 155, fols. 311–314v, Xochimilco, 1796.
41. AGN-TSJDF, Colonial Alcaldes Ordinarios, Criminal, box 35A, exp. 13, fols. 1–6, Mexico City, 1785.
42. AGN-TSJDF, Colonial Alcaldes Ordinarios, Criminal, box 35A, exp. 2, Mexico City, 1784. A similar complaint about insults to a noble official occurred between the subdelegate of Otumba and the assistant priest. AGN, Clero Regular y Secular, vol. 217, exp. 18, fols. 273–90, Otumba, 1808. In 1795 don Guillermo Brixis stated that he considered his actions in light of the "dignity of his post." AGN, Criminal, vol. 458, fol. 117, Mexico City, 1795.
43. AGN, Criminal, vol. 538, fols. 62–62v, Mexico City, 1808.

44. AGN, Criminal, vol. 487, fols. 46–47, Mexico City, 1804.

45. Castro Gutiérrez, *Historia Social*, 123.

46. Ibid., 51.

47. Deans-Smith, "Working Poor," 54.

48. Castro Gutiérrez, *Historia Social*, 73.

49. Villaseñor Black, *Creating the Cult*, 121.

50. Arrom, *Women*, 1985, 26. It helped that employers could also pay women less than men.

51. José Joaquin Fernández de Lizardi, *La Quijotita y su prima* (1818; repr., Mexico City: Porrua, 1967), 100–101.

52. Arrom, *Women*, 27.

53. Susan Deans-Smith, *Bureaucrats, Planters, and Workers: The Making of the Tobacco Monopoly in Bourbon Mexico* (Austin: University of Texas Press, 1992), 174, 210.

54. Castro Gutiérrez, *Historia Social*, 140. I am extending the argument made by this author.

55. Ochoa, "Por faltar," 358–59.

56. Lipsett-Rivera, *Gender*, 181, 215.

57. AGN, Bienes Nacionales, vol. 874, exp. 7, Ixtacalco, 1833.

58. Archivo Judicial de Puebla, 1791, no. 5535, San Juan de los Llanos.

59. Sonya Lipsett-Rivera, "Marriage and Family Relations in Mexico during the Transition from Colony to Nation," in *State and Society in Spanish America during the Age of Revolution*, ed. Victor Uribe-Uran (Wilmington: Scholarly Resources, 2001), 138–41.

60. Johnson, *Workshop*, 52.

61. Castro Gutiérrez, *Historia Social*, 162. Johnson, *Workshop*, 61, describes the dignity of craft that came with mastering skills.

62. AGN-TSJDF, Colonial Corregidores, Criminal, box 16A, exp. 30, Mexico City, 1632.

63. AGN-TSJDF, Colonial Corregidores, Criminal, box 16A, exp. 35, Mexico City, 1632.

64. AGN, Criminal, vol. 716, fols. 70–77, Mexico City, 1751. For other incidents involving stores, peddlers, or business owners, see the following: AGN-TSJDF, Colonial Alcaldes Ordinarios, Criminal, box 31A, exp. 31, Mexico City, 1641; AGN-TSJDF, Colonial Corregidores, Criminal, box 18, Mexico City, 1661; AGN-TSJDF, Colonial Corregidores, Marquesado del Valle, box 30A, exp. 52, Coyoacán, 1752; AGN-TSJDF, Colonial Alcaldes Ordinarios, Criminal, box 33A, exp. 39, Mexico City, 1804; AGN, Criminal, vol. 465, fols. 220–28, Mexico City, 1794; AGN-TSJDF, Colonial Corregidores, Criminal, box 17B, exp. 133, Mexico City, 1800; AGN-TSJDF, Colonial Corregidores, Criminal, box 17A, exp. 17, Mexico City, 1797.

65. AGN, Criminal, vol. 266, fols. 160–161v, Azcapotzaltongo (Tacuba), 1801.

66. AGN, Criminal, vol. 737, fol. 42, Mexico City, 1803.

67. AGN, Criminal, vol. 718, fols. 63–69, Mexico City, 1807; AGN, Criminal, vol. 718, fols. 196–99, Mexico City, 1809.

68. Johnson, *Workshop*, 68.

69. AGN-TSJDF, Colonial Libros y Expedientes Diversos, Hojas sueltas, box 96, exp. 26, Mexico City, 1783; AGN, Criminal, vol. 155, fols. 205–46, Coyocán, 1808; AGN, Criminal, vol. 132, fol. 414, Mexicalcingo, 1788; AGN, Criminal, vol. 176, fols. 184–91, Tlanepantla, 1787. Another interesting conflict occurred on a farm in Atizapan in the Tlanepantla area. Don Manuel González, a Spanish farmer, told an indigenous woman that she was performing her task poorly and that she should leave. She refused and began insulting and attacking him; then her husband joined in the assault. AGN, Criminal, vol. 176, fols. 195–210, Atizapan (Tlanepantla), 1788.

70. AGN, Criminal, vol. 176, fol. 368, Tlanepantla, 1808.

71. Deans-Smith, *Bureaucrats*, 205.

72. Castro Gutiérrez, *Historia Social*, 162; Deans-Smith, *Bureaucrats*, 190.

73. Castro Gutiérrez, *Historia Social*, 126, 132.

74. Carrera Stampa, *Los gremios*, 34; Johnson, *Workshop*, 61.

75. Cope, *Limits*, 94.

76. Castro Gutiérrez, *Historia Social*, 162–63.

77. AGN, Criminal, vol. 649, fols. 121–30, Azcapotzalco, 1744. Stern, *Secret History*, 161–62, writes that men gained status by demeaning their inferiors.

78. AGN, Criminal, vol. 155, fols. 32–61, Xochimilco, 1797; AGN, Criminal, vol. 730, fol. 375, Azcapotzalco, 1726. Stern, *Secret History*, 164, writes of similar punishments that demeaned and feminized.

79. AGN, Criminal, vol. 266, fols. 154–59, Tlanepantla, 1724.

80. AGN, Criminal, vol. 176, fols. 64–67, Tlanepantla (Tacuba), 1793.

81. Lipsett-Rivera, *Gender*, 101.

82. James C. Scott, *Weapons of the Weak: Everyday Forms of Peasant Resistance* (New Haven, CT: Yale University Press, 1985).

83. AGN, Criminal, vol. 727, fols. 183–223, Mexico City, 1796.

84. AGN, Criminal, vol. 267, fol. 87, Coaspusalco (Tacuba), 1772. In a similar case, a supervisor began to beat María Andrea de Fuentes for gathering plants at the edge of a field. Her husband, a worker, objected that the official should not hit a married woman. In essence he was asking not only for respect for his wife but also for the customary rights that allowed his family to eat. AGN, Criminal, vol. 176, fols. 195–210, Atizapan (Tlanepantla), 1788.

85. Richard Boyer, "Honor among Plebeians: *Mala Sangre* and Social Reputation," in *The Faces of Honor: Sex, Shame, and Violence in Colonial Latin America*, ed. Lyman Johnson and Sonya Lipsett-Rivera (Albuquerque: University of New Mexico Press, 1998), 164–65.

86. Robert Weis, *Bakers and Basques: A Social History of Bread in Mexico* (Albuquerque: University of New Mexico, 2012), 16–17; Cope, "Los ámbitos," 409;

Manuel Carrera Stampa, "El Obraje Novohispano," *Boletín Historial* 54, no. 146 (June 1969): 27; Greenleaf, "Obraje," 241–42; Carmen Viqueira and José I. Urquiola, *Los Obrajes en la Nueva España, 1530–1630* (Mexico City: Consejo Nacional para la Cultura y las Artes, 1990), 191; AGN-TSJDF, Colonial Corregidores, Criminal, box 17A, exp. 23, Mexico City, 1797; AGN, Criminal, vol. 265, fols. 43–48, Tacuba, 1766; AGN, Criminal, vol. 163, fols. 280–85, Tacuba, 1749; AGN, Criminal, vol. 228, fols. 259–60, Tlalmanalco, 1792.

87. AGN-TSJDF, Colonial Corregidores, Criminal, box 16A, exp. 27, Mexico City, 1631.

88. Carrera Stampa, "El Obraje," 27.

89. AGN, Criminal, vol. 670, fols. 67–69, Mexico City, 1806.

90. AGN, Criminal, vol. 625, fols. 350–78, Mexico City, 1804. For another incident of drunkenness in a bakery, see AGN-TSJDF, Colonial Alcaldes Ordinarios, box 35A, exp. 1, Mexico City, 1784.

91. AGN-TSJDF, Colonial Corregidores, Criminal, box 17A, exp. 23, Mexico City, 1797.

92. Castro Gutiérrez, *Historia Social*, 126.

93. AGN, Criminal, vol. 132, fols. 13–16, Tacubaya, 1727. Workers in many spheres owed money to their employers. This was also the case for Chalco hacienda workers. AGN, Criminal, vol. 228, fols. 259–60, Tlalmanalco, 1792.

94. Weis, *Bakers*, 17.

95. AGN-TSJDF, Colonial Libros y Expedientes Diversos, Hojas sueltas, box 96, exp. 33, Coyoacán, 1785.

96. Greenleaf, "Obraje," 246–47; Viqueira and Urquiola, *Los Obrajes*, 191.

97. Malvido, "El abandono," 552. Parents or guardians frequently pawned their children's work when their debts were too big. Many custody battles over orphans were a result of accusations of exploiting the children's labor. Cheryl E. Martin, *Governance and Society in Colonial Mexico: Chihuahua in the Eighteenth Century* (Stanford, CA: Stanford University Press, 1996), 60.

98. Carrera Stampa, "El Obraje," 29.

99. AGN-TSJDF, Colonial Corregidores, Criminal, box 16B, exp. 67, Mexico City, 1726.

100. AGN, Criminal, vol. 265, fols. 197–99, Tacuba, 1785.

101. Suárez Argüello, "Los arrieros," 86–87, 94, 98; Ivonne Mijares Ramírez, "La mula en la vida cotidiana del siglo XVI," in *Caminos y mercados de México*, ed. Janet Long Towell and Amalia Attolini Lecón (Mexico City: Universidad Nacional Autónoma de México, 2010), 294.

102. AGN-TSJDF, Colonial, section 4A, Hojas sueltas, box 107, Coyoacán, 1754.

103. AGN-TSJDF, Colonial Corregidores, Marquesado del Valle, box 30A, exp. 67, Coyoacán, 1754; AGN, Criminal, vol. 177, fols. 221–22, San Luis Acayucan (Tlanepantla), 1750.

104. AGN, Criminal, vol. 266, fols. 154–159v, Tlanepantla, 1724. In Tacuba the

administrator of the Hacienda la Lechería confiscated two donkeys from Phelipe de la Cruz, an indigenous man. AGN, Criminal, vol. 163, fols. 296–302, Tacuba, 1749.

105. AGN, Criminal, vol. 177, fols. 348–56, Tlanepantla, 1739.

106. AGN, Criminal, vol. 50, fols. 17–19v, Xochimilco, 1782; AGN, Criminal, vol. 227, fols. 120–146v, Coatepec Chalco, 1810.

107. AGN, Criminal, vol. 267, fols. 190–205, Cuautitlan, 1791. Silverio Antonio, an indigenous man from Coatepec, suffered a similar fate at the hands of employees of the Hacienda de Soquiapa in the Chalco region. AGN, Criminal, vol. 227, fols. 120–146v, Coatepec Chalco, 1810.

108. AGN, Criminal, vol. 587, fols. 138–47, Mexico City, 1809.

109. Cope, "Los ámbitos," 414–15; Cope, *Limits*, 86.

110. Mehl, *Forced Migration*, 125.

111. AGN, Criminal, vol. 272, fols. 200–220v, Chalco, 1780.

112. AGN, Criminal, vol. 267, fols. 206–7, Cuautitlan, 1729.

113. Arrom, *Containing the Poor*.

114. Cope, *Limits*, 90; Castro Gutiérrez, *Historia Social*, 153.

115. Alexandra Shepard, "'Swil-bols and Tos-pots': Drink Culture and Male Bonding in England, c. 1560–1640," in *Love, Friendship, and Faith in Europe, 1300–1800*, ed. Laura Gowing, Michael Hunter, and Miri Rubin (London: Palgrave MacMillan, 2005), 121–24.

116. Deans-Smith, *Bureaucrats*, 209.

117. Castro Gutiérrez, *Historia Social*, 153.

118. Cope, *Limits*, 34.

119. Castro Gutiérrez, *Historia Social*, 153. Cope, *Limits*, 33, argues that plebeians were very reluctant to inform on other members of their class, showing a kind of solidarity among working people. On the importance of the solidarity of friends in work settings, see Sergio Lussana, "'No Band of Brothers Could Be More Loving': Enslaved Male Homosociality, Friendship, and Resistance in the Antebellum American South," *Journal of Social History* 46, no. 4 (Summer 2013): 872–95.

120. Castro Gutiérrez, *Historia Social*, 161. Robles, *Diario*, 3:82, mentions a worker nicknamed El Fundidor.

121. AGN, Criminal, vol. 154, fols. 175–203, Coyoacán, 1802. On the importance of joking in workshops, see Johnson, *Workshop*, 52.

122. AGN, Criminal, vol. 718, fols. 63–69, Mexico City, 1807; AGN, Criminal, vol. 155, fols. 205–46, Coyoacán, 1808; AGN, Criminal, vol. 625, fols. 350–78, Mexico City, 1804; AGN, Criminal, vol. 399, fols. 140–74, Amecameca, 1800.

123. AGN, Criminal, vol. 625, fol. 361, Mexico City, 1804.

124. AGN, Criminal, vol. 236, fols. 146–146v, Xochimilco, 1801.

125. AGN, Criminal, vol. 41, fols. 92–104, Milpa Alta, 1761; AGN, Criminal, vol. 40, fols. 488–501v, Xochimilco, 1810; AGN, Criminal, vol. 625, fols. 350–78, Mexico City, 1804.

Chapter 5

1. AGN-TSJDF, Colonial Corregidores, Criminal, box 17B, exp. 78, Mexico City, 1802.

2. Giovanni Gemelli Carreri, *Viaje a la Nueva España: México a fines del siglo XVII* (Mexico City: Ediciones Libro-Mex, 1955), 1:181.

3. Sandra Lauderdale Graham, *House and Street: The Domestic World of Servants and Masters in Nineteenth-Century Rio de Janeiro* (Austin: University of Texas Press, 1988); Daphne Spain, *Gendered Spaces* (Chapel Hill: University of North Carolina Press, 1992); Stern, *Secret History*; Nancy Van Deusen, *Between the Sacred and the Worldly: The Institutional and Cultural Practice of Recogimiento in Colonial Lima* (Stanford, CA: Stanford University Press, 2001); Kanter, *Hijos*, 52; Lipsett-Rivera, *Gender*.

4. Cordóba, *Jardín*, pt. 2, chap. 3.

5. Amar y Borbón, *Discurso*, xxxvi–xxxvii.

6. John Tosh, *A Man's Place: Masculinity and the Middle-Class Home in Victorian England* (New Haven: Yale University Press, 1999), 4. Although domesticity was gendered, both men and women had roles in its development. Karen Harvey, *The Little Republic: Masculinity and Domesticity in Eighteenth-Century Britain* (Oxford, UK: Oxford University Press, 2012), 8–12. Men have been absent from accounts of domesticity mostly because the emphasis of a previous generation of feminist historians has been on women. There has been a tendency to look at male authority in the household rather than their connection to the home as space or domestic nest. Karen Harvey, "Men Making Home: Masculinity and Domesticity in Eighteenth-Century Britain," *Gender and History* 21, no. 3 (November 2009): 521. For the argument that domesticity emerged earlier, achieved by women but affecting men as well, see Witold Rybczynski, *Home: A Short History of an Idea* (New York: Viking, 1986), 75.

7. Rybczynski, *Home*, 75.

8. Nancy Van Deusen, "Determining the Boundaries of Virtue: The Discourse of recogimiento among Women in Seventeenth-Century Lima," *Journal of Family History* 22, no. 4 (October 1997): 373.

9. Cerda, *Libro intitulado*, 321, emphasizes that it was important to make sure that all in the household were morally upright.

10. Tosh, *A Man's Place*, 27.

11. AGN-TSJDF, Colonial Alcaldes Ordinarios, box 23B, exp. 70, fols. 1–4, Mexico City, 1790. See in particular the testimony of don José Suleta and Florentino Granillo.

12. AGN, Criminal, vol. 129, fol. 2, Mexico, 1799.

13. Kanter, *Hijos*, 53.

14. AGN, Criminal, vol. 163, fol. 379, Tacuba, 1767.

15. AGN, Criminal, vol. 41, fol. 101, Milpa Alta, 1761.

16. AGN-TSJDF, Colonial Alcaldes Ordinarios, Criminal, box 31A, exp. 49, fol. 1v, Mexico City, 1661; AGN, Criminal, vol. 176, fol. 79, Tlanepantla, 1773.

17. AGN-TSJDF, Colonial Corregidores, Teniente General de Xochimilco, Criminal, box 31A, exp. 31, fol. 6v, Xochimilco, 1749.

18. AGN, Criminal, vol. 465, fol. 221, Mexico City, 1794.

19. AGN, Criminal, vol. 398, fols. 3–44, Mexico City, 1799; AGN, Criminal, vol. 624, fols. 62–72, Mexico City, 1756.

20. Escoiquiz, *Tratado*, 117–19.

21. Muchembled, *History*, 59, notes that the home was considered an inviolable sanctuary and that breaching the walls of a home at night was considered just cause for homicidal violence. See also Riitta Laitinen, "Home, Urban Space, and Gendered Practices in Mid-Seventeenth-Century Tukku," in *The Routledge History Handbook of Gender and the Urban Experience*, ed. Deborah Simonton (London: Routledge, 2017), 145.

22. AGN, Criminal, vol. 40, fols. 521R–522r, Churubusco, 1770; AGN, Criminal, vol. 222, fol. 72, Tlayacapa (Tlalmanalco), 1779; AGN-TSJDF, Colonial Corregidores, Marquesado del Valle, box 30A, exp. 31, fol. 2, Coyoacán, 1749; AGN-TSJDF, Colonial Alcaldes Ordinarios, Criminal, box 31A, exp. 12, fol. 2, Mexico City, 1631; AGN, Criminal, vol. 398, fol. 8, Mexico City, 1799.

23. AGN, Criminal, vol. 236, fol. 52, Coyoacán, 1767.

24. AGN, Criminal, vol. 163, fol. 388, Tacuba, 1767; AGN, Criminal, vol. 131, fols. 192–93, Xochimilco, 1809; AGN-TSJDF, Colonial Alcalde del Crimen, Criminal, box 47B, exp. 49, fol. 2, Mexico City, 1804; AGN, Criminal, vol. 398, fol. 8, Mexico City, 1799; AGN, Criminal, vol. 129, fol. 4, Mexico City, 1799; AGN, Criminal, vol. 111, fol. 341, Tacuba, 1786; AGN, Criminal, vol. 398, fol. 8, Mexico City, 1799; AGN, Criminal, vol. 672, fol. 103v, Mexico City, 1801.

25. AGN, Criminal, vol. 176, fol. 79, Tlanepantla, 1773; AGN, Criminal, vol. 132, exp. 2, fol. 8, Tacubaya, 1647; AGN-TSJDF, Colonial Alcaldes Ordinarios, Criminal, box 31A, exp. 12, Mexico City, 1631; AGN-TSJDF, Colonial Alcaldes Ordinarios, Criminal, box 31A, exp. 4, fol. 4, Mexico City, 1628.

26. Lipsett-Rivera, *Gender*, 75, 130–33.

27. AGN-TSJDF, Colonial Corregidores, Teniente General de Xochimilco, Criminal, box 31A, exp. 31, fol. 7v, Xochimilco, 1749.

28. AGN-TSJDF, Colonial Alcalde del Crimen, Criminal, box 47B, exp. 49, fol. 2v, Mexico City, 1804.

29. AGN-TSJDF, Colonial Alcaldes Ordinarios, Criminal, box 31A, exp. 14, fols. 1–1v, Mexico City, 1632.

30. AGN, Criminal, vol. 176, fols. 419–422v, Tlanepantla, 1748.

31. AGN, Criminal, vol. 29, fol. 266v, Xochimilco, 1799.

32. AGN-TSJDF, Colonial Corregidores, Marquesado del Valle, Criminal, box 30B, exp. 115, Tacubaya, 1757; AGN, Criminal, vol. 129, fols. 1–133, Mexico City, 1799.

33. Lipsett-Rivera, *Gender*, 94–99.

34. AGN-TSJDF, Colonial, section 4A, Hojas sueltas, box 106, exp. 54, fols. 1–2v, Mexico City, 1683.

35. AGN-TSJDF, Colonial Juzgados Especiales, Libros y Expedientes Sueltos, box 100, exp. 7, fols. 1–7, Mexico City, 1803.

36. AGN-TSJDF, Colonial Alcaldes Ordinarios, box 28A, exp. 33, fols. 1–3, Mexico City, 1809.

37. Lipsett-Rivera, *Gender*, 71–82.

38. AGN-TSJDF, Colonial Alcaldes del Crimen, Criminal, box 47B, exp. 39, Mexico City, 1801.

39. Kanter, *Hijos*, 53.

40. On the threshold as a transitional object that "has traditionally enjoyed an almost ritual significance," see Henri Lefebvre, *The Production of Space*, trans. Donald Nicholson-Smith (Oxford: Blackwell, 1991), 210. See also Laitinen, "Home," 147.

41. Christine Stansell, *City of Women: Sex and Class in New York, 1789–1860* (Urbana, IL: University of Chicago Press, 1983), 56. On warm summer nights the women living in New York City tenements would gather on their stoops and talk to one another. They would also hang out windows and spend the evenings outdoors. Sloan, *Runaway Daughters*, 114, recounts how one couple courted in the woman's doorway. See also Taylor, *Honor and Violence*, 144.

42. Undurraga Schüler, *Los Rostros*, 145.

43. Muchembled, *History*, 60.

44. Laura Gowing, *Domestic Dangers: Women, Words, and Sex in Early Modern London* (Oxford: Clarendon Press, 1996), 98.

45. AGN, Criminal, vol. 446, fol. 117, Mexico City, 1784–1785.

46. AGN-TSJDF, Colonial Alcaldes Ordinarios, Criminal, box 31A, exp. 4, fols. 2v–3, Mexico City, 1628.

47. AGN-TSJDF, Colonial Alcaldes Ordinarios, Criminal, box 35B, exp. 63, fol. 2v, Mexico City, 1798.

48. AGN-TSJDF, Colonial Corregidores, Marquesado del Valle, box 30A, exp. 29, fol. 5, Coyoacán, 1748.

49. AGN, Criminal, vol. 177, fol. 10, Tlanepantla, 1777.

50. AGN, Criminal, vol. 154, exp. 1, fol. 9v, Coyoacán, 1807; AGN, Criminal, vol. 715, fol. 18v, Mexico City, 1779; AGN, Criminal, vol. 227, fols. 245–46, Coatepec, 1742; AGN, Criminal, vol. 677, fol. 245v, Cuautitlan, 1778; AGN, Criminal, vol. 537, fols. 1–18, Cuautla, 1804.

51. AGN, Criminal, vol. 137, fols. 34–51, Coyoacán, 1790.

52. AGN, Criminal, vol. 456, fol. 157v, Mexico City, 1783; AGN, Criminal, vol. 706, fols. 294–303, Mexico City, 1804; AGN, Criminal, vol. 227, fols. 245–46, Coatepec, 1742.

53. AGN, Criminal, vol. 624, fols. 62–72, Mexico City, 1756.

54. AGN, Criminal, vol. 111, fols. 340–44, Tacuba, 1786; AGN, Criminal, vol. 274, fols. 219–26, Tlalmanalco, 1723; AGN, Criminal, vol. 40, fols. 519–29, Churubusco, 1770; AGN, Criminal, vol. 649, fols. 279–282v, Cuautitlan, 1792; AGN-TSJDF, Colonial Alcaldes Ordinarios, Criminal, box 35B, exp. 87, Mexico City, 1809; AGN, Criminal, vol. 76, fols. 1–194, Tacuba, 1803.

55. Jennine Hurl-Eamon, *Gender and Petty Violence in London, 1680–1720* (Columbus: Ohio State University Press, 2005), 86. In a slightly similar pattern, Londoners used the liminal space of the threshold to accentuate the insult of their violence, such as by dragging householders out of their home.

56. AGN, Criminal, vol. 624, fols. 62–72, Mexico City, 1756.

57. AGN, Criminal, vol. 660, fols. 160–83, Mexico City, 1752. For the account of a man who went to collect on a debt in the middle of the night, see AGN-TSJDF, Colonial Corregidores, Marquesado del Valle, box 30A, exp. 31, Coyoacán, 1749. For a complaint about a dead pig, see AGN-TSJDF, Colonial Corregidores, Teniente General de Xochimilco, Criminal, box 31A, exp. 31, Xochimilco, 1749.

58. AGN, Criminal, vol. 83, fols. 119–40, Mexico City, 1808.

59. Taylor, *Honor and Violence*, 46.

60. Kanter, *Hijos*, 53. For an account of the smearing of excrement on the door of a shopkeeper in 1808, see Eric Van Young, *The Other Rebellion: Popular Violence, Ideology and the Mexican Struggle for Independence, 1810–1821* (Stanford, CA: Stanford University Press, 2001), 450.

61. AGN-TSJDF, Colonial Alcalde del Crimen, Criminal, box 47A, exp. 24, fols. 1–12, Mexico City, 1801.

62. AGN, Criminal, vol. 567, fol. 187v, Mexico City, 1798.

63. Hurl-Eamon, *Gender*, 79; Robert Muchembled, *La violence au village: Sociabilité et comportements populaires en Artois du XVe au XVIIe siècle* (Turnhout, Belgium: Brepols, 1989), 147–54.

64. Robert B. Shoemaker, *The London Mob: Violence and Disorder in Eighteenth-Century England* (London: Hambledon, 2004), 53.

65. Pilar Gonzalbo Aizpuru, *Introducción a la historia de la vida cotidiana* (Mexico City: El Colegio de México, 2006), 178.

66. AGN-TSJDF, Colonial, section 4A, Hojas sueltas, box 107, fols. 1–1v, Tacubaya 1757. For businessmen and artisans, the streets in front of their locales were a literal extension, for it was customary for their products to spill out into the streets. Rubial García, *Monjas*, 62.

67. Curcio-Nagy, *Great Festivals*, 29, says that individual Mexicans generally participated in the festival occasions for parish saints on a local level. This procession undoubtedly fit into that scenario.

68. AGN, Criminal, vol. 2, fols. 276–311, Tlayacapa, 1786.

69. Rybczynski, *Home*, 26, notes that historically, only important people could sit on chairs.

70. Cañeque, *King's Living Image*, 149 (and 119 for controversies over the use of cushions at Mass). See also Marc Eagle, "Beard-Pulling and Furniture Rearranging: Conflict within the Seventeenth-Century Audiencia of Santo Domingo," *Americas* 68, no. 4 (April 2012): 467–93; and Rybczynski, *Home*, 82–83, who notes that the type of chair and placement were also important indicators of status.

71. AGN, Criminal, vol. 2, fols. 276–311, Tlayacapa, 1786. But the indigenous residents rebelled and forced Arizaga out, and they celebrated by playing the chirimías (a type of flute).

72. Richard Conway, "Lakes, Canoes, and the Aquatic Communities of Xochimilco and Chalco, New Spain," *Ethnohistory* 59, no. 3 (Summer 2012): 545. I would like to thank Richard Conway for clarifying the meaning of *compuerta* (sluicegate) in this context and the mechanisms of this passage from one lake to another.

73. AGN, Criminal, vol. 155, fols. 134–135v, Mexico City, 1766.

74. AGN, Criminal, vol. 131, fols. 311–41, Xochimilco, 1796.

75. AGN, Criminal, vol. 398, fols. 45–55, Mexico City, 1799. For another interesting case involving a garita guard, see AGN, Criminal, vol. 265, fols. 219–223v, Tacuba, 1790.

76. AGN, Criminal, vol. 154, exp. 1, fols. 1–100, Coyoacán, 1807.

77. AGN, Criminal, vol. 265, fols. 61–102, Tultitlan, 1753.

78. AGN, Criminal, vol. 232, fols. 243–307, Coyoacán, 1806.

79. AGN-TSJDF, Colonial, Hojas sueltas, section 4A, box 107, fol. 1, Mexico City, 1749. The theft of agricultural produce from fields was central to other cases. See AGN, Criminal, vol. 40, fols. 488–501v, Xochimilco, 1810; and AGN, Criminal, vol. 131, fols. 201–202v, Xochimilco, 1810.

80. For another example of a conflict between residents and people traveling on the camino real, see AGN, Criminal, vol. 232, fols. 308–13, Tacubaya, 1685.

81. AGN, Criminal, vol. 176, fol. 182, Tlanepantla, 1749.

82. AGN, Criminal, vol. 176, fols. 491–498v, Tlanepantla, 1752. For a case in which a farmer blocked access to a spring because of damage to some magueys that he had planted, see AGN, Criminal, vol. 236, fol. 116, Churubusco, 1782.

83. AGN, Criminal, vol. 265, fols. 61–102, Tultitlan, 1753.

84. AGN, Criminal, vol. 537, fols. 19–48, Cuautla, 1804; AGN, Criminal, vol. 737, fol. 42, Mexico City, 1803.

85. Rubial García, *Monjas*, 71; Gemelli Carreri, *Viaje*, 1:163.

86. Rubial García, *Monjas*, 63.

87. AGN, Criminal, vol. 727, fols. 13–24v, Mexico City, 1796; AGN, Criminal, vol. 129, fols. 1–133, Mexico City, 1799; AGN, Criminal, vol. 265, fols. 211–215v, Tacuba, 1793.

88. Rubial García, *Monjas*, 72.

89. Gemelli Carreri, *Viaje*, 1:163.

90. Ibid., 1:177. Rubial García, *Monjas*, 72, asserts that San Augustín de las Cuevas was a place of assignation for young men and women.

91. Rubial García, *Monjas*, 72; Gemelli Carreri, *Viaje*, 108, 161–62, 163.

92. Viqueira Albán, *Propriety*, 112.

93. León Cázares, "A cielo abierto," 27; Rubial García, *Monjas*, 73; Gemelli Carreri, *Viaje*, 1:182, 1:184.

94. Viqueira Albán, *Propriety*, 172; Fray Agustín de Vetancurt, "Tratado de la ciudad de México y las grandezas que la ilustran después que la fundaron los españoles," in *La Ciudad de México en el siglo XVIII (1690–1780): Tres crónicas*, ed. Antonio Rubial García (Mexico City: Consejo Nacional para la Cultura y las Artes, 1990), 45; Viera, "Breve Compendiossa," 259.

95. AGN, Criminal, vol. 609, fols. 252v–53, Mexico City, 1797. In 1796 three young plebeian men were walking in the Alameda and conversing when they ran into another group of young men and fought. AGN-TSJDF, Colonial Alcaldes Ordinarios, Criminal, box 35A, exp. 52, fols. 1–28, Mexico City, 1796.

96. Viqueira Albán, *Propriety*, 171–72.

97. Gemelli Carreri, *Viaje*, 1:177.

98. AGN, Criminal, vol. 564, fol. 37v, Mexico City, 1801.

99. AGN, Criminal, vol. 614, fols. 215–18, Mexico City, 1796.

100. AGN, Criminal, vol. 402, fols. 21–22v, Mexico City, 1801.

101. AGN-TSJDF, Colonial Corregidores, Marquesado del Valle, Criminal, box 30B, exp. 115, fols. 1–2, Tacubaya, 1757. Also in Tacubaya, a widow named Dominga Marsela reported that two men came to her house to drink pulque and drank in her oratory. AGN-TSJDF, Colonial Corregidores, Marquesado del Valle, Criminal, box 30A, exp. 75, Tacubaya, 1757.

102. AGN-TSJDF, Colonial Libros y Expedientes Diversos, Hojas sueltas, box 96, exp. 33, Coyoacán, 1785.

103. AGN, Criminal, vol. 398, fols. 3–44, Mexico, 1799.

104. AGN, Criminal, vol. 40, fols. 142–51, Coyoacán, 1805.

105. AGN, Criminal, vol. 613, fol. 8, Cuautla Amilpas, 1754.

106. Stern, *Secret History*, 178.

107. AGN, Criminal, vol. 272, fols. 200–220v, Chalco, 1780.

108. Alfredo Nava Sánchez, "La Voz descarnada: Un acercamiento al canto y al cuerpo en la Nueva España," in *Presencias y miradas del cuerpo en España la Nueva*, ed. Estela Roslló Soberón (Mexico City: Universidad Nacional Autónoma de México, 2011), 30–31; Alvaro Ochoa Serrano, *Mitote, fandango y mariacheros*, 2nd ed. (Zamora, Mexico: El Colegio de Michoacán, 2000), 18.

109. Andrew Cashner, "Playing Cards at the Eucharistic Table: Music, Theology, and Society in a Corpus Christi Villancico from Colonial Mexico, 1628," *Journal of Early Modern History* 18, no. 4 (2014): 384, 388; Lourdes Turrent, *Rito, música y poder en la Catedral Metropolitana México, 1790–1810* (Mexico City: El Colegio de México, 2013), 137.

110. Ajofrín, *Diario del viaje*, 80–81; Rubial Garcia, *Monjas*, 164–65; Ochoa Serrano, *Mitote*, 32. Fandangos could be held for many reasons, including the wake for a dead infant. AGN, Criminal, vol. 537, fols. 19–48, Cuautla, 1804.

111. Alejandro Martínez de la Rosa, "Las mujeres bravas del fandango: Tentaciones del infierno," *RelacionesEstudios de Historia y Sociedad* 34, no. 134 (Spring 2013): 117–19, 121, 123; Stern, *Secret History*, 173.

112. AGN, Criminal, vol. 617, fols. 72–86, Mexico City, 1800; AGN-TSJDF, Colonial Alcalde Mayor de Xochimilco, Criminal, box 32B, exp. 48, Xochimilco, 1795; AGN, Criminal, vol. 76, fols. 1–194, Tacuba, 1803; AGN, Criminal, vol. 40, fols. 142–51, Coyoacán, 1805; AGN, Criminal, vol. 235, fols. 220–23v, Xochimilco, 1780; AGN, Criminal, vol. 110, fols. 135–75, Tacuba, 1745; AGN, Criminal, vol. 398, fols. 3–44, Mexico City, 1799; AGN-TSJDF, Colonial Corregidores (Coyoacán), Criminal, box 29B, exp. 100, fols. 1–6, Coyoacán, 1754; Stern, *Secret History*, 174.

113. Katie Barclay, "Singing and Lower-Class Masculinity in the Dublin Magistrate's Court, 1800–1845," *Journal of Social History* 47, no. 3 (2014): 749, 755, 759. For the analysis of one such song, the Chuchumbé, see Sergio Rivera Ayala, "Dance of the People: The Chuchumbé (Mexico, 1766)," in *Colonial Lives: Documents on Latin American History, 1550–1850*, ed. Richard Boyer and Geoffrey Spurling (New York: Oxford University Press, 2000), 178–84.

114. AGN, Criminal, vol. 617, fols. 74v–75, 78v–79v, Mexico City, 1800; Ochoa Serrano, *Mitote*, 40–43.

115. AGN, Criminal, vol. 537, fols. 19–48, Cuautla, 1804.

116. Cashner, "Playing Cards," 394–95.

117. AGN, Criminal, vol. 228, fols. 205–205v, Chalco, 1801.

118. Javier Villa-Flores, "Reframing a 'Dark Passion': Bourbon Morality, Gambling, and the Royal Lottery in New Spain," in *Emotions and Daily Life in Colonial Mexico*, ed. Javier Villa-Flores and Sonya Lipsett-Rivera (Albuquerque: University of New Mexico Press, 2014), 148–67.

119. AGN-TSJDF, Colonial Corregidores (Coyoacán), Criminal, box 29B, exp. 89, fols. 1–29, Coyoacán, 1749.

120. AGN, Criminal, vol. 176, fols. 256–65, Tlanepantla, 1789. For other examples of playing rayuela, see AGN-TSJDF, Colonial Libros y Expedientes Diversos, Hojas sueltas, box 96, exp. 33, Coyoacán, 1785; and AGN, Criminal, vol. 455, fols. 19–29, Mexico City, 1781.

121. AGN, Criminal, vol. 699, fols. 366–432, Mexico City, 1796.

122. AGN, Criminal, vol. 399, fols. 140–74, Amecameca, 1800. For another example of men playing card games, see AGN-TSJDF, Colonial Corregidores (Coyoacán), Criminal, box 29B, exp. 89, fols. 1–29, Coyoacán, 1749.

123. AGN-TSJDF, Colonial Alcaldes Ordinarios, Criminal, box 31A, exp. 4, Mexico City, 1628; AGN, Criminal, vol. 565, fols. 328–50, Mexico City, 1794.

124. AGN, Criminal, vol. 265, fols. 211–215v, Tacuba, 1793. For a discussion of the suppression of card games and other entertainments, see Gabriel Haslip-Viera, *Crime and Punishment in Later Colonial Mexico City, 1692–1810* (Albuquerque: University of New Mexico Press, 1999), 63–64.

125. Rubial García, *Monjas*, 164.

126. AGN, Criminal, vol. 723, fols. 2–21, Mexico City,1777; AGN, Criminal, vol. 672, fols. 100–103v, Mexico City, 1759; AGN-TSJDF, Colonial Alcaldes Ordinarios, box 31B, exp. 97, Mexico City, 1740; AGN, Criminal, vol. 738, fols. 90–130, Mexico, 1764. The Church disapproved of cockfights. Viqueira Albán, *Propriety*, 6.

127. AGN, Criminal, vol. 76, fols. 1–194, Tacuba, 1803; AGN, Criminal, vol. 30, fols. 245–303, Mexico, 1786; AGN, Criminal, vol. 228, fols. 185–208, Chalco, 1801.

128. Stern, *Secret History*, 172–73.

129. AGN-TSJDF, Colonial Corregidores, Criminal, box 17B, exp. 78, Mexico City, 1802. Behind the viceregal palace in Mexico City, there was also a garden big enough to hold horse races and bullfights. Rubial García, *Monjas*, 125. The viceroy organized bullfights to amuse his young son. Gemelli Carreri, *Viaje*, 1:185–86.

130. AGN-TSJDF, Colonial Corregidores, Criminal, box 16B, exp. 109, Mexico City, 1795. The two men knocked over some young boys during their race and were reported for this reason. For an incident of a man riding fast along a road in a more rural area but also hitting a boy, see AGN, Clero Regular y Secular, vol. 28, exp. 1, fols. 1–29, Jilotepec, 1794. Two diarists report accidents between either racing horsemen or carriages: Robles, *Diario*, 3:243–44; and Guijo, *Diario, 1648–1664*, 208–9.

131. AGN-TSJDF, Colonial Corregidores, Criminal, box 17B, exp. 100, Mexico City, 1802.

132. AGN, Criminal, vol. 644, fols. 201–33, Mexico City, 1802.

133. José Álvarez del Villar, *Historia de la charrería* (Mexico City: Editorial Londres, 1941), 125–26. Natural scientist Manjit Kerr-Uppal tells me that pulling the tail of a cow will make her advance.

134. AGN, Criminal, vol. 134, fols. 80–110, Mexico City, 1801.

135. Pizzigoni, *Life Within*, 153, makes the point that it was mostly the male testators in her sample who had animals to bequeath.

136. Jesús Salvador Ávila González, "Voces y ladridos: Ensayo sobre los perros de la ciudad de México, siglos XVIII y XIX," PhD dissertation, Universidad Iberoamericano, Mexico City, 2007, 63; Robles, *Diario*, 2:140, 2:166 (on a bull attacking a cleric in San Antón); AGN, Criminal, vol. 672, fols. 100–103v, Mexico City, 1759.

137. See the discussion in Muchembled, *La violence au village*, 144, 150–160. Sonya Lipsett-Rivera. "A New Challenge: Social History and Dogs in the Era of Post-Humanism," http://socindiana.hypotheses.org/320, accessed July 15, 2016.

138. Anita Maurstad, Dona Davis, and Sarah Oelws, "Co-being and Intra-action in Horse–Human Relationships: A Multi-Species Ethnography of Be(com)ing Human and Be(com)ing Horse," *Social Anthropology* 21, no. 3 (August 2013): 322–35.

139. Cañeque, *King's Living Image*, 124–25. On the previous viceroy's injury as a result of a riding accident, see Robles, *Diario*, 3:12, 3:58.

140. Rubial García, *Monjas*, 119; Gemelli Carreri, *Viaje*, 1:110.

141. Antonio Rubial García, *El Paraíso de los elegidos: Una lectura de la historia cultural de la Nueva España (1521–1804)* (Mexico City: Universidad Nacional Autónoma de México, 2010), 65.

142. Daniel Roche, "Equestrian Culture in France from the Sixteenth to the Nineteenth Century," *Past and Present* 199, no. 1 (May 2008): 113–45.

143. Schwaller, "La Identidad," 67–68.

144. Gemelli Carreri, *Viaje*, 2:194–95.

145. Paredes, *Folklore*, 215.

146. AGN-TSJDF, Colonial Corregidores, Marquesado del Valle, box 30A, exp. 29, fols. 2–10, Coyoacán, 1748.

147. There are numerous examples of such conduct. AGN, Criminal, vol., 267, fols. 128–135v, Tacuba, 1733; AGN-TSJDF, Colonial, Hojas sueltas, section 4A, box 107, Mexico City, 1756; AGN, Criminal, vol. 176, fols. 64–67, Tlanepantla (Tacuba), 1793; AGN, Criminal, vol. 79, fols. 511–24, San Bartolomé Naucalpan (Tacuba), 1738.

148. Ávila González, "Voces y ladridos," 33, 115.

149. Muchembled, *La violence*, 159–64, writes at length about the relationship between men and their dogs.

150. AGN, Criminal, vol. 1, fols. 1–10, Chalco, 1776.

151. AGN, Criminal, vol. 235, fols. 17, Xochimilco, 1780; Arnaud Exbalin Oberto, "Perros asesinos y matanzas de perros en la ciudad de México (siglos XXI–XVIII)," *RelacionesEstudios de Historia y Sociedad* 35, no. 137 (2014): 100.

152. Zeb Tortorici, "'In the Name of the Father and the Mother of All Dogs': Canine Baptisms, Weddings, and Funerals in Bourbon Mexico," in *Centering Animals in Latin American History*, ed. Martha Few and Zeb Tororici (Durham, NC: Duke University Press, 2013), 93–119; Frank Trey Proctor III, "Amores perritos: Puppies, Laughter and Popular Catholicism in Bourbon Mexico City," *Journal of Latin American Studies* 46, no. 1 (February 2014): 1–28.

153. AGN-TSJDF, Colonial Alcaldes Ordinarios, Criminal, box 33A, exp. 3, Mexico City, 1795. Robles, *Diario*, 1:281, recounts a fatal fight between men over a dog.

154. AGN-TSJDF, Colonial Alcaldes Ordinarios, box 32A, exp. 66, Mexico City, 1790.

155. AGN, Criminal, vol. 176, fols. 419–422v, Tlanepantla, 1748. For a fight on horseback between two hacienda administrators over intruding cattle, see AGN, Criminal, vol. 227, fols. 245–46, Coatepec, 1742.

156. AGN, Criminal, vol. 265, fol. 146, Cuautitlan, 1773. There is an eery similarity to an incident described earlier in which a man broke off a few stalks of corn as he was walking along the camino real.

157. AGN, Criminal, vol. 131, fols. 379–80, Mexicalcingo, 1783; AGN, Criminal, vol. 227, fols. 245–46, Coatepec, 1742; AGN-TSJDF, Colonial, Hojas sueltas, section 4A, box 107, Coyoacán, 1756; AGN, Criminal, vol. 79, fols. 511–24, San Bartolomé Naucalpan (Tacuba), 1738; AGN, Criminal, vol. 222, fols. 121–29, Chalco, 1796.

158. AGN-TSJDF, Colonial Corregidores, Teniente General de Xochimilco, Criminal, box 31A, exp. 31, Xochimilco, 1749. For another case over a pig, see AGN-TSJDF, Colonial Corregidores, Teniente General de Xochimilco, Criminal, box 31A, exp. 42, Xochimilco, 1779. For an incident in which the owners of a chinampa killed a horse that got into their plants and caused a lot of damage, see Pizzigoni, *Life Within*, 154.

159. AGN, Criminal, vol. 30, fols. 273–273v, Mexico City, 1786.

160. AGN-TSJDF, Colonial, Hojas sueltas, section 4A, box 107, Coyoacán, 1756.

161. AGN, Criminal, vol. 176, fols. 202–202v, Atizapan (Tlanepantla), 1788.

162. AGN-TSJDF, Colonial Corregidores, Marquesado del Valle, Criminal, box 30B, exp. 105, fols. 1–20, Cuajimalpa, 1747.

163. AGN, Criminal, vol. 50, fols. 17–19v, Xochimilco, 1782. For a similar case, see AGN, Criminal, vol. 227, fols. 120–146v, Coatepec Chalco, 1810.

164. AGN, Criminal, vol. 267, fol. 190, Cuautitlan, 1791.

165. AGN, Criminal, vol. 266, fols. 86–91, Santa Maria Quautepec (Tacuba), 1766. For a similar case, see AGN, Criminal, vol. 163, fols. 280–85, Tacuba, 1749. In Xochimilco and Azcapotzalco there was also tension over the cutting of *zacate*—a type of grass that could be used for fodder. AGN-TSJDF, Colonial Corregidores, Teniente General de Xochimilco, Criminal, box 31A, exp. 41, Xochimilco, 1779; AGN, Criminal, vol. 730, fols. 375–80, Azcapotzalco, 1726.

Chapter 6

1. AGN-TSJDF, Colonial Corregidores (Coyoacán), Criminal, box 28A, exp. 39, Mexico City, 1746.

2. James C. Scott, *Domination and the Arts of Resistance: Hidden Transcripts* (New Haven, CT: Yale University Press, 1990), 10.

3. Víctor Macías-González, "Masculine Friendships, Sentiment, and Homoerotics in Nineteenth-Century Mexico: The Correspondence of José María Calderón y Tapia, 1820s–1850s," *Journal of the History of Sexuality* 16, no. 3 (September 2007): 416–35; Kate Davison, "Occasional Politeness and Gentlemen's Laughter in 18th-Century England," *Historical Journal* 57, no. 4 (December 2014): 921–45; Shepard, "'Swil-bols and Tos-pots,'" 110–30; T. Reinke-Williams, "Misogyny, Jest-Books, and Male Youth Culture in Seventeenth-Century England," *Gender and History* 21, no. 2 (2009): 324–39.

4. Lussana, "No Band," 872–95; Ignacio Martínez, "The Paradox of Friendship: Loyalty and Betrayal on the Sonoran Frontier," *Journal of the Southwest* 56, no. 2 (2014): 319–44.

5. For one of the first critiques of the broad racial classifications, see John K. Chance and William B. Taylor, "Estate and Class in a Colonial City: Oaxaca in 1792," *Comparative Studies in Society and History* 19, no. 4 (October 1977): 454–87.

6. Isabel Cruz de Amenábar, *El traje: Transformaciones de una segunda piel* (Santiago, Chile: Universidad Católica de Chile, 1996), 35.

7. Cañeque, *King's Living Image*, 191, 227; Rubial García, *Monjas*, 56; Martínez. "Paradox," 329.

8. AGN, Criminal, vol. 165, fols. 224–42, Escapusalco, 1641.

9. Rubial García, *Monjas*, 2005, 97. Santos, *Cleansing Honor*, 77, argues that prosperity allowed men to be violent because they could afford to defend themselves in court and to post bail.

10. AGN-TSJDF, Colonial Corregidores, Teniente General de Xochimilco, Criminal, box 31A, exp. 40, Xochimilco, 1779.

11. AGN, Criminal, vol. 719, fols. 14–56, Amecameca, 1800.

12. Cruz de Amenábar, *El traje*, 36–37, 115; Fabián y Fuero, *Colección*, 528; Vetancurt, "Tratado," 47.

13. Martín, "La desnudez," 263, 266, 279.

14. Ibid., 279, 281; Deans-Smith, *Bureaucrats*, 205.

15. Marie François, "Cloth and Silver: Pawning and Material Life in Mexico City at the Turn of the Nineteenth Century," *Americas* 60, no. 3 (2004): 325–62.

16. Cruz de Amenábar, *El traje*, 29, 35.

17. AGN, Criminal, vol. 473, fols. 383–89, Mexico City, 1797.

18. AGN, Criminal, vol. 129, fols. 1–133, Mexico City, 1799; see also AGN, Criminal, vol. 83, fols. 119–40, Mexico City, 1808.

19. AGN, Criminal, vol. 110, fols. 86–95, Cuautitlan, 1750; AGN, Criminal, vol. 267, fols. 206–512, Cuautitlan, 1729; AGN, Criminal, vol. 176, fols. 64–67, Tlanepantla (Tacuba), 1793; AGN, Criminal, vol. 407, fols. 438–75, Mexico City, 1809; AGN-TSJDF, Colonial Alcaldes Ordinarios, box 31B, exp. 97, Mexico City, 1740; AGN-TSJDF, Colonial Alcalde Mayor de Xochimilco, Criminal, box 32B, exp. 48, Xochimilco, 1795; AGN-TSJDF, Colonial Corregidores, Teniente General de Xochimilco, Criminal, box 31A, exp. 41, Xochimilco, 1779; AGN, Criminal, vol. 176, fols. 256–65, Tlanepantla, 1789; AGN-TSJDF, Colonial Alcaldes ordinarios, box 35A, exp. 1, Mexico City, 1784; AGN, Criminal, vol. 496, fols. 159–202, Mexico City, 1808; AGN, Criminal, vol. 177, fols. 245–47, San Francisco Chilpa (Tultitlan), 1763.

20. AGN, Criminal, vol. 727, fols. 127–67, Mexico City, 1781; AGN-TSJDF, Colonial Alcaldes Ordinarios, Criminal, box 35A, exp. 38, Mexico City, 1791; AGN, Criminal, vol. 222, fols. 1–16v, Amecameca, 1783; AGN, Criminal, vol. 660, fols. 160–13, Mexico City, 1752. For an explanation of the way that insults were both verbal and corporeal, see Sonya Lipsett-Rivera, "*De Obra y de Palabra*: Patterns of Insults in Mexico, 1750–1856," *Americas* 54, no. 4 (April 1998): 511–39. See also Taylor, *Honor and Violence*, 142; and Iván Jurado Revaliente, "Las injurias cotidianas: Identidades e individuos en el siglo XVI," *Bulletin of Spanish Studies* 92, no. 5 (May 2015): 677–97, https://doi.org/10.1080/14753820.2015.1039385.

21. AGN, Criminal, vol. 83, fols. 119–40, Mexico City, 1808.

22. Cruz de Amenábar, *El traje*, 37, 60; Vetancurt, "Tratado," 47.

23. AGN, Criminal, vol. 624, fols. 129–213, Mexico City, 1657.
24. AGN, Criminal, vol. 110, fols. 86–95, Cuautitlan, 1750; AGN, Criminal, vol. 718, fols. 269–77, Mexico City, 1809; AGN, Criminal, vol. 537, fols. 1–18, Cuautla, 1804; AGN-TSJDF, Colonial Corregidores Alcalde Mayor de Xochimilco, Criminal, box 32B, exp. 66, Xochimilco, 1717; AGN-TSJDF, Colonial Corregidores, Marquesado del Valle, box 30A, exp. 67, Coyoacán, 1754; AGN-TSJDF, Colonial Alcaldes Ordinarios, Criminal, box 32A, exp. 16, Mexico City, 1785; AGN, Criminal, vol. 227, fols. 90–119, San Vicente Chicoaloapan, 1765; AGN, Criminal, vol. 131, fols. 311–41, Xochimilco, 1796; AGN, Criminal, vol. 715, fol. 14, Mexico City, 1779; AGN, Criminal, vol. 50, fols. 7–13, Xochimilco, 1779; AGN, Criminal, vol. 272, fols. 200–220v, Chalco, 1780.
25. AGN, Criminal, vol. 1, fols. 1–10, Chalco, 1776.
26. Cruz de Amenábar, *El traje*, 66; François, "Cloth and Silver," 355; Silvia Hunold Lara, "The Signs of Color: Women's Dress and Racial Relations in Salvador and Rio de Janeiro, ca. 1750–1815," *Colonial Latin American Review* 6, no. 2 (December 1997): 212; Rubial García, *Monjas*, 85, 129; Muchembled, *History*, 21, 80.
27. Castro Gutiérrez, *Historia Social*, 132; Rubial García, *Monjas*, 129. Hunold Lara, "Signs of Color," discusses the attempts of a *pardo* (black) man in eighteenth-century Brazil who asked for an exemption from the law forbidding pardos to carry swords. He argued that it would reflect and enhance his respectability and authority.
28. Teresa Lozano Armendares, *La criminalidad en la ciudad de México, 1800–1821* (Mexico City: Universidad Nacional Autónoma de México, 1987), 101–2.
29. Pieter Spierenberg, ed., "Knife Fighting and Popular Codes of Honor in Early Modern Amsterdam," in *Men and Violence: Gender, Honor, and Rituals in Modern Europe and America* (Columbus: Ohio State University Press, 1998), 107–10.
30. Cañeque, *King's Living Image*, 141.
31. Cruz de Amenábar, *El traje*, 64.
32. Cañeque, *King's Living Image*, 154. See also Undurraga Schüler, *Los Rostros*, 177, 224, 321.
33. In shocked tones, María Secundina Aguilar recounted how José Gregorio Aguilar left his home without a hat or a jacket. She used this fact to show how agitated he was, even though he did not go into the street, just onto the shared patio of a tenement. AGN, Criminal, vol. 565, fols. 70–117, Mexico City, 1793. See also AGN-TSJDF, Colonial Juzgados Especiales, Auditor de Guerra, box 20, exp. 192, Mexico City, 1810.
34. AGN-TSJDF, Colonial Juzgados Especiales, Auditor de Guerra, box 20, exp. 192, Mexico City, 1810.
35. AGN, Criminal, vol. 490, fols. 2–32, Mexico City, 1804; AGN-TSJDF, Colonial Corregidores (Coyoacán), Criminal, box 28A, exp. 1, Mexico City, 1708; AGN, Criminal, vol. 40, fols. 488–501v, Xochimilco, 1810.

36. AGN, Criminal, vol. 79, fols. 511–24, San Bartolomé Naucalpan (Tacuba), 1738. See also AGN, Criminal, vol. 718, fols. 269–77, Mexico City, 1809; AGN, Criminal, vol. 413, fols. 246–76, Chalco, 1806; AGN, Criminal, vol. 266, fols. 97–110, Tultitlan-Tacuba, 1760; AGN-TSJDF, Colonial Corregidores, Teniente General de Xochimilco, Criminal, box 31A, exp. 41, Xochimilco, 1779; AGN-TSJDF, Colonial, Corregidores, Teniente General de Xochimilco, Criminal, box 31A, exp. 36, Xochimilco, 1766; and AGN, Criminal, vol. 83, fols. 119–40, Mexico City, 1808.

37. Castro Gutiérrez, *Historia Social*, 132–33.

38. Scott, *Domination*, 10, 24.

39. AGN, Criminal, vol. 708, fols. 1–511, Chalco, 1757; Taylor, *Honor and Violence*, 142.

40. AGN-TSJDF, Colonial Corregidores, Criminal, box 17B, exp. 133, Mexico City, 1800.

41. AGN-TSJDF, Colonial Alcaldes Ordinarios, Criminal, box 33B, exp. 49, Mexico City, 1808. See also AGN-TSJDF, Colonial Alcaldes Ordinarios, Criminal, box 32A, exp. 44, Mexico City, 1790; AGN, Criminal, vol. 677, fols. 243–273v, Cuautitlan, 1778; AGN-TSJDF, Colonial Alcaldes Ordinarios, Criminal, box 35A, exp. 10, Mexico City, 1785; AGN, Criminal, vol. 490, fols. 2–32, Mexico City, 1804; AGN, Criminal, vol. 565, fols. 328–50, Mexico City, 1794; AGN, Criminal, vol. 142, fols. 234–48, Ayotzingo (Chalco), 1781; and AGN, Criminal, vol. 490, fols. 2–32, Mexico City, 1804.

42. AGN, Criminal, vol. 129, fols. 1–133, Mexico City, 1799; AGN, Criminal, vol. 176, fols. 419–422v, Tlanepantla, 1748; AGN-TSJDF, Colonial, Alcaldes Ordinarios, Criminal, box 35A, exp. 10, Mexico City, 1785; AGN-TSJDF, Colonial, Alcaldes Ordinarios, Criminal, box 31B, exp. 97, Mexico City, 1740; AGN, Criminal, vol. 738, fols. 90–130, Mexico City, 1764; AGN-TSJDF, Colonial Corregidores, Teniente General de Xochimilco, Criminal, box 31A, exp. 41, Xochimilco, 1779; AGN, Criminal, vol. 222, fols. 121–29, Chalco, 1796; AGN, Criminal, vol. 496, fols. 159–202, Mexico City, 1808; AGN, Criminal, vol. 232, fols. 396–99, Tacubaya, 1633; AGN, Criminal, vol. 187, exp. 19, fols. 289–295v, Mexico City, 1643. For similar acts in a different context, see Robert Muchembled, *History*, 79–80; Undurraga Schüler, *Los Rostros*, 171; and Jurado Revaliente, "Las injurias cotidianas," 687.

43. Cited in Nava Sánchez, "La Voz," 24.

44. Richard Boyer, "Respect and Identity: Horizontal and Vertical Reference Points in Speech Acts," *Americas* 54, no. 4 (1998): 505; Jurado Revaliente, "Las injurias cotidianas," 677–69; Sandra Gayol, *La Sociabilidad en Buenos Aires: Hombres, Honor y Café, 1862–1910* (Buenos Aires: Signo, 2000), 153; Undurraga Schüler, *Los Rostros*, 311. When masters scolded servants, they had to be careful about tone of voice; it had to remain "cool, reasoned, and calm." Masters had to be careful to avoid becoming heated or intemperate. Servants were supposed to be silently obedient. Richard Cullen Rath, *How Early America Sounded* (Ithaca, NY: Cornell University Press, 2003).

45. AGN, Criminal, vol. 139, exp. 12, fols. 210–32, Malinalco, 1794; AGN-TSJDF, Colonial Corregidores, Criminal, box 17A, exp. 17, Mexico City, 1797. See also Jurado Revaliente, "Las injurias cotidianas," 677–97.
46. AGN, Criminal, vol. 274, fols. 83–87, Amecameca (Chalco), 1780.
47. AGN, Criminal, vol. 465, fols. 220–28, Mexico City, 1794.
48. AGN, Criminal, vol. 154, exp. 1, fols. 1–100, Coyoacán, 1807; AGN, Criminal, vol. 537, fols. 19–48, Cuautla, 1804. In one example, the word *compañerito*, or little comrade, was used with sarcasm. AGN-TSJDF, Colonial Juzgados Especiales, Auditor de Guerra, box 13A, exp. 117, Mexico City, 1803.
49. Pardo, *Honor*, 81; Angela Rosenthal, "Raising Hair," *Eighteenth-Century Studies* 38, no. 1 (2004): 2; Earle, *Body*, 24; Michelle Perrot, *Mi historia de las mujeres* (Mexico City: Fondo de Cultura Económica, 2008), 67–68; Muchembled, *History*, 77, 79–80.
50. This seems anomalous compared with other accounts. See, e.g., Lyman Johnson, "Dangerous Words, Provocative Gestures, and Violent Acts: The Disputed Hierarchies of Plebeian Life in Colonial Buenos Aires," in *The Faces of Honor: Sex, Shame, and Violence in Colonial Latin America*, ed. Lyman Johnson and Sonya Lipsett-Rivera (Albuquerque: University of New Mexico Press, 1998), 127–51; and Marta Madero, *Manos violentas, palabras vedadas: La injuria en Castilla y León (siglos XIII-XV)* (Madrid: Taurus, 1992), 76, 81.
51. Robles, *Diario*, 1:115, 3:109–10. It was forcibly cut off him in the hospital. Rosales, *Catón Christiano*, 81, connected shaving with honoring Christ.
52. Undurraga Schüler, *Los Rostros*, 154–55; Rosenthal, "Raising Hair," 1–2.
53. Cañeque, *King's Living Image*, 227.
54. AGN, Criminal, vol. 227, fols. 90–111, San Vicente Chicoaloapan, 1765; AGN, Criminal, vol. 131, fols. 311–41, Xochimilco, 1796; AGN, Criminal, vol. 630, fols. 377–83, Cuautitlan, 1770; AGN, Criminal, vol. 227, fols. 1–56v, Quautepec, 1739; AGN, Criminal, vol. 630, fols. 198–207, Cuautitlan, 1740; AGN, Criminal, vol. 227, fols. 147–154v, Quatepec (Tlanepantla), 1785.
55. AGN-TSJDF, Colonial Corregidores, Marquesado del Valle, box 30A, exp. 31, Coyoacán, 1749; AGN-TSJDF, Colonial, Alcaldes Ordinarios, Criminal, box 35A, exp. 18, Mexico City, 1785; AGN-TSJDF, Colonial Corregidores, Criminal, box 17A, exp. 17, Mexico City, 1797; AGN-TSJDF, Colonial Corregidores, Marquesado del Valle, box 30A, exp. 29, Coyoacán, 1748; AGN, Criminal, vol. 339, fols. 40–43, Chalco, 1789.
56. Castro Gutiérrez, *Historia Social*, 163.
57. Osvaldo Pardo, "How to Punish Indians: Law and Cultural Change in Early Colonial Mexico," *Comparative Studies in Society and History* 48, no. 1 (2006): 86, 89, 93, 98; Madero, *Manos violentas*, 82. Perrot, *Mi historia*, 65, considers head shaving to be an erasure of identity and thus dishonoring.
58. AGN, Criminal, vol. 602, fols. 48–56, Mexico City, 1732; AGN, Criminal, vol. 265, fols. 61–102, Tultitlan, 1753; AGN, Criminal, vol. 129, fols. 1–133, Mexico City, 1799;

AGN, Criminal, vol. 227, fols. 90–119, San Vicente Chicoaloapan, 1765; AGN-TSJDF, Colonial Corregidores, Teniente General de Xochimilco, Criminal, box 31A, exp. 41, Xochimilco, 1779; AGN-TSJDF, Colonial Corregidores, Criminal, box 16B, exp. 74, Mexico City, 1749; AGN, Criminal, vol. 267, fols. 87–88, Coaspusalco (Tacuba), 1772; AGN, Criminal, vol. 649, fols. 306–317v, Tacuba, 1795; AGN, Criminal, vol. 176, fols. 73–77, Tlanepantla, 1773; AGN-TSJDF, Colonial Alcaldes Ordinarios, Criminal, box 35A, exp. 34, Mexico City, 1790; AGN, Criminal, vol. 131, fols. 311–41, Xochimilco, 1796; AGN, Criminal, vol. 176, fols. 284–367, Huehuetoca, Tlanepantla, 1809; AGN-TSJDF, Colonial Alcaldes Ordinarios, Criminal, box 35A, exp. 21, Mexico City, 1785; AGN, Criminal, vol. 617, fols. 72–86, Mexico City, 1800; AGN-TSJDF, Colonial Corregidores, Marquesado del Valle, box 30A, exp. 29, Coyoacán, 1748; AGN-TSJDF, Corregidores, Criminal, box 16B, exp. 74, Mexico City, 1749; AGN, Criminal, vol. 163, fols. 378–88, Tacuba, 1767; AGN, Criminal, vol. 176, fols. 224–28, Pueblo Sta María Zocoquaio, Tlanepantla, 1796; AGN, Criminal, vol. 222, fols. 1–16v, Amecameca, 1783; AGN, Criminal, vol. 715, fols. 14–23v, Mexico City, 1779.

59. They may have been referring to Nahua concepts. In Nahua ideas, hair protected the *tonalli*, an animistic entity that was lodged in the skull and imparted vigor and valor to the individual.

60. AGN, Criminal, vol. 227, fols. 1–56v, Quautepec, 1739. On how the hair of enslaved Africans was often associated with rebelliousness, see Shane White and Graham White, "Slave Hair and African American Culture in the Eighteenth and Nineteenth Centuries," *Journal of Southern History* 61, no. 1 (February 1995): 45–76. See also Pardo, *Honor*, 104, 187, 191; and Dana Murillo Velasco, *Urban Indians in a Silver City: Zacatecas, Mexico, 1546–1810* (Stanford, CA: Stanford University Press, 2016), 23–24.

61. AGN, Criminal, vol. 339, fols. 40–43, Chalco, 1789.

62. AGN, Criminal, vol. 131, fols. 311–41, Xochimilco, 1796.

63. Lussana, "No Band," 872–95; Boyer, "Respect," 161, 164.

64. Scott, *Domination*, 4.

65. Castro Gutiérrez, *Historia Social*, 161.

66. For a study of male friendship on the basis of letters, see Victor Macías-González, "Las amistades apasionadas y la homosociabilidad en la primera mitad del siglo XIX," *Historia y Grafía* 31 (2008): 19–48.

67. AGN-TSJDF, Colonial Alcalde del Crimen, Criminal, box 47A, exp. 14, Mexico City, 1743; AGN, Criminal, vol. 362, fols. 235–81, Mexico City, 1802.

68. AGN, Criminal, vol. 362, fols. 235–81, Mexico City, 1802; AGN, Criminal, vol. 537, fols. 19–48, Cuautla, 1804; AGN, Criminal, vol. 154, fols. 175–203, Coyoacán, 1802; AGN-TSJDF, Colonial Alcaldes Ordinarios, Criminal, box 31A, exp. 49, fol. 1v, Mexico City, 1661; AGN, Criminal, vol. 625, fols. 350–78, Mexico City, 1804; AGN-TSJDF, Colonial Corregidores, Criminal, box 17B, exp. 100, fols. 1–7v, Mexico City, 1802.

69. AGN-TSJDF, Colonial Alcalde del Crimen, Criminal, box 47A, exp. 14, Mexico City, 1743; AGN-TSJDF, Colonial Alcaldes Ordinarios, Criminal, box 35A, exp. 52, fols. 1–28, Mexico City, 1796; AGN, Criminal, vol. 564, fols. 19–143, Mexico City, 1801; AGN, Criminal, vol. 488, fols. 37–70, Tlanepantla, 1804; AGN-TSJDF, Colonial Alcaldes Ordinarios, Criminal, box 33A, exp. 3, Mexico City, 1795; AGN, Criminal, vol. 407, fols. 209–27, Mexico City, 1809. Rubial García, *Monjas*, 72, comments that paseos were one of the most important social activities. See also Viqueira Albán, *Propriety*, 104.

70. AGN-TSJDF, Colonial Corregidores (Coyoacán), Criminal, box 28A, exp. 29, Mexico City, 1742. During festivals there were masquerades and dances. Rubial García, *La plaza*, 58.

71. AGN-TSJDF, Colonial Alcaldes Ordinarios, Criminal, box 35B, exp. 67, Mexico City, 1800; AGN-TSJDF, Colonial Alcaldes Ordinarios, Criminal, box 35A, exp. 25, fols. 1–17, Mexico City, 1790; AGN-TSJDF, Colonial Alcaldes Ordinarios, Criminal, box 32B, exp. 92, fols. 1–8, Mexico City, 1792; AGN, Criminal, vol. 86, fols. 6–27, Mexico City, 1808; AGN, Criminal, vol. 488, fols. 37–70, Tlanepantla, 1804; AGN, Criminal, vol. 694, fols. 71–176, Mexico City, 1803; AGN-TSJDF, Colonial Corregidores (Coyoacán), Criminal, box 28B, exp. 82, Mexico City, 1769; AGN, Criminal, vol. 402, fols. 17–34, Mexico City, 1801; AGN-TSJDF, Colonial Corregidores, Criminal, box 17B, exp. 100, Mexico City, 1802; AGN, Criminal, vol. 727, fol. 13, Mexico City, 1796; AGN, Criminal, vol. 397, fols. 88–114, Mexico City, 1798; Gayol, *La Sociabilidad*, 150–63; Muchembled, *History*, 63–64; Shepard, "'Swil-bols,'" 120–24; Reinke-Williams, "Misogyny," 324–39. For men, drinking together built social cohesion. Muchembled, *History*, 63.

72. Nicknames were part of a plebeian subculture. Castro Gutiérrez, *Historia Social*, 161.

73. It is possible that higher-status men also had nicknames or aliases. Robles, *Diario*, notes that the presbiter don Juan Bautista was nicknamed El Chato (1:55) and that don Fernando Valenzuela—whose passing merited the tolling of bells all over the city—was called El Duende (2:237–38).

74. Stanley Brandes, "The Structural and Demographic Implications of Nicknames in Navanogal, Spain," *American Ethnologist* 2, no. 1 (1975): 143.

75. Castro Gutiérrez, *Historia Social*, 140, remarks that many poor Spaniards who worked in the Royal Mint ended up with the nickname of gachupín because they were perceived as pretentious.

76. James Lockhart, *The Nahuas after the Conquest: A Social and Cultural History of the Indians of Central Mexico, Sixteenth through Eighteenth Centuries* (Stanford, CA: Stanford University Press, 1992), 120–21.

77. David D. Gilmore, "Some Notes on Community Nicknaming in Spain," *Man* 17, no. 4 (December 1982): 686–700; Dennis Masaka, Ephraim Taurai Gwaravanda, and Jowere Mukusha, "Nicknaming as a Mode of Black Resistance: Reflections

on Black Indigenous People's Nicknaming of Colonial White Farmers in Zimbabwe," *Journal of Black Studies* 43, no. 5 (September 2012): 479–504.

78. Brandes, "Structural and Demographic Implications," 141–42. Muchembled, *History*, 59, remarks that young men often used insulting nicknames among themselves as part of competing masculinities.

79. Rubial García, *Monjas*, 185.

80. AGN, Criminal, vol. 663, fols. 10–19, Mexico City, 1735.

81. AGN, Criminal, vol. 463, fols. 1–153, Mexico City, 1790.

82. AGN-TSJDF, Colonial Alcaldes Ordinarios, Criminal, box 31B, exp. 91, Mexico City, 1726. Madero, *Manos violentas*, 22, argues that there was a fine line between humor and insults.

83. AGN, Criminal, vol. 1, fols. 1–10, Chalco, 1776.

84. AGN, Criminal, vol. 537, fols. 27–27v, Cuautla, 1804.

85. AGN, Criminal, vol. 537, fols. 159–78, Cuautla, 1805.

86. Rod A. Martin, *The Psychology of Humor: An Integrative Approach* (Amsterdam: Elsevier Academic Press, 2007), 17. For a historical perspective, see Davison, "Occasional Politeness," 934; and Taylor, *Honor and Violence*, 135.

87. AGN-TSJDF, Colonial Corregidores (Coyoacán), Criminal, box 28B, exp. 69, Mexico City, 1765.

88. AGN-TSJDF, Colonial Alcaldes Ordinarios, Criminal, box 32A, exp. 61, fols. 1–22, Mexico City, 1790.

89. Viqueira Albán, *Propriety*, 164–65.

90. AGN, Clero Regular y Secular, vol. 28, exp. 1, fols. 1–29, Jilotepec, 1794.

91. AGN, Criminal, vol. 176, fols. 368–91, Tlanepantla, 1808.

92. Taylor, *Honor and Violence*, 141–42, 145. See also Amanda Flather, "Male Servants, Identity and Urban Space in Eighteenth-Century England," in *The Routledge History Handbook of Gender and the Urban Experience*, ed. Deborah Simonton (London: Routledge, 2017), 97.

93. Fabián y Fuero, *Colección*, 451–52. Rubial García, *Monjas*, 87, comments that during festivals many Mexicans placed images, candles, incense burners, and vases with aromatic water on altars in the doorways of palaces and churches. This practice was common and also controversial in colonial Santiago, Chile. Laura Fahrenkrog, "Prácticas musicales durante la colonia: Reglamentando la vida musical; Santiago de Chile, siglo XVIII," in *Formas de control y disciplinamiento: Chile, América y Europa, siglos XVI–XIX*, ed. Verónica Undurraga Schüler and Rafael Gaume (Santiago: UQBAR, 2014), 225, 231.

94. Robles, *Diario*, 1:44, 1:47, 1:106, 1:112–13, 1:130–31, 1:158, 2:277, 3:139–40.

95. AGN-TSJDF, Colonial Alcalde Mayor de Xochimilco, Criminal, box 32B, exp. 4, Xochimilc, 1795.

96. AGN, Criminal, vol. 76, fols. 1–194, Tacuba, 1803. The lyrics are recorded only in part. Those in the document were: "de Veracruz he llegado viniendo por el Oriente solo por venir a darle a este Carajo de Teniente" (from Veracruz I have come

from the East just to give it to this prick of a lieutenant) as well as other verses. It ended with this verse: "Con esta y no digo mas agua de la mar bermeja pensaría en Teniente que mi china es muy pendeja." (With this and not saying any more, water of the crimson sea, I will think of the lieutenant and say that my china is a coward.)

97. Robles, *Diario*, 2:257. He also reports the use of other pasquines (3:42, 3:281).

98. AGN, Criminal, vol. 266, fols. 154–159v, Tlanepantla, 1724.

99. Richard Boyer, "Negotiating Calidad: The Everyday Struggle for Status in Mexico," *Historical Archaeology* 31, no. 1 (1997): 66–67.

100. Boyer, "Respect," 491–509.

101. Sinha, *Colonial Masculinity*, 41–42.

102. Undurraga Schüler, *Los Rostros*, 288, 311, 339, 341; Madero, *Manos violentas*, 90.

103. AGN-TSJDF, Colonial Corregidores (Coyoacán), Criminal, box 28B, exp. 117, Mexico City, 1804.

104. AGN Criminal, vol. 718, fols. 269–77, Mexico City, 1809.

105. AGN-TSJDF, Colonial Alcaldes Ordinarios, box 31B, exp. 111, Mexico City, 1767; see also AGN-TSJDF, Colonial Alcalde del Crimen, Criminal, box 47B, exp. 49, Mexico City, 1804. Keith Thomas, "The Place of Laughter in Tudor and Stuart England," *Times* [London] *Literary Supplement*, January 21, 1977, writes that humor was sometimes used to keep people in their place. For another example of such use of race as a way to push a person into outsider status, see Jurado Revaliente, "Las injurias cotidianas," 677–97; and María Albornoz Vásquez, "Desencuentro de afectos y de poderes: Variaciones para el estudio de un conflicto singular; Santiago de Chile, octubre 1793-noviembre 1797," *Nuevo mundo, mundos nuevos*, October 2008, http://nuevomundo.revues.org/240#tocto1n1.

106. Jurado Revaliente, "Las injurias cotidianas," 677–97.

107. AGN, Criminal, vol. 228, fols. 185–208, Chalco, 1801.

108. AGN-TSJDF, Colonial Libros y Expedientes Diversos, Hojas sueltas, box 96, exp. 33, Coyoacán, 1785.

109. AGN, Criminal, vol. 131, fols. 208–208v, Xochimilco, 1809.

110. AGN, Criminal, vol. 255, fols. 288–309, Coatepec (Chalco), 1802.

111. AGN, Criminal, vol. 421, fols. 1–24, Mexico City, 1810. For several examples of soldiers being ridiculed, see Vinson, *Bearing Arms*, 74, 77.

112. Scott, *Domination*, 15–18, notes that the public transcript is often broken in the anonymity of crowds and that those in power need to enact their superiority in order to protect this public persona of power.

113. AGN, Criminal, vol. 398, fols. 45–55, Mexico City, 1799; see also Taylor, *Honor and Violence*, 128.

114. AGN, Criminal, vol. 687, fols. 171–92, Mexico City, 1796.

115. Taylor, *Honor and Violence*, 49.

116. AGN, Criminal, vol. 265, fols. 146–54, Cuautitlan, 1773; AGN, Criminal, vol. 129, fols. 1–133, Mexico City, 1799; AGN-TSJDF, Colonial Corregidores, Marquesado

del Valle, Criminal, box 30B, exp. 137, Mexico City, 1804; AGN, Criminal, vol. 265, fols. 211–18, Tacuba, 1793; AGN, Criminal, vol. 176, fols. 184–91, Tlanepantla, 1787; AGN, Criminal, vol. 176, fols. 491–498v, Tlanepantla, 1751; AGN, Criminal, vol. 413, fols. 246–76, Chalco, 1806; AGN-TSJDF, Colonial Corregidores (Coyoacán), Criminal, box 29B, exp. 89, Coyoacán, 1749; AGN, Criminal, vol. 139, fols. 233–41, Malinalco, 1802. Madero, *Manos violentas*, 98, writes that wealthy men rode horses in front of another man and made them jump about as an insult. The horses also threw up dirt with their hooves, which intensified the affront.

117. AGN, Criminal, vol. 715, fol. 14, Mexico City, 1779. See also Undurraga Schüler, *Los Rostros*, 226; Gayol, *La Sociabilidad*, 207; Santos, *Cleansing Honor*, 99–100.

118. AGN, Criminal, vol. 716, fols. 151–53, Mexico City, 1760. See also AGN-TSJDF, Colonial Libros y Expedientes Diversos, Hojas sueltas, box 96, exp. 33, Mexico City, 1785; and Taylor, *Honor and Violence*, 110–11.

119. Felipe Castro Gutiérrez, ed., "El origen y conformación de los barrios de indios," in *Los Indios y las ciudades de la Nueva España* (Mexico City: Universidad Nacional Autónoma de México, 2010), 106.

120. Rodrigo Salomón Pérez, "Porque palabras duelen más que puñadas: la injuria en Nueva España, siglos XVI y XVI," *Fronteras de la Historia* 13, no. 2 (2008): 355–56.

121. Boyer, "Negotiating Calidad," 72; Sonya Lipsett-Rivera, "A Slap in the Face of Honor: Social Transgression and Women in Late-Colonial Mexico," in *The Faces of Honor: Sex, Shame, and Violence in Colonial Latin America*, ed. Lyman L. Johnson and Sonya Lipsett-Rivera (Albuquerque: University of New Mexico Press, 1998).

122. Salomón Pérez, "Porque palabras," 358, reports an incident in which one man called another a *hereje judío* (Jewish heretic). See also Taylor, *Honor and Violence*, 113; and Martin, *Governance*, 135.

123. Frances L. Ramos, "Myth, Ritual, and Civil Pride in the City of Angels," in *Emotions and Daily Life in Colonial Mexico*, ed. Javier Villa-Flores and Sonya Lipsett-Rivera (Albuquerque: University of New Mexico Press, 2014), 122–47.

124. Two authors report a similar pattern: Undurraga Schüler, *Los Rostros*; and Gayol, *La Sociabilidad*, 207.

125. Santos, *Cleansing Honor*, 99, reports that being called a thief was considered a terrible stain on one's honor and reputation.

126. Castro Gutiérrez, *Historia Social*, 164.

127. Robles, *Diario*, 3:254, recounts an incident in which a priest who was giving a sermon used the occasion to insult the Dominican monks in attendance, calling them *perros machados* (dirty dogs).

128. Margo DeMello, *Animals and Society: An Introduction to Human-Animal Studies* (New York: Columbia University Press, 2012), 284; Madero, *Manos violentas*, 150.

129. Albornoz Vásquez, "Desencuentro"; Stern, *Secret History*, 164.

130. Boyer, "Negotiating Calidad," 72; Undurraga Schüler, *Los Rostros*, 208, 286.

131. Boyer, "Respect," 497; Lipsett-Rivera, *De Obra*, 511–39.

132. Sandra Gayol, *Honor y duelo en la Argentina moderna* (Buenos Aires: Siglo XXI, 2008), 44.

133. Guijo, *Diario, 1648–1664*; Robles, *Diario*, 3:129.

134. Undurraga Schüler, *Los Rostros*, 231–32.

135. Albornoz Vásquez, "Desencuentro."

136. AGN-TSJDF, Colonial Alcaldes Ordinarios, Criminal, box 31A, exp. 12, Mexico City, 1631; AGN, Criminal, vol. 30, fols. 245–303, Xochimilco, 1786; AGN, Criminal, vol. 630, fols. 377–83, Cuautitlan, 1770.

137. AGN, Criminal, vol. 159, fols. 73–93, Chalco, 1808; AGN, Criminal, vol. 407, fols. 228–43, Mexico City, 1809; AGN, Criminal, vol. 727, fols. 183–223, Mexico City, 1796; AGN-TSJDF, Colonial Corregidores, Criminal, box 16B, exp. 82, Mexico City, 1790.

138. AGN, Criminal, vol. 110, fols. 135–75, Tacuba, 1745; AGN-TSJDF, Colonial Corregidores, Criminal, box 16B, exp. 82, Mexico City, 1790.

139. AGN-TSJDF, Colonial Alcaldes Ordinarios, Criminal, box 33A, exp. 34, Mexico City, 1804; AGN, Criminal, vol. 83, fols. 119–40, Mexico City, 1808; AGN, Criminal, vol. 538, fols. 60–91, Mexico City, 1808; AGN-TSJDF, Colonial Corregidores, Criminal, box 17A, exp. 20, Mexico City, 1797; AGN-TSJDF, Colonial Alcaldes Ordinarios, Criminal, box 35A, exp. 12, Mexico City, 1785.

140. AGN, Criminal, vol. 272, fols. 200–220v, Chalco, 1780; AGN, Criminal, vol. 708, fols. 1–511, Chalco, 1757.

141. AGN, Criminal, vol. 708, fols. 1–511, Chalco, 1757; AGN, Criminal, vol. 677, fols. 243–273v, Cuautitlan, 1778; AGN, Criminal, vol. 83, fols. 119–40, Mexico City, 1808; AGN, Criminal, vol. 76, fols. 1–194, Tacuba, 1803.

142. AGN, Criminal, vol. 131, fols. 311–41, Xochimilco, 1796; AGN, Criminal, vol. 613, fols. 1–28v, Cuautla Amilpas, 1754; AGN-TSJDF, Colonial Alcaldes Ordinarios, Criminal, box 32A, exp. 55, Mexico City, 1790; AGN, Criminal, vol. 76, fols. 1–194, Tacuba, 1803; AGN, Criminal, vol. 538, fols. 60–91, Mexico City, 1808. Van Young, *Other Rebellion*, 315, writes that many insurgents referred to defecating on those they despised as royalists.

143. AGN, Criminal, vol. 40, fols. 452–87, Zacualtipán, 1802; AGN, Criminal, vol. 177, fol. 468, Tlalnepantla, 1748; AGN-TSJDF, Colonial Corregidores, Criminal, box 16B, exp. 82, Mexico City, 1790; AGN, Criminal, vol. 40, fol. 519, Churubusco, 1770; AGN, Criminal, vol. 176, fols. 368–91, Tlanepantla, 1808; AGN, Criminal, vol. 715, fols. 14–23v, Mexico City, 1779.

144. Pierre Bourdieu, *Outline of a Theory of Practice*, trans. Richard Nice (Cambridge, UK: Cambridge University Press, 1977), 11.

145. William B. Taylor, *Drinking, Homicide, and Rebellion in Colonial Mexican Villages* (Stanford, CA: Stanford University Press, 1979), 81–82.

146. AGN-TSJDF, Colonial Alcaldes Ordinarios, Criminal, box 31A, exp. 12, Mexico City, 1631; AGN-TSJDF, Colonial Alcaldes Ordinarios, Criminal, box 31A, exp. 49, Mexico City, 1661; AGN, Criminal, vol. 421, fols. 25–39, Mexico City, 1810; AGN,

Criminal, vol. 176, fols. 195–210, Atizapan (Tlanepantla), 1788; AGN, Criminal, vol. 137, fols. 34–51, Coyoacán, 1790; AGN, Criminal, vol. 538, fols. 60–91, Mexico City, 1808; AGN-TSJDF, Colonial Alcaldes Ordinarios, Criminal, box 31A, exp. 4, Mexico City, 1628; AGN, Criminal, vol. 487, fols. 44–62, Mexico City, 1804; AGN, Criminal, vol. 723, fols. 2–21, Mexico City, 1777. See also Taylor, *Honor and Violence*, 48; Robles, *Diario*, 3:131–32; and Guijo, *Diario*, 1648–1664, 88.

147. AGN, Criminal, vol. 728, fols. 151–77, Apazingan, 1796; AGN, Criminal, vol. 225, fols. 5–38, Mexico City, 1808; AGN-TSJDF, Colonial Alcaldes Ordinarios, box 32 A, exp. 66, Mexico City, 1790.

148. AGN, Criminal, vol. 225, fols. 5–38, Mexico City, 1808; AGN, Criminal, vol. 694, fols. 45–61, Mexico City, 1803.

149. AGN-TSJDF, Colonial Juzgados Especiales, Auditor de Guerra, box 19, exp. 176, Mexico City, 1808; AGN, Criminal, vol. 660, fols. 160–83, Mexico City, 1752; AGN, Criminal, vol. 131, fols. 127–45, Tacubaya, 1760; AGN, Criminal, vol. 723, fols. 2–21, Mexico City, 1777; AGN, Criminal, vol. 84, fols. 169–80, Mexico City, 1809. See also Guijo, *Diario*, 1648–1664, 134; and Robles, *Diario*, 1:176, 1:306.

150. Undurraga Schüler, *Los Rostros*, 223, 262, notes that sometimes men refused a challenge if they believed the person making the challenge was socially inferior.

151. Robert B. Shoemaker, "The Taming of the Duel: Masculinity, Honour, and Ritual Violence in London, 1660–1800," *Historical Journal* 45, no. 3 (2002): 525–45; Muchembled, *History*.

152. AGN, Criminal, vol. 72, fols. 51–52v, Mexico City, 1722, reports on the Law and Royal Pragmatic, which prohibited duels and desafíos.

153. AGN-TSJDF, Colonial Alcaldes Ordinarios, Criminal, box 32B, exp. 71, Mexico City, 1791; AGN, Criminal, vol. 573, fols. 212–56, Mexico City, 1806; AGN, Criminal, vol. 129, fols. 1–133, Mexico City, 1799; AGN, Criminal, vol. 131, fols. 208–208v, Xochimilco, 1809.

154. Castro Gutiérrez, *Historia Social*, 162.

155. AGN, Criminal, vol. 660, fols. 160–83, Mexico City, 1752.

156. AGN, Criminal, vol. 723, fols. 22–35, Mexico City, 1780.

157. AGN, Criminal, vol. 266, fols. 97–110, Tultitlan (Tacuba), 1760; see also AGN, Criminal, vol. 723, fols. 2–21, Mexico City, 1777. Undurraga Schüler, *Los Rostros*, 327, writes that it was a sign of respect for the tavern owners to go into the street after a desafío.

158. AGN, Criminal, vol. 76, fols. 1–194, Tacuba, 1803; AGN, Criminal, vol. 232, fols. 243–307, Coyoacán, 1806; AGN, Criminal, vol. 84, fols. 169–80, Mexico City, 1809; AGN-TSJDF, Colonial Corregidores (Coyoacán), Criminal, box 28B, exp. 78, Mexico City, 1768; AGN, Criminal, vol. 176, fols. 195–210, Atizapan (Tlanepantla), 1788; AGN-TSJDF, Colonial Alcaldes Ordinarios, Criminal, box 33A, exp. 34, Mexico City, 1804; AGN, Criminal, vol. 719, fols. 14–56, Amecameca, 1800; AGN-TSJDF, Colonial Alcaldes Ordinarios, Criminal, box 35A, exp. 2, Mexico City,

1784; AGN, Criminal, vol. 129, fols. 1–133, Mexico City, 1799. Gayol, *La Sociabilidad*, 210, writes that the expression *ser hombre* (to be a man) was equivalent to the concept of manliness (hombría). Undurraga Schüler, *Los Rostros*, 326, notes the usage of verbal challenges and physical acts such as throwing a drink in another man's face.

159. AGN-TSJDF, Colonial Juzgados Especiales, Auditor de Guerra, box 19, exp. 176, Mexico City, 1808.

160. AGN, Criminal, vol. 131, fols. 379–380v, Mexicalcingo, 1783; AGN, Criminal, vol. 76, fols. 1–194, Tacuba, 1803; AGN, Criminal, vol. 129, fols. 1–133, Mexico City, 1799.

161. AGN, Criminal, vol. 177, fols. 348–56, Tlanepantla, 1739; AGN, Criminal, vol. 730, fol. 375, Azcapotzalco, 1726; AGN, Criminal, vol. 373, fol. 495, Mexico City, 1744; AGN, Criminal, vol. 176, fols. 195–210, Atizapan (Tlanepantla), 1788; AGN, Criminal, vol. 176, fols. 64–67, Tlanepantla (Tacuba), 1793; AGN, Criminal, vol. 649, fols. 306–317v, Tacuba, 1795; AGN, Criminal, vol. 602, fols. 48–56, Mexico City, 1732; AGN, Criminal, vol. 139, exp. 12, fols. 210–32, Malinalco, 1794.

162. AGN, Criminal, vol. 442, fols. 1–9, Mexico City, 1729.

163. Boyer, "Respect," 497–98; Twinam, *Public Lives*, 4.

164. AGN, Criminal, vol. 413, fols. 246–76, Chalco, 1806. Robles, *Diario*, 3:133, recounts that a mestizo refused an invitation for a second drink, and his companion killed him. See also Stern, *Secret History*, 153, 173.

165. Gayol, *La Sociabilidad*, 149–153; see also Shepard, "'Swil-bols,'" 110–30.

166. Eagle, "Beard-Pulling," 469, recounts that a Santo Domingo judge insulted the masculinity of another official by saying that he could not control his wife.

167. AGN-TSJDF, Colonial Alcaldes Ordinarios, Criminal, box 32B, exp. 71, fols. 1–30, Mexico City, 1791.

168. AGN-TSJDF, Colonial Alcalde del Crimen, Criminal, box 47A, exp. 24, Mexico City, 1801; AGN-TSJDF, Colonial Corregidores, Teniente General de Xochimilco, Criminal, box 31A, exp. 41, Xochimilco, 1779; AGN, Criminal, vol. 48, fols. 370–71, Xochimilco, 1800; AGN, Criminal, vol. 703, fols. 2–19, Mexico City, 1651; AGN-TSJDF, Colonial Corregidores (Coyoacán), Criminal, box 28B, exp. 117, Mexico City, 1804; AGN-TSJDF, Colonial Juzgados Especiales, Auditor de Guerra, box 20, exp. 185, Mexico City, 1809; AGN-TSJDF, Colonial Alcalde del Crimen, Criminal, box 47B, exp. 49, Mexico City, 1804; AGN-TSJDF, Colonial Alcaldes Ordinarios, Criminal, box 31A, exp. 12, Mexico City, 1631; AGN-TSJDF, Colonial Alcaldes Ordinarios, Criminal, box 31A, exp. 14, Mexico City, 1632.

169. Socolow, "Women and Crime," 39–54.

170. AGN-TSJDF, Colonial Corregidores (Coyoacán), Criminal, box 28B, exp. 117, Mexico City, 1804; AGN-TSJDF, Colonial Alcaldes Ordinarios, Criminal, box 35A, exp. 38, Mexico City, 1791; AGN, Criminal, vol. 595, fols. 366–390, Mexico City, 1801; AGN, Criminal, vol. 565, fols. 70–117, Mexico City, 1793; AGN, Criminal, vol. 266, fols. 97–110, Tultitlan (Tacuba), 1760; AGN-TSJDF, Colonial Corregidores,

Marquesado del Valle, box 30A, exp. 29, Coyoacán, 1748; AGN, Criminal, vol. 630, fols. 281–286v, Cuautitlan, 1760; AGN-TSJDF, Colonial Alcaldes Ordinarios, Criminal, box 31A, exp. 12, Mexico City, 1631; AGN, Criminal, vol. 670, fols. 54–80, Mexico City, 1806; AGN, Criminal, vol. 132, exp. 2, fol. 8, Tacubaya, 1647; AGN, Criminal, vol. 236, fols 116–28, Churubusco, 1782.

Chapter 7

1. AGN-TSJDF, Colonial Corregidores, Marquesado del Valle, box 30A, exp. 29, fol. 247, Coyoacán, 1748.
2. AGN, Criminal, vol. 267, fols. 127–135v, Tacuba, 1733.
3. AGN, Criminal, vol. 142, fols. 234–48, Ayotzingo (Chalco), 1781.
4. Van Young, *Other Rebellion*, 184–85.
5. Inga Clendinnen, "The Cost of Courage in Aztec Society," *Past and Present* 107 (May 1985): 44–89.
6. Mehl, *Forced Migration*, 125, 137, 162, 167.
7. AGN, Criminal, vol. 131, fols. 280–297v, Xochimilco, 1790.
8. Van Young, *Other Rebellion*, 171, writes about a man named José María González. Before the Hidalgo revolt, he was considered a troublemaker and a rabble-rouser, and he was instrumental in trying to organize the village residents to fight for land rights. He had no criminal record but was disrespectful of authority. He joined the Hidalgo revolt two to three weeks after the Grito. He was an example of the uppity conduct that the elites found worrying.
9. Van Young, *Other Rebellion*, 180, 184, 344.
10. Ibid., 313–15, 450, documents examples of calling Spaniards Jews and coyote dogs and of threatening to defecate on them.
11. Ibid., 169; María Antonieta Ilhui Pacheco Chávez, "Rebeldes y transgresores: Entre los murmullos de la insurrección; La intendencia de México, 1810–1814," *Historia mexicana* 59, no. 1 (2009): 332–33, http://www.jstor.org.proxy.library. carleton.ca/stable/pdf/40285233.pdf.
12. Stern, *Secret History*, 48–49, 151–60.

Bibliography

Ajofrín, Francisco de. *Diario del viaje que hizo a la América española en el siglo XVIII*. Vol. 1. Mexico City: Instituto Cultural Hispano, 1964.

Albornoz Vásquez, María. "Desencuentro de afectos y de poderes: Variaciones para el estudio de un conflicto singular; Santiago de Chile, octubre 1793–noviembre 1797." *Nuevo mundo, mundos nuevos*, October 2008. http://nuevomundo. revues.org/240#toctoini.

Álvarez del Villar, José. *Historia de la charrería*. Mexico City: Editorial Londres, 1941.

Amar y Borbón, Doña Josefa. *Discurso sobre la educación física y moral de las mugeres*. Madrid: D. Benito Cano, 1790.

Anonymous. *Breve instrucción a los Christianos casadas y útiles advertencias a los que pretenden serlo*. Puebla, Mexico: Don Pedro de la Rosa, 1790.

Anonymous. *Reglas de la buena crianza civil y christiana: Utilísimas para todos y singularmente para los que cuiden de la educación de los Niños, a quienes las deberían explicar, inspirándoles insensiblemente su práctica en todas ocurrencias*. Puebla, Mexico: Don Pedro de la Rosa, 1802.

Ariès, Philippe. *Centuries of Childhood: A Social History of Family Life*. Translated by Robert Baldiek. New York: Alfred A. Knopf, 1961.

Arrom, Silvia M. *Containing the Poor: The Mexico City Poor House, 1774–1871*. Durham, NC: Duke University Press, 2000.

———. *The Women of Mexico City. 1790–1857*. Stanford, CA: Stanford University Press, 1985.

Astete, Father Gaspar de. *Tratado del buen govierno de la familia y estado de las viudas y doncellas*. Burgos, Spain: Juan Baptista Varedio, 1603.

Atondo Rodríguez, Ana María. *El amor venal y la condición femenina en el México colonial*. Mexico City: Instituto Nacional de Antropología e Historia, 1992.

Ávila González, Jesús Salvador. "Voces y ladridos: Ensayo sobre los perros de la ciudad de México, siglos XVIII y XIX." PhD dissertation, Universidad Iberoamericana, Mexico City, 2007.

Barahona, Renato. *Sex Crimes, Honour, and the Law in Early Modern Spain: Viscaya, 1528–1735*. Toronto, ON: University of Toronto Press, 2003.

Barclay, Katie. "Singing and Lower-Class Masculinity in the Dublin Magistrate's Court, 1800–1845." *Journal of Social History* 47, no. 3 (2014): 746–68.

Bennett, Herman L. *Africans in Colonial Mexico: Absolutism, Christianity, and Afro-Creole Consciousness, 1570–1640*. Bloomington: Indiana University Press, 2003.

——. *Colonial Blackness: A History of Afro-Mexico*. Bloomington: Indiana University Press, 2009.

Bourdieu, Pierre. *Outline of a Theory of Practice*. Translated by Richard Nice. Cambridge, UK: Cambridge University Press, 1977.

Boyd-Bowman, Peter. "Los nombres de pila en México desde 1540 hasta 1950," *Nueva Revista de Filología Hispánica* 19 (1970):12–48.

Boyer, Richard. "Honor among Plebeians: *Mala Sangre* and Social Reputation." In *The Faces of Honor: Sex, Shame, and Violence in Colonial Latin America*, edited by Lyman Johnson and Sonya Lipsett-Rivera, 152–78. Albuquerque: University of New Mexico Press, 1998.

——. *Lives of the Bigamists: Marriage, Family, and Community in Colonial Mexico*. Albuquerque: University of New Mexico Press, 1995.

——. "Negotiating Calidad: The Everyday Struggle for Status in Mexico." *Historical Archaeology* 31, no. 1 (1997): 64–73.

——. "Respect and Identity: Horizontal and Vertical Reference Points in Speech Acts." *Americas* 54, no. 4 (1998): 491–509.

Brandes, Stanley. "The Structural and Demographic Implications of Nicknames in Navanogal, Spain." *American Ethnologist* 2, no. 1 (1975): 139–48.

Bristol, Joan Cameron. *Christians, Blasphemers, and Witches: Afro-Mexican Ritual Practice in the Seventeenth Century*. Albuquerque: University of New Mexico Press, 2007.

Burkholder, Mark. "Honor and Honors in Colonial Spanish America." In *The Faces of Honor: Sex, Shame, and Violence in Colonial Latin America*, edited by Lyman Johnson and Sonya Lipsett-Rivera, 18–44. Albuquerque: University of New Mexico Press, 1998.

Burns, Kathryn. *Into the Archive: Writing and Power in Colonial Peru*. Durham, NC: Duke University Press, 2010.

Cáceres Menéndez, Beatriz, and Robert Patch. "'Gente de mal vivir': Families and Incorrigible Sons in New Spain, 1721–1729." *Revista de Indias* 66, no. 237 (June 2006): 363–91.

Cañeque, Alejandro. *The King's Living Image: The Culture and Politics of Viceregal Power in Colonial Mexico*. New York: Routledge, 2004.

Carrasco, Rafael. *Inquisición y represión sexual en Valencia: Historia de los sodomitas (1565–1785)*. Barcelona: Laertes, 1985.

Carrera Stampa, Manuel. "El Obraje Novohispano." *Boletín Historical* 54, no. 146 (June 1969): 26–53.

——. *Los gremios mexicanos: La organización gremial en Nueva España, 1521–1861*. Mexico City: Iberoamericana, 1954.

Cashner, Andrew. "Playing Cards at the Eucharistic Table: Music, Theology, and Society in a Corpus Christi Villancico from Colonial Mexico, 1628." *Journal of Early Modern History* 18, no. 4 (2014): 383–419.

Castro Gutiérrez, Felipe, ed. "El origen y conformación de los barrios de indios." In *Los Indios y las ciudades de la Nueva España*, 105–22. Mexico City: Universidad Nacional Autónoma de México, 2010.

———. *Historia Social de la Real Casa de Moneda de México*. Mexico City: Universidad Nacional Autónoma de México, 2012.

———. "Salud, enfermedad y socorro mutuo en la Real Casa de Moneda de México." *Historia Social* 63, no. 1 (2009): 3–17.

Cerda, Juan de la. *Libro intitulado vida política de todos los estados de mugeres: En el qual dan muy provechosos y Christianos documentos y avisos, para criarse y conservarse debidamente las mugeres en sus estados*. Alcalá de Henares, Spain: Juan Gracian, 1599.

Cervantes, Fernando. *The Devil in the New World: The Impact of Diabolism in New Spain*. New Haven, CT: Yale University Press, 1994.

Chance, John K., and William B. Taylor. "Estate and Class in a Colonial City: Oaxaca in 1792." *Comparative Studies in Society and History* 19, no. 4 (October 1977): 454–87.

Clendinnen, Inga. "The Cost of Courage in Aztec Society." *Past and Present* 107 (May 1985): 44–89.

Connell, R. W. *Masculinities*. Berkeley: University of California Press, 1995.

Conway, Richard. "Lakes, Canoes, and the Aquatic Communities of Xochimilco and Chalco, New Spain." *Ethnohistory* 59, no. 3 (Summer 2012): 541–68.

Cope, R. Douglas. *The Limits of Racial Domination: Plebeian Society in Colonial Mexico City, 1660–1720*. Madison: University of Wisconsin Press, 1994.

———. "Los ámbitos laborales urbanos." In *Historia de la vida cotidiana en México*. Vol. 2, *La ciudad barroca*, edited by Antonio Rubial García, 407–32. Mexico City: El Colegio de México, 2005.

Córdoba, Martín de. *Jardín de las nobles doncellas*. N.p.: n.p., 1542.

Crenshaw, Kimberlé Williams. "The Structural and Political Dimensions of Intersectional Oppression." In *Intersectionality: A Foundations and Frontiers Reader*, ed. Patrick R. Grzanka. Boulder, CO: Westview Press, 2014.

Cruz de Amenábar, Isabel. *El traje: Transformaciones de una segunda piel*. Santiago, Chile: Universidad Católica, 1996.

Curcio-Nagy, Linda. *The Great Festivals of Colonial Mexico City: Performing Power and Identity*. Albuquerque: University of New Mexico Press, 2004.

———. "Magic, Sexuality, and the Manila Galleon Trade." Paper presented at the annual meeting of the Rocky Mountain Council on Latin American Studies, Santa Fe, NM, 2016.

Davison, Kate. "Occasional Politeness and Gentlemen's Laughter in 18th-Century England." *Historical Journal* 57, no. 4 (December 2014): 921–45.

Dean, Carolyn. "Sketches of Childhood: Children in Colonial Andean Art and Society." In *Minor Omissions: Children in Latin American History and Society*, edited by Tobias Hecht, 21–51. Madison: University of Wisconsin Press, 2002.

Deans-Smith, Susan. *Bureaucrats, Planters and Workers: The Making of the Tobacco Monopoly in Bourbon Mexico*. Austin: University of Texas Press, 1992.

———. "The Working Poor and the Eighteenth-Century Colonial State: Gender, Public Order, and Work Discipline." In *Rituals of Rule, Rituals of Resistance: Public Celebrations and Popular Culture in Mexico*, edited by William Beezley, William French, and Cheryl Martin, 47–75. Wilmington, DE: Scholarly Resources, 1994.

DeMello, Margo. *Animals and Society: An Introduction to Human-Animal Studies*. New York: Columbia University Press, 2012.

Du Bron, Valeri Marión Juliette. "El Caballo en la sociedad virreinal Novohispano de los siglos XVI y XVII: La caballería del Dios Marte." In *La Gesta del caballo en la historia de México*, edited by Miguel Ángel J. Márquez Ruiz, 71–77. Mexico City: Universidad Nacional Autónoma de México, 2010.

Dueñas-Vargas, Guiomar. *Of Love and Other Passions: Elites, Politics, and Family in Bogotá, Colombia, 1778–1870*. Albuquerque: University of New Mexico Press, 2015.

Eagle, Marc. "Beard-Pulling and Furniture Rearranging: Conflict within the Seventeenth-Century Audiencia of Santo Domingo." *Americas* 68, no. 4 (April 2012): 467–93.

Earle, Rebecca. *The Body of the Conquistador: Food, Race, and the Colonial Experience in Spanish America, 1492–1700*. Cambridge, UK: Cambridge University Press, 2012.

Escoiquiz, Don Juan de. *Tratado de las Obligaciones del Hombre*. Madrid: Real, 1803.

Exbalin Oberto, Arnaud. "Perros asesinos y matanzas de perros en la ciudad de México (siglos XXI-XVIII)." *Relaciones* 35, no. 137 (2014): 91–111.

Fabián y Fuero, Francisco. *Colección de providencias diocesanas del Obispado de Puebla de los Ángeles*. Puebla, Mexico: Real Seminario Palafoxiana, 1770.

Fahrenkrog, Laura. "Prácticas musicales durante la colonia: Reglamentando la vida musical; Santiago de Chile, siglo XVIII." In *Formas de control y disciplinamiento: Chile, América y Europa, siglos XVI-XIX*, edited by Verónica Undurraga Schüler and Rafael Gaume, 216–40. Santiago: UQBAR, 2014.

Farge, Arlette. *The Allure of the Archives*. Translated by Thomas Scott-Railton. New Haven, CT: Yale University Press, 2013.

Fernández de Lizardi, José Joaquin. *La Quijotita y su prima*. 1818. Reprint, Mexico City: Porrua, 1967.

Ferrer, Vicente. *Suma Moral para examen de curas y confesors en que a la luz del sol de las escuelas Santo Thomás, se desvanecen los perniciosos extremos de laxedad y rigor*.Valencia, Spain: Joseph Thomas Lucas, 1736.

Fisher, Andrew B. "Keeping and Losing One's Head: Composure and Emotional Out-bursts as Political Performance in Late-Colonial Mexico." In *Emotions and Daily Life in Colonial Mexico*, edited by Javier Villa-Flores and Sonya Lipsett-Rivera, 168–97. Albuquerque: University of New Mexico Press, 2014.

Flather, Amanda. "Male Servants, Identity, and Urban Space in Eighteenth-Century England." In *The Routledge History Handbook of Gender and the Urban Experience*, edited by Deborah Simonton, 91–114. London: Routledge, 2017.

François, Marie. "Cloth and Silver: Pawning and Material Life in Mexico City at the Turn of the Nineteenth Century." *Americas* 60, no. 3 (2004): 325–62.

Galindo, Pedro. *Excelencias de la castidad y virginidad*. Madrid: Matheo de Espinosa y Arteaga, 1681.

———. *Parte segunda del directorio de Penitentes, y practica de una buena y prudente confesión*. Madrid: Antonio de Zafra, 1680.

Gallant, Thomas. "Honor, Masculinity, and Ritual Knife Fighting in Nineteenth-Century Greece." *American Historical Review* 105, no. 2 (April 2001): 359–63.

Garza, James. "Dominance and Submission in Don Porfirio's Belle Époque: The Case of Luis and Piedad." In *Masculinity and Sexuality in Modern Mexico*, edited by Víctor M. Macías-González and Anne Rubenstein, 79–100. Albuquerque: University of New Mexico Press, 2012.

Garza Carvajal, Federico. *Butterflies Will Burn: Prosecuting Sodomites in Early Modern Spain and Mexico*. Austin: University of Texas Press, 2003.

Gayol, Sandra. *Honor y duelo en la Argentina moderna*. Buenos Aires: Siglo XXI, 2008.

———. *La Sociabilidad en Buenos Aires: Hombres, Honor y Café, 1862–1910*. Buenos Aires: Signo, 2000.

Gemelli Carreri, Juan F. *Viaje a la Nueva España: México a fines del siglo XVII*. 2 vols. Mexico City: Ediciones Libro-Mex, 1955.

Gerona, Carla. "With a Song in Their Hands: Incendiary Décimas from the Texas and Louisiana Borderlands during a Revolutionary Age." *Early American Studies* 12, no. 1 (Winter 2014): 93–142.

Gilmore, David D. "Some Notes on Community Nicknaming in Spain." *Man, New Series* 17, no. 4 (December 1982): 686–700.

Gómez de Terán, Don Juan Elías. *Infancia ilustrada y niñez instruida en todo género de virtudes Christianas, Morales, y Políticas, que conducen a la Santa Educación y buena crianza de los niños*. Madrid: Antonio Marin, 1735.

Gonzalbo Aizpuru, Pilar. "Familias y viviendas en la capital del Virreinato." In *Casas, vivienda y hogares en la historia de México*, edited by Rosalva Loreto López, 75–107. Mexico City: El Colegio de México, 2001.

———. *Familia y Orden Colonial*. Mexico City: El Colegio de México, 1998.

———. *Introducción a la historia de la vida cotidiana*. Mexico City: El Colegio de México, 2006.

———. "La Casa de niños expósitos de la ciudad de México: Una fundación del siglo XVIII." *Historia Mexicana* 31, no. 3 (1982): 409–30.

———. "Los primeros siglos de la Nueva España." In *Historia de la educación en la ciudad de México*, edited by Pilar Gonzalbo Aizpuru and Anne Staples, 49–116. Mexico City: El Colegio de México, 2012.

———. *Vivir en Nueva España: Orden y desorden en la vida cotidiana*. Mexico City: El Colegio de México, 2009.

Gonzalbo Aizpuru, Pilar, and Anne Staples, eds. *Historia de la educación en la época colonial: La educación de los criollos y la vida urbana*. Mexico City: El Colegio de México, 1990.

González, Ondina E., and Bianca Premo, eds. *Raising an Empire: Children in Early Modern Iberia and Colonial Latin America*. Albuquerque: University of New Mexico Press, 2007.

González Angulo Aguirre, Jorge. *Artesanado y ciudad a finales del siglo XVIII*. Mexico City: Secretaría de Educación Pública, 1983.

González Obregón, Luis. *La Vida de México en 1810*. Mexico City: Innovación, 1979.

Gowing, Laura. *Domestic Dangers: Women, Words, and Sex in Early Modern London*. Oxford, UK: Clarendon Press, 1996.

Graham, Sandra Lauderdale. *House and Street: The Domestic World of Servants and Masters in Nineteenth-Century Rio de Janeiro*. Austin: University of Texas Press, 1988.

Greenleaf, Richard. "The Obraje in the Late Mexican Colony." *Americas* 23, no. 3 (1967): 227–50.

Gruzinski, Serge. "The Ashes of Desire: Homosexuality in Mid-Seventeenth-Century New Spain." Translated by Ignacio López-Calvo. In *Infamous Desire: Male Homosexuality in Colonial Latin America*, edited by Pete Sigal, 210. Chicago: University of Chicago Press, 2003.

Guijo, Gregorio M. de. *Diario, 1648–1664*. Edited by Manuel Romero de Terreros. Vol. 1. Mexico City: Porrua, 1952.

Gutmann, Matthew C. *The Meanings of Macho: Being a Man in Mexico City*. Berkeley: University of California Press, 1996.

Halberstam, Judith. *Female Masculinity*. Durham, NC: Duke University Press, 1998.

Harvey, Karen. *The Little Republic: Masculinity and Domesticity in Eighteenth-Century Britain*. Oxford, UK: Oxford University Press, 2012.

———. "Men Making Home: Masculinity and Domesticity in Eighteenth-Century Britain." *Gender and History* 21, no. 3 (November 2009): 520–40.

Haslip-Viera, Gabriel. *Crime and Punishment in Later Colonial Mexico City, 1692–1810*. Albuquerque: University of New Mexico Press, 1999.

Hecht, Tobias. *Minor Omissions: Children in Latin American History and Society*. Madison: University of Wisconsin Press, 2002.

Hidalgo Nuchera, Patricio. "Los 'malos usos' y la reglamentación de los temascales públicos mexicanos (1686–1691)." *Anuario de Estudios Americanos* 69, no. 1 (January–June 2012): 91–108.

Hunold Lara, Silvia. "The Signs of Color: Women's Dress and Racial Relations in Salvador and Rio de Janeiro, ca. 1750–1815." *Colonial Latin American Review* 6, no. 2 (December 1997): 205–25.

Hurl-Eamon, Jennine. *Gender and Petty Violence in London, 1680–1720.* Columbus: Ohio State University Press, 2005.

Ilhui Pacheco Chávez, María Antonieta. "Rebeldes y transgresores: Entre los murmullos de la insurrección; La intendencia de México, 1810–1814." *Historia mexicana* 59, no. 1 (2009): 327–54. http://www.jstor.org.proxy.library.carleton.ca/stable/pdf/40285233.pdf.

Irwin, Robert McKee. *Mexican Masculinities.* Minneapolis: University of Minnesota Press, 2003.

Jaramillo, Carlos Eduardo. "Los guerreros invisibles: El papel de los niños en los conflictos civiles del siglo XIX en Colombia." In *Historia de la infancia en América Latina*, edited by Pablo Rodríguez Jiménez and María Emma Manarelli, 232–46. Bogotá: Universidad Externado de Colombia, 2007.

Jiménez Martínez, Angélica. "¿Somos de la basura? El mito fundador de la casa de niños expósitos de la ciudad de México (1767)." *Revista de historia de América* 139 (2008): 169–79.

Johnson, Lyman. "Dangerous Words, Provocative Gestures, and Violent Acts: The Disputed Hierarchies of Plebeian Life in Colonial Buenos Aires." In *The Faces of Honor: Sex, Shame, and Violence in Colonial Latin America*, edited by Lyman Johnson and Sonya Lipsett-Rivera, 127–51. Albuquerque: University of New Mexico Press, 1998.

———. "The Role of Apprenticeship in Colonial Buenos Aires." *Revista de historia de América* 103 (1987): 7–30.

———. *Workshop of Revolution: Plebeian Buenos Aires and the Atlantic World, 1776–1810.* Durham, NC: Duke University Press, 2011.

Jurado Revaliente, Iván. "Las injurias cotidianas: Identidades e individuos en el siglo XVI." *Bulletin of Spanish Studies: Hispanic Studies and Researches on Spain, Portugal, and Latin America* 92, no. 5 (May 2015): 677–97. https://doi.org/10.1080/14753820.2015.1039385.

Jurado Rojas, Yolanda. "Puppet Theater in Eighteenth-Century Mexico." *Americas* 67, no. 3 (January 2011): 315–29.

Kanter, Deborah. *Hijos del Pueblo: Gender, Family, and Community in Rural Mexico, 1730–1850.* Austin: University of Texas Press, 2008.

Kuznesof, Elizabeth Anne. "Gender Ideology, Race, and Female-Headed Households in Urban Mexico, 1750–1850." In *State and Society in Spanish America during the Age of Revolution*, edited by Victor M. Uribe-Uran, 149–70. Wilmington, DE: Scholarly Resources, 2001.

Laitinen, Riitta. "Home, Urban Space, and Gendered Practices in Mid-Seventeenth-Century Tukku." In *The Routledge History Handbook of Gender and the*

Urban Experience, edited by Deborah Simonton, 142–52. London: Routledge, 2017.

Lambert, Catherine Héau. "El caballo en el imaginario coletivo mexicano." In *La Gesta del caballo en la historia de México*, edited by Miguel Ángel J. Márquez Ruiz, 281–89. Mexico City: Universidad Nacional Autónoma de México, 2010.

Lavallé, Bernard. "Miedo reverencial versus justo miedo: Presiones familiares y vocación religiosa en Lima (1650–1700)." In *El miedo en el Perú, siglos XVI al XX*, edited by Claudia Rosas Lauro, 83–102. Lima: Pontificia Universidad Católica del Perú, 2005.

Lavrin, Asunción. "La sexualidad y las normas de la moral sexual." In *Historia de la vida cotidiana en México*. Vol. 2, *La ciudad barroca*, edited by Antonio Rubial García, 489–518. Mexico City: El Colegio de México, 2005.

———. "Lay Brothers: The Other Men in the Mendicant Orders of New Spain." *Americas* 72, no. 3 (July 2015): 411–38.

———. "Los hombres de Dios: Aproximación a un estudio de la masculinidad en Nueva España." *Anuario Colombiano de Historia Social y de la Cultura* 31 (2004): 283–309.

———. "Masculine and Feminine: Construction of Gender Roles in the Regular Orders in Early Modern Mexico." *Explorations in Renaissance Culture* 34, no. 1 (Summer 2008): 1–26.

———, ed. "Sexuality in Colonial Mexico: A Church Dilemma." In *Sexuality and Marriage in Colonial Latin America*, edited by Asunción Lavrin, 47–92. Lincoln: University of Nebraska Press, 1989.

Lefebvre, Henri. *The Production of Space*. Translated by Donald Nicholson-Smith. Oxford, UK: Blackwell, 1991.

León Cázares, María del Carmen. "A cielo abierto: La convivencia en plazas y calles." In *Historia de la vida cotidiana en México*. Vol. 2, *La ciudad barroca*, edited by Antonio Rubial García, 19–45. Mexico City: El Colegio de México, 2005.

Lipsett-Rivera, Sonya. "*De Obra y de Palabra*: Patterns of Insults in Mexico, 1750–1856." *Americas* 54, no. 4 (April 1998): 511–39.

———. *Gender and the Negotiation of Daily Life, 1750–1856*. Lincoln: University of Nebraska Press, 2012.

———. "'If I Can't Have Her, No One Else Can': Jealousy and Violence in Mexico." In *Emotions and Daily Life in Colonial Mexico*, edited by Javier Villa-Flores and Sonya Lipsett-Rivera, 66–86. Albuquerque: University of New Mexico Press, 2014.

———. "The Intersection of Rape and Marriage in Late-Colonial and Early-National Mexico," *Colonial Latin American Historical Review* 6, no. 4 (November 1997): 559–90.

———. "Marriage and Family Relations in Mexico during the Transition from Colony to Nation." In *State and Society in Spanish America during the Age of*

Revolution, edited by Victor Uribe-Uran, 121–48. Wilmington, DE: Scholarly Resources, 2001.

———. "A New Challenge: Social History and Dogs in the Era of Post-Humanism." Sociedad Indiana. http://socindiana.hypotheses.org/320.

———. "Scandal at the Church: José de Alfaro Accuses Doña Theresa Bravo and Others of Insulting and Beating His *Castiza* Wife, Josefa Cadena (Mexico, 1782)." In *Colonial Lives: Documents on Latin American History, 1550–1850*, edited by Richard Boyer and Geoffrey Spurling, 216–23. New York: Oxford University Press, 2000.

———. "A Slap in the Face of Honor: Social Transgression and Women in Late-Colonial Mexico." In *The Faces of Honor: Sex, Shame, and Violence in Colonial Latin America*, edited by Lyman L. Johnson and Sonya Lipsett-Rivera, 179–200. Albuquerque: University of New Mexico Press, 1998.

Lockhart, James. *The Nahuas after the Conquest: A Social and Cultural History of the Indians of Central Mexico, Sixteenth through Eighteenth Centuries*. Stanford, CA: Stanford University Press, 1992.

López Bejarano, Pilar. "Dinámicas mestizas: Tejiendo en torno a la jerarquía, al trabajo y al honor; Nueva Granada, siglo XVIII." Nuevo Mundo, February 17, 2008. http://nuevomundo.revues.org/19263.

Loreto López, Rosalva. "Familial Religiosity and Images in the Home: Eighteenth-Century Puebla de Los Angeles, Mexico." *Journal of Family History* 22, no. 1 (1997): 26–49.

Lozano Armendares, Teresa. *La criminalidad en la ciudad de México, 1800–1821*. Mexico City: Universidad Nacional Autónoma de México, 1987.

———. "Las sinrazones del corazón." In *Amor e historia: La expresión de los afectos en el mundo de ayer*, edited by Pilar Gonzalbo Aizpuru, 89–107. Mexico City: El Colegio de México, 2013.

———. *No codiciaras la mujer ajena: El adulterio en las comunidades domésticas Novohispanas ciudad de México, siglo XVIII*. Mexico City: Universidad Nacional Autónoma de México, 2005.

Lussana, Segio. "'No Band of Brothers Could Be More Loving': Enslaved Male Homosociality, Friendship, and Resistance in the Antebellum American South." *Journal of Social History* 46, no. 4 (Summer 2013): 872–95.

Macías-González, Victor. "The Bathhouse and Male Homosexuality in Porfirian Mexico." In *Masculinity and Sexuality in Modern Mexico*, edited by Víctor M. Macías-González and Anne Rubenstein, 25–52. Albuquerque: University of New Mexico Press, 2012.

———. "Hombres de mundo: La masculinidad, el consume, y los manuales de urbanidad y buenas maneras." In *Orden social e identidad de género, México, siglos XIX y XX*, edited by María Teresa Fernández Aceves, Carmen Ramos Escandón, and Susie Porter, 267–97. Guadalajara: Centro de Investigaciones y Estudios Superiores en Antropologia Social [CIESAS], 2006.

———. "Las amistades apasionadas y la homosociabilidad en la primera mitad del siglo XIX." *Historia y Grafía* 31 (2008): 19–48.

———. "Masculine Friendships, Sentiment, and Homoerotics in Nineteenth-Century Mexico: The Correspondence of José María Calderón y Tapia, 1820s–1850s." *Journal of the History of Sexuality* 16, no. 3 (September 2007): 416–35.

Macías-González, Víctor M., and Anne Rubenstein, eds. Introduction to *Masculinity and Sexuality in Modern Mexico*. Albuquerque: University of New Mexico Press, 2012.

Madero, Marta. *Manos violentas, palabras vedadas: La injuria en Castilla y León (siglos XIII–XV)*. Madrid: Taurus, 1992.

Malvido, Elsa. "El abandono de los hijos: Una forma de control del tamaño de la familia y del trabajo indígena; Tula (1683–1730)." *Historia mexicana* 26 (1980): 521–61.

Margadant, Guillermo F. "La Familia en el derecho Novohispano." In *Familias novohispanas: Siglos XVI al XIX*, edited by Pilar Gonzalbo Aizpuru, 27–56. Mexico City: El Colegio de México, 1991.

Martin, Cheryl E. *Governance and Society in Colonial Mexico: Chihuahua in the Eighteenth Century*. Stanford, CA: Stanford University Press, 1996.

Martín, Norman. "La desnudez en la Nueva España del siglo XVIII." *Anuario de Estudios Americanos* 29 (1972): 261–94.

———. *Los Vagabundos en la Nueva España, siglo XVI*. Mexico City: Jus, 1957.

Martin, Rod A. *The Psychology of Humor: An Integrative Approach*. Amsterdam: Elsevier Academic Press, 2007.

Martínez, Ignacio. "The Paradox of Friendship: Loyalty and Betrayal on the Sonoran Frontier." *Journal of the Southwest* 56, no. 2 (2014): 319–44.

Martínez, María Elena. "Sex and the Colonial Archive: The Case of 'Mariano' Aguilera.'" *Hispanic American Historical Review* 96, no. 3 (2016): 421–43.

Martínez de la Rosa, Alejandro. "Las mujeres bravas del fandango: Tentaciones del infierno." *Relaciones* 34, no. 134 (Spring 2013): 117–39.

Masaka, Dennis, Ephraim Taurai Gwaravanda, and Jowere Mukusha. "Nicknaming as a Mode of Black Resistance: Reflections on Black Indigenous People's Nicknaming of Colonial White Farmers in Zimbabwe." *Journal of Black Studies* 43, no. 5 (September 2012): 479–504.

Maurstad, Anita, Dona Davis, and Sarah Oelws. "Co-being and Intra-action in Horse-Human Relationships: A Multi-Species Ethnography of Be(com)ing Human and Be(com)ing Horse." *Social Anthropology* 21, no. 3 (August 2013): 322–35.

Mawson, Stephanie. "Unruly Plebeians and the *Forzado* System: Convict Transportation between New Spain and the Philippines during the Seventeenth Century." *Revista de Indias* 73, no. 259 (2013): 693–730.

Mehl, Eva. *Forced Migration in the Spanish Pacific World: From Mexico to the Philippines, 1765–1811*. Cambridge, UK: Cambridge University Press, 2016.

Mijares Ramírez, Ivonne. "La mula en la vida cotidiana del siglo XVI." In *Caminos y mercados de México*, edited by Janet Long Towell and Amalia Attolini Lecón, 291–310. Mexico City: Universidad Nacional Autónoma de México, 2010.

Milton, Cynthia. "Wandering Waifs and Abandoned Babes: The Limits and Uses of Juvenile Welfare in Eighteenth-Century Quito." *Colonial Latin American Review* 13, no. 1 (June 2004): 103–28.

Morales, María Dolores, and María Gayón. "Viviendas, casas y usos de suelo en la ciudad de México, 1848–1881." In *Casas: Vivienda y hogares en la historia de México*, edited by Rosalva Loreto López, 339–55. Mexico City: El Colegio de México, 2001.

Muchembled, Robert. *A History of Violence: From the End of the Middle Ages to the Present*. Translated by Jean Birrell. Cambridge, UK: Polity Press, 2012.

———. *La violence au village: Sociabilité et comportements populaires en Artois du XVe au XVIIe siècle*. Turnhout, Belgium: Brepols, 1989.

Murillo Velasco, Dana. "The Creation of Indigenous Leadership in a Spanish Town: Zacatecas, Mexico, 1609–1752." *Ethnohistory* 56, 4 (Fall 2009): 669–98.

———. *Urban Indians in a Silver City: Zacatecas, Mexico, 1546–1810*. Stanford, CA: Stanford University Press, 2016.

Nava Sánchez, Alfredo. "La Voz descarnada: Un acercamiento al canto y al cuerpo en la Nueva España." In *Presencias y miradas del cuerpo en España la Nueva*, edited by Estela Roselló Soberón, 21–44. Mexico City: Universidad Nacional Autónoma de México, 2011.

Nazzari, Muriel. "An Urgent Need to Conceal: The System of Honor and Shame in Colonial Brazil." In *The Faces of Honor: Sex, Shame, and Violence in Colonial Latin America*, edited by Lyman L. Johnson and Sonya Lipsett-Rivera, 101–26. Albuquerque: University of New Mexico Press, 1998.

Ochoa, Margarita R. "'Por faltar a sus obligaciones': Matrimonio, género y autoridad entre la población indígena de la ciudad de México colonial, siglos XVIII y XIX." In *Los Indios y las ciudades de la Nueva España*, edited by Felipe Castro Gutiérrez, 351–70. Mexico City: Universidad Nacional Autónoma de México, 2010.

Ochoa Serrano, Alvaro. *Mitote, fandango y mariacheros*. 2nd ed. Zamora, Mexico: El Colegio de Michoacán, 2000.

Ortega Noriega, Sergio, ed. "Teología novohispano sobre el matrimonio y comportamientos sexuales, 1519–1570." In *De la santidad a la perversión o de porqué no cumplía la ley de Dios en la sociedad novohispano*, 19–46. Mexico City: Grijalbo, 1986.

Osuna, Fray Francisco de. *Norte de los estados en que se da regla de bivir a los mancebos: Y a los casados; y a los viudos; y a todos los continentes; y se tratan muy por estenso los remedios del desastrado casamiento; enseñando que tal a de ser la vida del cristiano casado*. Seville: n.p., 1531.

Pardo, Osvaldo. *Honor and Personhood in Early Modern Mexico*. Ann Arbor: University of Michigan Press, 2015.

———. "How to Punish Indians: Law and Cultural Change in Early Colonial Mexico." *Comparative Studies in Society and History* 48, no.1 (2006): 79–109.

Paredes, Américo. *Folklore and Culture on the Texas-Mexican Border*. Translated by Richard Bauman. Austin: University of Texas Press, 1993.

Penyak, Lee. "Criminal Sexuality in Central Mexico, 1750–1850." PhD dissertation, University of Connecticut, Mansfield, 1993.

Pérez Martínez, Herón. "El caballo y la mujer en el refranero mexicano." *Relaciones* 26, no. 104 (Fall 2005): 169–87.

Pérez Toledo, Sonia. *Los Hijos del trabajo: Los artesanos de la ciudad de México, 1780–1853*. Mexico City: El Colegio de México, 1996.

Pérez y López, Don Antonio Xavier. *Discurso sobre la Honra y deshonra legal*. 2nd ed. Madrid: Real, 1786.

Perrot, Michelle. *Historia de las alcobas*. Translated by Ernesto Junquera. Mexico City: Fondo de Cultura Económica, 2011.

———. *Mi historia de las mujeres*. Mexico City: Fondo de Cultura Económica, 2008.

Pilcher, Jeffrey M. "The Gay Caballero: Machismo, Homosexuality, and the Nation in Golden Age Film." In *Masculinity and Sexuality in Modern Mexico*, edited by Víctor M. Macías-González and Anne Rubenstein, 214–33. Albuquerque: University of New Mexico Press, 2012.

Pizzigoni, Caterina. *The Life Within: Local Indigenous Society in Mexico's Toluca Valley, 1650–1800*. Stanford, CA: Stanford University Press, 2012.

Premo, Bianca. *Children of the Father King: Youth, Authority, and Legal Minority in Colonial Lima*. Chapel Hill: University of North Carolina Press, 2005.

Proctor, Frank Trey III. "Afro-Mexican Slave Labor in the Obrajes de Paños of New Spain, Seventeenth and Eighteenth Centuries." *Americas* 60, no. 1 (2003): 33–58.

———. "Amores perritos: Puppies, Laughter, and Popular Catholicism in Bourbon Mexico City." *Journal of Latin American Studies* 46, no. 1(February 2014): 1–28.

Quezada, Noemí. *Amor, magia amorosa entre los aztecas: Supervivencia en el México colonial*. Mexico City: Universidad Nacional Autónoma de México, 1975.

———. *Sexualidad, amor y erotismo: México prehispánico y México colonial*. Mexico City: Universidad Nacional Autónoma de México, 1996.

Quintana, Fray Augustín de. *Confesionario en lengua Mixe Con una construcción de las Oraciones Christiana y un Compendio de Voces Mixes para enseñarse a pronunciar dichas lenguas*. Puebla, Mexico: Viuda de Miguel de Ortega, 1773.

Ramos, Frances L. "Myth, Ritual, and Civil Pride in the City of Angels." In *Emotions and Daily Life in Colonial Mexico*, edited by Javier Villa-Flores and Sonya Lipsett-Rivera, 122–47. Albuquerque: University of New Mexico Press, 2014.

Rath, Richard Cullen. *How Early America Sounded*. Ithaca, NY: Cornell University Press, 2003.

Reinke-Williams, T. "Misogyny, Jest-Books, and Male Youth Culture in Seventeenth-Century England." *Gender and History* 21, no. 2 (2009): 324–39.

Rivera Ayala, Sergio. "Dance of the People: The Chuchumbé (Mexico, 1766)." In *Colonial Lives: Documents on Latin American History, 1550–1850*, edited by Richard Boyer and Geoffrey Spurling, 178–84. New York: Oxford University Press, 2000.

Robins, Nicholas A. *Of Love and Loathing: Marital Life, Strife, and Intimacy in the Colonial Andes, 1750–1825*. Lincoln: University of Nebraska Press, 2015.

Robles, Antonio de. *Diario de sucesos notables (1665–1703)*. 3 vols. Mexico City: Porrua, 1946.

Roche, Daniel. "Equestrian Culture in France from the Sixteenth to the Nineteenth Century." *Past and Present* 199, no. 1 (May 2008): 113–45.

Rosales, Padre Gerónimo de. *Catón Christiano y catecismo de la doctrina christiana para la educación y nueva crianza de los niños y muy provechosos para personas de todos estados*. Mexico City: Nueva de la Biblioteca Mexicana, 1761.

Rosas Lauro, Claudia. "El derecho de nacer y crecer: Los niños en la Ilustración; Perú, siglo XVIII." In *Historia de la infancia en América Latina*, edited by Pablo Rodríguez Jiménez and María Emma Manarelli, 214–28. Bogotá: Universidad Externado de Colombia, 2007.

Rosenthal, Angela. "Raising Hair." *Eighteenth-Century Studies* 38, no. 1 (2004): 1–16.

Rossell, Don Manuel. *La educación conforme a los principios de la religión christiana, leyes y costumbres, de la nación española en tres libros dirigidos a los padres de familia*. Madrid: Real, 1786.

Rubial García, Antonio. *El Paraíso de los elegidos: Una lectura de la historia cultural de la Nueva Españ (1521–1804)*. México: Universidad Nacional Autónoma de México, 2010.

———. *La plaza, el palacio y el convento: La ciudad de México en el siglo XVII*. Mexico City: Consejo Nacional para la Cultura y el Arte, 1998.

———. *Monjas, cortesanas y plebeyos: La vida cotidiana en la época de Sor Juana*. Mexico City: Taurus, 2005.

Ruiz Martínez, Christina. "La moderación como prototipo de santidad: Una imagen de la niñez." In *De la santidad a la perversión o de porqué no cumplía la ley de Dios en la sociedad novohispano*, edited by Sergio Ortega, 49–66. Mexico City: Grijalbo, 1986.

Rybczynski, Witold. *Home: A Short History of an Idea*. New York: Viking, 1986.

Salomón Pérez, Rodrigo. "Porque palabras duelen más que puñadas: La injuria en Nueva España, siglos XVI y XVI." *Fronteras de la Historia* 13, no. 2 (2008), 353–74.

Sánchez, Padre Matías. *El Padre de familias: Brevemente instruido en sus muchas obligaciones de padre*. Madrid: n.p., 1786.

Santos, Martha S. *Cleansing Honor with Blood: Masculinity, Violence, and Power in the Backlands of Northeast Brazil, 1845–1889*. Stanford, CA: Stanford University Press, 2012.

Schwaller, John Frederick. "La Identidad sexual: Familia y mentalidades a fines del siglo XVI." In *Familias novohispanas: Siglos XVI al XIX*, edited by Pilar Gonzalbo Aizpuru, 59–72. Mexico City: El Colegio de México, 1991.

Scott, James C. *Domination and the Arts of Resistance: Hidden Transcripts*. New Haven, CT: Yale University Press, 1990.

———. *Weapons of the Weak: Everyday Forms of Peasant Resistance*. New Haven, CT: Yale University Press, 1985.

Seijas, Tatiana. *Asian Slaves in Colonial Mexico: From Chinos to Indians*. New York: Cambridge University Press, 2014.

Shelton, Laura M. *For Tranquility and Order: Family and Community on Mexico's Northern Frontier, 1800–1850*. Tucson: University of Arizona Press, 2010.

Shepard, Alexandra. *Meanings of Manhood in Early Modern England*. Oxford, UK: Oxford University Press, 2005.

———. "'Swil-bols and Tos-pots': Drink Culture and Male Bonding in England, c. 1560–1640." In *Love, Friendship, and Faith in Europe, 1300–1800*, edited by Laura Gowing, Michael Hunter, and Miri Rubin, 110–30. London: Palgrave MacMillan, 2005.

Shoemaker, Robert B. *The London Mob: Violence and Disorder in Eighteenth-Century England*. London: Hambledon, 2004.

———. "The Taming of the Duel: Masculinity, Honour, and Ritual Violence in London, 1660–1800." *Historical Journal* 45, no. 3 (2002): 525–45.

Sigal, Pete, ed. "Gendered Power, the Hybrid and Homosexual Desire in Late Colonial Yucatan." In *Infamous Desire: Male Homosexuality in Colonial Latin America*, edited by Pete Sigal, 102–33. Chicago: University of Chicago Press, 2003.

Sinha, Mrinalini. *Colonial Masculinity: The "Manly Englishman" and the "Effeminate Bengali" in the Late Nineteenth Century*. Manchester, UK: Manchester University Press, 1995.

Sloan, Kathryn A. *Runaway Daughters: Seduction, Elopement, and Honor in Nineteenth-Century Mexico*. Albuquerque: University of New Mexico Press, 2008.

Socolow, Susan. "Women and Crime: Buenos Aires, 1757–1797." *Journal of Latin American Studies* 12, no. 1 (February 1980): 39–54.

Spain, Daphne. *Gendered Spaces*. Chapel Hill: University of North Carolina Press, 1992.

Spierenberg, Pieter, ed. "Knife Fighting and Popular Codes of Honor in Early Modern Amsterdam." In *Men and Violence: Gender, Honor, and Rituals in Modern Europe and America*, 103–27. Columbus: Ohio State University Press, 1998.

———. *Written in Blood: Fatal Attraction in Enlightenment Amsterdam*. Columbus: Ohio State University Press, 2004.

Stansell, Christine. *City of Women: Sex and Class in New York, 1789–1860*. Urbana, IL: University of Chicago Press, 1983.

Stearns, Peter N. "Obedience and Emotion: A Challenge in the Emotional History of Childhood." *Journal of Social History* 47, no. 3 (2014): 593–611.

Stern, Steve. *The Secret History of Gender: Women, Men, and Power in Late Colonial Mexico*. Chapel Hill: University of North Carolina Press, 1995.

Suárez Argüello, Clara Elena. "Los arrieros novohispanos." In *Trabajo y sociedad en la historia de México: Siglos XVI-XVIII*, edited by Gloria Artís Espriu, 86–99. Mexico City: CIESAS, 1992.

Suárez Escobar, Marcela. *Sexualidad y norma sobre lo prohibido: La ciudad de México y las postrimerías del virreinato*. Mexico City: Universidad Autónoma Metropolitana, 1999.

Tanck de Estrada, Dorothy. "Muerte precoz: Los niños en el siglo XVIII." In *Historia de la vida cotidiana en México*. Vol. 3, *El siglo XVIII: Entre tradición y cambio*, edited by Pilar Gonzalbo Aizpuru, 213–45. Mexico City: El Colegio de México, 2005.

———. *Pueblos de Indios y educación en el México colonial, 1750–1821*. Mexico City: El Colegio de México, 1999.

Taylor, Scott K. *Honor and Violence in Golden Age Spain*. New Haven, CT: Yale University Press, 2008.

Taylor, William B. *Drinking, Homicide, and Rebellion in Colonial Mexican Villages*. Stanford, CA: Stanford University Press, 1979.

Thomas, Keith. "The Place of Laughter in Tudor and Stuart England." *Times Literary Supplement*, January 21, 1977.

Thompson, Angela T. "Children and Schooling in Guanajuato, Mexico, 1790–1840." *SECOLAS Annals* 23 (March 1992): 36–52.

Torres Septién, Valentina. "Notas sobre urbanidad y buenas maneras de Erasmo al Manual de Carreño." In *Historia de la educación y enseñanza de la historia*, edited by Pilar Gonzalbo Aizpuru and Anne Staples, 89–111. Mexico City: El Colegio de México, 1998.

Torre V., Guadalupe de la, Sonia Lombardo de Ruiz, and Jorge González Angulo A. "La vivienda en una zona al suroeste de la Plaza Mayor de la ciudad de México (1753–1811)." In *Casas, vivienda y hogares en la historia de México*, edited by Rosalva Loreto López, 109–46. Mexico City: El Colegio de México, 2001.

Tortorici, Zeb. "Heran Todos Putos: Sodomitical Subcultures and Disordered Desire in Early Colonial Mexico." *Ethnohistory* 54, no. 1 (Winter 2007): 35–67.

———. "'In the Name of the Father and the Mother of All Dogs': Canine Baptisms, Weddings, and Funerals in Bourbon Mexico." In *Centering Animals in Latin American History*, edited by Martha Few and Zeb Tororici, 93–119. Durham, NC: Duke University Press, 2013.

———. "Sins against Nature: Sex and Archives in New Spain (1530–1821)." Unpublished manuscript, n.d.

Tosh, John. *A Man's Place: Masculinity and the Middle-Class Home in Victorian England*. New Haven, CT: Yale University Press, 1999.

Trujillo, Fray Thomas de. *Libro Llamado Reprobacion de Trajes, Con un Tratado de Lymosnas*. Navarre: n.p., 1563.

Turrent, Lourdes. *Rito, música y poder en la Catedral Metropolitana México, 1790–1810*. Mexico City: El Colegio de México, 2013.

Twinam, Ann. *Public Lives, Private Secrets: Gender, Honor, Sexuality, and Illegitimacy in Colonial Latin America*. Stanford, CA: Stanford University Press, 1999.

Underraga Schüler, Verónica, ed. "Fronteras sociales y sus intersticios: Usos y abusos de las categorías 'caballeros,' 'dones' y 'españoles' en Santiago de Chile, siglo XVIII." In *América colonial: Denominaciones, clasificaciones e identidades*, 285–313. Santiago: RIL, 2010.

———. *Los Rostros del Honor: Normas culturales y estrategias de promoción social en Chile colonial, siglo XVIII*. Santiago: Direccíon de Bibliotecas, Archivos y Museos [DIBAM], 2012.

Uribe-Uran, Victor M. *Fatal Love: Spousal Killers, Law, and Punishment in the Late Colonial Spanish Atlantic*. Stanford, CA: Stanford University Press, 2016.

Van Deusen, Nancy E. *Between the Sacred and the Worldly: The Institutional and Cultural Practice of Recogimiento in Colonial Lima*. Stanford, CA: Stanford University Press, 2001.

———. "Determining the Boundaries of Virtue: The Discourse of Recogimiento among Women in Seventeenth-Century Lima." *Journal of Family History* 22, no. 4 (October 1997): 373–89.

Van Young, Eric. *The Other Rebellion: Popular Violence, Ideology, and the Mexican Struggle for Independence, 1810–1821*. Stanford, CA: Stanford University Press, 2001.

Vetancurt, Fray Agustín de. "Tratado de la ciudad de México y las grandezas que la ilustran después que la fundaron los españoles." In *La Ciudad de México en el siglo XVIII (1690–1780): Tres crónicas*, edited by Antonio Rubial García, 39–129. Mexico City: Consejo Nacional para la Cultura y las Artes, 1990.

Vidal, Noële. "'El pequeño teatro del mundo': Les marionettes et l'histoire du Mexique." *Revue d'histoire moderne et contemporaine* 32 (January–March 1985): 99–113.

Viera, Juan de. "Breve Compendiossa narración de la ciudad de México, corte y cabeza de toda la América septentrional." In *La Ciudad de México en el siglo XVIII (1690–1780): Tres crónicas*, edited by Antonio Rubial García, 183–296. Mexico City: Consejo Nacional para la Cultura y las Artes, 1990.

Villa-Flores, Javier. *Dangerous Speech: A Social History of Blasphemy in Colonial Mexico*. Tucson: University of Arizona Press, 2006.

———. "Reframing a 'Dark Passion': Bourbon Morality, Gambling, and the Royal Lottery in New Spain." In *Emotions and Daily Life in Colonial Mexico*," edited by Javier Villa-Flores and Sonya Lipsett-Rivera, 148–67. Albuquerque: University of New Mexico Press, 2014.

Villarroel, Hipólito. *Enfermedades políticas que padece la capital de esta Nueva España en casi todos los cuerpos de que se compone y remedios qu se le deben aplicar para su curación si se requiere que sear útil al rey y al público*. 1785–1787. Reprint, Mexico City: Planeta 2002.

Villaseñor Black, Charlene. *Creating the Cult of St. Joseph: Art and Gender in the Spanish Empire*. Princeton, NJ: Princeton University Press, 2006.

Vinson, Ben III. *Bearing Arms for His Majesty: The Free Colored Militia in Colonial Mexico*. Stanford, CA: Stanford University Press, 2001.

———. "From Dawn till Dusk: Black Labor in Late Colonial Mexico." In *Black Mexico: Race and Society from Colonial to Modern Times*, edited by Ben Vinson III and Matthew Restall, 96–135. Albuquerque: University of New Mexico Press, 2009.

Viqueira Albán, Juan Pedro. *Propriety and Permissiveness in Bourbon Mexico*. Translated by Sonya Lipsett-Rivera and Sergio Rivera Ayala. Wilmington, DE: Scholarly Resources, 1999.

Viqueira, Carmen, and José I. Urquiola. *Los Obrajes en la Nueva España, 1530–1630*. Mexico City: Conejo Nacional para la Cultura y las Artes, 1990.

Von Germeten, Nicole. *Violent Delights, Violent Ends: Sex, Race, and Honor in Colonial Cartagena de Indias*. Albuquerque: University of New Mexico Press, 2013.

Weis, Robert. *Bakers and Basques: A Social History of Bread in Mexico*. Albuquerque: University of New Mexico Press, 2012.

White, Shane, and Graham White. "Slave Hair and African American Culture in the Eighteenth and Nineteenth Centuries." *Journal of Southern History* 61, no. 1 (February 1995): 45–76.

Wood, J. Carter. *Violence and Crime in Nineteenth-Century England: The Shadow of Our Refinement*. London: Routledge, 2004.

Index

~~